UCL
HUMAN RIGHTS
REVIEW

SECOND EDITION

2009

ISBN: 978-0-9560806-1-5

UCL Human Rights Review
UCL Student Human Rights Programme
Faculty of Laws
University College London
Bentham House
Endsleigh Gardens
LONDON WC1H 0EG

UCL Student Human Rights Programme

Published in the United Kingdom
By the Institute for Human Rights
Faculty of Laws
University College London
Bentham House
Endsleigh Gardens
London WC1H 0EG

On behalf of the UCL Student Human Rights Programme
http://www.uclshrp.com/review

ISBN: 978-0-9560806-1-5

UCL
HUMAN RIGHTS
REVIEW

2009

Patron:
The Rt. Hon. the Baroness Brenda Hale of Richmond

Editor-in-Chief:
Pasquale Annicchino

Deputy Editor-in-Chief:
Justin Leslie

Editorial Team:
Chris Appleby, Amy Bharucha, Harriet Holmes,
Yuvraj Joshi, Naureen Shameem, Ilias Trispiotis,
Kai Zhang

Graphic Design:
Tony Daly

Advisory Board:
Stephen Guest, Dawn Oliver, Colm O'Cinneide,
George Letsas, Phillipe Sands QC, Sonalini de Zoysa Gunasekera,
Christopher Campbell-Holt

Funding:
University College London

EDITORIAL

The second edition of the UCL Human Rights Review comes at a time of immense change in the way human rights are protected. In Strasbourg, attempts are being made to restructure the European Court of Human Rights (ECtHR) to avoid the pressures of an overwhelming case-load. It is 50 years since the European Convention on Human Rights (ECHR) was established and during that time it has demonstrated that human rights protection can be both effective *and* progressive.[1] However, its effectiveness is being severely curtailed by the ongoing challenge presented by a jurisdiction which covers over 800 million people. 'Protocol 14-bis' has been introduced as a stop-gap whilst Russia considers whether to agree to reform. However, as cynics might say, turkeys do not vote for Christmas. As to the progressiveness of the ECHR, there are those who are opposed to Strasbourg imposing a 'federal law of Europe'. The most notorious opponent of the ECHR in these terms is the now retired Lord Hoffmann who has accused the ECtHR of being 'unable to resist the temptation to aggrandise its jurisdiction and to impose uniform rules on member states'.[2] However, we believe that if a court decides that you *have* to know the case against you rather than the Kafkaesque nightmare of the alternative (see *A v United Kingdom*[3]) a common standard of human rights protection can only be a good thing. In this edition of the Review, Judge Rozakis and Eric Metcalfe take a critical look at Lord Hoffmann's position and provide spirited defences of the ECHR as a whole.

Closer to home, the dissolved Appellate Committee of the House of Lords has been reconstituted as the United Kingdom's Supreme Court. Their Lordships have stressed that the change is primarily symbolic and will not necessarily lead to a more activist, less-

---

[1] See further A Lester, *The European Court of Human Rights after 50 years* [2009] EHRLR 461 and JA Goldston, *Achievements and challenges – insights from the Strasbourg experience for other international courts* [2009] EHRLR 603

[2] See Lord Hoffmann, The Universality of Human Rights, Judicial Studies Board Annual Lecture (19 March 2009), Available at:
http://www.jsboard.co.uk/downloads/Hoffmann_2009_JSB_Annual_Lecture_Universality_of_Human_Rights.doc

[3] (2009) 49 EHRR 29. Lord Hoffmann accepted the judgment of Strasbourg but did so 'with very considerable regret, because I think that the decision of the ECtHR was wrong' *Secretary of State for the Home Department v AF (No 3)* [2009] UKHL 28 at para [71].

deferential court. Time will tell. A less high-profile but more profound change is currently under way by virtue of the Tribunals, Courts and Enforcement Act 2007 which shall bring together all of the many disparate tribunals into a two-tier structure. Cases are considered by First-Tier Tribunals and appeals on points of law can be considered by the second-tier known as the 'Upper Tribunal'. Whilst this change sounds innocuous it presents a threat to effective human rights protection since a central part of the government's plan is to exclude judicial review of the Upper Tribunal or at least to only allow judicial review in the most exceptional cases.

The principal focus of these changes has been the large number of immigration cases which have consistently represented the majority of all judicial reviews dealt with by the High Court. In cases where there is no right of appeal, such as in the immigration context, judicial review has been the only opportunity to scrutinise important decisions which, by their very nature, interfere with fundamental human rights. The attempt to exclude or severally restrict judicial review of the Upper Tribunal would have the practical effect of insulating the tribunal system, which would allow the entrenchment of bad law that could not be siphoned off by the High Court, and would inhibit access to the constitutional protections provided by judicial review.

The tribunal system is set to further become the engine-room of justice providing a quick and cost-effective method to challenge the executive's decisions on subjects such as asylum, housing, social security, pensions, tax, care standards, special educational needs and many more. Each of these areas directly impact on core human rights issues. The constitutional safety-net of effective judicial review is required to ensure these areas are not isolated from meaningful scrutiny. The judgment of Laws LJ in *Cart v Upper Tribunal* [2009] EWHC 3052 (Admin) deals directly with these issues and has recently received permission to appeal.

The UCL Human Rights Review has also undergone some changes. First, articles from academics beyond UCL are now accepted. In the next edition, we will also allow submissions from students beyond UCL. These changes are part of the Review's development from an internal, UCL-based publication towards a journal with international reach. A supplementary section – 'The Year in Human

Rights' – has been added to provide readers with a useful directory of recent decisions in human rights law. However, our focus remains on top-quality articles from high calibre academics and students.

Our thanks must go to several people. First and foremost, the efforts of Chris Appleby must be acknowledged. He has worked tirelessly to compile the Review and has provided the kind of dedication that money simply cannot buy. The other members of the Editorial Board – Harriet, Naureen, Yuvraj, Amy, Illias, Kai – have also played an vital role throughout the genesis of this edition. We must also extend our gratitude to the Board of the UCL Student Human Rights Programme (UCL SHRP) and, in particular, Tony Daly who has provided invaluable technical advice during the entire process.

The support of the UCL Faculty of Laws has been unwavering. We are particularly pleased to be closely associated with the newly founded Human Rights Institute whose financial support will ensure the long-term viability of the Review. The Staff Advisory Board has grown to include Professor Phillipe Sands and the Board has always been on hand to gently guide us whilst giving us the freedom to develop the Review in our own way. We are particularly grateful for Stephen Guest's prompt and authoritative replies to our queries.

Our final thanks must go to the contributors to this year's edition who have been very patient with the editorial process. This edition of the Review demonstrates the continued dynamism of thought inspired by human rights. It is unnecessary to précis each article here. Each piece is thought-provoking and deserves a thorough read. However, a special mention must be made for Helen Wildbore's article which discusses and challenges a report authored by members of the UCL SHRP. The article is evidence of the Review's ability to promote debate on the pressing issues raised by human rights. As the Review continues to grow, we hope that this commitment to providing a forum where current topics can be explored with scepticism and imagination will ensure its success. Given the challenges faced in effectively delivering human rights protection to those who need it most, the role of publications like the Review is becoming all the more important.

Pasquale Annicchino
Editor-in-Chief

Justin Leslie
Deputy Editor-in-Chief

PATRON'S FOREWORD

It is a delight to welcome this second edition of the UCL Human Rights Review. UCL has been a pioneer in the field of student-edited journals of high academic quality. This volume brings together scholarly contributions from students and from academic staff under a student Editor-in-Chief, this year Pasquale Annicchino, and Deputy Editor-in-Chief, this year Justin Leslie. They have proved that last year's outstanding volume was not just a flash in the pan.

This year the 'Law Lords' have left the House of Lords and been transformed into the Supreme Court of the United Kingdom. There has been much debate about whether, in time, the change in name and place will affect the way in which we conceive our role. We spend a good deal of our time on human rights issues in one form or another. Shall we get bolder or more cautious now we have left the protective cover of Parliament? If, which is not admitted, we were to get bolder might it be, not only in our relations with the UK Government and Parliament, but also in our relations with the European Court of Human Rights in Strasbourg?

Two of this year's papers engage with Lord Hoffmann's criticism of the European Court of Human Rights for 'teaching its grandmother to suck eggs.' Eric Metcalfe suggests that, if this is so, 'it is because grandmothers sometimes appear to have forgotten how.' As the only grandmother on the Supreme Court, I have never known how to suck eggs. But I do think that I can recognise a fair trial when I see one. The Strasbourg Court is trying to uphold some precepts which were once taken for granted in this country but have since been modified in the light of changing conditions. Just as the Human Rights Act involves the courts in a dialogue with Government and Parliament, it may increasingly involve us in a dialogue with Strasbourg as we seek to explain why we think that some of those modifications are justified.

The courts may be increasingly preoccupied with human rights but others are more sceptical. As Helen Wildbore argues, we need constantly to reaffirm and promote their importance outside the narrow confines of the courts. And that is what the UCL Human Rights Review seeks to do. Congratulations to all involved!

Brenda Hale of Richmond
October 2009

CONTENTS

ANNABEL LEE

Common Values, Common Sense: The Story of Rights and Freedoms in Modern Britain

SHAMI CHAKRABARTI[*]

Introduction

During his lifetime, Lord Mishcon was able to explode so many of the negative stereotypes that have confronted human rights defenders in recent years. Not least the myth that all lawyers are high-born, or out of touch, and the suggestion that long-standing differences between people, faiths and nations are somehow intractable.

In stark contrast to this theme, David Cameron – in an otherwise highly pertinent and freedom-friendly speech – has promised to:

> '...reign in and reverse the regulation of our lives by unaccountable judges who are changing Britain's legal landscape with their judgments in the courtroom.'

Forgive this long-time student of the dark tower remembering the ghosts of Home Secretaries past, when a phrase like that is uttered by an aspirant to power. Have the judges, as opposed to the executive or even the legislature really been the bad guys when it comes to constitutional overreach and erosions of our liberties? I think not. Nor did they crunch the credit, warm the planet, scandalise parliament or start wars - literal and metaphysical.

After a dozen years of New Labour Government, the once reasonable concern that the 'toffs in wigs' would impede progressive administration and the interests of the vulnerable sounds especially hollow from any politician's lips, let alone those of a Conservative leader.

I would even wager that a contemporary poll to measure the

---

[*] Director, Liberty. This piece was delivered on 29th June 2009 as part of the UCL Annual Mishcon Lecture series which were established at UCL in 1990 in honour of Lord Mishcon to mark his 75th birthday and in recognition of his achievements and service in the fields of law, education, religion, government and politics, both central and local.

trust index of various senior professionals would favour the judiciary over both MPs and bankers. However, this is not my point. For 'unaccountable judges', I read independent ones and the basic notion that even elected representatives and what Mr Cameron calls 'the wisdom of the crowd', must be tempered by the Rule of Law if democracy itself, is to survive. When the judges are too 'accountable' Barabbas will always go free.

This was the wisdom of an earlier generation, and in particular of Winston Churchill, when traditional British liberties were enshrined and expanded in international human rights instruments – such as the Universal Declaration of Human Rights – that would be a bulwark against tyranny at home, across Europe and in younger democracies everywhere.

In the future as in the past, it seems to me that our rights and freedoms must be fought for in the court room but also in the living room, news room, class room, cabinet room and parliament chamber. Here I want to explore our various challenges and opportunities by remembering some of the experiences of recent years.

As with most stories there will be villains and heroes, great victories as well as moments of disaster. And whilst all human rights sceptics are not knaves; nor are they all innocently misguided. Sound arguments and good intentions alone are unlikely to persuade those whose short-term and particular interests lie in remaining at least apparently un-persuaded. But mine is ultimately a hopeful tale in which people are slightly better than not, and a great old democracy is more than capable of reflection, self-correction and renewal.

Transforming the landscape

I begin in the mid-nineteen nineties when two lawyer-politicians shadowed each other in the brief of Home Affairs. 'Shadow boxed' is perhaps more descriptive. For they began an authoritarian duel or arms race for which Britain still pays the price today. Each went on to lead his own party and one of them to lead the country for a decade.

No more was the Home Department to be a sedate political graveyard where the incumbent Secretary of State did his best to balance freedom and security, manage risk and expectation and say a little prayer each night. This was to be a vote-winning department where the claims and counter-claims of the executive's ability to drive out crime, 'bogus asylum seekers' (the phrase being coined in this period), perhaps even offence and irritation seemed to become more inflated by the year.

It is that brutal (and for some time crowd-pleasing) joust that changed the legal landscape more than any judicial intervention, single or accumulative. The slogans were no-nonsense – "If you can't do the time; don't do the crime". "Tough on crime; tough on the causes of crime". The phrases launched what has seemed like a thousand criminal justice bills and an ocean of new offences as well as giving the state an armoury of intrusive powers. Many of these were drafted almost as quickly as the press releases that inspired them.

The transformed landscape is one of stop and search without suspicion, summary extradition and punishment without trial; of naming and shaming and umpteen short-cuts through traditional rules of fairness via civil, administrative or modified criminal process to an ever-bulging prison estate. It is the world of expanded surveillance and gargantuan databases. It is a less friendly place to be a refugee, however genuine, to be a protester or even just young.

Critics of the Human Rights Act

It is important to remember that the threats to our rights and freedoms did not begin on 9/11, nor with the ill-judged and mis-named 'War on Terror' which was adopted in response. That said, it is a cruel twist of fate indeed that on the day of the Twin Towers atrocity in New York, Britain's infant Human Rights Act was not quite 11 months in force. Any domestic Bill of Rights would have been sorely tested in the subsequent years, but such a young one was especially vulnerable, not least because the Governing party that had introduced (but hardly promoted) it now pursued anti-terror, criminal justice, policing and asylum policies that strained every sinew of its contents.

The lack of any public information about the Act meant that the human rights narrative was now one of real and imagined litigation as reported by the media. By unhappy coincidence, legal aid was also in decline, so even a completely impartial press would be likely to find that the bulk of newsworthy stories involved either terror suspects, criminal defendants and asylum seekers (wretched enough still to qualify for public funding) or the rich and famous who had no need of it. Most of the population were shut out of this litigation by the absence of legal aid and crucial protection against having to pay a public authority's costs in the event of losing.

Further, newspapers in particular were far from completely neutral as far as the Act was concerned. Certainly many editors seemed to fear privacy rights (for a long time at least), more than they welcomed the first-ever positive right to free expression in British law.

So the first problem was bad parenting. Critics of the Government often became knee-jerk critics of the Act without even reading or understanding it. In some cases it was a matter of partisan politics but in others, a growing disillusionment associated with its political parents. The parents didn't help by openly criticising court judgments and even judges they didn't like; on occasion attacking the whole idea of human rights in this new era that was, we were told, more dangerous than any previous moment in human history.

But as others have ably demonstrated, criticisms are mixed, incoherent and often contradictory. The biggest contradiction being that the Act is both too strong and weak simultaneously. It has failed, we are told, to prevent all kinds of authoritarian laws hitting the statute book but also saps power from parliament to the judiciary. So which is it? Both criticisms cannot stand.

Of course the Act hasn't prevented the passing of authoritarian laws from ID cards (yet to be implemented), to disproportionate DNA retention, stop and search, extensive snooping and so on. But nor did the US Bill of Rights prevent the passing of the Patriot Act or the establishment of internment at Guantanamo Bay. Almost by definition, Bills of Rights act as check on executive and legislative power after its exercise and few in Britain have argued for the line between legal advice and judicial determination of disputes to be blurred as in some kind of Conseil d'Etat. Further, and once more as others have pointed out, the mechanism of statements under section 19 of the Act does at least require officials to consider and Ministers to justify how new Bills sit with human rights standards, with a view to stimulating parliamentary and public debate.

As for sapping the power of parliament, it is hard to see how that charge can be pointed anywhere other than towards successive

Governments. The Section 4 declaration of incompatibility remains a compromise that preserves parliamentary sovereignty whilst being capable of shaming the executive into more enlightened remedial action.

Euro-sceptic hostility towards the Act is equally superficial and nonsensical. The very British provenance of much of the ECHR's contents and drafting aside, it is bizarre indeed to suggest that giving domestic judges less opportunity to interpret it before an international court intervenes in local disputes is any way of repatriating power.

In any event, as last year's *Marper* decision on DNA retention best demonstrates, continental judges (with relatively recent memories of totalitarian rule) might indeed have something to contribute to a formerly more complacent discussion, in the world's oldest unbroken democracy.[1]

Challenges to fundamental rights

Alongside predictable challenges to the Article 8 value of privacy, the years of the War on Terror brought profound compromises of due process rights under Articles 5 and 6 and even apologists for torture and inhuman and degrading treatment contrary to Article 3. But predictably at time of great and often quite legitimate fear, the greatest challenge was to the principle of equal treatment in Article 14, and even more fundamentally to the notion of human rights for all human beings as opposed to rights or even privileges for those deemed worthy of citizenship.

When future scholars and schoolchildren look back on this period and ask how various affronts to human dignity were allowed to pass, amongst their answers will surely be that in as far as mainstream society knew what was happening, it thought that the price would be paid by foreigners, and other people not like them. Extensive surveillance without warrant, lengthy pre-charge detention, detention and then control orders completely outside the criminal justice system, summary extradition, deportation and rendition to torture. When fear stalks the land, all of these measures can seem palatable, even desirable when you don't think the target could ever be you.

Despite promises of content to the contrary, talk of British Bills

[1] (2009) 48 EHRR 50.

of Rights and Responsibilities can in context blow a rather xenophobic dog whistle. Quite simply, a retreat from human to citizens' rights is the road to Guantanamo Bay. It is a very strange moment indeed to re-enact that journey. If my analysis seems overly cynical, consider one of the most vehement and repeated attacks on the HRA and Convention itself. Irritation that Article 3 prevents foreigners being deported to torture is not so much the elephant as the woolly mammoth in the room whenever human rights must be defended from instinctive critics whether on the left or right of politics.[2]

A former Home Secretary once said that he would resign on the steps of Number 10 and tell the world how he'd been prevented from doing his job if the Court upheld the *Chahal* principle in a then pending case. Fortunately perhaps, political developments hastened his departure long before the judgment in *Saadi v Italy*[3] but the ethical principle must be unpacked and fought for if the HRA or any other future progressive Bill of Rights is to take root.

It is an ill-wind indeed but the War on Terror has itself produced rather helpful illustration of why *Chahal* and *Saadi* must be right. If we abhor torture, as British and much world opinion does, its legal prohibition must be absolute. On this side of the Atlantic at least, few of those, even sceptical of human rights more generally, are prepared to argue against this principle. For human rights advocates it is completely non-negotiable. To permit deportation to places of torture you must trim the absolute prohibition on the basis either of binding governments only in what they do with their own hands, or to their own citizens. On either basis, the logical distinction between the deportation and extraordinary rendition of foreign nationals becomes a muddy one of precise intention rather than any difference of principle.

Perhaps even more importantly, the convenient exaggeration of the problem needs to be addressed. Where there are evidential issues about whether a person would be tortured, they must ultimately be resolved in court. But where a non-deportable foreign national is

---

[2] See *Chahal v United Kingdom* (1997) 23 E.H.R.R. 413. The '*Chahal* principle' is that a government cannot make a deportation order to a country where a person is likely to suffer inhuman or degrading treatment as this would be a breach of Article 3, which is an absolute right.

[3] (2009) 49 EHRR 30. In *Saadi*, the Grand Chamber of the European Court of Human Rights reasserted the absolute nature of Article 3.

considered a threat they must be watched or prosecuted like any British citizen whose deportation is also impermissible under international law.

In this regard, it is worth remembering the broad range of serious criminal offences over which Britain now asserts extraterritorial jurisdiction, allowing prosecution here for alleged acts even on the other side of the world. The CPS, under the direction of Sir Ken Macdonald and now Keir Starmer, has been incredibly successful at prosecuting terrorism cases. We need to start thinking of their triumphs, not only as evidence of terrible dangers, but as proof of democracy's capacity to address them within a human rights framework.

The 'Charge or Release' campaign

Liberty's opinion polling and focus group work during our 'Charge or Release' campaign against 42-day pre-charge detention, demonstrated a public that was fairer than not, even in the face of the terrorist threat. When presented with practical alternatives to lengthy detention without charge, the overwhelming majority preferred them to the more draconian option. This heartening view of British public opinion is also borne out by our more general surveys of commitment to human rights values.

Twice in a recent six-month period we asked a cross-section of people whether it is important that there is a law in Britain that protects fundamental rights and freedoms. Over 95 per cent on each occasion said yes. We asked the same sample whether rights against torture and arbitrary detention, to free speech, fair trials and personal privacy were vital, important, useful or unnecessary. In each case an overwhelming majority found these principles vital or important. Finally, we asked the participants if they remembered ever having received any public information about the Human Rights Act. Only around 10 per cent had such a memory. They must have been deluded.

So clearly people don't believe everything they read in the papers. Further the media itself is no monolith but a growing range of minds and voices capable of both apparent contradiction and positive change.

At the start of the "Charge or Release" campaign Liberty could boast editorial support from only two rather predictable national daily newspapers. By the end, only two remained unconvinced of the view that 42 days was unnecessary, counterproductive and wrong. True enough, Article 8 can be a significant commercial concern when it impedes some of the kiss-and-tell stories that shift a lot of print from the shelves. But when the intrusive camera belongs to the state not a paparazzo, many editors and readers become champions of personal privacy and cheerleaders even for the Court of Human Rights. See *Marper* again. 'Big Brother Humbled' was the best headline to a news report of that judgment and I am not quoting the Guardian or the Independent.

The other side of the coin

Although technological advancement and countervailing concerns (crime detection, child and health protection etc.) have brought significant threats to privacy, these have in turn brought real opportunities for the advancement of the popular rights discourse in Britain. Whilst many people find it hard to imagine that they would ever be the subject of arbitrary detention or torture, most people enjoy their privacy and resent unjustified attacks upon it. From the embarrassment of communal changing rooms in clothing shops to the sense of violation that follows a domestic burglary, most of us have experienced uncomfortable scrutiny and have instincts rather similar to human rights principles of proportionality, legality and even-handedness when judging whether we object.

The rise of surveillance and the database society has also probably impacted greater numbers of ordinary enfranchised people than any other attack on rights and freedoms. It has illustrated the law of cock-up and unintended consequences when sensitive information is compromised and powers taken in the name of serious crime and terrorism are used to police wheelie bins and school catchment areas. It is a short hop from valuing your privacy to cherishing the presumption of innocence and so it begins. I have watched a number of journalists, politicians and others who once thought themselves antipathetic to the human rights agenda, start with a rather instinctive and cultural concern about ID cards and begin down the path of opposition to arbitrary detention and rendition.

Now some will actively seek to prevent this process by jumping on particular bandwagons and advocating a pick-and mix approach to which values are worthy of promotion and which people of protection, but they are usually transparent and always fighting the tides of both logic and imagination. Oppression may be infectious but so its antidote. I have long believed that the human instinct for justice is as deeply ingrained as those that prompt fear or revenge.

Ironically, the War on Terror that once so threatened our infant human rights discourse may yet, with hindsight, prove its making. After all, hasn't it provided fairly concrete proof that authoritarian adventures all the way up to war itself, can leave us less rather than more safe? Hasn't it debunked the nonsense that only far away third world places need worry about human rights violations because democracies would never indulge in the really bad stuff like kidnap and torture? Hasn't it demonstrated to legal and political commentators across the spectrum that the common law alone cannot suffice in the face of a dominant executive hell-bent on circumventing parliament and in many instances expressly ousting the jurisdiction of the courts in primary legislation?

Britain may finally be tiring of the political and legislative arms race, not least because it has inevitably failed over the last fifteen years to deliver on exaggerated promises of the risk free society. Instead, sarcastic pensioners have received ASBOs, peace protesters and Icelandic assets have been impeded under anti-terror powers and a vulnerable hacker with Aspergers syndrome faces summary extradition to the United States.

Meltdowns in financial and parliamentary systems clearly present real dangers to human rights, not least in the potential rise of racism and extremism in a time of recession. But the other side of that coin is that a healthy distrust of the powerful may bring a greater appetite for holding the powerful to account and a greater empathy on the part of the mighty for those who face the wrath rather than the wisdom of the crowd.

To be fair, as campaigns against 42-days, secret inquests and various blanket data retention and sharing projects have now demonstrated, politics has not been a complete rights-free zone of late. Even the House of Commons is slowly beginning to catch up with the House of Lords in its attempts to apply human rights concerns to the scrutiny of Government policy and legislation. Only time will tell what the next Parliament will bring but one can only hope that rafts of new MPs of all complexions, if elected on a more independent or independent-minded ticket, are likely to continue in this vein, whether or not party leaders deliver on current promises to diminish the power of their whips.

But to really thrive, human rights values need not only elite application and public education but a local, daily and above all even-handed demonstration of how the principles can assist in what Eleanor Roosevelt famously called the 'small places close to home'. This will be more not less important in times of economic constraint, when the competition for resources could make access to justice the difference between rubbing along and losing everything and could make equal treatment the difference between rubbing along together and descending into distrust and hostility along the lines of age, race or even country.

In addressing the apparent stirring of the far right in particular there may be much to learn from counter-productive approaches to other forms of extremism that have undermined the democrat's moral high ground in freedom's name. It is one thing in my view, and quite possibly a necessary and proportionate limitation on freedom of conscience, to vet those seeking sensitive public employments (for example those jobs involving coercive power or the care of the vulnerable), for their commitment to race equality and ability to serve and protect all those in their charge. It is quite another and almost an own goal, I would argue, to seek to ban extreme but ostensibly non-violent political parties, via the front or back door, by the forced sanitisation of their constitutions so that they look more human-rights friendly.

As with previous threats, it might be wise to roll up our sleeves and expose the fascists at school, street and community level before running to court or sharpening our quills for another round of quick-fix legislation. A racist party forced to take non-white members by law would still be a racist party. The additional layer of sheep's clothing would merely make it more dangerous.

The question of religion

Whilst far from providing computer programmes or magic bullets to issues of societal tension, human rights values can assist us in negotiating the limits of both tolerance and cohesion. Issues of faith identity and expression are another important case in point, in an age where global identities may feel as important to some as they do threatening to others. It seems to me that any society has but three choices in dealing with the small question of religion.

The first is to select and elevate an approved faith, to the point of giving it dominant status over all other belief systems. It is completely and formally interweaved into the entire legal, political and social system; every sphere of public life and as much of private life as can be achieved. An extreme example might be Afghanistan under the Taliban; a more moderate one - Britain at earlier stages in its history.

The second option is in many ways both equal and opposite. It is based on the view that faith conviction is all dangerous and divisive mumbo jumbo. No good can come of it. If it cannot be eradicated altogether it must be chased from the public sphere to the private one; confined to a place of worship or the home, upstairs under the bed with the pornography. An extreme example would be Stalin's Russia; a more moderate one - the French Republic.

From the way that I have caricatured the first two options, it is easy to guess that I favour the third option, which is the human rights approach and is an approach that resonates well with a society like Britain, where the struggle for religious freedom has been so connected with the struggle for democracy itself.

I believe that human beings are creatures of both faith and logic, emotion and reason and it is as well that human rights reflect this. It may be true that religion has inspired much war and prejudice but also much art, music and compassion. It is true that scientists and engineers have produced some of the greatest advancements in human history, but also some of the stuff of nightmares. If we believe in freedom of thought, conscience and religion, that must include the right to the faith of your choice, the right to no faith and crucially to be a heretic to any religion.

As with other forms of individual expression and autonomy, we should be slow to interfere, doing so only when such intervention is necessary and proportionate to protecting the rights and freedoms of others. This is of course a difficult and often controversial exercise in practice, which even the courts sometimes understandably struggle with. I think that it is easier to justify intervention in the context of young children than with adults. It is easier to justify in the context of employment when a public official in particular, cannot practically perform their reasonable duties or refuses to apply the law of the land and the principle of non-discrimination to those that he or she serves.

It may be easier to justify in particular security or safety scenarios, where for example, an item of clothing must be temporarily removed to allow a respectful identity check at an airport or sterile conditions in parts of a hospital. But the rights and freedoms of others, in my view, do not include protection from difference, irritation and offence, as opposed to real harm, whether the individual concerned is in a religious, political or other minority. In this vein, I do not have much admiration for the French President's recent comments on the Burkha and his apparent desire to free people from the prisons of their own choices (as opposed to making other choices more readily available to them).

Resolutions

When clashes appear between competing societal and individual interests, the human rights framework is a vital tool for attempting resolution. Some have always scoffed at the inevitable balancing acts involved in applying qualified rights in particular, but here it is the principle of equal treatment that provides the best discipline. Few of us have doubts about our own rights to dignity and fairness. It is *other people* who 'give human rights a bad name'. My speech is free but yours more expensive. I am innocent; you inevitably more suspicious and so on. So when we make the inevitable compromises to various freedoms and protections, there is rarely a better safeguard than imagining ourselves in the vulnerable position, or the interference to an interest of our own.

Surely this is the kind of empathy that everyone teaches their children and the best way of advancing any cause, let alone that of human rights? Surely this is what Tom Paine really meant by rights creating duties by reciprocity, not some conditional agreement capable of stripping the 'unworthy' of consideration?

In conclusion, today is a day of both adversity *and* great

opportunity for rights and freedoms in Britain. Minimising the former and harnessing the latter will depend upon more and clearer public engagement than many in the political, legal and wider human rights communities have committed to in the past. I do not say that further constitutional innovations will not or must not come but that they should be built on genuine public understanding and support if they are to advance protections rather than constituting a race to the bottom.

The good news is that whilst many attempt to trash the Human Rights Act, as with many a battered old suitcase, the population still warms to the treasure inside. These values are their values. When articulated and demonstrated, in particular with an even hand, people are still fairer than not. As an eminent lawyer renowned for social engagement, I hope that Lord Mishcon would have approved of this practical rather than theoretical approach to the promotion of dignity, equality and fairness in our country. Remembering his achievements leaves me more inspired and optimistic than ever.

Human Rights and the Royal Assent (on Sark): A Case Comment on *R (on the application of Barclay) v Secretary of State for Justice and the Lord Chancellor*

STUART LAKIN[*]

Introduction

In the recent *Barclay* case,[1] two land owners on the island of Sark (one of the islands which form the Crown Dependency of the Bailiwick of Guernsey) contended that the Reform (Sark) Law 2008 ('the Reform Law') was contrary to the European Convention on Human Rights, European Community law and the International Covenant on Civil and Political Rights. One aspect of their legal challenge may well have sent seismic tremors simultaneously along the corridors of the Royal Courts of Justice, Westminster, Whitehall and Buckingham Palace. Among the different forms of relief sought by the applicants was an order quashing the decision by the Secretary of State for Justice, the Lord Chancellor, and Her Majesty's Privy Council to recommend to the Queen that she give the Royal Assent to the 2008 law. In other words, the applicants wanted the court to rule that the Royal Assent *should not* have been given.

The *Barclay* case is interesting for a variety of different reasons,[2] but I shall focus only on the audacious argument just described, an argument which raises the following intriguing constitutional question: is a recommendation by a Government minister (and/or by other officials) to the Monarch that she give the Royal Assent susceptible in

---

[*] University of Reading. I would like to thank Professor Patricia Leopold for her extremely helpful thoughts, suggestions and references.

[1] *R (Barclay and others) v Lord Chancellor and Secretary of State for Justice and others)* [2008] EWHC 1354 (Admin), [2008] 3 WLR 857; *R (on the application of Barclay v Secretary of State for Justice and the Lord Chancellor* [2008] EWCA Civ 1319.

[2] One particularly important issue to arise out of the case is whether British overseas territories are subject the Human Rights Act 1998 in domestic law, or merely to the European Convention of Human Rights in international law. For a discussion, see G Dawes, 'Sark bites' (2008) 22(30) *The Lawyer* 30.

principle to judicial review (whether under the Human Rights Act 1998 ('HRA 1998') or under the common law)? To place this question in its broader constitutional context, is there a sense in which the *Barclay* decision extends the ideal of government under the rule of law in the UK constitution? Before coming to these questions, it will first be necessary to set out the background to the case, and the judgments of the High Court and Court of Appeal.

Background to the Barclay Case

The legislature and executive of Sark is called Chief Pleas. Prior to the Reform Law, it comprised a (unelected) Seigneur whose historic role was to keep the island inhabited with 40 men (the population is now approximately 600), 36 landowners, 12 elected deputies, and a person called the Seneschal who was appointed by the Seigneur, and who acted both as President of Chief Pleas and also as the island's judge. The Reform Law was introduced principally to change the composition of Chief Pleas to 28 elected conseillers, the Seigneur and the Seneschal. Under the terms of the Reform Law, the Seigneur and Seneschal both remain unelected,[3] and both lose their right to vote in Chief Pleas.[4]

Two features of the Sark legislative process should be emphasized in preparation for the discussion below. First, the enactment of Laws (as opposed to Ordinances) on Sark requires the approval of Her Majesty by Order in Council.[5] Secondly, a Law (or technically a 'Project de Loi') is presented to Her Majesty only once the Secretary of State for Justice (the first defendant), a Committee for the Affairs of Jersey and Guernsey (the second defendant),[6] and Her Majesty's Privy Council (the third defendant) have considered and/or approved it. In the present case, the third defendant explained its decision to recommend the Reform Law for Royal Assent in the following terms:

---

[3] s21 Reform Law.
[4] *Ibid.*, s35.
[5] [2008] EWHC 1354 (Admin) para [15].
[6] This committee was set up by Order in Council dated 22 February 1952.

'The Reform Law would not violate any of the Crown's international obligations, and that therefore those international obligations provided no basis for refusing the Royal Assent.'[7]

As noted above, the claimants sought, *inter alia*, an order quashing this decision and each of the other various decisions by the defendants to approve or recommend the Reform Law for Royal Assent. They argued a) that the continuing membership of the Seigneur and the Seneschal in Chief Pleas was contrary to Article 3 of the First Protocol to the ECHR; b) that the Reform Law was contrary to Article 3 of the First Protocol, Article 14 of the ECHR, and Article 19(1) of the EC Treaty in that it prohibited 'aliens' (as defined in the Reform Law) from standing for election; and c) that the dual role of the Seneschal (as a judge and member of Chief Pleas) was contrary to Article 6 of the ECHR.

The Judgments

In the High Court, Williams J rejected each of the applicants' arguments. Given the very limited role and powers of the Seigneur and Seneschal, he found that the Reform Law did not 'impair the very essence of the rights conferred under Article 3.'[8] As to whether the prohibition on 'aliens' standing for election contravened the ECHR, the judge found that a contracting state was entitled to decide that only its citizens can stand for election (just as a state was entitled to decide that only its citizens could form the electorate).[9] These were the types of decisions on which states enjoyed a wide margin of appreciation.[10] Nor were elections to Chief Pleas 'municipal elections' for the purpose of Article 19 of the EC Treaty.[11] In relation to the claimants' Article 6 claim, the judge found that, given the small amount of power held by the Seneschal, and the fact that there were several other judges on Sark, the Seneschal '[did not lack] the required impartiality and/or

---

[7] [2008] EWCA Civ 1319 para [3].
[8] [2008] EWHC 1354 (Admin) para [32] (applying the decision in *Mathieu-Mohin and Clerfayt v Belgium* (1987) 10 EHRR 1).
[9] *Ibid.*, para [50].
[10] *Ibid.*, para [31].
[11] *Ibid.*, para [58].

independence and/or the appearance thereof demanded by Article 6(1).'[12]

Having dismissed each of the applicants' substantive claims, the judge proceeded to consider (in anticipation of an appeal) whether any form of relief was, in principle, available to the applicants. On the question of whether the applicants could avail themselves of a remedy under the HRA 1998, the judge decided in the negative. Since the 1998 Act did not expressly extend to overseas territories, the only obligations on the United Kingdom in relation to Sark were the international obligations which arose by virtue of Article 56 of the ECHR.[13] If the HRA 1998 offered no assistance, could the applicants, in principle, challenge the validity of an Order in Council by reference to one or more of the well-established principles of judicial review? Applying the Court of Appeal decision in R *(Bancoult) v Secretary of State for Foreign and Commonwealth Affairs (No 2)*,[14] the judge answered this question firmly in the affirmative and indicated that he would have quashed each of the defendants' recommendations, together with the resulting Order in Council, had the applicants succeeded in their substantive claims.[15]

The Court of Appeal agreed with the judge on each of his substantive findings bar one.[16] Contrary to the judge, the Court of Appeal found that the multiple roles of the Seneschal were inconsistent with the Article 6 requirement to establish by law an independent and impartial tribunal. Pill LJ said:

'A judge independent of the legislature and executive is in my judgment required even for the comparatively modest litigation in the Seneschal's

---

[12] *Ibid.*, paras [70] and [71] (applying the decision in *McGonnell v United Kingdom* (2000) 30 EHRR 289).
[13] *Ibid.*, para [87] (applying the decision in R *(Quark Fishing Ltd) v Secretary of State for Foreign and Commonwealth Affairs* [2006] 1 AC 529).
[14] [2007] EWCA Civ 498. The House of Lords decision in *Bancoult* had not yet been delivered at the time of the High Court decision in *Barclay*. In any event, the House of Lords supported the Court of Appeal in ruling that Orders in Council were subject to judicial review. See (R *(Bancoult) v Foreign Secretary (No. 2)* [2008] UKHL 61 paras [35] and [105].
[15] [2008] EWHC 1354 (Admin) para [101].
[16] Although Etherton LJ dissented from Pill and Jacob L.JJ on the question of whether the position of the Seneschal was contrary to Article 3 of the First Protocol: [2008] EWCA Civ 1319 para [137].

diary. A constitution should also make provision for the litigation capable of arising in a complex modern society.'[17]

The Appeal Court also differed from the judge on the question of remedies. Where the judge had been willing, in principle, to quash each of the relevant decisions by the defendants, Pill LJ gave numerous reasons for preferring to grant only a declaration in relation to the Article 6 infringement. Chief amongst these reasons was the fact that the Reform Law marked a significant improvement (in ECHR terms) on the previous composition of Chief Pleas.[18]

Discussion

At the start of this case comment, I posed the following question: is a recommendation by a Government minister (and/or by other officials) to the Monarch that she give the Royal Assent susceptible in principle to judicial review (whether under the HRA 1998 or under the common law)? To place this question in its broader constitutional context, is there a sense in which the *Barclay* decision extends the ideal of government under the rule of law in the UK constitution? It will be apparent from my brief description above that the judgments in *Barclay* contain relatively little direct consideration of these types of questions. They centre instead on the applicants' substantive arguments (alongside some consideration of jurisdictional questions). This emphasis can be explained, I think, by the fact that the legal instrument under challenge was an Order in Council. Given that the *Bancoult* decision had established beyond question that this form of 'executive legislation' is itself subject to judicial review,[19] it would have been surprising had there been an issue about the susceptibility to judicial review of a *recommendation* to create such executive legislation.

In order to appreciate the potential implications of the *Barclay* judgment for the questions that I have posed, we need to strip away the peculiarities arising from the status of Sark as an overseas territory (principally the non-applicability of the HRA 1998), and put to one side the fact that the Reform Law depended for its validity on an Order in

[17] *Ibid.*, para [66].
[18] *Ibid.*, para [111].
[19] n 14.

Council. Imagine, instead, that the Minister for Justice in the UK had recommended to the Monarch that she give the Royal Assent to the (fictitious) Lord Chancellor and Law Lords Bill 2009 which sought to restore the role of the Lord Chancellor as a member of each branch of government, and to restore the Law Lords to the Upper chamber of Parliament. Let us assume, for argument's sake, that the 2009 Bill is incompatible with Article 6 and Article 3 of the First Protocol to the ECHR. Could a suitable applicant mount a successful challenge to the 2009 Bill based on the illegality of the Minister of Justice's recommendation to the Monarch?

The first difficulty with such a challenge is that it would arguably entail the courts adjudicating on questions relating to 'proceedings in Parliament' contrary to art 9 of the Bill of Rights 1689.[20] The granting of the Royal Assent is typically notified to each House of Parliament separately by the Speaker of that House.[21] If this *notification* falls within the scope Article 9, then it would not be a huge leap to contend that the ministerial advice behind the grant should also be covered.[22] On the other hand, the English courts have demonstrated an increasing willingness to adjudicate on questions relating to Parliament where there are 'rule of law' issues in question.[23] And, given that the very *point* of Article 9 was historically to insulate Parliament against the influence of the Sovereign, it seems more likely that the courts would treat a ministerial recommendation to grant the Royal Assent, and perhaps even the Monarch's act in granting the Royal Assent, as straightforward executive acts or decisions subject to the full range of judicial review

---

[20] See, for example, *Pickin v British Railways Board* [1974] AC 765.

[21] See O Hood, Phillips and Jackson, *Constitutional and Administrative Law* (8th ed. Sweet & Maxwell, London 2001) 158.

[22] There have been no attempts to provide an exhaustive definition of the phrase 'proceedings in Parliament'. The proper meaning of this phrase has recently been the subject of widespread debate following the Parliamentary expenses saga and the introduction of the Parliamentary Standards Bill 2009.

[23] The most salient recent example is the willingness of the House of Lords to rule on the validity of the Hunting Act 2004 in *Jackson v Her Majesty's Attorney-General* [2005] UKHL 56. See, in particular, paras [25] and [110] distinguishing the case from *Pickin*. See also *Pepper v Hart* [1993] AC 593.

principles.[24] This is certainly the tenor of the judgments in *Barclay*. As Williams J put it:

> 'It seems to me that if a decision-maker or advice-giver sets out to make a decision or give advice on the basis that his interpretation of the Convention is the correct one, and his decision or advice is erroneous...none the less judicial review lies.'[25]

Assuming that a legal challenge to the minister's recommendation is not ruled out by Article 9 of the Bill of Rights, the next potential difficulty is whether, or at what point, the English courts could *quash* (or grant some other remedy in respect of) the Lord Chancellor and Law Lords Bill or Act. There are two routes which the courts might take to this end. First, it could be argued that a *lawful* recommendation made by a minister to the Monarch that she grant the Royal Assent is a condition precedent to – or one of the substantive or 'manner and form' requirements necessary for – the enactment of a valid Act of Parliament. If so, then it would arguably be open to the courts to quash (or perhaps grant an injunction blocking the enactment of) the 2009 *Bill*.[26] More controversially still, it may be that the courts could quash the 2009 *Act* (or '*Act*') at some point after its formal enactment (or 'purported' enactment). The availability of one or other of these routes must depend, I think, on how we understand the HRA 1998 and, more broadly, on how we conceive of the legal powers of institutions and officials in the UK constitution.

   On one reading of the HRA 1998 – call it the 'Parliamentary sovereignty' reading – each of the routes just described is arguably blocked by ss4, 6 and 19 of the Act. s19 ('Statements of Compatibility') clearly empowers a minister to recommend that one or other House of Parliament should proceed with a Bill notwithstanding that he or she has certified the Bill as being incompatible with the Convention. And

---

[24] For an extremely progressive argument to this effect in relation to the Home Rule Bill 1914, see H Calvert, *Constitutional Law in Northern Ireland a study in regional government* (Stevens & Sons Ltd and Northern Ireland Legal Quarterly Inc, London 1968) 31.

[25] [2008] EWHC 1354 (Admin) para [101].

[26] For a powerful argument on the potential for a legal challenge to a Parliamentary Bill which is contrary to EC law, see P Leopold, 'Parliamentary Free Speech, Court Orders and European Law' (1998) 4 *Journal of Legislative Studies* 53-69.

s6(3)(b) of the Act ('Acts of Public Authorities') clearly excludes Parliament and those exercising functions 'in connection with proceedings in Parliament' from the definition of a 'public authority'. These express statutory powers in relation to Parliament, the argument might run, must, by necessary implication, negate any common law bases for quashing a Bill following an (otherwise unlawful) ministerial recommendation to the Monarch. At the same time, s4 of the 1998 Act ('Declaration of Incompatibility'), with its reference to 'primary legislation', and its proviso that a declaration 'does not affect the validity, continuing operation or enforcement of the provision in respect of which it is given', arguably embodies Parliament's absolute sovereign power to leave an ECHR-incompatible Act on the statute books even in the face of a declaration of incompatibility, and in the face of any would-be common law illegality on the part of the recommending minister.[27]

I think there is a better way of reading of the HRA 1998. This reading – call it the 'rule of law' reading – supposes that the HRA 1998 depends for its force and meaning on certain fundamental legal principles, principles which determine the *basis and extent* of Parliament's legislative powers.[28] On this reading, it is not enough to treat ss4 and 19 of the 1998 Act as simple expressions of Parliamentary sovereignty; if these sections preclude the judicial quashing of a Bill or Act which is contrary to the ECHR, then this can only be in virtue of some *justification* to that effect. The most plausible justification, it is suggested, is that these sections reflect a particular distribution of institutional

---

[27] Some commentators have defended this Parliamentary power on the basis that it promotes representative (majoritarian) democracy in the UK. See, for example, C Gearty, *Principles of Human Rights Adjudication* (Oxford University Press, Oxford 2004) 8-30. For a powerful competing rights-based conception of democracy, see R Dworkin *Freedom's Law: The Moral Reading of the American Constitution* (Oxford University Press, Oxford 1996) Introduction: The Moral Reading and the Majoritarian Premise.

[28] This view has gathered judicial momentum in recent years, most notably in the *Jackson* decision *op.cit.* in which Lord Hope (para 107) said that the rule of law is 'the controlling factor on which our constitution is based'. For an attempt to develop this view, see S Lakin, 'Debunking the Idea of Parliamentary Sovereignty: the Controlling Factor of Legality in the British Constitution' (2008) 28 *Oxford Journal of Legal Studies* 709. For a similar type of argument directed specifically at the HRA 1998, see, TRS Allan, 'Parliament's Will and the Justice of the Common Law: The Human Rights Act in Constitutional Perspective' (2006) 59 *Current Legal Problems* 27-50.

powers and responsibilities in relation to the protection of individual rights. s19 is perhaps best understood as a means of alerting Parliament and/or courts to possible conflicts with the ECHR,[29] and affording Parliament an opportunity to amend (or vote down) an ECHR-incompatible provision.[30] And s4 is perhaps best understood as providing a means of assigning particular types of remedial action to Parliament (or the Government) rather than courts.[31]

If ss4 and 19 of the HRA 1998 stand as an obstacle to a legal challenge to our fictitious 2009 Bill or Act, then I think this can only be the result of the types of principled reasons that I have just suggested (as opposed to reasons based on Parliament's supposed absolute sovereign powers). The HRA 1998 enshrines a particular conception of the separation of powers according to which judges do not have the power to quash an ECHR-incompatible Parliamentary Bill or Act. This arrangement no doubt reflects the particular legal history and tradition of the UK constitution.[32] But legal history and tradition can change very quickly.[33] If ministers were, say, routinely to recommend ECHR-incompatible Bills to Parliament and then to the Monarch with little prospect of such Bills receiving adequate Parliamentary scrutiny, then it may be that we could justify a judicial power to quash such Bills under a

---

[29] This seemed to be the basis on which the Secretary of State made a statement of *incompatibility* in relation to s321(2) of the Communications Act 2003. See *R (Animal Defenders International) v. Secretary of State for Culture, Media and Sport* [2008] UKHL 15; [2008] AC 312 at para 13 per Lord Bingham.

[30] It is unfortunate, in my view, that far more attention is paid to s19 as a possible 'manner and form' limitation on Parliamentary sovereignty than on the *justification* for this provision. For a recent example of this tendency, see A Young, *Parliamentary Sovereignty and the Human Rights Act* (Hart Publishing, Oxford 2009) chapters 1-3.

[31] Thus in *Bellinger v Bellinger* [2003] 2 A.C. 467 the House of Lords made a declaration of incompatibility on the basis that Parliament (or the Government) is better placed to assess the implications of a change to gender-recognition for such things as tax law, inheritance law, criminal records and insurance. s3 of the Human Rights Act, conversely, is best understood, I think, as empowering *courts* to remedy particular types of incompatibilities with the ECHR, for instance, those touching on matters of procedure and evidence in criminal trials. See *R v A* (No 2) [2002] 1 AC 45 per Lord Steyn.

[32] See the Government white paper 'Rights Brought Home: the Human Rights Bill' (Cm 3782, 1997) paras [2.10]-[2.16]. The Court of Appeal attached great weight to the history and tradition of Sark in reaching its decisions. See, for instance, [2008] EWCA Civ 1319 at para 121 per Jacob LJ.

[33] See R Dworkin, *A Bill of Rights for Britain*, (Chatto & Windus, London 1990) 26-27.

developed notion of 'common law constitutionalism.'[34] And should Parliament (or the Government) routinely fail to remedy an Act following a declaration of incompatibility, then it may be that this failure would similarly trigger a residual common law power to quash or 'strike down' the offending 'Act'.[35]

Conclusion

Whether our imaginary applicant would succeed in his or her challenge to the fictitious Lord Chancellor and Law Lords Act 2009 must depend on how we read the *Barclay* decision and, more generally, how we conceive of the powers of officials and institutions in the UK constitution. A narrow reading of *Barclay* merely confirms the (relatively uncontroversial) proposition of law to emerge from *Bancoult*: than an Order in Council should be subject to the same principles of judicial review as any other executive act or decision. This reading sits comfortably within traditional accounts of the constitution in so far as it treats executive decisions as being inferior (in democratic terms) to Parliamentary decisions.[36]

A broader reading of *Barclay* supposes that *each* of the actions and decisions of *all* officials and institutions – whether it be a ministerial recommendation, a Parliamentary Bill or Act, or the decision of the Crown in the person of the Queen to grant the Royal Assent – are subject to the ideal of government under the rule of law. Whether this means that judges in the UK have the power to *quash* a measure or decision which is contrary to the ECHR or common law, must depend on the particular conception of the separation of powers to which the UK is committed through its past institutional decisions. Should a minister decide in future to recommend the equivalent to the Lord Chancellor and Law Lords Bill 2009 to Parliament, or to the Monarch for Royal Assent, or should Parliament (or the Government) decide in

---

[34] For a helpful survey of different theories of common law constitutionalism, see T Poole, 'Back to the Future? Unearthing the Theory of Common Law Constitutionalism' (2003) 23 *Oxford Journal of Legal Studies* 435.

[35] The possibility of such radical judicial action is entertained explicitly by Lord Hope, Lord Steyn and Baroness Hale in *Jackson op.cit.* For an excellent discussion, see J Jowell, 'Parliamentary Sovereignty under the New Constitutional Hypothesis', [2006] *PL* 562-580.

[36] See, for instance, *International Transport Roth GmbH v Secretary of State for the Home Department* [2002] EWCA Civ 158 per Laws LJ at para 81.

future to not to remedy the equivalent Act following a declaration of incompatibility under the HRA 1998, it may be that the *Barclay* case would be the springboard for our own UK *Marbury v Madison*.[37]

---

[37] 5 US (1 Cranch) 137 (1803).

The Strange Jurisprudence of Lord Hoffmann: Human Rights and the International Judge

ERIC METCALFE[*]

'Strange jurisprudence that is bounded by a river! Truth on one side of the Pyrenees, error on the other!'

Blaise Pascal

Introduction

After a distinguished career on the bench, including fourteen years spent as a Lord of Appeal in Ordinary, Lord Hoffmann retired in 2009. Shortly before doing so, he gave a lecture to the Judicial Studies Board entitled 'The Universality of Human Rights'. In his speech, Lord Hoffmann acknowledged the universality of the *concept* of human rights in general. He also commended the European Convention on Human Rights in particular. But he derided the role of the European Court of Human Rights having ultimate jurisdiction to determine the meaning of the Convention. The Strasbourg Court, he said, 'lacks constitutional legitimacy' to 'impose uniform rules on Member states' in the area of fundamental rights. Indeed, for the Court to decide on issues such as noise pollution, hearsay evidence and the rule against self-incrimination under the rubric of human rights was to 'trivialise and discredit the grand ideals of human rights'.

The European Court of Human Rights is an unusual court in many respects. With a jurisdiction that stretches from Reykjavik in the North Atlantic to Vladivostok on the Pacific coast of the Russian Federation, it is the linchpin for the protection of human rights in the 47 member states of the Council of Europe, encompassing more than 770 million inhabitants. First established in 1959,[1] it became the model

---

[*] Director of human rights policy at JUSTICE.

[1] The Court was originally established alongside the European Commission on Human Rights, with the Commission as the first tier and the Court as the second tier. The modern structure of the Court, which saw the Commission subsumed by the Court, dates from 1998 following the implementation of Protocol 11 to the Convention.

for other regional human rights courts: the Inter-American Court of Human Rights established in and the African Court on Human and People's Rights established in 2006. Indeed, despite its regional jurisdiction, it is arguably the most influential of any international court: certainly when measured in terms of its impact on the daily lives of nearly a sixth of the world's population, it is a far more important body than either the International Court of Justice or even the International Criminal Court.

The European Court of Human Rights may be no ordinary court but neither is Lord Hoffmann an ordinary judge. Described by the BBC as the 'cleverest Law Lord of his generation',[2] he is perhaps most famous for his criticism of the indefinite detention provisions of the Anti-Terrorism Crime and Security Act 2001: 'the real threat to the life of the nation, in the sense of a people living in accordance with its traditional laws and political values, comes not from terrorism but from laws such as these'.[3] Almost as well-known was his ringing denunciation of the use of torture evidence the following year: 'The use of torture is dishonourable. It corrupts and degrades the state which uses it and the legal system which accepts it'.[4] Lord Hoffmann is only slightly less famous for his role in the original Pinochet judgment,[5] having failed to declare his interest as a director of Amnesty International's charitable arm in a case in which Amnesty was a third party intervener, thereby inadvertently contributing to the law on apparent bias and the importance of not being perceived to be a judge in one's own cause.[6] It is perhaps unsurprising, therefore, that Lord Hoffmann gained a reputation in the media as 'one of Britain's most famously liberal law lords'.[7]

The irony, of course, is that Hoffmann is very far from the Daily Mail caricature of a liberal judge. For, if he is a liberal, he was

---

[2] BBC News, 15 January 1999.

[3] *A and others v Secretary of State for the Home Department (No 1)* [2004] UKHL 56 at para [97].

[4] *A and others v Secretary of State for the Home Department (No 2)* [2005] UKHL 71 at para [82].

[5] *R v Bartle and the Commissioner of Police for the Metropolis ex parte Pinochet (No 1)* (2000) 1 AC 61.

[6] *In re Pinochet* (2000) 1 AC 119.

[7] 'Lord Hoffmann's star historical witness' by Graham Stewart, *The Times,* 11 April 2009. See also e.g. 'A liberal judge gets it right', *Mail on Sunday,* 4 April 2009; Ian Burell, 'Pinochet Ruling: A landmark in British legal history', *Independent,* 26 November 1998, referring to Hoffmann as one of 'Britain's two liberal South-African born judges'; Bruce Anderson, 'How South African judges undermined the rule of law in Britain', *Spectator,* 5 December 1998.

certainly not a predictable one whilst on the bench. Indeed, by the time
of his retirement, he was probably one of the more reliably conservative
Law Lords of recent times. In appeals to the Privy Council from the
Caribbean, for instance, he consistently upheld the death penalty as a
lawful punishment in the face of powerful contrary arguments
advanced on constitutional and human rights grounds.[8] And his
pronouncements in the Belmarsh case and the Torture evidence case
were all the more striking for being exceptions to an otherwise deeply-
conservative track-record when it came to cases involving national
security. His speech in the *Rehman* case, for instance, delivered a month
after the 9/11 attacks was notable for its postscript, which stressed the
need for the judiciary to defer to executive decision-making in the fight
against terrorism.[9] In the control order appeal of JJ and others, Lord
Hoffmann was in the minority who thought that house arrest for
periods up to 18 hours a day could not constitute a deprivation of
liberty contrary to article 5;[10] in the control order appeals of MB and
AF, Lord Hoffmann was the sole dissenter who maintained that the
public interest in the prevention of terrorism outweighed any concerns
about the unfairness of using secret evidence against controlees.[11]
Hearing the appeals of RB, U and OO against their deportation to
possible torture in Algeria and Jordan respectively, Lord Hoffmann was
content to accept that the assurances of the Algerian and Jordanian
governments were sufficient to justify SIAC's conclusion that it was
safe to return them, notwithstanding considerably evidence that both
governments regularly failed to honour their promises under other
international agreements.[12] Revisting AF's case in June 2009, Hoffmann
expressed 'very considerable regret' that the February judgment of the

---

[8] See e.g. the majority judgment delivered by Lord Hoffmann in *Higgs and Mitchell v Minister for National Security* (2000), 2 WLR 1368; Robert Mendik and Sophie Goodchild, 'Amnesty judge sent 13 to gallows', *Independent,* 23 January 2000.

[9] *Secretary of State for the Home Department v Rehman* [2001] UKHL 47 at para [62]: 'I wrote this speech some three months before the recent events in New York and Washington. They are a reminder that in matters of national security, the cost of failure can be high. This seems to me to underline the need for the judicial arm of government to respect the decisions of ministers of the Crown on the question of whether support for terrorist activities in a foreign country constitutes a threat to national security'.

[10] *Secretary of State for the Home Department v JJ and others* [2007] UKHL 45.

[11] *MB v Secretary of State for the Home Department* [2007] UKHL 46.

[12] See e.g. *RB and another v Secretary of State for the Home Department* [2009] UKHL 10 at para [192].

Grand Chamber in *A and others v United Kingdom* obliged him to allow AF's appeal against the use of secret evidence:[13]

> 'because I think that the decision of the [European Court of Human Rights] was wrong and that it may well destroy the system of control orders which is a significant part of this country's defences against terrorism.'

It is one thing to disagree with the decisions of a court. After all, reasonable people disagree and judges are meant to be reasonable *par excellence*. It is quite another to attack the institution of the court itself, to assert that it lacks legitimacy or to suggest that its decisions tend to undermine rather than reinforce respect for rights. What, then, are we to make of Lord Hoffmann's jeremiad against the Strasbourg Court? This article looks in turn at the various claims advanced in his speech, including: (1) the national character of human rights; and (2) the Strasbourg Court's lack of constitutional legitimacy.

The universality of human rights

More than sixty years after the Universal Declaration on Human Rights, the idea of human rights continues to draw controversy. Most criticism of human rights falls into one of two camps.

The first camp is critical of the idea of human rights altogether – whether because of concerns about the individualistic character of rights, a relativist critique of their claim to universality, or because of some general metaphysical scepticism about the nature of moral values in general. These are certainly not the only criticisms of the idea of human rights but they are among the most common.

By contrast, the second camp agrees with the *idea* of human rights but are critical of how they are applied. Again, there are a variety of criticisms but one of the most frequent is that it is anti-democratic to enable unelected judges to use human rights principles to limit or overrule the laws and decisions of democratically-elected governments.[14] Even in the UK, where the judges have no power to

---

[13] *Secretary of State for the Home Department v AF and others* [2009] UKHL 28 at para [70].
[14] See e.g. J Waldron, 'The Core of the Case Against Judicial Review' (2006) 115 *Yale Law Journal* 1346.

strike down legislation inconsistent with human rights,[15] the Human Rights Act has somehow managed to draw criticism for being 'anti-democratic'.[16]

At first glance, Lord Hoffmann's arguments appear more akin to the second camp than the first. He seems to accept the proposition that human rights are universal,[17] and he describes the European Convention on Human Rights as a 'perfectly serviceable abstract statement of the rights which individuals in a civilised society should enjoy'.[18] Instead, Hoffmann directs his scorn at the judges of the Strasbourg Court and their decisions. But despite his superficial acceptance of human rights in principle, the basis of Hoffmann's arguments against the Court are actually much closer to foundationalist critiques of human rights than he seems to think.

Hoffmann starts by citing Bentham's famous critique of the French Declaration of the Rights of Man as 'nonsense on stilts'. But whereas Bentham's ire was raised by the metaphysical pretensions of the National Assembly, Hoffmann is more interested in Bentham's arguments against the vague nature of the rights declared. For Bentham, talk of rights was only meaningful by reference to a particular

---

[15] See section 4(6)(a) of the Human Rights Act 1998: 'A declaration ... of incompatibility ... does not affect the validity, continuing operation or enforcement of the provision in respect of which it is given'. See also e.g. the Grand Chamber of the European Court of Human Rights in *Burden v United Kingdom* (2008) 47 EHRR 38 at para [40]: 'the Human Rights Act places no legal obligation on the executive or the legislature to amend the law following a declaration of incompatibility and that, primarily for this reason, the Court has held on a number of previous occasions that such a declaration cannot be regarded as an effective remedy within the meaning of Article 35(1)'.

[16] See e.g. 'The proper response to the Human Rights Act is to get rid of it', *Daily Mail*, 9 December 2008; Melanie Phillips, 'Yes, Big Brother is a menace. The irony is, it's the civil liberties lobby which is to blame', *Daily Mail*, 2 March 2009.

[17] See e.g. Hoffmann, 'The Universality of Human Rights' at para [23]: referring to human rights as 'universal in abstraction but national in application'.

[18] *Ibid.*, para [21]. On closer inspection, Lord Hoffmann's support for the Convention and the Human Rights Act seems to derive from the fact that it reflects common law values: 'At the national level, the precise wording of the document is not important, *because the values which it expresses have deep roots in our national history and culture*' (para [21], emphasis added); and '[The Convention] *was largely drafted in London, intended to reflect common law understandings of human rights* and, interpreted by United Kingdom courts as the American Bill of Rights is interpreted by American courts, would be a perfectly serviceable British bill of rights' (para [44], emphasis added). In other words, Lord Hoffmann seems happy with human rights so long as they reflect British values, which is about as grudging as an acceptance of universality as you are likely to find.

legal system, and particular laws that were clear and predictable. The lesson that Hoffmann draws from this is that rights are 'universal in abstraction but national in application'.[19] Focusing on the US Bill of Rights , he notes that, despite their general similarity to the rights in the French Declaration, 'the abstractions of the American Bill of Rights are interpreted differently from very similar abstractions in the legal systems of other countries'.[20] This is because, while the broad principles may be the same:[21]

> '[a]t the level of application ... the messy detail of concrete problems, the human rights which these abstractions have generated are national. Their application requires trade-offs and compromises, exercises of judgment which can be made only in the context of a given society and its legal system.'

Now, as a purely descriptive claim, the thesis that abstract principles of human rights only gain meaning in the context of particular legal systems is not an especially controversial one. But Hoffmann's argument is not so narrow. He notes the 'remarkable power' of the US Supreme Court to strike down legislation inconsistent with the Bill of Rights, while at the same time retaining 'more or less universal respect'.[22] Hoffmann identifies several reasons for this, the most important of which is that: [23]

> '[The US Supreme Court justices] are an American court, created by the Constitution, appointed by the President, confirmed by the Senate, an essential and historic part of the community which they serve. They have a special constitutional legitimacy for the citizens of the United States.'

For Hoffmann, this underlines what he takes to be 'the essentially national character of rights, embedded in a national legal system'. [24] And it forms the basis of his critique of the Strasbourg Court. For if, as

---

[19] *Ibid.*, para [23].
[20] *Ibid.*, para [13].
[21] *Ibid.*, para [15].
[22] *Ibid.*, para [14].
[23] *Ibid.*
[24] *Ibid.*, para [5].

Hoffmann claims, rights are 'universal in application but national in application':[25]

> 'it is not easy to see how in principle an international court [could] perform this function of deciding individual cases, still less why the Strasbourg court was thought a suitable body to do so. At the time that the Convention was drafted and negotiated, the example of the United States was there for everyone to see. Even supposing that the Convention had reproduced the precise language of the American Bill of Rights, one could hardly imagine a court of judges from various nationalities telling the people of the United States that their courts had applied their constitution incorrectly, or telling the people of other nations that, for example, the balance between freedom of the press and a fair trial should be struck in the same way as in the United States.'

It should be obvious, however, that Lord Hoffmann is here confusing *legitimacy* with *desirability*. It is indeed difficult to imagine the American people ever deciding that it would be better to have their constitution determined by an international court. They are unlikely to think such an arrangement desirable. But that would not mean it would be illegitimate. Assuming that the US government consented to such a bizarre arrangement and all the necessary constitutional amendments were in place to facilitate it, the international court would have the same legitimacy to decide on the meaning of the US Bill of Rights as the US Supreme Court currently does.

 The fact that a state may agree to give an international court jurisdiction to decide domestic questions of rights is clearly a challenge to Hoffmann's theory about the 'national character' of such rights. Plainly, his theory is normative rather than descriptive. When, for example, he claims that judgments about rights 'can be made only in the context of a given society and its legal system',[26] he obviously means 'should' rather than 'can'. For surely there is no *legal* barrier to domestic questions about rights being decided at the international level. Hoffmann nonetheless claims that the Strasbourg Court lacks legitimacy and I deal with that part of his argument later on, but the gravamen of his complaint is that international judges are ill-suited to

---

[25] *Ibid.*, para [23].
[26] n 211. Emphasis added.

decide domestic questions of human rights. This is because they are not part of the 'national legal system', not 'integral' with the 'given society',[27] nor 'part of the community which they serve'.[28] Lord Hoffmann does acknowledge the Court's own doctrine of the margin of appreciation, which affords a degree of latitude to member states in certain areas, but argues that 'the Court has not taken the doctrine … nearly far enough'.[29]

This emphasis on such non-legal concepts as 'nation', 'society', and 'community' is not accidental. On the contrary, Hoffmann attaches great importance to them. This is particularly clear from his analysis of Article 15 of the Convention in the Belmarsh case, which allows state parties to derogate from certain Convention rights 'in time of war or other public emergency threatening the life of the nation'. Most of the Law Lords approached this question in terms of the Strasbourg Court's own jurisprudence, predicting that the Court would be likely to find that the threat of terrorism posed by Al Qaeda constituted such a threat[30] – a prediction later shown to be correct.[31] Lord Hoffmann, by contrast, preferred to interpret the text of Article 15 afresh, unencumbered by any previous authority:[32]

---

[27] n 17, para 39.

[28] *Ibid.* Emphasis added.

[29] *Ibid.*, para [43]: 'The court treats the margin as a matter of concession to Member States on the ground that they are likely to know more about local conditions than the judges in Strasbourg. In other words, they assume that in principle they are competent to decide any question about the law of a Member State which is arguably touched by human rights but sometimes abstain from exercising this vast jurisdiction on the ground that it is something which the local judges are better equipped to do'.

[30] See e.g. Lord Bingham, *A and others (No 1)* (n 3), paras [28] ('If, however, it was open to the Irish Government in *Lawless* to conclude that there was a public emergency threatening the life of the Irish nation, the British Government could scarcely be faulted for reaching that conclusion in the much more dangerous situation which arose after 11 September') and [44] ('Assuming, as one must, that there is a public emergency threatening the life of the nation, measures which derogate from article 5 are permissible only to the extent strictly required by the exigencies of the situation, and it is for the derogating state to prove that that is so').

[31] See *A and others v United Kingdom*, 19 February 2009, at para [179]: 'the Court has in previous cases been prepared to take into account a much broader range of factors in determining the nature and degree of the actual or imminent threat to the "nation" and has in the past concluded that emergency situations have existed even though the institutions of the State did not appear to be imperilled to the extent envisaged by Lord Hoffmann'.

[32] *A and others (No 1)* (n 3), para [91]. See also para [92]: 'Nor do I find the European cases particularly helpful. All that can be taken from them is that the Strasbourg court allows a wide "margin of appreciation" to the national authorities in deciding 'both on the presence of such

'What is meant by 'threatening the life of the nation'? The 'nation' is *a social organism*, living in its territory (in this case, the United Kingdom) under its own form of government and subject to *a system of laws which expresses its own political and moral values*. When one speaks of a threat to the 'life' of the nation, the word life is being used in a metaphorical sense. The life of the nation is not coterminous with the lives of its people. *The nation, its institutions and values, endure through generations.* In many important respects, England is the same nation as it was at the time of the first Elizabeth or the Glorious Revolution. The Armada threatened to destroy the life of the nation, not by loss of life in battle, but by subjecting English institutions to the rule of Spain and the Inquisition. The same was true of the threat posed to the United Kingdom by Nazi Germany in the Second World War. This country, more than any other in the world, has an unbroken history of living for centuries under institutions and *in accordance with values* which show a recognisable continuity.'

At the core of Hoffmann's argument is the concept of a national legal system that is coextensive with a 'nation', 'society' or 'community' and through which the values of that nation or society are expressed. After all, on a purely positivist conception of the 'national legal system', the workings of the Strasbourg Court are now as much a part of UK law as those of the Royal Courts of Justice. But although the judges in Strasbourg may be part of our legal system, they are not part of our nation or society.

In truth, Lord Hoffmann's speech in the Belmarsh case may be great law but it is lousy sociology.[33] The problem with concepts like 'nation' and 'society' are that they are vague and indeterminate, and marked by strong disagreement.[34] It is very easy to talk of the 'political and moral values' of a nation, for instance, but how are these values determined and known? By government ministers elected by majority vote? By unelected judges? And who counts as a member of UK society? Those who are citizens (even if they reside elsewhere)? Those

---

an emergency and on the nature and scope of derogations necessary to avert it': *Ireland v United Kingdom* (1978) 2 EHRR 25, at para [207]. What this means is that we, as a United Kingdom court, have to decide the matter for ourselves'.

[33] It is also, as David Dyzenhaus has noted, a judgment that is much more conservative in its implications than is commonly appreciated: see *The Constitution of Law: Legality in a time of emergency* (Cambridge University Press, Cambridge 2006) 181-184.

[34] What Gallie called an 'essentially-contested concept'.

eligible to vote (not just UK citizens but Irish and Commonwealth nationals too)? Is an asylum seeker who has lived in the UK for 7 years a member of UK society? What about one who has lived in the UK for 14 years? Hoffmann's appeal to the UK's 'political and moral values' seems fine until one begins to ask what they are. As lawyers, we are accustomed to legal questions with determinate answers because the law requires certainty. But questions about values rarely yield right answers – only value judgements and disagreements about values.

It is therefore a mistake to suppose that an international judge is inherently ill-placed to decide questions about rights. For disagreements about rights do not simply occur on a nation-by-nation basis, wherein Spanish values differ from Polish values. Instead, disagreements about rights are endemic to every plural and democratic society, on issues in which there are likely to be Spaniards and Poles on both sides of the argument in both countries.[35] From that standpoint, an international judge is no worse placed than a national judge to render a dispassionate judgment.

The weakness of Hoffmann's analysis becomes apparent when one looks at the examples he gives of the Strasbourg Court's overreach: namely, the rule against self-incrimination, the hearsay rule and noise pollution.

In the cases of the rule against self-incrimination, Hoffmann criticised the decision of the Strasbourg Court in *Saunders v United Kingdom* for its failure to have regard to the earlier English cases on the right to silence, particularly the analyses of Lords Mustill and Templeman suggesting that the right to refuse to answer questions is only justifiable 'on the grounds that it discourages ill-treatment of a suspect'.[36] Hoffmann notes that, in areas where the risk of ill-treatment was minimal, Parliament had enacted a number of exceptions to the general rule. In Saunders' case, however, the Strasbourg Court held that a right against self-incrimination was implicit in the right to a fair trial, stating that 'the right to silence and the right not to incriminate oneself are generally recognised international standards which lie at the heart of

---

[35] In truth, no social group ever exhibits that kind of internal homogeneity and consensus over values that Hoffmann attributes to nations. Even religious groups, for whom shared values are the *sine qua non*, are typically marked by strong internal disagreements.
[36] n 17, para [28].

the notion of a fair procedure under article 6'. Hoffmann describes this as an instance of 'what Bentham called teaching grandmothers to suck eggs'.[37]

Concerning the Court's case law on the hearsay rule, Hoffmann is even more trenchant. Claiming that the rule 'has generally [been] thought irrational and an obstacle to justice', he notes that the rule was abolished by Parliament in civil cases following the Civil Evidence Act 1985 and substantially scaled back in criminal cases under the Criminal Justice Act 2003.[38] Nonetheless, in the recent case of *Al-Khawaja and Tahery v United Kingdom*, 'the Strasbourg court has discovered that the hearsay rule is a fundamental human right'. This is because the evidence was based 'solely or to a decisive degree' on a statement by a person whom the accused has had no opportunity to examine. Hoffmann proclaims:[39]

> 'It is quite extraordinary that on a question which had received so much consideration in the Law Commission and Parliament, the Strasbourg court should have taken it upon themselves to say that they were wrong.'

Hoffmann's main complaint is that the Strasbourg Court has overruled the decisions of the British Parliament and British courts. The question is not whether Strasbourg's decision is right or wrong (although Hoffmann plainly thinks they are wrong), but that the ultimate decision on the interpretation of human rights in the UK has been made by international judges who are not part of 'the nation, its institutions and values', nor a 'part of the community which they serve'. Strasbourg's rulings on self-incrimination and hearsay seem to ignore the fact that the UK is 'subject to a system of laws which expresses its own political and moral values'.

But Lord Hoffmann's choice of examples is curious, to say the very least. First of all, they are obviously issues upon which reasonable people could disagree. Secondly, and more significantly, they are issues upon which reasonable people *in the* UK disagree upon. In other words, the rule against self-incrimination and the rule against hearsay are

---

[37] *Ibid.*, para [34].
[38] *Ibid.*, para [31].
[39] *Ibid.*

plainly matters upon which people who are part of the UK nation, or society or whatever take different views. It is true that Parliament and the courts have weighed in on both issues and reached a particular point of view but that does not mean that they are necessarily right. More to the point, that does not even mean that they are consistent with the UK's own 'political and moral values'.

Lord Hoffmann's error lies in confusing the 'moral and political values' of the UK with the decisions of its Parliament and courts. Consider indefinite detention under Part 4 of the Anti-Terrorism Crime and Security Act 2001. Its compatibility with fundamental rights – far from being obvious at the time – was in fact marked by disagreement. Its introduction was strongly opposed many members of the public and by a significant number of parliamentarians but the government won the day and the Act was passed. At first instance, the Special Immigration Appeals Commission held that indefinite detention was compatible with the Convention in one respect (the right to liberty) but not in another (the right to non-discrimination). The Court of Appeal disagreed, and unanimously ruled that Part 4 was compatible with the Convention. Now, suppose that the House of Lords had not ruled the way that they did, and indeed upheld the judgment of the Court of Appeal. Would it have been wrong for the Strasbourg Court to reach a different conclusion? Would this have been an act of arrogance by an international court? Or would it in fact have been entirely consistent with fundamental rights, including the UK's own values?

The same is true the rules against hearsay and self-incrimination.[40] Not only was the Strasbourg Court entitled to come to the conclusion that it did, but its decisions were also entirely consistent with common law values.[41] Indeed, what is striking about Lord Hoffmann's choice of examples is that it might easily be said that – as with secret evidence and the retention of DNA evidence – the Strasbourg Court has often done a better job of standing up for British values than Britain's Parliament and Britain's courts have. If the

---

[40] On the issue of noise pollution, the Strasbourg Court ultimately sided with the British government against the complainants – Hoffmann's complaint seems only to be that noise pollution didn't really seem to be a human rights issue.
[41] This is even more remarkable given that most Strasbourg judges come from the civil law tradition – historically much more accepting of hearsay than the common law.

Strasbourg Court were truly teaching grandmothers to suck eggs, it is because grandmothers sometimes appear to have forgotten how.

The legitimacy of the Strasbourg Court

Even if the Strasbourg Court is not inherently ill-placed to decide national questions of rights, what are we to make of Lord Hoffmann's claims that it lacks the 'constitutional legitimacy'[42] to do so? He complains that:

> 'The fact that the 10 original Member States of the Council of Europe subscribed to a statement of human rights in the same terms did not mean that they had agreed to uniformity of the *application* of those abstract rights in each of their countries, still less in the 47 states which now belong'

If, however, the original signatories to the Convention never intended Convention rights to be applied consistently throughout the Council of Europe, then their decision to establish a Court with jurisdiction 'in all matters concerning the interpretation and application of the present Convention' was surely perverse.[43] Consistency is, after all, a basic aspect of the rule of law – what other function does a court serve, if not to ensure a degree of consistency? There was certainly no obligation on the States Parties to the Convention to establish a Court and yet they did so. They could presumably have settled for another unenforceable statement of abstract principle, along the lines of the Universal Declaration of Human Rights: plainly they meant to go further. Hoffmann nonetheless claims that uniformity of application was never considered,[44] and describes as 'a remarkable fact' that:[45]

---

[42] n 17, para 38.

[43] See Articles 45 and 46(1) of the original text of the Convention – c.f. article 32(1) of the Convention as subsequently amended.

[44] The only evidence offered by Hoffmann are two quotes: the first a sceptical aside from Hartley Shawcross and the second an excerpt from an inter-departmental working group of British officials involved in negotiations on the text of the First Protocol. Hoffmann cites the working group's statement that the 'original purpose of the Council of Europe Convention on Human Rights was to enable public attention to be drawn to any revival of totalitarian methods of government', as though this were somehow evidence of a general intention of the drafters of the Convention against uniformity of application. In fact, the purpose of the statement was to rebut Shawcross's attempt to limit the right to property, as Simpson makes clear: 'The working party took the view that Shawcross's draft provided no defence whatever against totalitarianism,

'during the drafting and negotiation of the European Convention, which is chronicled in detail by Professor Brian Simpson, no one seems to have drawn attention to [the] basic flaw in the concept of having an international court of human rights to deal with the concrete application of those rights in different countries.'

Bizarrely, although Hoffmann cites Simpson's study, he pays no heed to its extensive coverage of the debates surrounding the creation of the Court, which was seen by the drafters as 'central to the system of supervision, and to the evolution of a jurisprudence of rights'.[46] Contrary to Hoffmann's claims that nobody raised objections to the Court's role during its drafting, it is apparent that there was in fact very strong resistance to the Court on the part of several Member States – the UK included – on precisely the grounds that Hoffmann claims were never thought of. Jowitt, the Lord Chancellor, complained for instance that:[47]

'It was intolerable that the code of common law and statute law which had been built up over many years should be made subject to review by an international Court administering no defined system of law.'

Indeed, the very strength of the British government's concern was testament to the very clear intention of the drafters to establish a Court to ensure that Convention rights were applied in a consistent manner. Far from being unthought-of or overlooked, the objections to the Court were confronted squarely by the drafters and addressed in the scheme of the Convention itself. Consequently, it was agreed to make both the jurisdiction of the Court and the right of individual petition optional and to leave the enforcement of the Court's judgments in the

---

and was therefore unlikely to be acceptable' (Simpson, *Human Rights and the End of Empire: Britain and the genesis of the European Convention* (Oxford University Press, Oxford 2002) 777.

[45] n 17, para [25].

[46] Simpson (n 444) 719.

[47] *Ibid.*, 728. Simpson goes on to detail Jowitt's rearguard attempts to resist the Convention, noting the 'strangeness of the fact that a person with such an uncritical understanding of the British legal system, and with such parochial opinions, should nevertheless have risen to so high an office .... It must ... be borne in mind that Jowitt, like most senior lawyers of the period, had never received anything which could be dignified as a legal education. What they knew about law was learned, as in the case of manual labourers, on the job' (*ibid.*, 743).

hands of the Council of Ministers – a political body rather than a judicial one.[48] In other words, it would be left to the Court to establish the meaning of Convention rights through its jurisprudence, but it would be for each Member State to decide whether to accept the Court's jurisdiction, whether to accept the right of individual petition, and whether to incorporate the Convention into its domestic law.

How, then, can the Court be said to lack legitimacy? The Convention gives it jurisdiction over 'all matters' concerning its 'interpretation and application'. The UK government signed the Convention and recognised the Court's jurisdiction and, later, the right of individual petition. Fifty years on, Parliament passed the Human Rights Act 1998, making Convention rights effective in UK law. Hoffmann does not suggest that any of these steps were invalid or unlawful. It is again difficult to avoid the conclusion that Hoffmann is simply confusing legitimacy with what he sees as the undesirability of the role of the Court.

Conclusion

It should not have escaped notice that there is a certain irony in a Law Lord criticising international judges, for according to a recent Ministry of Justice report,[49] the Law Lords spend no less than 40% of their time sitting as the final court of appeal for not only most of the UK but also a significant number of foreign jurisdictions and self-governing overseas territories, including Antigua, the Bahamas, Barbados, Belize, Bermuda, the Cayman Islands, the Cook Islands, Dominica, the Falkland Islands, Gibraltar, Jamaica, Kiribati, Mauritius, Saint Lucia, Saint Vincent and the Grenadines, Trinidad and Tobago, Tuvalu and – until very recently – New Zealand. British judges also act from time to time as national judges in such common law jurisdictions as Hong Kong. This also does not include, of course, what many British judges can expect to do in retirement, arbitrating on international disputes which have given jurisdiction to the courts of England and Wales, resolving commercial disputes in such foreign climes as Brunei or Doha.

---

[48] See *ibid.*
[49] *Fees in the United Kingdom Supreme Court* (February 2009) 9.

Why should there be such controversy about international judges deciding on human rights matters when there is so little about their role in resolving commercial disputes? One answer is that commercial disputes don't involve the same kinds of value disagreements that disputes about rights do, but this seems simplistic. The foundation of any contract is, after all, an exchange of promises and can it really be said that the virtue of keeping one's promise is a more suitable subject for an international judge than, say, the right not to be tortured?

Presumably the reason that so many companies around the globe are willing to have their disputes hammered out in Breams Buildings, the Strand or St Dunstan's House is because there is a value to certainty and consistency, but also because there is a benefit on getting someone else's perspective, someone who does not have a vested interest – and who is more disinterested than a foreigner? Foreign judges too may enrich the law that they decide upon – consider the contribution made to English law and the common law in general by Lord Hoffmann. It was a mistake, then, for him to condemn the European Court of Human Rights – for what better way to arrive at the truth than to have judges from both sides of the Pyrenees?

Is the Case-Law of the European Court of Human Rights a Procrustean Bed? Or is it a Contribution to the Creation of a European Public Order? A Modest Reply to Lord Hoffmann's Criticisms

CHRISTOS ROZAKIS[*]

Introduction

This article constitutes, as its subtitle announces, a modest reply to a number of points raised by Lord Hoffmann in his erudite speech, given as the 2009 Annual Lecture organised by the Judicial Studies Board.[1] In the course of his lecture Lord Hoffmann criticised the European Court of Human Rights[2] for habitually embarking on expanded interpretations of the European Convention on Human Rights,[3] going beyond the intentions of its drafters and its Contracting States; but also for disregarding the decisions of national authorities – mainly courts – where it overturns them, by applying indiscriminately a uniform case-law to different domestic legal regimes, and without considering that in a Europe of 47 States (the Contracting States to the Convention) different treatment of the same situation may be justified by the social, cultural or other realities which exist in their domestic orders and are properly reflected in their laws and practices.

Lord Hoffmann works from the assumption that human rights are, by and large, universal in abstraction but national in application. By that he means that although a number of human rights have acquired the status of universal rights, widely accepted by the international community as a whole, their application in the domestic order of the various States should nevertheless be adapted to the particularities of

---

[*] Vice President, European Court of Human Rights.

[1] Lord Hoffmann, 'The Universality of Human Rights', Judicial Studies Board Annual Lecture, 19 March 2009. Available at :
http://www.jsboard.co.uk/downloads/Hoffmann_2009_JSB_Annual_Lecture_Universality_of_Human_Rights.doc (Last visited 28th September 2009).

[2] Hereinafter 'the Court' or 'Strasbourg'.

[3] Hereinafter 'the Convention'.

the society concerned. This assumption is made for the application of the Convention: that it is an international treaty containing a number of universally accepted rights which should not necessarily apply uniformly to all its 47 Contracting States. To use his own words:

> 'The fact that the 10 original Member States of the Council of Europe subscribed to a statement of human rights in the same terms did not mean that they had agreed to uniformity in their *application* of those abstract rights in each of their countries, still less in the 47 which now belong… The Strasbourg court… has no mandate to unify the laws of Europe on the many subjects which may arguably touch upon human rights. Because, for example, there is a human right to a fair trial, it does not follow that all the countries of the Council of Europe must have the same trial procedure. Criminal procedures in different countries may differ widely without any of them being unfair. Likewise, the application of many human rights in a concrete case, the trade-offs which must be made between individual rights and effective government, or between the rights of one individual and another, will frequently vary from country to country, depending upon the local circumstances and legal tradition.'[4]

Lord Hoffmann focuses his criticism not on the Convention itself but on the Court's interpretation and application of it. He states:

> 'If one accepts … that human rights are universal in abstraction but national in application, it is not easy to see how in principle an international court was going to perform this function of deciding individual cases, still less why the Strasbourg court was thought a suitable body to do so.'[5]

Equally, Lord Hoffmann expresses his dissatisfaction with the dynamic interpretation that the Court has adopted in a large number of cases through the application of the judge-made concept of the Convention as a 'living instrument, to be interpreted in the light of present day conditions.'[6] A concept which, apart from allowing the Court to adapt its case-law to situations which have emerged since the Convention

---

[4] n 1, para [24].

[5] *Ibid.*, para [23].

[6] *Ibid.*, para [27]. Reference to the Convention as 'a living instrument' was first made in the judgment of *Tyrer v the United Kingdom* (25 April 1978) Application No. 5856/72.

entered into force and had obviously not been foreseen by its drafters - and even to depart from its own precedents - also allows it to add new rights not specifically referred to in the text of the Convention. In his speech he particularly refers to the acceptance by the Court in its body of case-law of the new right to a healthy environment, mainly by applying, in this connection, Article 8 of the Convention. He comments in paragraph 36:

> 'I would entirely accept that the practical expression of concepts employed in a treaty or constitutional document may change. To take a common example, the practical application of the concept of a cruel punishment may not be the same today as it was even 50 years ago. But that does not entitle a judicial body to introduce wholly new concepts, such as the protection of the environment, into an international treaty which makes no mention of them, simply because it would be more in accordance with the spirit of the times.'

With all due respect for Lord Hoffmann's approaches, which go so far as to negate the very legitimacy (or even utility?) of the Court in ensuring the proper implementation of the Convention, when it deals with the inter-State or individual applications submitted to it, I would like to express my disagreement with his views. A disagreement which is coupled with a slight amazement. For these criticisms come from an eminent common-law lawyer, who through his training and experience is undoubtedly knowledgeable of the particular powers that courts have in norm-creation when they operate under such a legal system. And Strasbourg undoubtedly operates rather more as a common-law court than as a continental European (civil law) court.

In the lines which follow I shall attempt to show that the Strasbourg Court not only cannot be said to abuse its powers under the Convention, but, on the contrary, complies perfectly with the mandate conferred on it by the drafters and by the present States Parties; also that its case-law is not a Procrustean bed, where the clauses of the Convention are stretched in order to accommodate the idiosyncratic tendencies of the Strasbourg judges, but that it is in real harmony with the spirit of the Convention and the original intentions of those who invented the pan-European protection of human rights and placed their trust in the Court for the accomplishment of such an endeavour.

Intentions of the drafters

The Convention traces its pre-history, which can be identified with the political developments in the then Western Europe, back to the immediate aftermath of the Second World War. At the time Europe was witnessing the tragic repercussions, economic and otherwise, of that catastrophic war, and simultaneously the emergence of the two great powers, the USA and the USSR. These two phenomena contributed to the birth of a conviction that in order for Europe to avoid the repetition of such events, and in order to survive, as an independent entity, the harsh competition from the emerging superpowers, the States belonging to the same *ideological family* (countries with a common past and historical roots, democratic regimes in a free market economy) had to coordinate, in an institutional manner, their policies. In order to achieve greater integration, allowing them to develop a common front to the challenges arising out of the omnipresence of the two superpowers on the international scene, and to combat the perceived threats that one of them, the USSR, presented to their socio-political choices. These concerns led, at the end of the forties and in the fifties, to the creation of a number of European Organisations, whose main task was to lay down conditions for gradual social and economic rapprochement between the participating States, and tighten up their cooperation in a multiplicity of fields of human activity. The fundamental concept which prevailed in the minds of those who inspired the organisation of Europe, through regional mechanisms of integration, was that the continent was in a need both of co-ordinating instruments to provide, in the short term, for a collective approach to matters requiring urgent solutions, and of long-term policies to further the unification of like-minded States within a supranational entity with political aspirations.[7]

For the realisation of this last ambitious goal the founding fathers of the European idea opted for a step-by-step approach which appeared, at the time, the most realistic and feasible means of achieving these difficult goals. Indeed, they considered that in the circumstances

---

[7] See C Rozakis 'Multiple Institutional Protection in the New European Landscape' in *Zeus* (1998) 475. There I presented a view of the European architecture, as conceived by its post-war founding fathers, by considering that each European Organisation, created to serve an integration scheme, had its own (exclusive) share in the division of labour, intended to lead to the gradual unification of European States.

prevailing in post-war Europe, immediate political unification was impossible. Instead, a (lengthy) preparation for the gradual attainment of the conditions which would allow unification to fall as a ripe fruit at a more propitious moment was regarded as a viable alternative. A preparation that would touch upon all the crucial fields of human activity, whether social, economic, cultural or otherwise, allowing all States participating in this experiment to align their policies and practices in a manner which would make political integration the natural consequence of such a harmonisation of infrastructure.

With these ideas in mind, many prominent European leaders put forward a proposal for a political and economic union which was formally discussed at the Congress of Europe, organised by the International Committee of Movements for European Unity at The Hague in May 1948.[8] In a number of resolutions of the Congress there was a call for the establishment of a political and economic union. The Congress culminated with the preparation of a statute for the creation of the first (viable) European Organisation, the Council of Europe.[9] The Statute, adopted in London on 5 May 1949, provides that the Council of Europe's aim is to achieve unity amongst its members, through common actions in various fields (social, economic, cultural, scientific, legal, administrative), and through the maintenance and further realisation of fundamental freedoms. It is to be noted that throughout that standard-setting and value-creating period of preparation of the European integration mechanisms, human rights had been considered, together with democratic governance and the rule of law, as indispensable and inalienable founding concepts of European construction. In the declaration of principles for a European Union, adopted at The Hague Congress, the Movement for European Unity, which had proposed the drafting of a Charter of Human Rights, stated that:

> '[no] other State may belong to the European Union unless it accepts fundamental principles of a charter of human rights and declares its readiness to guarantee their application.'[10]

---

[8] See, *inter alia*, D Gomien, S Harris and L Zwaak, *Law and Practice of the European Convention on Human Rights and the European Social Charter* (Council of Europe Publishing, Strasbourg 1996) 11.

[9] *Ibid.*

[10] *Ibid.*

And it had equally proposed the establishment of a 'Court of Justice' with the capacity to impose sanctions in the event of violations by States of its provisions.[11]

Similarly, in Article 3 of the Statute of the Council of Europe, the member States agreed that:

> 'Every Member of the Council of Europe must accept the principles of the rule of law and of the enjoyment by all persons within its jurisdiction of human rights and fundamental freedoms.'

With the initiative of the Council of Europe, and under its auspices, and as a step towards fulfilling its obligations to promote and further the protection of human rights, the Convention was drafted. It was adopted on 4 November 1950. The Convention, despite its being an independent instrument, governed by international law and more particularly by the Law of Treaties, is institutionally linked to the Council of Europe, and, as a consequence, to the causes that it serves. The institutional interdependence of the Convention – and particularly of its organs – with the Council is evident. In the original text of the Convention, before the amendments introduced by the 11th Protocol,[12] the Committee of Ministers of the Council of Europe constituted one of the judicial organs of the Convention, together with the now defunct European Commission of Human Rights, as well as the Court. Even today the Committee of Ministers virtually remains an organ of the Convention: it is authorised by the 11th Protocol to monitor the execution of the Court's judgments – and, according to existing practice, to propose proper individual or general measures of compliance by a State with the Court's findings –; while the administration of the Court, including the crucial element of the budget, is also linked to the administration of the Council of Europe.

One may reach, at this juncture, the conclusion that from the foregoing analysis a mathematical equation emerges showing the close inter-relation between the intentions of the western Europeans in the aftermath of the war to achieve further unity and integration with the creation of the Council of Europe, as one organisation serving these

---

[11] *Ibid.*
[12] *Ibid.*

purposes, and the adoption of the Convention, which itself was to fulfil part of the overall visionary scheme of the founding fathers.

Drafters' Intentions Reflected in the Text of the Convention

I respectfully submit that the intentions of the drafters, as described in the previous lines, are moreover directly or indirectly reflected in the very text of the Convention, more particularly as follows:

First, the Preamble to the Convention, in which all the Contracting States express their expectations and describe their goals to be achieved through the implementation of the provisions, clearly states that the principles upon which the Convention as a whole rests are *inter alia* 'the achievement of *greater unity* between the Members... to be pursued [through] the maintenance and *further realisation* of Human Rights and Fundamental Freedoms' and 'effective political democracy and... a *common understanding and observance*... of Human Rights.'[13]

A textual interpretation of this part of the Preamble reveals, without difficulty and without stretching the meaning of the words to eccentric results, that the drafters of the Convention did not envisage that the Convention would solely serve to protect individuals against possible violations of the rights contained therein, but that it had a more ambitious future. The 'collective enforcement of human rights', to which the Convention's Preamble also refers, was to serve the cause of achieving greater unity between the European States participating in the scheme. It is also evident that the instrument was designed not only to safeguard respect for the rights contained therein, by maintaining them intact, but also to contribute to their further realisation. In other, more simple, words, the drafters invited those applying and interpreting the Convention – States parties, judicial organs of the Convention – to broaden the purview of the rights provided for by the text, presumably by streamlining its provisions to account for the ever-changing realities of life and the demands of progress which are typical of every modern society.

Finally, the reference in the Preamble to a 'common understanding and observance of... Human Rights', taken together with the reference, in the same part of the Convention, to 'greater unity', undoubtedly supports the assumption that the drafters of the

---

[13] Emphasis added.

Convention intended to use the Convention, and its jurisdictional mechanisms, to operate as harmonising tools, gradually imposing a common reading of the rights protected by it on all participating States. The end result would, of course, be to achieve greater unity between them, thus serving the cause of European integration.

Second, connected to these initial observations is the fact that the choice of the drafters was to produce a rudimentary and general text which enumerates a number of rights without actually defining or determining the exact content or extent of their application. Characteristically – but not exclusively – Article 3 of the Convention speaks of 'torture, inhuman or degrading treatment', without defining the terms; Article 8 speaks of 'private and family life', without delineating the exact scope of these notions.

Why is this so? It would seem logical to assert that the drafters of the Convention were led to approve such an elementary description of the protected rights, not because they were unable to agree on detailed definitions, but because they wanted to leave them open-ended, to be exposed to changes in their content with the passage of time and the concomitant differentiation which might occur as a result.

Third, the question which arises is whom the drafters had in mind, when leaving the definitions and scope of the Convention's provisions open-ended, for the task of determining their adaptation to contemporaneous conditions. It goes without saying that those primarily responsible for the interpretation and application of the Convention are the States parties; and no one could deny that it falls within their competence, when doing so, to determine the exact content and scope of the particular Convention provisions at a given time. Nevertheless, if one left the crucial issue of the adjustment of the Convention rights solely in the hands of the individual States, that is to say the 47 different States which today make up the Council of Europe, the most plausible end result would be a variety of interpretations based on the particularities of each country and their preferences and choices.

Was that the intention of the drafters when they spoke of 'the achievement of greater unity', and of a 'common understanding and observance' of the rights contained in the Convention? It does not seem so. The apparent intentions of the drafters are reflected more in their decision to create judicial organs which, through adjudication of specific cases, would create a homogeneous corpus of interpretation of the relevant substantive clauses of the Convention. Although, admittedly, the organs provided for by the Convention were vested with the competence to deal exclusively with individual cases, whether submitted to them by States (inter-State applications) or by individuals (individual applications), and to decide on the concrete issues before them, each time without *erga omnes* effect, the potential repercussions of their decisions have extended in reality far beyond the specific situations of those involved in a particular dispute.

These potential repercussions were known to the drafters of the Convention when they decided not only to produce a conventional regime for the protection of human rights to be applied in the domestic order of the Contracting States, but also to endow it with jurisdictional organs to decide on alleged violations of the Convention. They could clearly anticipate that the conjunction in the Convention of two elements concerning the organs' jurisdiction, namely the element of *stare decisis* and the binding force of the decisions taken by the organs, would lead to the creation of authoritative jurisprudential precedents that would be binding indiscriminately upon all the Contracting States.

It is true that nowhere in the Convention can one find an express obligation for the judicial organs to follow their own precedents, when dealing afresh with a new case resembling factually and legally one already decided. It may be deduced from the text of Article 30, however, that the drafters not only considered such an eventuality but also wanted to ensure consistency in the case-law. Indeed Article 30 (relinquishment of jurisdiction to the Grand Chamber) provides that:

'...where a resolution of a question before the Chamber might have a result inconsistent with a judgment previously delivered by the Court, the Chamber may, at any time before it has rendered its judgment, relinquish jurisdiction in favour of the Grand Chamber, unless one of the parties to the case objects.'

Thus the drafters, by providing for the regime of relinquishment, both exhorted Strasbourg to adhere to its own case-law, and at the same time offered it a process through which the *stare decisis* could be better maintained. Article 30 makes the Grand Chamber the ultimate and highest authority of the Convention to determine what the law is and how the instrument should be properly interpreted.

The Strasbourg organs have invariably followed the intentions of the drafters in this respect (as in many others). And now comes the second, concurring element which acts, together with the *stare decisis*, as the mainspring for the harmonisation of the protection of human rights in Europe: the binding force of the Strasbourg decisions. Article 46 of the Convention (binding force and execution of judgments), in its paragraph 1, provides:

> 'The High Contracting Parties undertake to abide by the final judgment of the Court in any case to which they are parties.'

In reality the fact that Strasbourg follows its own precedents and creates case-law to which it adheres, in a situation where the judgments have binding force, means that a State against which a violation has been found is obliged not only to compensate its victim for the established transgression, but also to proceed to make changes to the regime (legislation, practice) which is the 'culprit' for the violation found. If it omits to do so victims of the same State conduct which had led to a finding of a violation in a previous case will submit their complaints knowing that Strasbourg applies its own case-law; and the Court, adhering to its own precedent, will again find a violation. So the only remedy for the avoidance of a series of similar violations is the removal of the source of a violation. Equally, other States which are parties to the Convention can also make changes to their own regimes if they are similar to those that the Court has found defective, in order to avoid, in turn, findings of violations against them through the interaction of *stare decisis* and the binding force of Strasbourg judgments. It should be underscored that the history of the Convention's implementation offers many examples not only of States which have rectified their impugned regime because of a finding of a violation against them, but also of other Contracting States not involved in a given case which, by acting pre-emptively, have also rectified their regimes to bring them into line with a Strasbourg ruling. It goes without saying then that the consequence of such indirect 'competence' of Strasbourg leads to a gradual harmonisation of the protection of human rights among the countries participating in the Council of Europe's system, and to the creation of a 'European public order'.

The Court's position

I now turn to the Court's activity to see how Strasbourg has perceived its role, not only as a mechanism for settling individual disputes, but also as a tool for consolidating and furthering the protection of human rights in Europe. In this respect the following general jurisprudential principles can be identified as emanating from its case-law as a whole:

a) Despite the fact that the Court's role in protecting human rights is a subsidiary one, and the primary responsibility for maintaining and furthering human rights in Europe lies with the Contracting Parties to the Convention, Strasbourg has never denied that it has been entrusted with the weighty task of scrutinising and supervising the correct application of the Convention throughout the continent of 47 States. Even in situations where it accepts that a State enjoys a 'margin of appreciation', in deciding a case – and I will come to back to that discussion below – it nevertheless warns States that their privilege of discretion is not unlimited and is subject to a 'European' supervision.

b) Since its judgment in *Tyrer v the United Kingdom*[14] the Court has reiterated many times that the Convention is a *living instrument* to be interpreted in the light of the conditions existing at the time of the examination of a particular case. This means that the Court is not obliged to interpret its constitutive instrument on the basis of the original conditions which were known to the drafters of the Convention, and which in the meantime may have drastically changed; and, even more so, that the Court is not obliged to maintain its own case-law in situations where the social, cultural, economic substructure which supported a certain finding by the Court no longer exists.

The body of Strasbourg case-law contains a large number of judgments showing how the Court perceives the effect of changed circumstances on the determination of cases before it. This can be seen, to mention only two examples, in its judgments in the cases of

---

[14] n 6.

Christine Goodwin v the United Kingdom[15] and *Hénaf v France.*[16] In that first case the Court overturned its previous case-law which had accepted that the lack of official recognition of the new gender of a post-operative transsexual by the United Kingdom authorities – through a change in the birth records – did not constitute a violation of Article 8 of the Convention (private life). In the new judgment, departing from its previous position and finding a violation of Article 8, the Court recognised that between the period of its former judgment and the period of consideration of the new case, societal and other changes had occurred that justified a different approach. In that second case, the Court considered that the notions of 'torture, inhuman and degrading treatment' were not immutable, and that the passage of time might change their scope. An act of the authorities which had been identified as inhuman treatment in the past could be reclassified as torture at a later stage, in a new case.

c) The Court has, in a number of cases, adopted dynamic interpretations of the Convention, either through expansive interpretation of the existing text, or by inferring from that text the existence of new rights not specifically contemplated in it. A characteristic example in that first category is the interpretation given by the Court to the terms 'civil rights' and 'criminal charge' as contained in Article 6 (fair trial).[17] The drafters of the Convention, at the time of its preparation, intended to limit the applicability of the fair trial guarantees to purely civil or criminal cases. The Court has nevertheless taken the view that these guarantees should also be extended to other categories of judicial procedure, such as administrative or disciplinary procedures, in situations where such procedures present strong elements of resemblance with civil or criminal processes; and not to leave national authorities the unfettered right to exclude them from the

---

[15] *Christine Goodwin v the United Kingdom* (11 July 2002) Application No. 28957/95.

[16] *Hénaf v France* (27 November 2003) Application No. 65436/01.

[17] The approach followed by Strasbourg in this respect, which has incrementally extended the purview of protection under Article 6, has never been disputed by the Contracting States. On the contrary it seems that it has met with their approval. It is to be noted that the guarantees of the Charter of Fundamental Rights of the European Union (see *infra*) of a fair trial cover all possible categories of court proceedings, without any exception whatsoever (see Article 47 of the Charter).

protection of the Convention simply because their domestic characterisation is not covered by the literal terms of Article 6.[18] In so far as the second category is concerned, the most characteristic field of 'law-making' activity by the Court is the protection of the environment. The *locus classicus* of the expansive interpretation of the Court on this matter is the case of *Lopez Ostra v Spain*,[19] where Strasbourg decided that Article 8, protecting private and family life and the home, had been violated because of serious environmental pollution caused by the operations of a waste-treatment plant situated near the applicant's house. That Spanish case heralded the beginning of an era of environmental protection cases where environmental damage was associated with a violation of the Convention. It should nevertheless be emphasised that in order for the Court to admit that an environmental hazard constitutes a violation of the Convention, applicants must show that the hazard affects them personally and rights already afforded to them by the Convention; it cannot be an abstract complaint amounting to an *actio popularis*.

d) The methods of interpreting the Convention that have just been described reflect the role that the Court assumes, with regard both to the harmonisation of the protection of human rights, as part of the integrational activity of the European institutions, and to furthering the ambit of the protected rights by expanding them in accordance with contemporaneous needs at each moment of the Convention's application. Both these attributes of the Court's jurisdictional activity would seem to be perfectly consonant with the intentions of the drafters, as expressed in the Preamble to the Convention.

It should be pointed out, however, that Strasbourg uses this power, and the legacy of the drafters, with considerable caution. Prudence and self-restraint are the keywords for an understanding of the manner in which the Court builds its case-law or departs from its precedents. In principle, whenever the Court delineates new boundaries in its case-law, it reaches its decision after carefully examining the existing approaches of the European States to the matter before it. In a situation where the Court realises that there is either a strong national

---

[18] *Oztürk v Germany* (21 February 1984) Application no. 8544/79.
[19] *Lopez Ostra v Spain* (9 December 1994) Application no. 16798/90.

consensus accepting a certain legal regime, or a wide acceptance of it, or at least a clear trend which does not seem to meet with objections on the part of those States which have not expressed their views, then, and only then, will it proceed to the establishment of a new jurisprudential principle. By contrast, in a situation where it realises that a matter before it presents an issue which European States have not touched upon, or in respect of which they are strongly opposed to a particular solution, the Court refrains from ruling in a manner that would impose a departure from national preferences and would make the Court the first to 'legislate' on a generally sensitive issue.[20]

It should also be noted that there is another dimension to the self-restraint principle in the Court's jurisprudential history, and that is the invocation and application by the Court of the margin of appreciation, to which Lord Hoffmann referred in his lecture. In accordance with this concept – which is of jurisprudential inspiration and is not provided for by the Convention – Strasbourg accepts that in certain categories of cases national authorities, and more particularly domestic courts, are better positioned than the international judge to assess which measures should be taken to balance conflicting rights or interests (on the one hand the rights of an individual – as protected by the Convention -, and, on the other, the rights or interests of the wider democratic society within which the individual lives and acts). In a large number of cases Strasbourg has refrained from proceeding with the balancing of the rights and interests involved in a case, at the stage of the examination of proportionality, by accepting that the national authorities, which had already done so, are more competent to assess such interests on the basis of the domestic realities.

However, acceptance of the margin of acceptation does not mean a total surrender of the Court to the choices made by the national authorities. In the *Handyside v the United Kingdom* judgment,[21] the Court stressed that '[t]he domestic margin of appreciation... [went] hand in

---

[20] The case of *Pretty v the United Kingdom* (17 July 2003) Application no. 2346/02 clearly illustrates the Court's reluctance to take the initiative of deciding on an issue which cannot find support in any legal order among the Contracting States, and which is still controversial in many European countries: that of legalising euthanasia. In this case the Court found that there had been no violation of the Convention, leaving the matter to mature before deciding otherwise.
[21] *Handyside v the United Kingdom* (7 December 1976) Application no. 5493/72.

hand with a European supervision', while in *Klass v Germany*[22] the Court said: 'this does not mean that the Contracting Parties enjoy an unlimited discretion... the Contracting States may not... adopt whatever measures they deem appropriate.' In the real world of the everyday application of the margin of appreciation, the Court first scrutinises the facts of the case and the response given by the national authorities to the issues relevant to the Convention, before giving the green light for the application of the margin and the exercise of its self-restraint. It can be said that the control made by the Court when it finally applies the margin of appreciation differs minimally from the control it exercises when it proceeds with its own tools to apply the proportionality test.

Further, the margin of appreciation is not applicable to all those cases for which the Court has given its own answers concerning the balancing of the rights and interests involved, through an established case-law developed in previous similar cases. Equally the margin of appreciation cannot be justifiably applied in cases for which European standards have developed, showing that the States Parties to the Convention have adopted positions on the relevant matter that indicate a *consensus* towards a common solution. Applying the margin of appreciation in these conditions would be tantamount to allowing a State, through the Court's judgment, to depart from a harmonious application of standards of protection already existing in Europe on a specific matter.

In any event, although the margin of appreciation continues to be invoked in many cases, the frequency of its application is constantly losing ground. This is the result of the ever-growing enrichment of the Strasbourg case-law with new detailed answers to a great number of issues concerning the rights protected by the Convention; but it is also the result of the fact that European States are increasingly in agreement on common standards of protection of human rights in many areas. Because of these phenomena the margin of appreciation is shrinking, for the benefit of more harmonised protection around Europe.

The Approval of Case-Law by the Contracting States
The Strasbourg Court has now been working for fifty years. It is submitted that a good test to assess its success or failure and the

---

[22] *Klass and Others v Germany* (6 September 1978) Application no. 5029/71.

approval or disapproval of its contribution to the protection of human rights in Europe and of its case-law, is to look at the reaction of those who are involved in its operation and who are affected by the consequences of its pronouncements, namely, the applicants and the Contracting States.

Admittedly, when a court of law decides in cases of opposing interests, there is always one party who is satisfied and one who is dissatisfied. Then in each individual case there is most often someone who complains and who usually considers that a court has decided unjustly. From this fate no court can escape - certainly not the Court in Strasbourg. Yet the question is not whether there may be disagreements between the parties with regard to specific cases, or allegations as to erroneous assessments of facts or laws, but whether, overall, the Court is considered to be a trustworthy institution which is correctly interpreting and applying its law and whether it meets the expectations of its visionary drafters and of those States which have entrusted it with the function of protecting human rights in Europe.

The continuous increase in the Court's case-load, with more than a hundred thousand cases pending, unquestionably shows that Strasbourg has gained, as a result of its work over the years, a good reputation throughout Europe; and this is despite the fact that it generally rejects more than ninety per cent of the applications lodged by individuals without detailed reasoning as to the grounds of rejection. Most applicants complain about this anomaly – unreasoned judicial decisions – which is unfortunately the price to pay for the flood of applications that the Court faces.

Then come the Contracting States. It is appropriate to look at the attitudes of States *vis-à-vis* the Court's pronouncements, first because the focus of this article is to show that Strasbourg acts within the limits of the mandate that was defined by the drafters and the Contracting States; and second because its survival largely depends upon the latter. The execution of its judgments is in their hands. The Court does not have any mechanism of enforcement, and the Committee of the Ministers of the Council of Europe – a political body composed of representatives of the Contracting States –, although entrusted with the power to monitor the proper compliance by States with the Court's pronouncements, is still a slow-moving organ and its reactions are rather lenient when it comes to the imposition of sanctions on a recalcitrant State. Hence if the States did not readily execute judgments, the whole Strasbourg system would find itself in serious trouble; not to mention, moreover, the fact that the Court is financially dependent on States for its unimpeded operation.

The indications available concerning the disposition of States towards the Court is, in principle, positive. One may safely proceed with such an assumption on the basis of the strong inferences that support it. The crucial elements that convincingly point to this conclusion are as follows:

a) The degree of compliance by States with the judgments of the Court. With few insignificant exceptions, States have always complied with its pronouncements; and, most of the time, with the requests made by the Committee of Ministers to extend the scope of these pronouncements by taking individual or general measures intended to align the domestic legal order of States with the essence of a pronouncement, thus going beyond the simple monetary compensation provided for in the judgment's operative part.

b) The approval of the interpretation that the Court gives to the clauses of the Convention. Indeed the very compliance by States with the Court's judgments attests to such approval; but not only that. The fact that during the fifty years of its operation no State has asked for withdrawal from the Convention – with the exception of Greece, but for other political reasons[23] or for amendment of its text is a good indication of States' satisfaction in this respect. It should not be forgotten that Contracting States have legislative power at their disposal. They could easily have used it to amend the Convention in a way that would preclude the Court from adopting interpretations that could be considered by them as incommensurate with the letter and spirit of the Convention. On the contrary, all the Protocols which have followed the coming into force of the Convention have either added new rights, extending the protection to new fields, or have increased the power of the Court to adjudicate on matters of human rights.

---

[23] Greece, during the colonels' dictatorship (1967-74), and in order to avoid a humiliating 'condemnation' by Strasbourg, voluntarily withdrew from the Council of Europe.

Characteristically, both the 11th and the ill-fated (for the moment, at least) 14th Protocols contain provisions which increase the obligations of the Contracting States – limiting their manoeuvring capacity when applying the Convention – and, at the same time, are intended to equip Strasbourg with effective tools so that the Court will be able to cope better with its ever-increasing case-load.[24]

c) The role that the Court's case-law plays in relation to European actors outside the close circuit of the Contracting States. Indeed, one of Strasbourg's major achievements is that it has gradually become, through its case-law, the beacon which, to varying degrees, directs third parties (in the strict legal sense of entities not participating in the Convention) towards a uniform application of human rights. It is clear that courts outside Europe frequently refer to the Strasbourg case-law in their decisions. But what is really more interesting – and pertinent from the point of view of our analysis – is that the European Community/Union has been strongly influenced by the Strasbourg case-law when dealing with human rights issues. The Court of Justice of the European Communities has relied on it in a large number of cases, considering that it is part, together with the constitutional principles of the Member States of the Community/Union, of the law applicable whenever issues of human rights arise in cases pending before it.[25]

Equally important, if not more so, is the fact that the EU's Charter of Fundamental Rights, which is mainly intended to deal with the protection of human rights within the institutional framework of the Union, expressly provides that the interpretation to be given by the Union's organs to the rights in that Charter that are similar to those laid down by the Convention must follow the case-law of the Court.[26] There

---

[24] The 11th Protocol merged the jurisdictional organs of the Convention, replacing them with a single court. It has also imposed an obligation on all the Contracting States to observe a regime, whereby, without any other formality, all individuals under their jurisdiction have the right to submit an application to the Court, after exhausting domestic remedies, to allege a violation of the Convention and seek the Court's protection. The 14th Protocol has come as a 'life-saver' for the Court, by providing for procedures to simplify and accelerate the Court's decision-making capacity.

[25] See, *inter alia*, TC Hartley, *The Foundations of European Community Law* (5th ed. Oxford University Press, Oxford 2003), Chapter 5; P Craig, and G Burca, *EU Law: Text, Cases and Materials* (3rd ed. Oxford University Press, Oxford 2002), Chapter 7.

[26] See Article 52 (3) of the *EU Charter of Fundamental Rights*.

is also an obligation for the Union to accede to the Convention, allowing individuals, in due course, to have direct recourse to Strasbourg against any acts or omissions of the Union's organs that may be alleged to violate the Convention.

If one takes into account the fact that all the members of the European Union – 27 for the time being – are equally Contracting States of the Convention, one can readily conclude that their strong emphasis on the applicability of the Court's case-law to the Union's own protection, apart from attesting to their continuous desire to ensure harmonisation of protection, is a good indicator of their confidence in the work being accomplished by Strasbourg.

Some Concluding Remarks

This modest reply to Lord Hoffmann's criticisms is not, of course, intended to establish the infallibility and omniscience of the Court. Like all human creations, the Court suffers from imperfections in both its structure and procedure, and, sometimes, in the decisions that it takes. This article's main aim has been to show that Lord Hoffmann's scheme that human rights are universal in abstraction but national in application does not apply in situations where States, belonging to the same ideological or geopolitical family – or aspiring to become members of that family – decide by common consent to strengthen their ties through a gradual harmonisation of their institutions, laws and practices. And this is the case for those countries that participate in the Council of Europe, which are, at the same time, Contracting Parties to the Convention. Their willingness to share common values and principles is manifested not only in the text of the constitutive Convention ratified by them, but also in the continuous support that they provide to ensure the operation of the Strasbourg system and its main product, its case-law.

National Security and Fundamental Rights: the Redundancy or Illegitimacy of Judicial Deference

RONNIE DENNIS[*]

Introduction

In the course of determining whether legislation or executive action is compatible with fundamental rights, the courts frequently refer to the notion of 'deference' as a relevant or even determinative consideration. The use of this term has been disapproved for bearing 'overtones of servility',[1] but the alternatives conceived by the courts are no different in substance.[2] Whether by reference to 'deference',[3] 'latitude',[4] 'relative institutional competence',[5] the 'discretionary area of judgment'[6] or 'margin of discretion',[7] the courts have recognised limits to the legitimate scope of judicial decision-making. These limits constrain the extent to which they will be willing to interfere with decisions reached by Parliament or the executive as to how a particular social problem

---

[*] Ronnie Dennis studied for an LLB degree at UCL.

[1] R (ProLife Alliance) v British Broadcasting Corporation [2002] EWCA Civ 297 at para [75] (Lord Hoffmann).

[2] See, for example, Tweed v Parades Commission for Northern Ireland [2006] UKHL 53 at [36], where Lord Carswell refers to 'a margin of discretion, frequently referred to as deference or…latitude.' Lord Hoffmann's disapproval of the term 'deference' is a consequence of His Lordship's understanding of the limits to judicial decision-making being a matter of law arising out of the separation of powers, rather than one of 'gracious concession' (see n 1 at para [75]). This is discussed further below.

[3] Secretary of State for the Home Department v Rehman (Consolidated Appeals) [2001] UKHL 47 at para [49] (Lord Hoffmann).

[4] A and Others v Secretary of State for the Home Department [2004] UKHL 56 at para [80] (Lord Nicholls).

[5] Ibid., at para [29] (Lord Bingham).

[6] International Transport Roth GmbH and others v Secretary of State for the Home Department [2002] EWCA Civ 158 at para [81] (Laws LJ).

[7] R (Farrakhan) v Secretary of State for the Home Department [2002] EWCA Civ 606 at para [71] (Lord Phillips MR). This should be distinguished from the 'margin of appreciation' afforded by the European Court of Human Rights ('ECtHR') to national authorities (including national courts), which reflects the principle of subsidiarity peculiar to the European Court as an international tribunal (A and Others v The United Kingdom, Application No. 3455/05, 19 February 2009 (ECtHR) at para [173]).

should be resolved. Where they are placed is ostensibly not the subject of any disagreement, but in fact there are two discernable approaches.

In some instances, the limits imported by reference to deference are conceived as preventing the court from exercising a primary decision-making function, or from interfering with the decision under review if it falls within the range of legitimate choices open to the primary decision-maker. One example of such an expression is that in Fordham's *Judicial Review Handbook*,[8] which was cited with approval by Lord Carswell in *Tweed v Parades Commission for Northern Ireland*:[9]

> '[The] concept of "latitude"…recognises that the court does not become the primary decision-maker on matters of policy, judgment and discretion, so that public authorities should be left with room to make legitimate choices.'

Conceived in this way, recognition of the need for deference merely recalls the limits already inherent in the grounds of review. These prescribe that the court may only interfere with the decision under challenge if it is shown to be incompatible with the rights of those affected. It follows that the court does not exercise a primary decision-making function on matters of policy, and that the primary decision-maker is left with room to make legitimate choices between all of the available measures that can be shown to be compatible with fundamental rights. This understanding of deference is unobjectionable since it reflects the legitimate limits of judicial decision-making necessitated by the separation of powers, and is in fact conducive to the protection of fundamental rights. But conceived in this way, 'deference' has no autonomous significance.

In other instances, the need for deference is conceived as having a more restrictive effect, preventing the court from exercising its own independent judgment as to whether the decision under review is in fact compatible with fundamental rights. According to Lester and Pannick's definition, the 'margin of discretion' refers to the courts' willingness to 'accept that there are some circumstances in which the legislature and the executive are better placed', 'to assess the needs of

---

[8] M Fordham, *Judicial Review Handbook* (3rd ed., Hart, Oxford 2001), para [58.2].
[9] At para [36].

society, and to make difficult choices between competing considerations…'[10] In *Tweed* Lord Carswell cites this passage with approval alongside Fordham's definition, without averring to any distinction between the two.[11] This is indicative of the courts' failure to distinguish between these competing conceptions, despite the importance of the distinction. It is only in this more restrictive manifestation that deference has any illegitimate impact. Accepting that the legislature or the executive is better placed to resolve the particular social problem in view, the court abstains from exercising its own independent judgment on the rights-compatibility of the impugned decision. This degree of deference leaves the complainant without recourse to any genuinely independent tribunal for the resolution of his dispute with the state, undermining the protection of his fundamental rights.

This distinction is the same as that drawn by Trevor Allan, who moves from a study of the limits necessitated by the separation of powers to his conclusion that:

> '[T]here is no role for any distinct doctrine of deference to fulfil: its invocation above and beyond the ordinary constraints inherent in judicial review amounts to…a failure to protect legal rights.'[12]

However, the conclusion that this more restrictive conception of deference is illegitimate does not necessarily follow from this objection. This conclusion depends on showing that the considerations seen as justifying this degree of judicial restraint are misguided, and therefore incapable of supporting the argument that the courts should, in some circumstances, abstain from exercising their own independent judgment on review.

In this discussion my focus is on the courts' approach to deference in cases involving fundamental rights and issues of national security. This is to do justice to the particular considerations arising in this context, particularly as regards the judiciary's supposedly

---

[10] A Lester and D Pannick (eds), *Human Rights Law and Practice* (1st ed., Butterworths, London 1999) para [3.21].

[11] At para [36].

[12] TRS Allan, 'Human rights and judicial review: a critique of "due deference"' (2006) 65(3) *Cambridge Law Journal* 671, 680.

insufficient access to information and expertise, and alleged lack of democratic legitimacy. It is also in recognition of the contemporary relevance of the interaction between fundamental rights and national security, in circumstances where the Government has at times been ambivalent about protecting rights in its efforts to address the threat from international terrorism. At its worst, this friction led the nation's second most senior Law Lord to express the view that:

> 'The real threat to the life of the nation, in the sense of a people living in accordance with its traditional laws and political values, comes not from terrorism but from laws such as these.'[13]

This approach also takes the arguments in favour of judicial deference at their strongest, since it is in this context that some of the most outspoken assertions of the need for judicial restraint have been expressed.[14] This is in recognition of the fact that:

> 'It is the first responsibility of government…to protect and safeguard the lives of its citizens…and…the duty of the court to do all it can to respect and uphold that principle.'[15]

However, the distinction drawn here between the two conceptions of deference, and the argument made that the one is redundant and the other illegitimate, are equally applicable beyond the context of national security.[16]

In developing each of these arguments in turn I hope to establish that the notion of deference, however conceived, should no longer be recognised as an autonomous principle in cases involving fundamental rights and issues of national security.

---

[13] *A* (n 4) at para [97] (Lord Hoffmann).
[14] *Ibid.*, at para [192] (Lord Walker).
[15] *Ibid.*, at para [99] (Lord Hope).
[16] See further Allan (n 12).

The limits inherent in the grounds of review

In *Secretary of State for the Home Department v Rehman*,[17] the Special Immigration Appeals Commission ('SIAC') was invited to review the Secretary of State's decision to deport the appellant in the interests of national security under s3(5)(b) of the Immigration Act 1971. The Commission concluded that it had not been established, 'to a high civil balance of probabilities', that the appellant 'ha[d] engaged in conduct that endanger[ed] the national security of the United Kingdom'.[18] On appeal before the House of Lords, Lord Hoffmann held that the Commission had erred in law by failing to recognise 'certain inherent limitations…within the judicial function' arising 'from the need…to show proper deference to the primary decision-maker'.[19] Later His Lordship explained what he meant by reference to the need for deference:

> 'First, the Commission is not the primary decision-maker…Secondly…the appellate body…should not ordinarily interfere with a case in which…the view of the Home Secretary is one which could reasonably be entertained.'[20]

This is the most conspicuous formulation of deference in its limited sense that I take issue with here as having no autonomous significance. Others are arguably capable of more than one understanding, but Lord Nicholls' expression of 'latitude' in *A v Secretary of State for the Home Department*[21] certainly falls into the same category:

> '[T]he courts will accord…an appropriate degree of latitude…interven[ing] only when it is apparent that…the primary decision-maker must have given insufficient weight to the human rights factor.'[22]

Each of these examples defines the need for deference as preventing the court from exercising a primary decision-making function, or from

---

[17] n 3.
[18] Cited by Lord Slynn in the House of Lords at para [3].
[19] At para [49].
[20] At para [57].
[21] n 4.
[22] At para [80].

interfering with the decision under review if it falls within the range of legitimate choices open to the primary decision-maker. But neither of these restrictions is dependent on the recognition of any notion of deference. Both are already inherent in the limited grounds of review, which reflect the legitimate limitations to judicial decision-making prescribed by the separation of powers.[23]

The principle of the separation of powers recognises that there are three main functions of government – legislative, executive and judicial – each of which should be performed by a different institution. Broadly, the first involves the enactment of law and holding the executive to account; the second, the administration of law and the conduct of foreign affairs; and the third, the application of laws of general application to individual cases.[24] In the British constitution, there is no rigid distinction between the legislature and the executive, but for our purposes it is sufficient that the judiciary is strongly independent from both.[25]

In this context, the judiciary's role involves the review of legislation and executive action, when challenged, for compatibility with fundamental rights. In the exercise of this jurisdiction, a court may be invited to review the compatibility of a sensitive decision taken by the executive and, potentially, approved by Parliament, which is likely to be the result of the balancing of competing interests and the culmination of a thorough process of consultation. But the court is limited to assessing the rights-compatibility of the decision actually taken, rather than deciding the issue again for itself. As Jeffrey Jowell puts it:

> 'They ask not: "would we decide this question differently?" but "does this action fit the necessary qualities of a rights-based democracy…?"'[26]

In the particular context of national security, this distinction is drawn in the following way by Lord Nicholls in *A*:

---

[23] Allan (n 12) 679.

[24] NW Barber, 'Prelude to the Separation of Powers' (2001) 60(1) *Cambridge Law Journal* 59, 60.

[25] See, for example, *R (Anderson) v Secretary of State for the Home Department* [2002] UKHL 46 at para [39] (Lord Steyn).

[26] J Jowell, 'Judicial deference: servility, civility or institutional capacity?' (2003) *Public Law* 592, 598.

'[T]he Government alone is able to…decide what counter-terrorism steps are needed…The duty of the courts is to check that…[it] do[es] not overlook the human rights of persons adversely affected.'[27]

It follows that the courts are not entitled to exercise a primary decision-making function, in the sense of determining what the best measures might be to address the particular social problem in view, and that Parliament and the executive are afforded the freedom to make legitimate choices, since they may choose from any of the range of options that are compatible with fundamental rights. These are the limits referred to in the formulations of deference extracted at the beginning of this section. But their existence is not contingent on the recognition of any such principle. In fact they are already implicit in the 'ordinary mechanisms of judicial review',[28] specifically in the limits inherent in the grounds of review.

According to the limited grounds of review the court may only interfere with a decision, when challenged, if it is shown to be incompatible with the rights of those affected. If the decision is incompatible with some absolute right, which is to say one that is incapable of abrogation under any circumstances, then it clearly falls outside the range of legitimate decisions open to the primary decision-maker. As per Lord Hoffmann in *Rehman*:

'If there is a danger of torture, the Government must find some other way of dealing with a threat to national security.'[29]

Conversely, if the decision only infringes some qualified right, which is to say one capable of abrogation in the pursuit of a legitimate objective, it is not shown to be unlawful unless it is unreasonable or disproportionate in the pursuit of the objective in view. It follows that the court must recognise that the primary decision-maker is entitled to reach any of the range of decisions open to him that, while infringing the qualified rights of those affected, can nonetheless be shown to be legitimate in the pursuit of some competing objective.

---

[27] At para [79].
[28] Allan (n 12) 680.
[29] At para [54].

In respect of those rights capable of abrogation at common law, the position is clear. As per Lord Bridge in *R v Secretary of State for the Home Department, ex parte Brind*:[30]

> 'The primary judgment as to whether the particular competing public interest justifies the particular restriction…falls to…the Secretary of State…[W]e are entitled to…as[k] whether a reasonable Secretary of State…could reasonably make that primary judgment.'

The court will only interfere if the infringement is 'unreasonable in the sense of being beyond the range of responses open to a reasonable decision-maker…'[31] These expressions of the limits to judicial decision-making, while recognising the constraints imposed by the less restrictive notion of deference, are not dependent on the recognition of any such principle. If Lord Bridge were to refer to 'deference' in this context, it would not add anything to the limits already inherent in the reasonableness approach applicable at common law.

As for those rights capable of limitation under the Convention, the position is more contentious. The court applies a proportionality analysis, according to which the primary decision-maker may reach any decision that is proportionate to the legitimate aim in view.[32] But it has been argued that the public authority does not retain any scope for discretion under this approach, since it requires the court to determine whether 'the means used to impair the right…are no more than is necessary to accomplish the objective.'[33] Danny Nicol argues that this effectively negates 'the ability of the public authority to choose between a range of lawful options', '[s]ince the only lawful solution will be that which involves minimum interference'.[34]

This argument overlooks the difference in approach taken by the courts in the exercise of their particular functions on review. It has been held that in the exercise of the proportionality analysis the court

---

[30] [1991] 1 AC 696 at para [749].
[31] *R v Secretary of State for the Home Department, ex parte Simms* [2000] 2 AC 115 at para [144] (Lord Hope).
[32] *R (Daly) v Secretary of State for the Home Department* [2001] UKHL 26 at para [27] (Lord Steyn).
[33] *Ibid.*
[34] D Nicol, 'Law and politics after the Human Rights Act' (2006) *Public Law* 722, 734.

does not become the primary decision-maker on matters of policy.[35] As such it is not interested in what the least restrictive measures might be, but merely whether the measures actually taken can be shown to be no more restrictive than necessary. Thus in *A*, which is discussed further below, the House of Lords concluded that the incarceration of foreign terrorist suspects without trial had not been shown to be 'strictly required', because British nationals who posed the same threat were subject to less restrictive measures.[36] The court did not undertake its own investigation into what the least restrictive measures might be. It simply looked at the arguments and the evidence adduced by both sides to determine whether it had been shown that the measures under challenge were no more restrictive than necessary. The Government was effectively free to choose from any of the range of options that it could have convinced the court in argument satisfied that test.

It is apparent, therefore, that the court does not exercise a primary decision-making function on matters of policy, and that the primary decision-maker is permitted to choose from any of a range of legitimate options, each of which could be shown to be compatible with fundamental rights. These limitations are unobjectionable, both because they are the necessary result of restrictions inherent in the separation of powers, and because they do not have a prejudicial effect on the protection of fundamental rights.[37] But these limitations are not dependent on the recognition of any notion of deference. Insofar as the limits imported by reference to deference only have this limited effect, that notion is unobjectionable, but it has no autonomous significance.

Deference as inimical to the protection of fundamental rights

In its stricter formulation, deference is conceived as imposing limits beyond those inherent in the grounds of review. When the need for deference is expressed in these terms, the court betrays an unwillingness to interfere with the impugned decision, not because the balance of argument suggests that it is compatible with fundamental rights, but because it feels itself to be less well placed than the primary decision-

---

[35] See, for example, *Huang v Secretary of State for the Home Department* [2007] UKHL 11 at para [13] (Lord Bingham).
[36] At para [132] (Lord Hope).
[37] See further below.

maker to resolve that question. This degree of deference therefore constrains the court's decision as to whether the measures under review are compatible with fundamental rights, rather than merely limiting it to the resolution of that question. As per Lord Steyn:

> '[Deference] refers to the idea of a court…declining to make its own independent judgment on a particular issue.'[38]

The effects of this degree of judicial restraint are apparent from the decision of the Court of Appeal in R *(on the application of Farrakhan) v Secretary of State for the Home Department.*[39] The court was invited to review the Home Secretary's decision to refuse entry to the spiritual leader of the 'Nation of Islam', which Lord Phillips MR described as 'a religious, social and political movement whose aims include 'the regeneration of black self-esteem, dignity and self-discipline".[40] The Home Secretary had formed the view that the appellant posed a threat to public order, specifically to relations between the Muslim and Jewish communities.[41]

At first instance, Turner J held that 'the contemporary, and undisputed, evidence' was that the claimant had 'endeavoured to follow a path of reconciliation between Jews and Black Muslims'.[42] The learned judge also noted that there was no record of disorder at any public gathering associated with the appellant, some of which Jews had been invited to attend, and one of which had even taken place in Israel. He concluded that it had not been shown that there was a more than 'nominal risk' posed by Mr Farrakhan's visit,[43] and therefore that the refusal constituted an unjustified infringement of his common law and Article 10 rights to freedom of expression. Granting leave to appeal, Sedley LJ expressed the view that the Home Secretary did not have any realistic prospect of success because of the 'exiguousness of the grounds for [the] decision.'[44]

---

[38] Lord Steyn, 'Deference: a tangled story' (2005) *Public Law* 346, 349.
[39] [2002] EWCA Civ 606.
[40] At para [1].
[41] At para [2].
[42] 2001 WL 949875 at para [53].
[43] *Ibid.*
[44] Cited in the House of Lords at para [4] (Lord Phillips MR).

The Court of Appeal reversed Mr Justice Turner's decision, but not because it took a different view of the weight of the evidence and arguments adduced by the Home Secretary. The court's reasoning moves from a simple recognition of the need to afford the Home Secretary 'a particularly wide margin of discretion',[45] to the conclusion that he had provided 'sufficient explanation'[46] for his decision, which had therefore not been shown to be disproportionate in the interests of preventing public disorder. There is no doubt that the court's willingness to defer to the Home Secretary was determinative of the outcome of the appeal, where closer scrutiny of the reasons for his decision had revealed them to be 'exiguous'.

The considerations that lead the courts to exercise this degree of restraint are referred to by Lord Hoffmann in *Rehman* as the basis for His Lordship's disapproval of another aspect of the Commission's decision. SIAC held that the appellant's deportation could not be conducive to national security unless he was involved in violent activity targeted at 'the United Kingdom, its system of government or its people.'[47] This was contrary to the Home Secretary's submission that the appellant should be deported because of his involvement with Islamic terrorist organisations operating in the Indian subcontinent. Lord Hoffmann emphasised 'the need for the judicia[ry] to respect the decisions of ministers' on what national security required. This was for two reasons:

> 'It is not only that the executive has access to special information and expertise in these matters. It is also that such decisions, with serious potential results for the community,[48] require a legitimacy which can be conferred only by entrusting them to persons responsible to the community through the democratic process.'[49]

---

[45] At para [71].

[46] At para [79].

[47] Cited in the House of Lords at para [43].

[48] It is somewhat paradoxical that His Lordship was willing to reach a different conclusion to that of the executive on the existence of a threat to the life of the nation in *A*, where that decision had far more serious potential results for the community. His Lordship's willingness to agree with the Home Secretary in *Rehman* may in fact betray his sympathy for the arguments adduced. As Allan argues, '[D]eference…is likely, in practice, to disguise an endorsement of the views acceded to…' (n 12, 681).

[49] At para [62].

In yet other cases the courts have evinced an absolute unwillingness to interfere with the decision under review, on the basis of limits taken to be inherent in the separation of powers. Thus in *Rehman,* Lord Hoffmann went further than expressing the need for the judiciary to respect the decisions of ministers on what national security required, holding that SIAC was 'not entitled' to differ from the Home Secretary on the issue of whether the appellant's deportation could, in the circumstances alleged by the Home Secretary, be conducive to national security.[50] This was on the grounds that:

> 'Under the constitution of the United Kingdom…decisions as to whether something is…in the interests of national security are not a matter for judicial decision.'[51]

In both scenarios, the court betrays an unwillingness to disagree with the decision under review because of its recognition of its own perceived democratic, institutional or constitutional limitations. In doing so, it agrees with the primary decision-maker that the decision is compatible with fundamental rights not because it finds its arguments persuasive, but because of extraneous considerations that do not go to the weight of the evidence and arguments adduced to support the decision.

This has a number of effects. Firstly, as Allan argues, it amounts to an abdication of the judicial function for the protection of fundamental rights. As per Lord Bingham in *A:*[52]

> '[T]he court's role under the 1998 Act is as the guardian of human rights. It cannot abdicate this responsibility.'[53]

The effective performance of this responsibility is dependent on the courts attaching determinative weight to the arguments and evidence adduced by both sides that go to the rights-compatibility of the impugned decision. While democratic accountability and access to a

---

[50] At para [53].
[51] At para [50].
[52] At para [41].
[53] This responsibility was equally incumbent on the courts before the introduction of the 1998 Act; see *A* at para [88] (Lord Hoffmann).

wide range of information and expertise may be generally conducive to good governance, neither characteristic can provide an argument for the rights-compatibility of a given decision. As Allan puts it:

> 'A weak argument for infringing rights gains no additional strength from its being adopted by a[n]…accountable decision-maker…'[54]

A reasoned conclusion on the rights-compatibility of a given decision cannot be one founded on arguments that are not rationally connected to the determination of that issue. This degree of deference therefore 'threatens to displace law and reason…[with] expediency and arbitrariness'.[55] Where the decision under challenge is incompatible with fundamental rights, the effect of this degree of restraint is also to compound the infringement by giving it what Sullivan J has called a 'veneer of legality'.[56]

　　This degree of deference also undermines the legitimacy of judicial decision-making, which is contingent on the judiciary's independence and impartiality, as well as its duty to give reasons for its decisions.[57] By acknowledging the need for this degree of deference, the court is effectively predisposed to side with one party to the dispute, regardless of the lawfulness of the decision under review.[58] As regards the duty to give reasons, this cannot be satisfied where the court affords the primary decision-maker this degree of deference, since it is in the nature of such a decision that it is no longer incumbent on the court to reach its own fully reasoned decision on the appropriate outcome of the dispute. Both of these considerations are also likely to undermine the acceptability of the decision from the point of view of the complainant, who will not be satisfied that justice has been done if he has been denied recourse to an independent tribunal, and where that tribunal cannot offer adequate reasons for him to accept the decision as a just outcome.[59]

---

[54] Allan (n 12) 688.
[55] *Ibid.*, 695.
[56] *Secretary of State for the Home Department v MB* [2006] HRLR 29 at para [103].
[57] See further below.
[58] Allan (n 12) 676.
[59] TRS Allan, 'Common Law Reason and the Limits of Judicial Deference' in D Dyzenhaus (ed.), *The Unity of Public Law* (Hart Publishing, Oxford 2004) 289.

In spite of these arguments, it remains for proponents of judicial reticence to argue that these costs are merely the unfortunate consequences of necessary limitations to judicial decision-making. As was seen above, these limitations may be said to arise because of the court's limited role under the separation of powers, or because of its inferior democratic credentials and insufficient access to information and expertise. If it can be shown that these arguments are misguided, then it becomes clear that the abdication of function in these cases is illegitimate, and that the costs that it entails are therefore unjustifiable. It follows, in that case, that the courts should no longer recognise deference as having any constraining effect beyond that already inherent in the grounds of review.

The separation of powers

Lord Hoffmann elaborated on his understanding of the limits imposed by the separation of powers in R *(ProLife Alliance) v British Broadcasting Corporation*:[60]

> '[T]he independence of the courts is necessary for a proper decision o[n]...claims of violation of human rights...[and] majority approval is necessary for a proper decision on policy...'[61]

His Lordship's conclusion in *Rehman* therefore followed inexorably from his conclusion that 'the question of whether something is 'in the interests' of national security is...a matter of...policy'.[62]

Read literally, Lord Hoffmann's approach is internally inconsistent for being founded on an unsustainable distinction between decisions on policy and decisions on the violation of legal rights.[63] The assessment of the rights-compatibility of legislation or executive action frequently, if not necessarily, involves the determination of the lawfulness of a given policy decision. As Lord Steyn points out, 'Most legislation is passed to advance a policy'[64] and the same can be said of

---

[60] n 1.

[61] At para [76].

[62] At para [50].

[63] This has been characterised as the 'separate spheres' approach; see D Feldman, 'Human rights, terrorism and risk: the roles of politicians and judges' (2006) *Public Law* 364.

[64] n 38, 357.

most executive action. It follows that the courts cannot make decisions on rights without interfering with policy decisions. Similarly, the determination of whether a right has been unlawfully infringed may depend on whether its infringement is legitimate in the pursuit of some competing policy objective, for example whether it is necessary in the interests of national security. Questions of policy are therefore inextricably bound up with the determination of whether a particular decision is compatible with fundamental rights.[65]

His Lordship may be drawing the distinction set out above between policy formation and the review of the lawfulness of a particular policy decision, but this does not seem to be the case. This is because it follows, on His Lordship's view, that the courts cannot interfere with decisions as to what is in the interests of national security. On the view espoused earlier of the proper constraints imposed by the separation of powers, the court might legitimately interfere with such a decision if it found it to be incompatible with fundamental rights.

This apparent contradiction can only be avoided if His Lordship is understood as expressing the view that, in some cases, the independence of the courts is really not necessary for a proper decision on rights. On this view, the courts cannot come to their own decisions on rights where the issue of their infringement involves the resolution of sensitive policy questions. This effectively negates the judicial protection of fundamental rights. In *Rehman*, for example, it was no longer incumbent on the executive to justify the appellant's deportation as being proportionate in the interests of national security, since what was in the interests of national security was a matter exclusively for him. The appellant would have no remedy from the courts if his deportation was deemed to be conducive to national security because, for example, he was a supporter of a political organisation, committed to achieving its objectives peacefully, that the Secretary of State deemed to be involved in terrorism.[66]

---

[65] *Ibid.*, 355.

[66] See *Lord Alton of Liverpool and others v Secretary of State for the Home Department* [2008] 1 WLR 2341, where the Secretary of State proscribed the People's Mojahadeen Organisation of Iran – a political organisation whose members included thirty-five members of the two Houses of Parliament – as a terrorist organisation for the purposes of the Terrorism Act 2000. Rejecting the Home Secretary's application to appeal, Lord Phillips CJ expressed the view that, '[T]he

In any event, Lord Hoffmann's dicta on the subject in *Rehman* should be treated as *obiter*, since His Lordship was the only member of the House of Lords to rely on the absolute impunity of the Secretary of State in determining what national security required. Lord Slynn seemed to recognise the absurdity of this approach,[67] before reaching to the same conclusion as that of Lord Hoffmann by a more legitimate course of reasoning. Having considered the evidence and arguments adduced by both sides, His Lordship simply concluded that:

> '[R]eciprocal co-operation between the United Kingdom and other states in combating international terrorism is capable of promoting the United Kingdom's national security…'[68]

The proper limits imposed by the separation of powers have already been referred to as being secured by the limited grounds of review. The separation of legislative, executive and judicial functions is secured by the difference in approach taken by those institutions to the exercise of their particular functions. Thus, as David Feldman argues:

> 'One can respect the role of the executive as makers of policy while upholding the obligation of the courts to ensure that the policy is not unlawful…'[69]

Lord Hoffmann's approach confuses this distinction by seeking to distinguish spheres of legal and political decision-making according to the subject-matter of the decision, rather than by reference to the particular questions asked by the different institutions of government in the performance of their particular functions. The duty incumbent on the courts to review the compatibility of legislation and executive action does not admit of any qualification according to the subject-matter of the impugned decision.

If authority were needed for this proposition it can be taken from the House of Lords' decision in *A*. The courts were invited to review the lawfulness of s23 of the Anti-terrorism, Crime and Security

---

decision-making process in this case has signally fallen short of the standards which our public law sets…' (at para [57]).

[67] See para [15].

[68] At para [17].

[69] n 63, 376.

Act 2001, which provided for the indefinite detention without trial of foreign terrorist suspects who could not be deported because of the risk that they might be subject to torture or inhuman or degrading treatment in their country of origin.[70] In the Court of Appeal, Lord Woolf CJ referred to Lord Hoffmann's dicta in *Rehman* as authority for his conclusion that:

> 'Whether…action was only necessary in relation to non-national[s]…is an issue on which it is impossible for this Court to differ from the Secretary of State.'[71]

Before the House of Lords, the Attorney-General made submissions to the same effect:

> '[I]t was for [Parliament and the executive]…to judge the response necessary…These were matters…calling for an exercise of political and not judicial judgment.'[72]

The majority of the House of Lords rejected this contention, recognising that such an approach could not be reconciled with the duty incumbent on the courts to assess the proportionality of any interference with Convention rights.[73] The majority concluded that the measures taken were not rationally connected to the exigencies of the situation, for failing to address the threat posed by suspected terrorists who were British nationals, and for leaving those subject to detention free to leave the United Kingdom for any country willing to receive them.[74] The measures taken had also not been shown to be strictly required, in circumstances where the same threat posed by UK nationals was being dealt with by less restrictive measures.[75] In reaching this conclusion their Lordships clearly felt entitled to interfere with the Home Secretary's assessment of what national security required. This was necessary if the court was to fulfil its obligations under the

---

[70] See *Chahal v United Kingdom* (1996) 23 EHRR 413.
[71] [2002] EWCA Civ 1502 at para [40].
[72] As per Lord Bingham at para [37].
[73] See paras [44] (Lord Bingham) and [108] (Lord Hope).
[74] See paras [44] (Lord Bingham) and [133] (Lord Hope).
[75] *Ibid.*

separation of powers to review legislation and executive action for compatibility with fundamental rights.

Specialist information and expertise

It will be recalled that in *Rehman* Lord Hoffmann emphasised the need for the courts to respect the executive's assessment of what was in the interests of national security, given its superior access to specialist information and expertise. Similarly, in *Farrakhan* the Court of Appeal's willingness to afford the Home Secretary 'a particularly wide margin of discretion' was partly in recognition of 'the very detailed consideration, involving widespread consultation, that [he] has given to his decision…'[76] This objection was put even more strongly by Laws LJ in his dissenting judgment in *International Transport Roth GmbH and others v Secretary of State for the Home Department*,[77] where His Lordship expressed the view that the 'factual merits' of decisions dealing with matters of defence 'cannot sensibly be scrutinised by the courts'.[78]

The fundamental objection to arguments couched in these terms is that they do not provide any reason why the courts might be incapable of effectively performing their particular functions on review. The effective performance of the courts' functions for the protection of fundamental rights is not dependent on their having access to the same wealth of information and expertise as that available to Parliament and the executive. This is only necessary for the formulation of initial policy decisions, where there is a need for the primary decision-maker to have regard to all of the available information and expertise in order to determine the most appropriate measures to address the particular social problem in view.

Conversely, in the exercise of its jurisdiction on review, the court's only concern is the rights-compatibility of the impugned decision, which should be capable of demonstration in argument, and all the more so if it is the result of a thorough process of consultation and the balancing of the competing interests of those affected.[79] If not, then the decision cannot represent a legitimate exercise of public

---

[76] At para [72].
[77] n 6.
[78] At para [85].
[79] Allan (n 12) 692.

power, at least not in a society that values 'the supremacy of reason' over 'expediency and arbitrariness'.[80] In such a society, as David Dyzenhaus argues:

> 'What justifies all public power is the ability of its incumbents to offer adequate reasons for the[ir] decisions…'[81]

This argument can be put even more forcefully than this, since not only are the courts not inhibited in the performance of their particular functions by these considerations, but their particular brand of expertise, and the adversarial process itself, are both conducive to the effective performance of their responsibilities for the protection of fundamental rights.

The courts are plainly better equipped to assess the reasonableness and proportionality of different courses of action, since they possess a greater degree of experience and expertise with regard to the proper application of those legal standards.[82] They are also well placed to assess the probity and reliability of evidence, having at their disposal the tools of forensic examination that are conducive to its accurate assessment. These include the facility for cross-examination, which has the additional potential of eliciting information that might not otherwise have been discovered,[83] as well as the ability to assess the demeanour of witnesses giving evidence in person.[84] The nature of the adversarial process is itself conducive to producing the best decision on rights, by focusing on the rights-compatibility of the impugned decision, and providing a forum for the citizen and the state to challenge each other by way of reasoned argument.[85]

---

[80] *Ibid,* 694.

[81] D Dyzenhaus, 'The Politics of Deference: Judicial Review and Democracy' in M Taggart (ed.), *The Province of Administrative Law* (Hart Publishing, Oxford 1997) 305.

[82] T Scaramuzza, 'Judicial deference versus effective control: the English courts and the protection of human rights in the context of terrorism' (2006) 11(2) *Coventry Law Journal* 2, 10.

[83] See, for example, *The Queen on the Application of Binyan Mohamed v Secretary of State for Foreign and Commonwealth Affairs* [2008] EWHC 2048, where the cross-examination of a witness for the Security Services led to the discovery of information that would not otherwise have been disclosed to the Parliamentary Intelligence and Security Committee.

[84] I Dennis, *The Law of Evidence* (3rd ed. Sweet and Maxwell, London 2007) 661.

[85] D Feldman (n 63) 381.

The House of Lords' decision in *A* provides authority for the rejection of arguments in favour of this degree of deference founded on concerns of institutional capacity. As has been seen, the court in that case scrutinised the factual merits of the measures introduced under s23 in order to determine the proportionality of that provision. Lord Bingham referred to the Newton Committee's finding that of the people suspected to be involved in international terrorism, 'nearly half are British nationals'.[86] Their Lordships were also alert to the fact that one individual had 'simply got the Eurostar to France',[87] Lord Bingham expressing the commonsensical view that this was 'hard to reconcile with a belief in his capacity to inflict serious injury to the people…of this country'.[88] In those circumstances the majority concluded that the measures employed had not been shown to be proportionate to the exigencies of the situation. They were not inhibited from doing so by any lack of information or expertise.

On the view espoused here, Jeffrey Jowell is wrong to suggest that the court should have conceded sole responsibility for the assessment of whether there existed a threat to the life of the nation within the meaning of Article 15(1) to the executive, on the basis of 'institutional [in]capacity'. Jowell argues that:

> '[T]here is no reason why the courts may not concede the superior intelligence-gathering capacity of the executive to answer that question…'[89]

But it does not follow that the answer to that question should be surrendered up to the executive. If the decision is legitimate this should be capable of demonstration in argument, if necessary by the presentation of the same evidence and expertise as that relied upon by the government in making its own assessment. In *A*, Lord Hope expressed the view that '[t]he judgment that has to be formed…lies

---

[86] At para [32].
[87] K Starmer, 'Setting the record straight: human rights in an era of international terrorism' (2007) 2 *European Human Rights Law Review* 123, 124. See para [33] (Lord Bingham).
[88] At para [33].
[89] n 26, 598.

outside the expertise of the courts',[90] but His Lordship also recognised that:

> 'There is ample evidence…to show that the Government were fully justified in taking the view…that there was an emergency threatening the life of the nation.'[91]

The former statement might refer to the formation of the initial judgment which, as I have argued here, is the exclusive prerogative of the executive. But Lord Hope implicitly acknowledges that any defensible conclusion on the issue was capable of demonstration in argument, and therefore not beyond the court's institutional capacity.[92]

It also follows that there is no place for the graduated approach advocated by Laws LJ in *Roth*, according to which:

> '[G]reater or lesser deference will be due according to whether the subject matter lies more readily within the…expertise of the democratic powers or the courts.'[93]

Conceived in this way, the expertise of the courts does not differ depending on the subject-matter of the decision under review. It always involves the assessment of competing arguments and the evaluation of evidence, whether the decision has been taken in the interests of national security or in the pursuit of any other policy objective.

A peculiar feature of cases touching on issues of national security is that some of the information relevant to the determination of whether a decision is compatible with fundamental rights may be subject to measures restricting its disclosure in the public interest. In those circumstances the Government has been inclined to oppose judicial intervention on the grounds that:

---

[90] At para [116].

[91] At para [118].

[92] Thomas Poole argues that 'traces of deference' are apparent in their Lordships' treatment of this question ('Courts and conditions of uncertainty in "times of crisis"' (2008) *Public Law* 234, 243). The better view, however, is that the majority's conclusion followed from the expansive interpretation of Article 15(1) adopted by the ECtHR in *Lawless v Ireland (No 3)* 1 EHRR 15. See [28] (Lord Bingham) and [208] (Lord Walker). See also Allan (n 12) 685.

[93] At para [87].

'[O]nly [it], being privy to the intelligence resources, is in a position to…identify the best course of action.'[94]

However, the fact that such information cannot be disclosed to the affected individual or made public does not preclude the court from demanding its disclosure, subject to the necessary safeguards, to facilitate the effective performance of its functions on review. The court has the power to order a closed hearing for the assessment of sensitive information, and to request the appointment of a security-cleared 'Special Advocate' to represent the affected individual, who is prohibited from communicating with his client once he has seen the closed material.[95] The court's jurisdiction to make use of these procedures arises out of the principle that they 'are masters of their own procedure subject [only] to any limitation imposed by legislation.'[96] Several amendments to the Civil Procedure Rules have also been made to accommodate the use of closed hearings and Special Advocates in particular circumstances, including control order proceedings under the Terrorism Act 2005.[97]

In *Farrakhan*, the Court of Appeal chose to appease the Home Secretary's decision not to 'describe…the purport of [his] information', noting only that 'it would have been better had he been less diffident' about doing so.[98] A better example was set by the European Court of First Instance ('CFI') in *People's Mojahedin Organization of Iran ('PMOI') v Council of the European Union*.[99] The CFI was invited to review the decision to include the PMOI in the Annex to Council Regulation No. 2580/2001, which sets out the organisations subject to restrictive measures within the European Union with a view to combating terrorism. The court held that:

'[T]he Council is not entitled to base its funds-freezing decision on information…if the…Member State is not willing to authorise its

---

[94] Poole (n 92) 247.
[95] See *A* (n 4) at para [223] (Baroness Hale).
[96] *R (Roberts) v Parole Board and another* [2005] UKHL 45 at para [44] (Lord Woolf CJ).
[97] See Rules 76.22 and 76.23. For discussion of the proposed amendment to cater for the use of these procedures in financial restrictions proceedings under the Counter-Terrorism Act 2008, see *Hansard*, HL Vol 707, col 432 (29 January 2009).
[98] At para [78].
[99] [2008] ECR 00.

communication to the Community judicature whose task is to review the lawfulness of that decision.'[100]

The court concluded that it had not been established that the decision was adopted in accordance with the Regulation, and therefore that the PMOI's inclusion on the list was unlawful.[101] Domestic courts should adopt the same approach, especially in circumstances where they may be acting incompatibly with the Convention if they fail to do so. In *Al-Nashif v Bulgaria*,[102] the European Court held that the appellant's deportation was incompatible with Article 8(2), on the grounds that the infringement of his Article 8 rights was not in accordance with the law for the purposes of the Convention. The court held that:

> 'Even where national security is at stake...measures affecting fundamental human rights must be subject to...proceedings before an independent body competent to review the...relevant evidence...'[103]

Democratic legitimacy

Without doubt the most popular argument in favour of judicial reticence in cases involving issues of national security is that founded on the allegedly superior democratic credentials of the elected powers of government. As per Laws LJ in *Roth*:

> 'Where the decision-maker is...exercising power conferred by Parliament, a degree of deference will be due on democratic grounds...where the decision-maker is Parliament...the tension...is at its most acute.'[104]

Those 'democratic grounds' were fleshed out by Lord Hoffmann in his postscript to *Rehman*, as extracted above.[105] On this view the courts should refrain from exercising their own independent judgment on the rights-compatibility of policy decisions that have 'serious potential

---

[100] At para [73].
[101] At para [78].
[102] (2003) 36 EHRR 37.
[103] At para [123].
[104] At para [83].
[105] n 48. See also *Farrakhan* (n 39) at para [74].

results for the community',[106] given that they are neither democratically
elected nor politically accountable for their decisions.

Arguments couched in these terms are symptomatic of what
Ronald Dworkin calls 'the majoritarian premise', according to which the
guiding rationale of democracy is that public power should be exercised
in the way that the majority of citizens prefer.[107] On this view it follows
that:

> '[T]he community should defer to the majority's view about
> what…individual rights are, and how they are best…enforced.'[108]

This conclusion, and the majoritarian premise that sustains it, should be
rejected in favour of 'the constitutional conception of democracy',
according to which 'the defining aim of democracy' is to 'treat all
members of the community…with equal concern and respect'.[109] On
this view the value of democracy is not majoritarian-rule, but that every
individual is treated as having equal value.[110] It is incidental to this
overriding rationale that, 'in most respects…the will of the majority
must prevail', but it also follows that, 'the will of the majority cannot
prevail if it is inconsistent with the equal rights of minorities'.[111]

These arguments apply equally when the rights at issue are
those of individuals who threaten to cause terrible suffering and loss of
life by their own actions. The protection of the rights of those
individuals is expressive of society's guiding and overriding
commitment to a belief in the inherent and inviolable dignity of every
individual.[112] But it is in this connection that some of the more
fundamental objections to judicial activism are expressed, specifically to
the very legitimacy of judicial protection of fundamental rights where
the rights at issue are those of individuals who pose a threat to the
liberty and security of others. Writing in the *Daily Telegraph* in response

---

[106] n 49.

[107] R Dworkin, *Freedom's Law* (Harvard University Press, Cambridge 1996) 16.

[108] *Ibid.*

[109] *Ibid.*, 17.

[110] See *Ghaidan v Godin-Mendoza* at para [132] (Baroness Hale), 'Democracy is founded on the
principle that each individual has equal value.'

[111] *A* (n 4) at para [237] (Baroness Hale).

[112] M Cohn, 'Judicial activism in the House of Lords: a composite constitutionalist approach'
(2007) *Public Law* 95, 112.

to the Lords' decision in *A,* the then Conservative Party leader Michael Howard expressed the view that:

> 'Aggressive judicial activism…could…put our security at risk – and with it the freedoms the judges seek to defend.'[113]

Arguments couched in these terms are misleading for drawing on a false distinction between liberty and security, before suggesting that those values cannot coexist unless one is traded off against the other. This dichotomy is unsustainable in a liberal democracy, where society's understanding of what it means to be secure presupposes an enduring commitment to its own core values.[114] This was recognised by President Aharon Barak of the Supreme Court of Israel, in the course of ruling that the use of torture in the fight against terrorism would be unlawful:

> 'A democracy must sometimes fight with one hand tied behind its back…The rule of law and the liberty of [the] individual constitute important components in its understanding of security.'[115]

In those circumstances, far from being inimical to national security, the protection of fundamental rights is a necessary prerequisite for it.

Conceived in this way, democracy demands that Parliament and the executive exercise their powers subject to conditions – 'the democratic conditions'[116] – which prescribe that their decisions must respect the fundamental rights of those affected, regardless of the threat that they might pose to the lives of others. Otherwise those institutions cannot claim to be exercising democratic legitimacy, in circumstances where the guiding rationale of democracy is not majoritarian tyranny, but that every individual should be treated as having equal value.

If this conception of democracy is accepted, it follows that there must necessarily be some institution entrusted with the task of demarcating the boundaries to legitimate majoritarian decision-making or, which amounts to the same thing, with the interpretation and

---

[113] BBC News Website, 10 August 2005.

[114] D Kostakopoulou, 'How to do things with security post 9/11' (2008) 28(2) *Oxford Journal of Legal Studies* 317, 323.

[115] *Public Committee against Torture v The State of Israel and the General Security Service* (1999) 7 BHRC 31 at para [39].

[116] Dworkin (n 107) 17.

application of fundamental rights. This function cannot be entrusted to Parliament or the executive, since those institutions would then be setting the limits to their own powers, in the exercise of those powers, which would be meaningless. The value of rights, in the sense of what makes them worth having, is contingent on their enforceability, if necessary, against the will of the majority. It is therefore dependent on the inviolability of their scope and meaning, and of questions of their proper application, from majoritarian decision-making. The alternative approach effectively divulges rights of any independent content. As Allan argues, if an individual's rights may be unjustly infringed by an accountable decision-maker, his rights have no independent content 'distinct from the procedure that…le[ads] to their infringement'.[117]

If we accept the legitimacy of the enforcement of individual rights as constraints on the exercise of public power, we must conclude that, as Lord Steyn has argued, 'The guarantor of those rights is and can only be an independent, neutral, and impartial judiciary.'[118] If the enforcement of fundamental rights is a necessary condition of democracy, and if the courts are the only institution capable of performing that function, then it seems illogical to suggest that they are not endowed with democratic legitimacy for the protection of fundamental rights. On this view, there is a loss to democracy whenever the courts refuse to exercise their own independent judgment on review.

The argument from accountability is particularly absurd in the context of national security, where the courts' unaccountability is precisely what enables them to protect the rights of unpopular individuals, even in the face of public and media pressures that are likely to lead the elected powers to give overriding importance to national security considerations.[119] The dangers inherent in the opposite approach can be illustrated by reference to another aspect of the decision in *A*, this time to their Lordships' conclusion that the

---

[117] n 12, 688.
[118] Lord Steyn, 'Democracy, the rule of law and the role of judges' (2006) 3 *European Human Rights Law Review* 243, 246.
[119] E Barendt, 'Separation of powers and constitutional government' (1995) *Public Law* 599, 616. See further A Barak, 'A judge on judging: the role of a Supreme Court in a democracy' (2002) 116 *Harvard Law Review* 16, 150.

measures under review were discriminatory in contravention of Art.14 of the Convention.

In a Discussion Paper issued by the Home Office before their Lordships' decision, David Blunkett, the then Home Secretary, dismissed Lord Newton's recommendation that 'new legislation should apply equally to all nationalities, including British citizens' on the grounds that 'such draconian powers would be difficult to justify.'[120] This assertion was met with indignation by the Parliamentary Joint Committee on Human Rights, which recognised that it seemed to betray a belief on the part of the Government that the liberty of foreign nationals was less important than that of British citizens.[121] The Commission concluded that this was 'impermissible under the Convention', but from a normative perspective it was also indicative of the Government's failure to adhere to the principles of non-discrimination and equal treatment that permeate liberal democratic society.

This failure can be taken as symptomatic of the difficulties with entrusting the protection of fundamental rights to majoritarian decision-making processes, in circumstances where the rights at issue are those of unpopular individuals. As per Jackson J of the United States Supreme Court, in a passage cited with approval by Lord Bingham in *A*:[122]

> '[N]othing opens the door to arbitrary action so effectively as to allow officials to…choose only a few to whom they will apply legislation and thus to escape the political retribution that might be visited upon them if larger numbers were affected.'[123]

That the Home Office was influenced by a desire to avoid such retribution seems to be implicit in its reasons for rejecting Lord Newton's recommendation that new measures apply equally to British

---

[120] 'Counter-Terrorism Powers: Reconciling Security and Liberty in an Open Society' February 2004 (Cm 6147), para [36].
[121] Eighteenth Report of the Session 2003-2004 (21 July 2004), HL Paper 158, HC 713, para [44].
[122] At para [46].
[123] *Railway Express Agency Inc v New York* (1949) 336 US 106 at para [112].

citizens. In its Discussion Paper the Government rejected this suggestion, arguing that:

> 'Experience has demonstrated the...damage [such an approach] can do...to the support from all parts of the public that is so essential to countering the terrorist threat.'[124]

A related problem is the peculiar susceptibility of public authorities to one-way pressures, according to which they should always prioritise national security over the rights of the individual. As the then serving Prime Minister Tony Blair admitted in a speech to the Institute of Public Policy Research in 2005:

> 'It is in th[e] interests [of public authorities] never to be accused of having missed a problem. So...[t]hey will always err on the side of caution.'[125]

The courts are not subject to the same pressures when called upon to review the legitimacy of a decision that has already been taken, in circumstances where the affected individual no longer poses an immediate threat to national security. Lord Hoffmann recognised this advantage of judicial review proceedings in *A and Others v Secretary of State for the Home Department (No 2)*:[126]

> '[T]here may be cases in which [the Home Secretary] is required to act urgently...The function of SIAC...is to form its own opinion, *after calm judicial process*, as to whether...there are reasonable grounds for [his] suspicion...'[127]

Judicial legitimacy for the protection of fundamental rights therefore stems predominantly from the courts' relative inviolability from public pressure and independence from the elected powers of government, which gives them the capacity to act exclusively in the interests of protecting individual rights. It should also be noted that it is dependent on two other characteristics of the judicial system, namely the

---

[124] n 120, para [36].
[125] Cited by Feldman (n 63) 378.
[126] [2005] UKHL 71 at para [94].
[127] Emphasis added.

obligation incumbent on judges to justify their decisions by way of rational arguments that are open to public and professional scrutiny, and their obligation to do so by reference to 'objective, publicly accessible standards', deriving their authority 'from a source other than the opinions of an individual judge'.[128] These characteristics help to ensure that the conclusions reached by the courts on the application of rights are rationally defensible, and that the applicable standards are not derived from the subjective value-system of the particular judge but from commitments shared by society as a whole.

In the United Kingdom arguments in favour of judicial deference on the grounds of the courts' allegedly inferior democratic credentials may be on the wane. This is because the incorporation of the European Convention into domestic law by the enactment of the Human Rights Act 1998 has been perceived as conferring express democratic legitimacy on the courts for the protection of fundamental rights. As per Lord Bingham in *A*:

> 'The 1998 Act gives the courts a...wholly democratic, mandate...The courts are charged by Parliament with delineating the boundaries of a rights based democracy.'[129]

Conclusion

It may now safely be concluded that the notion of deference is either redundant or illegitimate in cases involving fundamental rights and issues of national security. In its less restrictive formulation, deference merely recalls the limits already inherent in the grounds of review. While there is nothing objectionable about referring to those limits in terms of 'deference', 'latitude' or the primary decision maker's 'margin of discretion', conceived in this way, none of those expressions has any independent content.

Conversely, where deference is conceived as preventing the courts from exercising their own independent judgment on the rights-compatibility of the measures under review, it is inimical to the protection of fundamental rights and to the legitimacy of judicial decision-making. These qualities are contingent on the courts coming

[128] Feldman (n 63) 374.
[129] At para [42].

to their own reasoned conclusions on the evidence and arguments adduced by both sides, rather than siding with one party to the dispute for reasons that are irrelevant to a rational determination of the rights-compatibility of the impugned decision. These consequences cannot be excused by reference to the courts' constitutional, institutional or democratic limitations, since none of these inhibits the performance of their particular functions on review.

The House of Lords' decision in *A* should be read as an endorsement of this approach. However, that this area remains the subject of contention is apparent from the casual references to the need for deference in many of their Lordships' opinions, and the emphasis placed by some of their Lordships on the gravity of the infringement as the basis for their particular willingness to interfere.[130]

That the Government remains opposed to this degree of judicial intervention is also apparent from arguments made on its behalf before the European Court in *A and Others v The United Kingdom*,[131] where it argued that the House of Lords in *A* 'had erred in affording the State too narrow a margin of appreciation in assessing what measures were strictly necessary.'[132] Domestic courts should take encouragement from the European Court's rejection of that objection.[133] In performing their responsibilities for the delineation of 'the boundaries of a rights-based democracy', the courts should always be willing to exercise their own independent judgment on the compatibility of legislation and executive action, when challenged, with the rights of those affected.

---

[130] See paras [81] (Lord Nicholls) and [107] (Lord Hope).

[131] n 7.

[132] At para [150].

[133] At para [184].

Is the Anti-Terror Legislation passed by the British Government in the period 2001 – 2006 compatible with Articles 5 and 6 of the European Convention on Human Rights, incorporated into British law by the Human Rights Act 1998?

ZOE JACOB[*]

1. Introduction

'No judicial decision is necessarily the right decision.'[1]

I propose a philosophical approach[2] to the principles of which the Convention Rights[3] consist. The Convention Rights form the substantive element of the European Convention on Human Rights,[4] and the Human Rights Act[5] incorporates these rights into British law. Using this principled understanding of legal rights, I examine the compatibility of the Anti-Terror Legislation[6] with Article 5, the right to liberty and security, and Article 6, the right to a fair hearing. I challenge the House of Lords decisions using this approach.

My argument is methodologically grounded in Dworkin's theory of law.[7] Dworkin views law as an interpretative concept;[8] in

---

[*] Zoe received an MA in Human Rights at UCL and is currently studying for the BVC at City University.

[1] R Dworkin, *Taking Rights Seriously* (Duckworth, London 1977) 185.

[2] G Letsas, 'The Truth in Autonomous Concepts: How to Interpret the European Convention on Human Rights' (2004) 14 *European Journal of International Law* approaches the ECHR using this methodology. This method has not been directly applied to the HRA however, as although C Gearty, *Principles of Human Rights Adjudication* (Oxford University Press, Oxford 2004) looks at the HRA in terms of its consistent principles he does not use a philosophical theory of rights to define these principles, nor does challenge the case the law on the basis of his principled approach.

[3] Convention Rights are held by the individual, against the state.

[4] Henceforth known as the ECHR.

[5] Henceforth known as the HRA.

[6] Henceforth known as the ATL.

[7] R Dworkin, *Laws Empire* (Hart Publishing, Oxford 1998).

[8] *Ibid.*, 87.

order to determine what law is, we have to interpret it in the best possible moral light given its coercive purpose.[9] The concept of 'law as integrity'[10] places law in this light, viewing the law as consisting of moral principles present, but not necessarily explicit, in existing case law and legislation. Firstly, 'law as integrity' interprets law as consisting of temporally consistent principles - meaning law's coercive power is applied non-arbitrarily. Secondly, it views law as consisting of historically grounded and communally shared principles, hence views law as coercing individuals on grounds that are societally endorsed.[11] It provides the best possible moral interpretation of law given its coercive purpose. 'Law as integrity's' view of law as historically grounded ethical principles requires that the judiciary take an interpretative approach to prior case law and legislation; an assessment of the principles present in these enables a judicial determination of the law in a particular case.[12] A Dworkinian approach to the HRA implies it consists of the principles present in the legislation itself; those in the European Court of Human Rights;[13] and pre- and post-HRA British jurisprudence, which elucidates the nature of the Convention Rights. A principle is present where the case law and legislation, considered as a body, are explicable in these terms.[14] Those judicial decisions that do not reflect the principles present in the case law considered as a body can be rejected as flawed.

I adopt a Dworkinian approach to the HRA. In Section 2, I undertake an exploration of the major philosophical positions on the nature of human rights and find a philosophical position that reflects the principles expressed in the jurisprudence relevant to the HRA. Various theories of rights are rejected on the basis of their failure to reflect the principles present in the relevant jurisprudence. In Section 3, I elucidate on the exact protection Articles 5 and 6 provide on the basis

---

[9] *Ibid.*, 110.

[10] *Ibid.*, 176-274.

[11] G Postema, 'Integrity: Justice in Workclothes' in J Burley (ed.) *Dworkin and His Critics* (Blackwell, Oxford 2006).

[12] n 7, 256; he also argues that if more than one theory 'fits' preceding legal practice, then the theory that places the practice in the best possible moral light is chosen. In the case of the HRA as only one theory of rights is present in the relevant case law thus it is unnecessary to take this further analytical step.

[13] Henceforth known as the ECtHR.

[14] n 7, 255.

of the principles expressed by this philosophical position. In Section 4, I test whether Articles 5 and 6 are incompatible with the ATL. Using the British case law on the issue as a framework for my analysis, I challenge the House of Lords conclusions on the basis of the principles of which the HRA consists. I additionally refer to various independent reports on the issue.[15] I use primary sources here as they provide the principle forum in which deliberations on compatibility have occurred. Academic articles either address the issue tangentially,[16] or reflect on these primary sources.[17] I too reflect on the primary sources, but from my unique, principled perspective.

I define incompatibility as the HRA does; this exists where legislation cannot be read other than in a manner that violates Convention Rights.[18] If legislation can be read as compatible with the HRA, Section 3[19] deems applications of that legislation, which violates the HRA, impermissible in that legislation's own terms.[20] The HRA considers compatibility solely in relation to the nature of the Convention Rights, explained in the relevant jurisprudence. The British legal principle of parliamentary sovereignty[21] is irrelevant to the determination of compatibility as this principle is given effect after a Declaration of Incompatibility has been made. 'A declaration made under this section… does not affect the validity, continuing operation or enforcement of the provision in respect of which it is given';[22] the prerogative to act on a declaration remains legislative. The Courts thus determine incompatibility on the sole basis of the consideration of the nature of the Convention Rights. I too follow this approach focusing

---

[15] For example, *Review of Counter-Terrorism Powers,* Joint Committee on Human Rights, 18th Report of Session 2003-04, HL Paper 158.
[16] For example, C Gearty, '11th September 2001, Counter Terrorism and the Human Rights Act' in (2005) 32 *Journal of Law and Society,* which discusses the important role of civil society in preventing rights violations in the context of the 'war against terror'.
[17] For example D Hoffman and J Rowe QC, *Human Rights in the UK: An Introduction to the Human Rights Act* (Pearson Longman, Harlow 2006).
[18] HRA Sections 2-4.
[19] HRA Section 3.
[20] A Section 3 reading mitigates against 'as-applied' violations of the HRA; R Fallon, 'As-Applied and Facial Challenges and Third-Party Standing' (2000) 113 *Harvard Law Review.*
[21] See http://www.parliament.uk/about/how/laws/sovereignty.cfm.
[22] HRA Section 4(6)(a).

on the principles in which the Convention Rights consist and determining compatibility on the basis of these principles.

I focus on two specific, controversial elements of the ATL passed in the period following the September 11th 2001 terrorist attacks.[23] Firstly, Part 4 of the Anti-Terrorism Crime and Security Act 2001,[24] which permitted the indefinite detention of foreign terror suspects who could not be deported to their country of origin;[25] and secondly, Sections 1-4 the Prevention of Terror Act 2005[26] which permit the serving of control orders under specific procedural conditions. The 2005 Act was a response to the House of Lords 'Declaration of Incompatibility' in *A*[27] in relation to Part 4 of the ATCSA. Article 5 and 6 compatibility challenges have since been made to the 2005 Act.[28]

I hypothesise that where Articles 5 and 6 are considered in terms of the principles of which they consist, Part 4 of the 2001 Act will be found to be incompatible with Articles 5 and 6; Section 1(4) of the 2005 Act will require a Section 3 reading given Article 5; and the procedure for imposing a control order set out in Sections 1-4 of the 2005 Act will be found to be incompatible with Article 6.

2. The Principles of the Human Rights Act
I. Hart's Will Theory?

Hart develops his 'Will Theory' as a general theory of legal and moral rights – the approach is best explained through example. In the case of a promise[29] made by James to John to pick up John's son from school, a right is entailed by this promise if, and only if, John can, at any point, say to James 'you do not have to pick up my son from school'. Thus,

---

[23] See http://www.gpoaccess.gov/911/pdf/fullreport.pdf.

[24] Henceforth known as the ATCSA.

[25] See *Chalal v UK* [1997] EHRR 413.

[26] Henceforth known as the 2005 Act.

[27] *A (FC) and others (FC) v Secretary of State for the Home Department* [2004] UKHL 56.

[28] *Secretary of State for the Home Department v E* [2007] UKHL 47; *Secretary of State for the Home Department v JJ* [2007] UKHL 45; *Secretary of State for the Home Department v MB* [2007] UKHL 46.

[29] HLA Hart, 'Are There Any Natural Rights' in J Waldron (ed.) *Theories of Rights*, Oxford University Press, Oxford 1984) 82.

the ability to exercise a right is defined in terms of the right-holder's power to waive his right at any point.[30]

The principle of rights as waiveable powers is not present in the jurisprudence relevant to the HRA. A number of Convention Rights are unwaivable. Article 3, which provides 'No one shall be subject to torture or to inhuman or degrading punishment,' is not qualified by a proviso stating an individual's consent makes torture permissible. The ECtHR ruled that secondary obligations of the state to prevent torture could not be overridden where individuals consented to sado-masochistic practices.[31] Further, even in cases where a right can be waived (for example transsexuals' Article 8[32] right to recognition of post-operative gender), the court does not focus on this power, but rather the rights substantive content.[33] For these reasons Hart's 'will theory' does not provide the principle in which the Convention Rights consist.

II. *Raz's Interest Theory?*

Raz proposes a theory of rights in general, rather than human rights specifically. He defines the term 'right' separately from a substantive theory of the rights individuals possess.[34] 'X has a right if and only if X can have rights, and all other things being equal, an aspect of his well-being (his interest), is a sufficient reason for holding some other person(s) under a duty.'[35] Rights are founded on interests and 'an interest is sufficient to base a right on if and only if there is a sound argument of which the conclusion is that a certain right exists, and among its non-redundant premises is a statement of some interest of the right holder, the other premises supplying grounds for attributing to it the required importance';[36] the 'weightier' the interest, the stronger the foundation it provides for a right. Rights-grounding interests are 'objective'; they are predicated objective values such as autonomy.[37]

---

[30] *Ibid.*, 53.
[31] *Laskey, Jaggard and Brown v United Kingdom* [1997] 24 EHRR 39.
[32] Right to respect for private and family life.
[33] *Bellinger v Bellinger* [2003] UKHL 21.
[34] J Raz, *The Morality of Freedom* (Clarendon, Oxford 1986) 166.
[35] *Ibid.*
[36] *Ibid.*, 181.
[37] *Ibid.*, 210-15.

This distinguishes interests from utilitarian preferences.[38] Raz views rights as grounding duties for others.[39]

Morality is not, according to Raz, rights based; 'in [many] respects a rights-based morality is impoverished.'[40] Although the interests that form the bases of rights have moral weight, a morality grounded solely in rights claims excludes the many morally normative claims that are not grounded in the interests of others. Moral claims can be grounded in the value of a particular institution such as friendship, or a socially valuable good such as tolerance.[41] Additionally, a rights-based morality cannot explain why entities such as art which give value to human life, are in themselves morally valuable.[42] As a response to Dworkin's rights-based morality[43] this approach is flawed; it portrays Dworkin's as failing to accept moral value apart from that which arises in relation to rights. In fact, Dworkin argues that rights-claims have moral priority over other, existent, forms of moral claim.[44] It is thus better to read Raz as contesting the moral priority of rights; instead he morally prioritises the objective values on which rights and non-rights based moral claims are predicated.[45]

Two elements of Raz's theory contradict the principles of which the HRA consists. Firstly, Raz's argument against the moral priority of rights contradicts the HRA's approach to compatibility, in which Convention Rights are the pre-eminent concern.[46] As Lord Bingham argued,[47] it is not the court's role to engage with policy concerns regarding the value of social goods or independently morally valued entities such as art, to which no individual has a rights-based claim.[48] Thus Raz's willingness to subordinate rights claims to such concerns

---

[38] See R Crisp, *Mill on Utilitarianism* (Routledge, London 1997) for a discussion of utilitarianism.
[39] n 34, 168.
[40] *Ibid.*, 195.
[41] *Ibid.*, 196.
[42] *Ibid.*, 212-3.
[43] n 1.
[44] *Ibid.*, 202-5.
[45] For a discussion of this see J Raz, 'Human Rights Without Foundations', Unpublished Paper, 2007, 4-5.
[46] See Section 1.
[47] *R v Secretary of State for Environment, Transport and the Regions* [2003] HLR 30.
[48] See Section 2(III) for further discussion of the principle of rights prioritisation.

contradicts the principle of rights prioritisation present in HRA jurisprudence on compatibility.

Secondly, Raz's theory does not contain a mechanism for the prioritisation of rights beyond the notion of the 'weightiness' of the interest[49] upon which the right is predicated. 'Weightiness' depends on the relationship of the interest to the objective value on which it rests; for example my interest, in and consequent right to, choice of a career path is weighted according to its relatively loose relationship with the objective value of autonomy on which it is based. This approach diverges in two ways from the principles present in the jurisprudence relevant to the HRA. Firstly, the notion of 'weightiness' of interests does not appear to capture the stringency of the Convention Rights that the HRA prioritises.[50] Secondly, if rights are grounded in weighted interests that depend on objective values, then the fact of incommensurable values, which Raz accepts,[51] leads to an irresolvable clash of rights.[52] The HRA lexically prioritises rights, and thus does not accept incommensurability.

I use an example to illustrate that 'weightiness' of interest does not provide a foundation for rights that adequately captures the stringency accorded by the HRA, to the rights it enshrines. James, who is innocent of a crime, has an objective interest in not being sent to prison, based on the value of autonomy, to which a free-life outside of prison is intimately connected. This weighty interest grounds his right to a fair trial in which his innocence will be objectively assessed. This Razian response does not however capture the stringency which pre and post-HRA British case law accords to James' 'Right to a Fair Hearing'.[53] The stringency accorded to the right to a fair hearing must derive from a source other than the individual's objective interest in

---

[49] n 34, 181.
[50] FM Kamm, 'Rights' in J Coleman and S Shapiro (eds.) *The Oxford handbook of Jurisprudence and Philosophy of Law* (Oxford University Press, Oxford 2004) 495; Raz recognises this problem when he ponders why the strength of a right often seems greater than the interest it protects.
[51] n 34, 212-4.
[52] L Zucca, *Constitutional Dilemmas: Conflicts of Fundamental Legal Rights in Europe and the USA* (Oxford University Press, Oxford 2007) views rights conflict as inevitable on the basis of incommensurability.
[53] See Viscount Sankey's speech in *Woolmington v DPP* [1935] AC 462 and Bingham in *Attorney General Reference No 2*.

autonomy. Although provisions such as the provision of higher education in prison, which enhances autonomy, can be used to mitigate against the loss of this objective value entailed by an unfair prison sentence, the British courts do not accept such a trade-off as permissible, maintaining the right to a fair trial is absolute and of intrinsic moral value;[54] loss of this right cannot be compensated for using other means. Raz, however, would view the compensatory response acceptable, provided the prison's higher education provisions protected the objective value of autonomy. Thus Raz's theory again contradicts the principles present in the jurisprudence relevant to a HRA decision on incompatibility.

In many cases it is possible for Raz to resolve conflict with reference to the relative weights of the rights in question; for example he would argue that the weight of my interest in a fair trial is objectively greater than the weight of my interest in freedom to choose my occupation. Both of these interests are based on the objective value of autonomy but the former protects this more closely. Where, however, a lexical ordering of rights on the basis of the relative weight of interests is impossible, Raz accepts conflict as irresolvable.[55] This runs contrary to the legal approach to human rights, adopted under HRA. Here the courts aim to resolve rights-conflict though lexical prioritisation. In *Roberts*[56] two arguably equally weighty interests were pitted against one another. A prisoner's interest in having access to the complete case against him in a parole hearing came into conflict with the interests of a witness whose continued life would be threatened if his/her identity were revealed. Raz would argue we have two incommensurable interests based on incommensurable values – autonomy and human life – of equal weight and we should not attempt to further analyse these rights' relative importance. The Court took the opposite approach, deeming a restriction of Article 5(4), the right to fairly challenge one's detention, permissible given the stringent demands made by Article 2, the right to life. Raz's willingness to accept incommensurability runs

---

[54] *Brown v Stott* [2000] AC 681 (Privy Council).

[55] n 34, 215.

[56] R *(on the application of Roberts) v Parole Board* [2005] UKHL 45; for further discussion see the following section.

contrary to the principle of commensurability of Convention Rights in ECtHR and British jurisprudence.

III. The Theory of Equal Agency – a Revised Version of Dworkin's 'Rights as Trumps'

I demonstrate that the principle of equal agency provides the foundational moral principle on which the Convention Rights are based, using a constructivist approach.[57] Constructivism uses accepted facts as a foundation for the construction of moral precepts.[58] My theory is based on the existence of moral constructs. This is accepted by the HRA, which enshrines moral constructs relating to the state's legal treatment of individuals. Given this fact, I ask 'what are the fundamental conditions necessary the existence moral constructs?' and answer 'foundational moral precepts which protect agency, for if individuals are unable to act as agents, they are unable to take the directed action additional moral constructs require, hence the existence of these constructs is threatened'. This answer is grounded in a view of moral constructs as definitionally normative; they are defined by their provision of a moral guide for action. If it is impossible to act on the basis of a moral construct, that construct is by definition undermined. If any other moral constructs are to exist, moral agency must be protected. A set of rights that protect the agency upon which moral constructs rest is entailed by the acceptance of the fact of the existence of such constructs. These rights provide the foundation of morality as without them morality itself is threatened.

Rights are derived from the principle of protection of agency, and agency itself is defined through use of constructivism. This conception of agency reflects the notion of agency employed in the jurisprudence relevant to the HRA. In line with the above constructivist analysis, a person's status as an agent is dependent on the fulfilment of the conditions that enable him to undertake the normative demands made by a moral construct. Anything that wholly undermines his capacity to undertake these demands invalidates his status as an agent.

---

[57] A Gewirth, 'Human Dignity as the Basis of Rights' in Meyer and Parent (eds.) *The Constitution of Rights* (Cornell University Press, Ithaca 1992) endorses a constructivist approach to rights.
[58] O O'Neill, 'Constructivisms in Ethics' in *Proceedings of the Aristotelian Society,* 1988.

The Convention Rights are derived from the principle of protection of agency, as an exploration of Articles 2 and 9[59] illustrates. Article 2's provision, 'no-one shall be deprived of his life intentionally' has been strictly enforced by the ECtHR.[60] This notion is fundamentally linked to agency; a person is wholly unable to undertake the normative demands made by a moral construct if they are deprived of their life; a deprivation of the right to life invalidates agency status. Further to this the ECtHR viewed a violation of Article 9 to have occurred in a case where applicants were unable to act on the normative demand made by their religious morality, to engage in communal worship.[61] This invalidated their agency status; hence the ECtHR jurisprudence contains the principle of inviolability of agency status.

Constructivism can also be used to define the 'equality' element of agency. If we accept the fact that all human beings possess an equal capacity to act on the normative demands made by moral constructs,[62] then all possess agency equally. Rights derived from agency must therefore be accorded to all equally. If equal accordance of agency is an inherent feature of that agency, then protecting an individual's agency entails not only ensuring that agent's agency status is not invalidated, but also each individual's agency status is treated with the same degree of concern and respect. To treat all individuals' agency with equal concern and respect means: firstly, rights predicated on the protection of agency status; and secondly, policies that enhance the individuals' agency status, for example the provision of free secondary education, must be applied equally. If they are not, a rights violation occurs, as rights are predicated on equal concern and respect for agency. Equality does not, however, entail identical treatment in all situations; where two agents are relevantly different, differential treatment is permissible. For example, a French citizen's inability to vote in the UK whilst British citizens have this right, does not treat the French citizen's agency with unequal concern and respect. The British citizen has a reason to be

---

[59] Freedom of Thought and Conscience.

[60] *McCann v UK* (1995) 21 EHRR 97 Application No. 324; the principle that the force can use against an individual is "no more than absolutely necessary in defence of persons from unlawful violence" was upheld, at para [213].

[61] *Manoussakis v Greece* 1996-IV 1346 (1996) 23 EHRR 187.

[62] The HRA's applicability to all those who fall under the UK's jurisdiction implies acceptance of this fact.

more morally concerned with the manner in which the UK is governed than the French citizens, and this relevant difference allows the UK citizen to be treated differently without this creating inequality.

This principle of equal concern and respect for agency is reflected in post HRA-British and ECtHR jurisprudence. Article 14 states, "the enjoyment of rights and freedoms set forth in this Convention shall be secured without any discrimination"; the Convention Rights, which protect agency status, must be accorded equally.[63] Whist Convention Rights protect individuals' status as agents, and Article 14 appears only to protect against unequal application of these rights, the British approach to Article 14 extends beyond this and demonstrates a second principle of equal agency; where policy enhances an individual's agency, and another individual is relevantly similar, the policy must be similarly applied to the latter agent.[64] Like Dworkin,[65] I accord priority to equality, as a violation of equal concern and respect for agency amounts to an invalidation of agency status, and hence a violation of rights. I do not view equality as the foundation of rights, although Dworkin does.

I modify Dworkin's notion of 'rights as trumps',[66] which views rights derived from the principle of equality, unrelated to agency, as the foundational moral principle. I instead argue the 'protection of equal agency principle' is morally pre-eminent, given the preceding constructivist analysis, which demonstrates it is this principle that provides a foundation on which all other moral constructs rest. I also modify two of his possible justifications of the limitation of rights,[67] in line the principle of the equal protection of agency status in which the HRA consists. This modification allows for an understanding of the principle from which the HRA's notion of the commensurability of rights derives, something the Razian approach was unable to provide.

---

[63] *Belgian Linguistic case (No 2)* (1968) 1 EHRR 252 Application No. 6; the right to respect for family and private life, which protects agency must be applied similarly to all agents regardless of gender, as gender has no affect on agency status.

[64] http://www.equalityhumanrights.com/en/aboutus/pages/aboutus.aspx; the Equality and Human Rights Commission, a quasi-governmental organisation which encourages individuals to use the HRA, views equality and human rights as wholly inter-relational issues.

[65] n 1.

[66] R Dworkin, 'Rights as Trumps' (n 29).

[67] n 1, 262.

Firstly, if two rights based on the protection of equal agency status come into conflict, then the right that provides the most effective protection of that status is prioritised.[68] The principle of commensurability of rights present in ECtHR and British jurisprudence, which enables lexical prioritisation of rights, derives from the principle of the protection of equal agency from which all rights derive. Given their common principled derivative, rights can be prioritised with reference to the intimacy of their relationship with this principle. The permissible limitations of the 'Right to Liberty' enshrined in Article 5(1)(a)-(f), explored at greater length in Section 3(I), can be rationalised according to this principle; one individual's right to liberty, predicated on the principle of the protection of equal agency, is restricted only where protection of another individual's equal agency demands this.

Secondly, procedural elements enshrined in definitions of a right do not in every case act to protect an individual's equal agency; where they do not, equal agency permits their sacrifice. This principle was evident in Lord Woolf's judgement in *Roberts*,[69] mentioned in the previous section. Here the procedural protection in Article 5(4), which requires full disclosure of information to an individual applying for parole, was not deemed necessary to ensure the non-violation of his status as an equal agent, on which the right to a fair hearing is based, given other procedural safeguards. Procedural 'rights' can be restricted on the basis of non-rights based concerns, for example road-safety, where these 'rights' do not protect the principle of equal protection of agency.[70] Where procedures do not protect the principle on which rights are based, they do not have the 'trumping' power that stems directly from the morally foundational nature of that principle.

My modified version of Dworkin's rights prioritarianism views rights that protect equal agency status as trumps; where rights protect such status they can be limited only on the basis that another right that protects equal agency is at stake. This approach reflects the principles present in the jurisprudence relevant to British courts considering

---

[68] n 50, 500-502 advocates such an approach, arguing the relative importance of rights is determined by the intimacy of their relation to the principle on which they are grounded.
[69] n 56.
[70] n 54.

compatibility under the HRA. The foundational principle of protection of equal agency status is the principle on which the Convention Rights are based.

3. Articles 5 and 6: A Principled Perspective
I. Article 5 – Right to Liberty and Security
In contrast to Dworkin's portrayal of liberty as a 'misguided right'[71] to which no independent claim can be made, an equal agency approach entails the existence of a limited but independent right to liberty. This right is enshrined in Article 5. I agree with Dworkin's assertion that there is no general right to liberty defined in Berlin's negative sense as 'freedom from curtailment of action'.[72] Freedom in this sense can often be justifiably restricted in relation to non-rights based concerns and given that rights trumps, where these restrictions justifiably occur, rights cannot exist.[73] If I had a right to negative liberty, I would have a right to drive down Oxford Street wherever another's rights were not violated by my doing so; equal agency does not view the pedestrianisation of Oxford Street, for the non-rights based reason of crowd control, an unjustified rights restriction. Here I am in agreement with Dworkin. I do not, however, agree that no right exists in this instance because there are no liberty rights at all.[74] Dworkin illustrates his argument by taking the right classical liberty right to political participation, and showing that its moral fundamentality derives equal concern and respect for individuals, rather than from a right to negative liberty.[75] 'Liberty rights', which do not protect equality, including the 'right' to drive down Oxford Street, are not, in Dworkin's view, rights at all; only equality can provide a foundation for rights. I approach the 'closing of Oxford Street' example from a different perspective; no right exists here, because this curtailment of action does not invalidate agency status; the policy is not applied unequally, nor does it invalidate an individual's ability to act on the normative demands made by

---

[71] n 1, 266.
[72] I Berlin, 'Two Concepts of Liberty' in *Four Essays on Liberty* (Oxford University Press, Oxford 1969) 122-131.
[73] *Ibid.*, 267-269.
[74] *Ibid.*, 269.
[75] *Ibid.*

morality. My argument does not, however, entail the non-existence of liberty rights, it in fact entails the opposite; where a restriction liberty is applied unequally or where it invalidates an individual's ability to act on the normative demands made by morality, an independent liberty right against such action exists.

The paradigm example of a restriction of liberty which invalidates an individual's agency status is a closed-prison sentence. Here an individual is isolated from the outside world. He thus severs the bonds formed in relationships prior to his imprisonment. In the outside world these relationships created a number of morally normative demands; for example, many conceive the friendship as imposing the moral duty to spend time with individuals considered ones friends;[76] in a prison-cell, however, an individual is unable to act on this and many other normative demands which arise in the context of social interaction, from which he has been excluded.

The independence of this liberty right from rights founded on the moral necessity to treat individuals with equal concern and respect is demonstrated when we the address the question 'are the rights of each separate individual violated if every relevantly similar individual is also is imprisoned in a separate cell?' In this case all are being treated with a low, but equal, level of concern and respect. The rights of each individual are, however, still being violated here as, for the reasons outlined above, the agency status of each member of the population is invalidated by imprisonment and the fact of equal treatment does not mitigate this. Equal agency entails an independent liberty right to freedom from imprisonment, as well as a right to freedom conditions that replicate the invalidation of agency status imprisonment creates. Article 5 therefore protects against such invalidation of agency status. It provides this protection to all individuals equally, given their equal status as agents.

The notion of equal concern and respect for individuals' agency helps explain circumstances under which restrictions of the right to liberty, defined above, are justifiable. As I mentioned in Section 2(III), Article 5(1) (a)-(f) defines the permissible limitations to liberty. An individual's liberty right can be sacrificed only where another's rights

---

[76] http://plato.stanford.edu/entries/friendship/#3.

have been, or are highly likely to be restricted, and the sacrifice of the former individual's rights will relate to this. Article 5(1)(a) allows a sacrifice of liberty following "conviction by a competent court". The high burden of proof imposed in criminal cases[77] and the other procedural provisions of Article 6 as well as the fact that a sentence is imposed in relation to the seriousness of the crime,[78] which relates to its effect on another individual's agency, ensures liberty is deprived only where impact on another individual's agency status requires this.[79] The principle of equal protection of agency status, which Article 5 is based on, requires such an approach.

To sum up, equal agency entails a limited, but independent, right to liberty where this right protects an individual's agency status. The right must be applied to individuals equally and can be sacrificed only where the rights of other agents are highly likely to be protected.

II. *Article 6 – An Equality Based on Agency Approach.*

Article 6, the right to a fair hearing, is a procedural right which outlines the protections that must be accorded to an individual subjected to legal proceedings. The consistency of Article 6 in the principle of the protection of equal agency entails three specific features.

Firstly, a distinction must be made between civil and criminal proceedings, as imprisonment, a possible outcome of the latter, but not the former, proceedings, will invalidate agency status, hence stringent proof of the agency-effect of the action of the individual being tried is necessary here. The *Engel* tests used by the ECtHR to define proceedings as 'criminal' reflect this approach; greater severity of punishment indicates a criminal case. Given that where a case is defined as criminal, the procedures used to prove guilt under Article 6 are more stringent – for example in a criminal case, the right to cross-examine witnesses applies,[80] whereas this is not a procedural requirement of a civil hearing – equal agency provides the principle inherent in the

---

[77] For a discussion of the burden of proof necessary in criminal trials see B Emmerson QC, *Criminal Justice and Human Rights* (Sweet and Maxwell, London 2001) 240-247.
[78] See http://www.sentencing-guidelines.gov.uk/docs/assault-against-the%20person.pdf.
[79] Contrary to Dworkin I believe that a convicted criminal has a right to liberty of which he is being justifiably deprived. This right is not predicated on equality; hence his equal treatment at trial does not negate the existence of such a right.
[80] ECHR Article 6(3)(d).

criterion. More stringent procedural provisions are required given the possibility of imprisonment, which is a rights violation. An individual's equal agency status requires his rights only be deprived where this is justified given the rights of others and the procedural provisions of a criminal trial ensure the existence of such justification is proved. In a civil case there is not likely to be a penalty that invalidates agency status, thus procedures need only ensure individuals are equally respected as agents. The necessity of an 'independent and impartial'[81] hearing, which applies in both civil and criminal cases, provides such procedural protection.

Secondly, equal agency requires that the procedural rights contained under Article 6's auspices ensure that the outcome of a hearing is non-speculative. A non-speculative procedure must be free from bias and hence objective; for example the judge presiding over a case cannot have any interest in a particular outcome.[82] A non-speculative outcome must also be proved with a high degree of certainty; this is a particularly pressing concern where an individual stands to have his/her rights violated as a result of the case's outcome. If speculation does occur, the agent whose agency stands to be certainly compromised by the outcome of the case is being treated unequally as compared to the individual whose agency the case enhances on a speculative basis. If agents' agency is to be treated with equal concern and respect, those agency claims grounded in certainty must be must be prioritised over agency claims grounded in speculation as the certainty is the only distinguishing factor here. Thus, procedurally ensuring non-speculation through Article 6 ensures equal protection of agency, the principle on which the Article is based.

The third requirement relates to the first two. All the procedural elements of a fair hearing must be directly related to foundational principle of equal protection of agency from which the Convention Rights are derived, if a violation of these procedural elements is to count as a rights violation. 'The right to a fair trial cannot be compromised but the constituent rights within that overall rights can be limited.'[83] Equal agency entails we must refer directly to this principle

---

[81] ECHR Article 6(1).
[82] See *Millar v Procurator Fiscal* [2002] 1 WLR 1615 (Privy Council).
[83] n 54, per Lord Bingham.

when assessing whether an Article 6 violation has occurred rather than viewing the procedural rights entailed by this principle as absolutes.

In sum, equal agency views Article 6 as consisting of procedural rights directly related to the protection of equal agency status principle. Given the possibility of an invalidation of agency status as a result of the punishment accorded in a criminal case, the procedural rights requirements in such cases are more demanding.

4. Belmarsh and Control Orders: Are the Principles Betrayed?

In the preceding chapters I demonstrated that the HRA consists of the principle of equal agency and is derivatives, and explored the implications of this for Articles 5 and 6. In this Section I examine the three major House of Lords decisions on the compatibility of the ATL with Article 5 and 6, and identify the flaws in the judgements given the equal agency principle on which these Articles are based, expaining a judgement entailed by an equal agency approach.

I. Article 5 and 6 Incompatibility with the Anti-Terrorism Crime and Security Act 2001.

Secretary of State for the Home Department v A[84] was a challenge to the legality of Part 4 of the ATCSA, which permitted indefinite detention without charge for non-nationals, using Article 5(1) of the ECHR. The case reached the House of Lords. The facts of the case are as follows. All the detainees in *A.* were suspected terrorists and were not UK nationals. They had not been criminally charged, and as the evidence against them was not admissible in court, a criminal trial was not a prospect. All had been subject to indefinite detention without charge in Belmarsh high security prison. They could not be deported to their country of origin given the ECtHR's ruling in *Chalal*[85] that it was a violation of secondary obligations under Article 3 to deport an individual where he faces a real risk of death or torture in custody on his return. The applicants faced such treatment in their country's of origin. The *Chalal* precedent applies even where the individual is deemed to pose a threat to national security. The ATCSA's solution to

---

[84] n 27.
[85] [1997] EHRR 413.

the impermissibility of deportation in these cases was derogation from Article 5(1)(f)[86] using Article 15, which allows derogation in times of national emergency, so as to allow 'indefinite detention on the basis of reasonable suspicion of terrorist offences, without charge or trial.'[87]

Three main issues arose in this case. Firstly, the existence of the 'national emergency' on which the derogation from Article 5 (which allowed the detainees to be held indefinitely) rested was questioned. Secondly, where the emergency's existence was accepted, the proportionality of the legislation in light of the emergency questioned. Thirdly, the legitimacy of the application of the legislation only to non-nationals was brought into doubt. The Lords took the fact that the detainees' liberty had been deprived was taken as a given, as the government's derogation was predicated on this assumption.[88] I too accept that liberty has been deprived, as an individual is unable to act on the normative demands made by morality when he is indefinitely detained in a high security prison.[89]

The Lords took a deferential approach to the first issue, judging the government's conclusion that a state of emergency existed as sufficient evidence of such an emergency.[90] The existence of an emergency is of paramount importance in an assessment of the legality of Part 4 using the equal agency principle. As outlined in Section 3, the right to liberty can only be restricted where another's agency has been proved non-speculatively to be highly likely to be undermined. The detention of those linked to terrorist activity can, in theory, be justified on rights protection grounds as the government has a secondary duty to protect its citizens' right to life; if there is a high likelihood of terrorist attack, on the basis of which an emergency can be declared, and detention of those highly likely to commit that attack is highly likely to prevent this attack, and hence considerable loss of life, then the derogation on which Part 4 relies is justified.[91] If the existence of this

---

[86] This article permits detention of non-nationals where deportation is imminent.

[87] n 27, at para [12].

[88] *Ibid.*, paras [1]-[5].

[89] See Section 3(II).

[90] *Ibid.*, per Lord Bingham at paras [26]-[30], Baroness Hale at para [226].

[91] *Review of Counter-Terrorism Powers,* Joint Committee on Human Rights, 18th Report of Session 2003-04, HL Paper 158, 7: 'security itself is a fundamental right', which can justify the deprivation of a terrorist's liberty after a fair trial.

emergency cannot be proved non-speculatively, however, the analysis in Section 3(II) shows equal agency does not permit the derogation. In this instance, as the Joint Committee on Human Rights[92] and the Newton Report[93] highlighted, the information released by the government did not adequately prove non-speculatively the existence of an emergency.[94] Further to this, Lord Hoffman, in dissent, makes the compelling point that though terrorism poses a threat, this does not amount to 'a threat to the life of the nation', on which an emergency must be grounded; in fact the threat to liberty made by the derogation is more dangerous to the UK's 'survival' as a democratic nation, that a terrorist attack. On these grounds an emergency cannot be said to exist.[95] Given the fact that an invalidation of agency status cannot justified on non-speculative grounds, and here the emergency on which the invalidation of the detainees' agency status was justified had not been proved non-speculatively, the equal agency analysis identifies a violation of Article 5, which consists in the principle of equal protection of agency status by Part 4 of the ATCSA. As Part 4 cannot be read other than being predicated on the existence of a national emergency, the ATCSA is incompatible with the HRA.

Even if we follow the Lords' judgement and assent to the view that an emergency existed, the second issue of compatibility remains – was Part 4 of the ATCSA a necessitated by the emergency in question. Equal agency views rights to 'trump' such that a restriction of rights can be deemed necessary only where the rights of other individuals are at stake. Ordinarily we would need a clear understanding of the nature of the emergency to judge whether a rights restriction could be justified given the threat to rights posed, however in this case the limited applicability of Part 4 to only non-national terror suspects highlights the non-necessity of the provision, regardless of the government's precise understanding of the emergency in question. Lords Bingham and Craighead[96] both deem Part 4 unnecessary, given the government's

[92] Henceforth known as the JCHR.
[93] *The Newton Report*, Privy Counsellor Review Committee, presented to Parliament pursuant to Section 122(5) of the Anti-terrorism, Crime and Security Act 2001, 18th December 2003, HC 100.
[94] HL Paper 158 at paras [15]-[17].
[95] n 27, at paras [92]-[97] and [109].
[96] *Ibid.*, at paras [49]-[53] and [102]-[105].

reasoning that it is not necessary to indefinitely detain UK nationals who are terror suspects, despite the fact they pose a similar threat. If two cases are relatively similar, and in one a rights-based reason for liberty deprivation is not necessitated, then logic entails there is no rights-based reason for liberty deprivation in the second. Equal agency provides the principle present in this reasoning; given the priority of rights concerns, liberty cannot be deprived in either instance. This analysis can be applied in *A*, with reference to the notion of relevant similarity and difference on which equal agency's understanding of equality rests.[97] The argument made in the government's submissions that the immigration status of the detainees is evidence of relevant difference is flawed given the *Chalal* ruling which deems deportation the case of the detainees impermissible, and *Singh*[98] which rules the time an individual can be held pre-deportation is limited; the detainees were relevantly similar to the British terror suspects in that they had a right to remain at liberty within the UK.[99] The only reason to deprive them of their liberty was the suspicion of terrorist engagement; this is, however, a reason that also applies to the British terror suspects.[100] As indefinite detention was not deemed proportionate to the threat posed by the British terror suspects, it cannot be deemed proportionate in relation to non-national terror suspects pose a relevantly similar threat, and possess not relevant differences.[101] This reasoning proves the indefinite detention of the detainees cannot be justified on necessity grounds, as the government's decision not to apply the policy to all relevantly similar individuals highlights their belief that the emergency does not necessitate a limitation of the detainees Article 5 right, on the basis of the rights of others. Given the specifity of Part 4 of the ATCSA, which cannot be read otherwise, it can be deemed incompatible with the HRA.

The above analysis aids our consideration of the third issue in this case. Given the difference in the treatment of UK-national terror

---

[97] Section 2(III).

[98] *R v Governor of Durham Prison Ex P Singh* [1984] 1 WLR 704.

[99] The government cannot have viewed the deprivation of liberty permissible on this basis or it would not have felt the need to derogate from this provision. See n 27, per Baroness Hale at para [237].

[100] See http://news.bbc.co.uk/1/hi/uk/1731568.stm.

[101] n 27, at para [256].

suspects, to whom the detainees are relatively similar, the Lords concluded unequal treatment, and thus a violation of Article 14, had occurred;[102] I am in agreement. The principle of equal agency entails that where a right that protects agency status is not protected equally, there is a rights violation. The fact that Article 5 was unequally applied in this instance provides a third argument for the incompatibility of Part of the ATCSA with the HRA on the basis of the equal agency principle in which the HRA consists. An equal agency approach endorses the Lords conclusion of incompatibility on the basis of the three reasons expressed above. This reasoning diverges from that of the Lords.

I also raise the additional issue of Article 6 incompatibility. The manner in which the detainees were tried, prior to detention, signals such incompatibility, given the equal agency principle in which the HRA consists. The procedural provisions of the hearings in which orders to detain the detainees, violating their right to liberty, were made, did not provide non-speculative, objective proof that the detention ordered would be highly likely to protect the rights of others.[103] This highlights a failure to treat the detainees as equal agents that will be explored in greater depth in the Section 4(III). Here the compatibility of the very similar judicial proceedings used to impose control orders with Article 6 is examined, given the equal agency principle in which the HRA consists.

II. Secretary of State for the Home Department v JJ and Secretary of State for the Home Department v E – A Section 3 reading of the Prevention of Terror Act 2005 on the basis of Article 5.

Following the decision of the Lords in *A*, the government passed new legislation to combat the problem of terror suspects with a right to remain in the UK who could not be prosecuted due to a lack of evidence, but were deemed by the government a 'threat to public security'. The 2005 Act created a system of control orders;[104] these restrict the actions of the individuals – known as controlees – to

---

[102] *Ibid.*, see Lord Scott at para [158].

[103] n 91, at paras [21]-[23].

[104] *Ibid.* Suggested civil restriction orders with a 'fully adversarial procedure' (para [79]) when imposed, as a possible solution to the problem addressed by Part 4 of the ATCSA.

varying degrees. Given the range of restrictions that can be imposed by a control order, it can be derogating or non-derogating. A derogating control order implies a violation of Article 5; as yet no derogating control orders have been made.

In both *JJ*[105] and *E*[106] the compatibility of 2005 Act with Article 5 with non-derogating control orders was challenged. Where it imposes a non-derogating control order the government maintains its obligation to protect the controlee's Article 5 rights; no derogation has been made and placing of a control order does not fall under 5(1)(a-f)'s permissible restrictions to liberty. The facts of the *JJ* case demonstrate that the restrictions on liberty imposed by a control order can be high. In this case the 6 Iraqi respondents who all had either temporary or permanent leave to remain in the UK, were each 'required to remain in [their] residence at all times save a period of six hours between 10am and 4pm';[107] in this 18 hour curfew each had to remain in the one-bedroom council flat, in which he lived alone, without access even to communal areas.[108] Additional restrictions included the permissibility of only those visitors who had Home Office approval, the requirement to wear an electronic tag, the attendance of only one specified mosque, the prohibition of the use of any communications equipment aside from one monitored landline, and a prohibition on pre-arranged meetings. In contrast *E*[109] was subject only to a 12-hour curfew from 7pm-7am, and during that curfew he remained within his own family home, shared by his wife and children. In the hours not covered by the curfew he was able live an ordinary life, going shopping, picking up his children from school and seeing family members in the area.[110] Just as *E*'s control order was less stringent than that applied to *JJ*, there have also been orders accorded that simply deprive individuals of their passport and forbid foreign travel.[111]

---

[105] *JJ* (n 28).
[106] *E* (n 28).
[107] *JJ* (n 28).
[108] *Ibid.*, at para [20].
[109] *E* (n 28).
[110] *Ibid.*, at paras [6]-[14].
[111] *MB* (n 28). *MB* was only asked to surrender his passport, and was denied permission to leave the UK.

The question the Lords had to address in the cases of *E* and *JJ* was 'has liberty been deprived?' An account of the nature of liberty is necessary to address this question, but in the Lords' judgements no fully elucidated account of liberty was given. In line with the ECtHR in *Guzzardi*, the Lords viewed detention in a four-walled prison the paradigm example of liberty deprivation, on the basis of its qualitative features of the detention in question; and endeavoured find out whether these qualitative features were also present in the control orders challenged under Article 5. In the *Guzzardi* case the sheer isolation of the prisoner on a small island[112] was deemed relevantly similar to a prison-sentence such that a deprivation of liberty had occurred. The Lords reached a similar decision in *JJ* arguing 'The effect of the 18-hour curfew, coupled with the effective exclusion of social visitors, meant the controlled persons were in practice in solitary confinement for a lengthy period of every day with very little opportunity for contact with the outside world.'[113] This position can be elucidated on the basis of the equal agency principle. If imprisonment is considered the paradigm example of liberty deprivation then the question is: 'what conditions can similarly undermine an individual's agency by rendering him unable to act on the normative demands of morality?' The notion of social isolation plays a major role in the answer to this question, as examined in Section 3(I).

In the case of *JJ*, the controlees' opportunities to socially interact are severely restricted; in their 18-hour a day curfew they are prevented from engaging in any but the most regulated interaction;[114] further to this in their 6-hours 'free' time the prohibition of pre-arranged meetings and the prohibition of attendance of any mosque apart from one previously defined severely limits the form of interaction that can take place. The restriction on interaction is so extreme that the individuals in question are unable to act on the normative demands made by morality; they are excluded from the socially interactive situations in which an individual has the opportunity to act on the normative demands made by morality. If the example of

---

[112] *Guzzardi v Italy* [1980] 3 EHRR 333.

[113] *JJ* (n 28), at para [7].

[114] *Ibid.* As Bingham highlights the need for Home Office approval disincentives visitors at para [24].

friendship explored in Section 3(I) is taken, a controlee in *JJ* would be unable to act on the normative moral demand to spend time with his friend given the order placed on him; this is indicative of the fact his status as an agent is invalidated by the restrictions on action, hence a violation of Article 5 has occurred. In *E*'s case the factors the Lords noted as relevant, such as his ability to live in his own home with his family,[115] evidence an ability to act on the normative demands made by morality in the context of relationships with other individuals; he is still able to fulfil his moral duty as a father to spend time with his children; this would not be the case in prison. *E's* agency status is not invalidated by the restrictions on action imposed by the control order; hence the order does not violate Article 5.

In these cases an equal agency approach entails the same conclusion reached by the Lords, but provides a principle on which to base this conclusion. The restrictions set out in Section 1(4) of the 2005 Act do not necessarily deprive an individual of liberty, as these restrictions can be applied with varying degrees of stringency, and in different combinations. Certain applications of the restrictions, such as those imposed on *E* do not invalidate agency status, and thus do not violate Article 5. Certain applications of the restrictions such as those applied to the controlees in *JJ* however, have precisely this effect. Given the possibility of the a non-derogating control order being applied thus in a manner which violates Article 5, a Section 3 reading of the 2005 Act is essential; it must be read such that non-derogating control orders which violate Article 5 are invalid in the act's own terms. Equal agency views a non-derogating control order as one predicated on a governmental view that the rights of other individuals do not stand to be deprived such that a deprivation of the controlee's right to liberty is justified to prevent this. To deprive the controlees of their right to liberty where others agency-based rights are not at stake is to fail to treat the controlees as equal agents. This is an impermissible violation of Article 5 that a Section 3 reading of the 2005 Act cannot deem valid.

---

[115] *E* (n 28).

III.   Secretary of State for the Home Department v MB – Article 6 Incompatibility with the Prevention of Terrorism Act 2005.

A control order is not imposed on the basis of a criminal trial as control orders were devised to provide a solution to the problem of terror suspects believed to pose a threat, but against whom there is not sufficient admissible evidence to ground a criminal prosecution.[116] A control order is therefore made on the basis of civil proceedings. A non-derogating control order is made by the Home Secretary where she 'reasonably suspects'[117] an individual of terrorist activity. Except in an emergency, where 7 days leeway is given, the order must be immediately approved in a court hearing, where the Home Secretary's decision is assessed for obvious flaws. The order is then automatically judicially reviewed; in these proceedings 'the decision of the Secretary of State will be upheld unless shown to be founded on a mistake of law, or disproportionate assessment of the facts in their legal context, or [to be] perverse.'[118] A similar test is used if the controlee appeals the order.

In *MB*[119] it was argued that the proceedings under *MB* and *AF's* (a party to the proceedings) control orders were imposed violated their Article 6 right to a fair hearing. The procedure set out above was followed in the imposition of a control order on both *MB* and *AF;* additionally the decision to impose both orders was partially based on a closed statement to which the controlees had no access, given its sensitive nature due to its relation to national security. Where deliberation on the closed material took place a special advocate, – 'a trained and security cleared independent lawyer who represents the controlee'[120]– was appointed to represent the issues of the controlees. Once the closed information was revealed to the special advocate he was no longer allowed any contact with the controlee he represented.

Two issues were raised by Lord Bingham in *MB* in relation to Article 6. Firstly, 'does the imposition of a control order amount to a criminal charge under the ECHR?', and secondly, 'is the 2005 Act

---

[116] The First Report of the Independent Reviewer Pursuant to Section 14(3) of the Prevention of Terror Act 2005, Lord Carlile of Berriew QC, 2nd February 2006 at paras [54]-[55].
[117] Prevention of Terrorism Act 2005, Section 2(1)(a).
[118] The First Report of the Independent Reviewer, 2nd February 2006 at paras [64]-[65].
[119] MB (n 28).
[120] n 118, at para [15].

incompatible with the Article 6, or is a Section 3 reading possible?' The first question is relevant because as discussed in Section 3(II) procedural protections accorded in criminal trials are more stringent than in civil hearings. The stringent procedural requirements applied in criminal hearings under Article 6 ensure that a deprivation of liberty is only accorded where it has been objectively and non-speculatively proved that another individual's rights will be protected by the rights restriction. In the case of *MB*, I agree that many of the other *Engel* criteria necessary to classify proceedings as criminal are not met, in particular if an individual has a control order imposed on them, they are not being charged with a criminal offence under British law.[121] However, the restrictions on agency that could occur as a result of a control order hearing are far greater than in ordinary civil proceedings[122] as *AF*'s case of a 14-hour curfew and a nine-mile radius of confinement in his 10 non-curfewed hours demonstrates. The element of the *Engel* criteria relevant to an equal agency approach therefore applies in the case of hearings for non-derogating control orders,[123] although to a lesser degree than in cases where Article 5 rights stand to be deprived as a result of the hearing. Procedural safeguards to ensure an objective and non-speculative outcome should be more stringent than in ordinary civil proceedings given the possibility of such agency restricting outcomes.[124]

The second issue of the possibility of Article 6 incompatibility, raised in *MB*, gives rise to two concerns when considered from an equal agency perspective. Firstly, that the Home Secretary has the power to make a control order, and that his decision is then subject only to the standards of judicial review, raises questions regarding the objective and non-speculative nature of the decision to make a control order. The considerable agency restriction, outlined above, which can result from a control order hearing, means the controlee should be stringently

---

[121] *MB* (n 28) at para [96].

[122] n 77, 223 on restrictions resulting from ordinary civil hearings.

[123] Similar reasoning was applied in R *(on the application of McCann) v Manchester Crown Court*, [2002] UKHL 39, regarding the use of criminal standards of proof where stringent Anti-Social Behaviour Orders are imposed.

[124] Counter Terrorism and Human Rights: Draft Prevention of Terrorism Act 2005 (Continuance in Force of Sections 1-9), Joint Committee on Human Rights, 8th Report of Session 2006-7, 4th March 2007, HL Paper 60 at para [38].

procedurally protected at the hearing, yet this is not the case. The fact that the Home Secretary, who has an obvious and declared interest in ensuring he or she does everything possible to protect public safety and avoid recrimination imposes control orders on the basis of her 'reasonable suspicion' raises issues of objectivity. Wherever suspicion exists, even where this suspicion is not objectively reasonable, the Home Secretary has an incentive to impose a control order.[125] Further to this 'there remains an important difference between judicial review and full appellate jurisdiction where the court is subject to no restrictions as to the nature of its functions,'[126] as evidence is tested against a higher burden of proof in the latter instance, yet in this case it is the former procedure that is followed in control order cases. As discussed in Section 3(II), a low burden of proof creates a speculative outcome and speculation undermines an individual's Article 6 rights by failing to treat him as an equal agent. This is particularly problematic where considerable agency restrictions can be imposed as a result of the hearing, as is the case in control order hearings. Although the Lords did not raise these issues in *MB*, they are hugely significant from an equal agency perspective and contribute greatly to my conclusion that the 2005 Act is incompatible with the Article 6. These provisions, which create a speculative restriction on agency, impermissible given the equal agency principle in which the HRA consists, are central to the 2005 Act, such that a Section 3 reading of the Act, which views cases in which these procedures apply impermissible, is impossible.

Secondly, putting aside the above momentarily, the 2005 Act's provisions regarding non-disclosure and the special advocate procedure designed to mitigate the negative effects of these provisions can also be examined with regard to compatibility with Article 6. As discussed in Section 3, the procedural requirements of Article 6 are rights only so far as they serve the equal protection of individuals' agency. If the special advocate procedure can be demonstrated to ensure objectivity and non-speculation in the face of non-disclosure of material to the controlee, then both non-disclosure and the special advocate procedure are permissible under Article 6. The argument made by Baroness Hale in

---

[125] *Prevention Of Terrorism Bill,* Joint Committee on Human Rights, 10th Report of Session 2004-5, 2nd March 2005, HL Paper 68 at para [16].
[126] *Ibid.,* at para [12].

MB on this issue is convincing; where firstly sufficient information is revealed to the defendant in the open case, such that he is able to contest his control order, and secondly an adequate summary of the closed material is presented to the him, Article 6 is protected.[127] Equal agency is not then invalidated, as the controlee has sufficient opportunity to rebut the case against him,[128] such that the judge is able to make an objective and non-speculative judgement. A Section 3 reading of the 2005 Act's provisions regarding non-disclosure is then possible, as in certain instances the special advocate procedure can be used, such that equal agency is protected, even where non-disclosure occurs. In *MB* and *AF*'s cases a Section 3 reading of the 2005 legislation these orders is invalid as neither controlee had sufficient information openly disclosed to contest his order, and the no summary was served; '*MB* was confronted by a bare, unsubstantiated assertion which he could do no more than deny.'[129] In these cases a Section 3 reading requires more information be revealed to the controlees if that information is to be used in the case against them.[130] The protest made by the special advocates in relation to their compromised position also provides evidence that present the special advocate procedure in its current form is in need of reform.[131] A Section 3 reading of this element of the 2005 Act does not, however, save it from incompatibility with Article 6 on the grounds outlined in the preceding paragraph; the standards of judicial review following the Home Secretary's judgement are speculative regardless of the nature of the special advocate proceedings, hence the 2005 Act is incompatible with the HRA regardless of the manner in which the special advocate provisions are applied.

Although *MB* related to a non-derogating control order, as no derogating control orders have yet been imposed, there is an issue of legislative compatibility regarding Article 6 and the procedure used to impose a derogating control order. A derogating control order

---

[127] *MB* (n 28) at paras [65]-[66].

[128] The importance of an adversarial trial is emphasised in *Rowe and Davis v UK* [2000] Crim LR 584.

[129] *MB* (n 28) at para [40].

[130] *Ibid.*, at para [44].

[131] See http://news.bbc.co.uk/1/hi/uk_politics/4405415.stm (as of 04/08/08).

invalidates agency status by definition; hence an equal agency understanding of the Engel criteria entails stringent procedural requirements to ensure such liberty deprivation does not apart from for non-speculative rights-based reasons. The 2005 Act does not, however, provide procedures to ensure this. Although the Court, rather than the Home Secretary, makes derogating control orders, the test in 4(7) of the 2005 Act is whether on a 'balance of probabilities' controlee poses a threat to rights linked to the public emergency on the basis of which a derogation was made. The 'balance of probabilities' is a far lower standard of proof than the criminal standard 'beyond reasonable doubt'; unlike the criminal standard it does not prove non-speculatively a rights-based reason for a control order than will invalidate the agency status of the controlee. The principle of equal agency on which the HRA is based is therefore violated, and as the legislation cannot be read other than to authorise such procedures it is therefore incompatible with Article 6. The procedural requirements laid out by the ATCSA for indefinite detention was to be imposed on foreign terror suspects are very similar to those regarding the imposition of a derogating control order, thus the ATCSA can also be deemed incompatible with Article 6.

For all the above reasons an equal agency approach entails disagreement with the Lords, and the conclusion that the 2005 Act is incompatible with Article 6. Non-disclosure, mitigated by the special advocate procedure, on which the Lords focussed, is permissible under the HRA subject to a Section 3 reading, but the executive and judicial procedures for imposing derogating and non-derogating control orders cannot be read to meet the non-speculative and objective standards required by the principle of protection of equal agency status on which the HRA is based; thus they are incompatible with Article 6.

Conclusion: A Principled Approach to Compatibility

I conclude, as I hypothesised, that where the HRA is viewed as consisting of principles present in the legislation itself, and those present in the relevant jurisprudence,[132] the judgements of the House of Lords on the issue of the compatibility of the ATL with the HRA, are flawed. An exploration of a number of theories of rights demonstrated

---

[132] n 7.

that the principle of equal protection of agency, on which the equal agency theory of rights rests, is the principle from which all principles expressed in the legislation and jurisprudence relevant to the HRA derive. It is therefore the principle on which the Convention Rights enshrined in the HRA are based. An exploration of Articles 5 and 6, in light of the principle of equal protection of agency, and the subsequent application of these rights in the context of their compatibility with the ATL results in conclusions divergent from those of the Lords on this issue. Part 4 of the 2001 ATCSA was found to be incompatible with Article 5, not simply because of the lack of proportionality with which deprivations of liberty were applied under the Act, but also because the existence of a state of emergency, on which liberty deprivations were predicated, was not been proved non-speculatively, hence the equal protection of agency was undermined. Further, this failure to enshrine procedures that ensured detention was imposed by the executive and judiciary without speculation, and failed to protect equal agency status, which amounted to a violation of Article 6. The non-derogating control order provisions outlined in Section 1(4) of the 2005 Act are found, using a Section 3 reading of the Act, to be valid in the Act's on terms only where no liberty deprivation that prevents individual's from acting on the normative demands made by morality, thus invalidating agency status, occurs. Finally, the procedural provisions regarding the imposition of a derogating and non-derogating control orders outlined in Sections 1-4 of the 2005 Act are found to be incompatible with Article 6 as they fail to ensure any conclusion, on the basis of which an order is made, is non-speculative, thus failing to protect the equal agency status of the controlees. 'No judicial decision is necessarily the right decision,'[133] and in the case of the House of Lords' decisions on cases regarding the compatibility of the ATL with the HRA, a principled approach to the HRA demonstrates flaws in the judgements made.

---

[133] n 1.

The Protection of Freedom Under the Human Rights Act: What We've Gained

HELEN WILDBORE[*]

Introduction

This article is a response to the report by the UCL Student Human Rights Programme called 'The Abolition of Freedom Act 2009' with an introduction entitled 'What We've Lost'.[1] The report was compiled for the Convention on Modern Liberty (which took place in February 2009 in London) and is edited by the writer and journalist, Henry Porter. The report documents the 'erosion of liberty in Britain over the last decade' and describes the 'wholesale removal of rights that were apparently protected by the [Human Rights Act]'. It is an 'inventory of the loss' and lists the measures passed which have eroded our rights. They centre around traditional civil liberties areas such as freedom of expression, assembly, association, privacy, torture and fair trial.

This article will respond to the report (hereinafter 'the UCL report'). It will show that the Human Rights Act 1998 (HRA) is not to blame for the erosion of liberty outlined in the UCL report, that the Act has in fact protected rights and freedoms and without it the situation would have been far worse. It recognises that, of course, no bill of rights is a magic wand that can stop all draconian legislation being passed. Nor can a bill of rights be the final word on rights and freedoms. The US Bill of Rights has not stopped rights-curtailing legislation being passed, nor has it stopped debate in the US on rights and freedoms. But the HRA has introduced 'checkpoints' to help us to resist rights-curtailing legislation and assist Parliament to act as a watchdog. It is argued that vigilance and participation in the human rights dialogue created by the HRA are necessary to prevent the erosion of hard-won rights and freedoms.

---

[*] Human Rights Futures Project, London School of Economics and Political Science.

[1] Available at http://www.modernliberty.net/downloads/abolition_of_freedom.pdf (Last visited 30th October 2009).

The article does not condone or attempt to justify the measures outlined in the UCL report. Nor does it seek to attack or defend the policies of any one political party, whilst acknowledging that that the measures outlined in the UCL report were passed under the Labour government. It argues that the HRA, as our bill of rights, needs to be promoted so that we can all use it to stand up to the executive when they seek to erode our rights, in the same way that Americans do with their Bill of Rights.

The article is divided into six parts. First, the article puts the debate into context by setting out the constitutional effect of the HRA, explaining that it is our bill of rights. The second part points out that bills of rights alone will not be able to stop draconian measures being passed but that vigilance and political will are required. What bills of rights can do is introduce 'checkpoints' through which such legislation has to pass to help us stop rights-curtailing legislation getting through. The third part of the article explains the checkpoints the HRA has introduced. Fourth, the article points out that, whilst, of course, it is always theoretically possible to have a stronger and more comprehensive bill of rights, replacing the HRA with a new bill of rights will not solve the problems identified in the UCL report. Fifth, the article will set out some examples of how the HRA has protected rights and freedoms, demonstrating that not only would the situation have been far worse without the HRA, but that the Act has helped by safeguarding our rights and freedoms in a constitutional document. Finally, the article will briefly describe how human rights thinking has developed from the approach taken in the UCL report of individual freedom from state interference, towards positive obligations on states to protect rights and the emergence of key human rights values such as dignity, equality and community.

1. Our Bill of Rights

The HRA was designed to be far more than just the incorporation of a human rights treaty into our law.[2] As Jack Straw said as Home Secretary in 2000 when the HRA came into force, it was 'the first Bill of Rights

---

[2] The Human Rights Act 1998 incorporated the European Convention on Human Rights into UK law and came into force on 2 October 2000.

this country has seen for three centuries'.[3] The legal and constitutional characteristics that make up a bill of rights are all present in the HRA.[4]

First, like most post-war bills of rights, the HRA draws its principles from the Universal Declaration of Human Rights and the broad ethical values it contains which are partly reflected in the European Convention on Human Rights (ECHR). It is different to usual 'black letter' law statutes in that it contains broadly expressed, open-textured values. The Act has to be interpreted generously and purposefully, rather than narrowly and literally, to reflect its spirit.

Second, the rights in the HRA are binding on the government. The executive and all public authorities, including the courts, are explicitly prohibited from acting incompatibly with the rights it upholds.[5] But, whilst exhibiting many features of a 'higher law' to which all other laws must conform where 'possible',[6] the courts have no power under the HRA to strike down Acts of Parliament. Instead higher courts can make a declaration of incompatibility, which leaves it to Parliament to decide whether and how to proceed. In reality, the government has never ignored such declarations. Of the 17 declarations made that are still standing and not subject to appeal (out of 26 made altogether), the government has responded by either amending, or committing to amend, the legislation or policy at issue, or changing the offending practice.[7]

Third, the HRA provides redress for violations of the rights. It sets out in fairly simple terms the rights everyone in the jurisdiction of the UK can use to hold public authorities to account, both inside and outside the court. Where unjustified violations of those rights occur, the court may grant a remedy.

---

[3] Speech to Institute of Public Policy Research, 13 January 2000.
[4] See F Klug, 'A Bill of Rights: Do We Need One or Do we Already Have One?' Irvine Lecture 2007, Human Rights Centre, University of Durham, 2 March 2007, published in [2007] *Public Law* 701.
[5] Section 6 HRA.
[6] Section 3(1) HRA states: 'so far as it is possible to do so, primary legislation and subordinate legislation must be read and given effect in a way which is compatible with the Convention rights.'
[7] To date, 26 declarations of incompatibility have been made, of which 18 are still standing (although one is under appeal) and 8 have been overturned on appeal. In two cases the government is still considering how to remedy the incompatibility (R *(Wright et al) v Secretary of State for Health and Secretary of State for Education and Skills* [2009] UKHL 3 and R *(Baiai and others) v Secretary of State for the Home Department* [2008] UKHL 53).

This so-called 'dialogue model' was a response to criticisms of bills of rights in the Labour Party about handing over too much power to judges. The model adopted in the HRA protects the doctrine of parliamentary sovereignty but it also addresses what many bills of rights critics view as the 'democratic deficit' of bills of rights with strike down powers, where judges are given the power to determine the meaning of the broad values in the bill of rights and to repeal laws which don't conform to that meaning.[8]

The 'dialogue model' has begun to be replicated in other countries. In Australia, the Australian Capital Territories and the state of Victoria have both recently passed human rights legislation based on the model of the UK HRA.[9] Australia is also consulting on a national bill of rights. The terms of reference of the consultation committee explicitly rule out a constitutionally entrenched bill of rights and instead ask the committee to identify options to preserve the sovereignty of Parliament, as in the HRA.[10]

2. No magic wand

We all have our part to play in the dialogue on human rights created by the HRA and in preventing rights-curtailing legislation – Parliament, civil society and the public. As Shami Chakrabarti (the Director of Liberty) has said, 'like all bills of rights, the Human Rights Act is neither magic wand nor computer program'.[11] A bill of rights alone will not stop draconian legislation being passed. We can turn to the USA for evidence of this. The US Bill of Rights, a famously staunch and popular bill of rights, is constitutionally entrenched and the judges of the Supreme Court have the power to strike down legislation they find to be unconstitutional. However, the US Bill of Rights did not stop the passage of, say, the USA Patriot Act 2001, the Homeland Security Act 2002, the Real ID Act 2005, the Detainee Treatment Act 2005 or the

---

[8] See *Sceptical Essays on Human Rights*, T Campbell, K Ewing and A Tomkins (eds.) (Oxford University Press, Oxford 2001).
[9] A.C.T. Human Rights Act 2004, Victorian Charter of Rights and Responsibilities Act 2006.
[10] See http://www.humanrightsconsultation.gov.au/ (Last visited 30th October 2009).
[11] 'In 2009, the fight for liberty is about to go up a gear', *The Guardian*, 22 January 2009.

Military Commissions Act 2006.[12] This legislation curtails rights and freedoms in areas similar to those highlighted in the UCL report. For example, it increased the powers of the state to search email, telephone and other records, gave more discretion to the government to detain and deport suspected terrorists, it made changes to driver's licenses creating a uniform identity card, it removed the right of habeas corpus for persons the President designated as 'unlawful enemy combatants' and gave the President the power to define what is and what is not torture and abuse.

The erosion of rights and freedoms in the US over the past 8 years demonstrates that if the political will exists to pass draconian legislation, a bill of rights alone cannot stop it. Dominic Grieve the Shadow Justice Secretary (and Shadow Attorney General), has made this point: 'On its own a Bill of Rights will not provide all the solutions to the threat we face from creeping state authoritarianism in the face of terrorism and the fear of social disintegration.'[13]

The UCL report focuses on the loss of liberty over the last decade. The HRA was passed in 1998 so the implication is that the HRA is to blame, or has not helped, in failing to prevent the loss of liberty. Crucial to this debate is the fact that the HRA was in force less than a year before the terrorist attack on the USA in September 2001. The loss of liberty over the last decade has to be seen in the light of those events and the attacks on London in 2005, and the response to them, termed 'the war on terror'. Less than a year in force, before it had the chance to bed down, the HRA was faced with a world shifted on its axis and a barrage of new legislative measures passed in response. As shown above, there was a similar response in the USA, with new legislative measures being passed in the wake of 'the war on terror'. Sir Ken McDonald, the former Director of Public Prosecutions, has pointed out that the HRA stood up to the pressures created by global terrorism even more effectively than the US Bill of Rights. Speaking at the Liberty 75th anniversary conference in June 2009 he said that the HRA passed its test during the war on terror and stood up to the

---

[12] However, in June 2008 the US Supreme Court held that the removal of habeas corpus from persons the President designates as "unlawful enemy combatants" in the Military Commissions Act 2006 was unconstitutional. *Boumediene v Bush* 553 US (2008).

[13] 'Liberty and Community in Britain', Speech for Conservative Liberty Forum, 2 October 2006.

buffeting more effectively than the US Bill of Rights as interpreted by
the Supreme Court.[14] Lord Bingham, a retired senior law lord, has also
pointed out that the loss of liberty can be traced back even further than
the last decade and that the passage of the HRA was a step in another
direction, which he has expressed strong support for.[15] Speaking at the
Convention on Modern Liberty he said: 'It seems clear that the last half
century has seen an erosion of values once held dear. This is not the
work of one party or one government.'[16]

Not an end to debate

Bills of rights are not like 'computer programs' either. They do not
contain an equation which legislation can pass through and come out
human rights compliant and guarantee agreement by all. Bills of rights
are, by their nature, expressed in broad terms and contain ethical values
which are subject to interpretation by the courts. As the White Paper
for the 1990 New Zealand Bill of Rights said, 'In a great many cases
where controversial issues arise for determination, there is no "right"
answer.'[17] As such, bills of rights do not stop debates and all of them
have to balance competing rights and interests. But bills of rights do
provide a framework in which to approach these debates, providing
mechanisms to balance competing rights and setting out the principles
on which rights can be limited (including limitations having to be
prescribed by law, necessary in a democratic society and proportionate).
The model of the HRA was predicated on civil society playing its part
in the debates about where the boundaries of rights and freedoms lie
and using the mechanisms provided in the Act to protect our rights. No
bill of rights will guarantee freedoms in testing times if people do not
remain vigilant. As Justice Learned Hand said: 'Liberty lies in the hearts
of men and women; when it dies there, no constitution, no law, no
court can save it.'[18]

---

[14] Speech at Liberty 75th anniversary conference, London, 6 June 2009.
[15] See Lord Bingham speech at Liberty 75th anniversary conference, London, 6 June 2009.
[16] Lord Bingham, speech at the Convention on Modern Liberty, London, 28 February 2009.
[17] 'A Bill of Rights for New Zealand: A White Paper', 1985 [1984-85] 1 AJHR A 66. Presented
to the House of Representatives by the Hon. Geoffrey Palmer, Minister of Justice.
[18] 'The Spirit of Liberty', speech at *I Am An American Day* ceremony, Central Park, New York
City, 21 May 1944.

3. Checkpoints

Although a bill of rights is not a magic wand that can stop legislation which curtails rights, a bill of rights does introduce 'checkpoints' at which such legislation will be tested. The HRA introduced several of these checkpoints, which did not exist prior to its passage.

Statement of compatibility

First, on introducing a Bill to Parliament ministers in charge of a Bill have to make a statement under section 19 of the HRA that in their view it is compatible with the Convention rights, or if they are not able to make such a statement, that they nevertheless wish to proceed with the Bill. Whilst it is fair to say that this requirement has not led to the rigorous Parliamentary scrutiny of legislation that was hoped (for example, there have only been three Bills carrying a statement that they are not compatible with Convention rights[19]), it ensures an assessment within Whitehall, in the very early stages of the development of new legislation, of compatibility with human rights standards and triggers an effort to consider alternative means of achieving the legislative objectives in a manner more compatible with rights.[20] Lord Lester has said 'few, if anyone, in Whitehall or Westminster appreciated just how significant the practical impact of [the section] 19 procedure would be upon the preparation and interpretation of proposed legislation.'[21]

Joint Committee on Human Rights

As a consequence of the passage of the HRA, there is now a joint Parliamentary committee, the Joint Committee on Human Rights (JCHR), to scrutinise legislation for human rights compatibility. The

---

[19] The only Government Bill that on introduction has borne a section 19(1)(b) statement was the Bill that became the Communications Act 2003, in respect of the prohibition on paid political advertising on television and radio in what became section 321 of that Act. The Civil Partnership Bill was given a section 19(1)(b) statement upon introduction into the House of Commons on the basis of amendments made in the House of Lords, which were later removed in the Commons. The Local Government Bill 2000 was given a section 19(1)(b) statement following a House of Lords amendment to prevent the repeal of the prohibition on promoting homosexuality in teaching. The offending provision was later removed.
[20] See J Hiebert, 'Parliament and the Human Rights Act: Can the JCHR help facilitate a culture of rights?' (2006) 4(1) *International Journal of Constitutional Law* 1.
[21] Lord Lester and K Taylor, 'Parliamentary scrutiny of human rights', in *Human Rights law and Practice*, Lord Lester and D Pannick (eds.), (2nd ed, LexisNexis London, 2004).

Committee provides another checkpoint to assess legislation for human rights compliance and they report to Parliament to feed into the debate on new legislation as it passes through both Houses. Changes were made to the working practices of the JCHR following recommendations made by Professor Francesca Klug in 2006, who was appointed as a specialist advisor.[22] Pointing out that key to the whole scheme of the HRA is that Parliament has a central role in the protection of human rights and is entitled to take its own view about compatibility with Convention rights, Professor Klug recommended that the JCHR should express its *own view* on compatibility in its reports, rather than trying to predict whether a court would find a particular provision incompatible, especially where the case law is undeveloped or uncertain. This recommendation was taken up by the Committee. The JCHR's advice is crucial in helping Parliament play its role in the 'dialogue' on human rights; assisting Parliament to debate the impact of new legislation on rights, whether legislation encroaches on rights, whether that is necessary and proportionate, or indeed whether a Bill provides an opportunity to further protect rights.

Murray Hunt, the legal advisor to the Committee, points out that the standard of human rights debates in Parliament is increasing, as evidenced by the debates on proposals to increase the amount of time a suspect may be held for questioning without charge. In the more recent Parliamentary debate on increasing pre-charge detention to 42 days in 2008, the standard of debate on the human rights implications of the proposal was much higher than when 90 day detention was debated in 2005.[23] The more recent proposal to extend pre-charge detention beyond 28 days was rejected by Parliament in October 2008.[24]

---

[22] See F Klug, 'Report on the Working Practices of the JCHR', published in 'The Committee's Future Working Practices', JCHR, Twenty-third report of session 2005-06; F Klug and H Wildbore, 'Breaking new ground: the Joint Committee on Human Rights and the role of Parliament in human rights compliance' [2007] 3 *European Human Rights Law Review* 231.

[23] M Hunt, 'Scrutinising legislation for human rights compatibility', speech at the Institute of Advanced Legal Studies, 8 June 2009.

[24] The proposal to extend pre-charge detention beyond 28 days was included in the Counter-Terrorism Bill 2008. The proposal narrowly passed in the House of Commons on 11 June 2008 by 315 to 306 votes. The House of Lords rejected the proposal by 191 votes in October 2008. The Home Secretary announced that the Government was dropping the proposal shortly afterwards.

Duty on public authorities

A further checkpoint comes from section 6 of the HRA which makes it unlawful for public authorities to act in a way incompatible with the rights in the HRA. In addition to this legal obligation, this provision encourages public authorities to consider how to comply with human rights standards in the planning and delivery of public services. The recent Human Rights Inquiry by the Equality and Human Rights Commission (EHRC) provides evidence of how a 'human rights approach' can be used to drive systemic change in public services and can deliver real improvements to service delivery.[25] Although sporadic, it found that where public service providers had adopted a human rights approach to service delivery (rather than a basic compliance approach) they reported improved services, better and more coherent delivery procedures and heightened staff morale. At the launch of the Human Rights Inquiry in June 2009, Jack Straw, Justice Secretary, said:

> 'The Human Rights Act has therefore decisively changed the culture of government and public authorities by placing a positive obligation on the State to treat people with dignity, equality and respect. As a *Guardian* editorial acknowledged: "… it is not just suspects but soldiers, victims and care recipients who are served by an act which is all about arming the individual against the authority … By forcing public bodies to factor rights into their thinking, it prevents even more abuses than it cures."'[26]

Courts

A final 'checkpoint' is the courts, although they have a much stronger role than the word 'checkpoint' suggests and, like Parliament, they are central to the scheme of the HRA. Under the HRA the courts are able to provide redress where people feel their rights have been breached, allowing claimants to bring proceedings against a public authority, or to raise human rights arguments in other legal proceedings. The HRA has brought about three significant changes to protecting our fundamental rights in the courts. First, challenges to the decisions and actions of public authorities no longer have to be based on *Wednesbury*

---

[25] Human Rights Inquiry, Equality and Human Rights Commission, June 2009. See www.equalityhumanrights.com/humanrightsinquiry (Last visited 30th October 2009).
[26] Speech at the launch of the Human Rights Inquiry, London, 15 June 2009.

unreasonableness,[27] which the European Court of Human Rights (ECtHR) found to afford insufficient scrutiny of the justification for interferences with qualified Convention rights.[28] Since the HRA was passed, this test has been replaced by the more searching test of necessity and proportionality in cases concerning Convention rights.[29]

Second, before incorporation, the courts confirmed that use of the Convention as a guide to statutory interpretation was *only* applicable where there was an ambiguity in the wording of legislation. The duty imposed on courts by section 3 of the HRA (to construe legislation compatibly with Convention rights 'so far as it is possible to do so') represents a 'significant departure from the past'.[30]

Third, prior to incorporation of the ECHR, the common law protected 'basic interests' as opposed to 'positive rights'. Rights such as free speech and assembly were protected only in the negative sense, that people were entitled to do what they wished, so long as they didn't break the law or infringe the rights of others.[31] The inclusion of courts and tribunals as public authorities under section 6 of the HRA was clearly intended to put the common law within the reach of the Act. Convention rights are now applied both in common law proceedings involving public authority respondents and in proceedings between private parties.[32] Thus the HRA has brought about a 'constitutional shift' to protect rights like freedom of assembly which were previously not protected as 'positive rights' by the common law.[33]

Before the HRA was passed, none of these checkpoints were in place and we were much more vulnerable to the government eroding

---

[27] *Associated Provincial Picture Houses Ltd v Wednesbury Corporation* [1948] 1 KB 223.

[28] *Smith and Grady v UK* (2000) 29 EHRR 493.

[29] See F Klug and K Starmer, 'Incorporation through the 'front door': the first year of the Human Rights Act' [2001] *Public Law* 654; F Klug and K Starmer, 'Standing back from the Human Rights Act: how effective is it five years on?' [2005] *Public Law* 716.

[30] F Klug and C O'Brien, 'The first two years of the Human Rights Act' [2002] *Public Law* 649 at 650.

[31] F Klug, K Starmer and S Weir, *The Three Pillars of Liberty: Political Rights and Freedoms in the United Kingdom* (Routledge, London 1996).

[32] *Ibid.* See *Ahmad Raja Ghaidan v Antonio Mendoza* [2004] UKHL 30; *Campbell v Mirror Group Newspapers* [2004] UKHL 22; *Douglas v Hello! Ltd* (2005) EWCA Civ 595; *HRH Prince of Wales v Associated Newspapers* [2006] EWCA Civ 1776; *Venables and Thompson v News Group Newspapers Ltd* [2001] 1 All ER 908.

[33] See *R (Laporte) v Chief Constable of Gloucestershire* [2006] UKHL 55 quoted below.

our rights and freedoms. The introduction of the HRA brought these mechanisms with it to help us resist such measures, whilst at the same time preserving Parliamentary sovereignty. If the HRA were to be repealed, the checkpoints outlined above would be lost, or put at risk were the Act to be replaced with a weaker bill of rights.

4. A New Bill of Rights?

In response to the UCL report, the leader of the Conservative Party, David Cameron, in a written statement to the Convention on Modern Liberty said:

> 'This report from the Convention on Modern Liberty adds even more weight to the evidence of [the] erosions [of our historic liberties]. It shows very clearly that the Human Rights Act has not protected us from these erosions, and may even have given them a veneer of respectability. That is why a Conservative government would replace the Act with a British bill of rights - to better tailor, but also strengthen, the protection of our core rights in keeping with the great tradition of freedom under law that has been nurtured in this country for centuries.'[34]

However, as quoted above, Cameron's Shadow Justice Secretary (and Shadow Attorney General) Dominic Grieve said, on its own a bill of rights will not provide all the solutions to the threat we face from creeping state authoritarianism. As previously argued, even a constitutionally entrenched bill of rights with the power for judges to strike down legislation, like the US Bill of Rights, will not prevent draconian legislation being passed if the political will is not there to oppose such measures and Parliament, the courts and civil society do not remain vigilant. Therefore, calls for a new bill of rights will not necessarily solve the problem of the executive passing measures which curtail rights.

There is now cross-party support for a bill of rights for the UK. However, there is not cross-party support for the same *type* of bill of rights and a closer look at the debate reveals that some of the arguments being put forward for a new bill of rights may result in a weaker bill of rights than we currently have, not a stronger one.

---

[34] Written statement for the Convention on Modern Liberty, 28 February 2009.

Political arguments

David Cameron started the current debate in 2006 in a speech entitled 'Balancing Freedom and Security: A Modern British Bill of Rights' by promising to 'replace'[35] the HRA with a British Bill of Rights but stay signed up to the ECHR.[36] Cameron has repeated his commitment to abolish the HRA several times since then. As the title of Cameron's 2006 speech suggests, many of his arguments centre around security: 'the HRA has made it harder to protect our security...It is hampering the fight against crime and terrorism.'[37] Cameron says 'we've got to a position where the Home Secretary doesn't seem able to deport people who could put the country at risk'.[38] Thus, Cameron has made the case for a new bill of rights by talking about *increasing* the powers of the state.

The deportations Cameron was referring to presumably stem from a ECtHR ruling which pre-dates the HRA and relates to a case which took place during the life of the last Conservative government. In the 1993 decision of *Chahal v UK*, the ECtHR held that to deport a person to a country where they would be likely to face torture, inhuman or degrading treatment would be in violation of Article 3 of the ECHR (the prohibition of torture, inhuman or degrading treatment), an absolute right which could not be limited by national security considerations.[39] This has recently been upheld by the ECtHR despite the UK government intervening in a case to argue that the threat presented by the person to be deported must be a factor to be assessed in relation to the possibility and the nature of the potential ill-treatment. The ECtHR did not accept these arguments and reaffirmed the principle in *Chahal*.[40] Therefore, even if the HRA were repealed and

---

[35] David Cameron, 'Balancing Freedom and Security: A Modern British Bill of Rights', speech at the Centre for Policy Studies, London, 26 June 2006.

[36] Cameron's now Secretary of State for Business, Ken Clarke, dismissed this as 'xenophobic and legal nonsense' in the *Daily Telegraph*, 27 June 2006.

[37] n 35.

[38] *Cameron on Cameron: Conversations with Dylan Jones*, Fourth Estate, 2008.

[39] *Chahal v UK* (1996) 23 EHRR 413. The case concerned an Indian national who the Home Office wanted to deport to India on national security grounds as they accused him of being involved in Sikh terrorism. The ECtHR said where there is a real risk that a person faced torture, inhuman or degrading treatment, it would be a breach of Article 3 to deport them, irrespective of their conduct.

[40] *Saadi v Italy* ECtHR Grand Chamber, 28 February 2008.

replaced by a British Bill of Rights, as the Conservatives have pledged to do, the UK would still be bound by the decision of the ECtHR. The Conservatives could not enact a bill of rights with less protection for deportees without being in violation of our international legal obligations under the ECHR (unless they were to withdraw from the ECHR and the Council of Europe).

An unusual constitutional argument for a bill of rights was made by the former Shadow Justice Minister, Nick Herbert. He argued that 'one of the greatest impacts of the [Human Rights] Act has been the undermining of Parliamentary sovereignty' by 'transfer[ing] significant power out of the hands of elected politicians into the hands of unelected judges'. He said that 'essentially political questions that should be decided by Parliament are now being decided by judges.'[41] This is an argument that has been made for *opposing* bills of rights altogether. Dominic Grieve has also said he wants to restore a better balance between Parliament and the courts, indicating that he wants to weaken the enforcement mechanisms in sections 3 and 10 of the HRA:

> 'It is wrong that primary legislation can be altered by Statutory Instrument if found incompatible with the Human Rights Act. Nor should our courts have power to stand a statute on its head. All these things can be addressed in our proposals for a Bill of Rights.'[42]

To argue that we should give power back to Parliament *through* a Bill of Rights is an odd position. Herbert is right that the HRA has made the executive more accountable to the courts but the Act preserves Parliamentary sovereignty by not allowing the courts to strike down Acts of Parliament. If, as Herbert and Grieve suggest, a bill of rights were to involve *less* judicial scrutiny than the HRA, would it be legally or constitutionally a bill of rights at all?

In March 2009 the Ministry of Justice published the Green Paper 'Rights and Responsibilities: Developing our Constitutional Framework'. Whilst committing not to resile from the HRA, the Green

---

[41] 'Rights without Responsibilities - a decade of the Human Rights Act', British Library lecture, 24 November 2008.

[42] Dominic Grieve, 'It's the interpretation of the Human Rights Act that's the problem – not the ECHR itself', Conservative Home's Platform, 14 April 2009. http://conservativehome.blogs.com/platform/2009/04/dominic-grieve-.html (Last visited 30th October 2009).

Paper sets out options for a Bill of Rights and Responsibilities, such as a declaratory, symbolic statement, a set of rights and responsibilities directly enforceable by the individual in the courts, or some form of statement of principles which might inform legislation while not necessarily giving rise to enforceable individual rights (see *'Responsibilities'* section below.).

The Liberal Democrats on the other hand, long time supporters of a bill of rights, have expressed strong reservations about the way the current debate is being framed by both the other main political parties. Chris Huhne, the Shadow Secretary of State for the Home Department, responded to the Conservative Party proposals, summarised by his opposite number, Chris Grayling, as 'fewer rights, more wrongs'[43] and their promise to repeal the HRA:

> 'We believe that this is a fundamentally misguided conclusion. There is a danger of great mischief if this debate puts the Human Rights Act itself into contention. Both Conservative and Labour front benches seem to be responding to the frankly hysterical anti-human rights campaign in the media and by Europhobes.'[44]

The Liberal Democrats have also produced a Freedom Bill, which gives details of how they 'intend to roll back the draconian laws passed by successive Labour and Conservative administrations'. It brings 'all of the laws which have undermined civil liberties together in one piece of legislation so that they can be easily repealed.'[45] Many of the laws listed are those referred to in the UCL report. David Cameron recently announced a similar proposal to repeal a raft of such laws under a Conservative government.[46] But the crucial difference between the Liberal Democrat and Conservative approaches is that the Liberal Democrats remain committed to and support the HRA and wish to build on it. They want to see the HRA enshrined in a written constitution, making it more difficult to change and amend than

---

[43] 'Labour is soft on crime and soft on the causes of crime', speech 23 February 2009.
[44] 'The Bill of Rights and Responsibilities and the role of a Freedom Bill', British Institute of Human Rights lecture, 5 May 2009.
[45] See www.freedom.libdems.org.uk/the-freedom-bill/ (Last visited 30th October 2009).
[46] David Cameron, 'Giving power back to the people', Imperial College London, 25 June 2009.

ordinary law.[47] In contrast to the Conservatives, the Liberal Democrats view their Freedom Bill and the HRA as 'closely connected in one vital way. Rights are fundamental to how we live our lives – to enabling us to live our lives freely. The Freedom Bill aims to remove the obstacles to the free enjoyment of these rights that have been erected by successive Conservative and then Labour governments.'[48]

Responsibilities
One of Labour's main concerns in their proposals for a Bill of Rights and Responsibilities is to underlie 'the responsibilities we owe to each other and to the community'.[49] This was outlined in the 'Rights and Responsibilities' Green Paper:

> 'Although not necessarily suitable for expression as a series of new legally enforceable duties, it may be desirable to express succinctly, in one place, the key responsibilities we all owe as members of UK society, ensuring a clearer understanding of them in a new, accessible constitutional document and reinforcing the imperative to observe them.'[50]

The Conservatives also want to use a bill of rights to 'spell out the fundamental duties and responsibilities of people living in this country.'[51] As many commentators have pointed out, responsibilities are inherent in the human rights framework.[52] Most rights can be limited to the extent necessary to protect the rights of others or the wider community. But very few bills of rights contain legally enforceable duties on individuals, which are imposed by a raft of other statutes.[53]

---

[47] Chris Huhne, 'The Bill of Rights and Responsibilities and the role of a Freedom Bill', British Institute of Human Rights lecture, 5 May 2009.
[48] *Ibid.*
[49] Jack Straw, Uncorrected evidence to the JCHR, 20 January 2009. http://www.publications.parliament.uk/pa/jt200809/jtselect/jtrights/uc174-i/uc17402.htm (Last visited 30th October 2009).
[50] 'Rights and Responsibilities: Developing our Constitutional Framework', Ministry of Justice, 2009.
[51] n 35.
[52] See F Klug, 'Solidity or Wind? What's on the Menu in the Bill of Rights debate?' (2009) 80(3) *Political Quarterly* 420. See also E Metcalfe, 'Rights and Responsibilities', *Justice Journal*, December 2007.
[53] Exceptions include some African bills of rights and the constitution of the former Soviet Union. The Victorian Charter of Human Rights and Responsibilities passed in 2006 contains

Nor can a new bill of rights that complies with the ECHR make rights contingent on responsibilities.[54]

Role of the courts and 'margin of appreciation'
According to Dominic Grieve, a bill of rights under a Conservative government is an 'opportunity to define the rights under the European Convention in clearer and more precise terms and provide guidance to the judiciary and government in applying human rights law when the lack of responsibility of a few threaten the rights of others', whilst remaining compliant with the ECHR.[55] He refers to the 'margin of appreciation' as an example of how provision for different interpretations of the ECHR already exists. However, if the UK is to remain signed up to ECHR, any new bill of rights would reproduce the rights in the ECHR as a minimum floor of protection, otherwise we would be in breach of our international obligations at the ECtHR. Dominic Grieve concedes as much when he says 'this change won't remove all controversy. There will still be some people for instance we cannot deport because of the fate that awaits them in their own country would constitute a violation of Article 3 on protection from inhuman and degrading treatment.'[56] (A new bill of rights could, of course, go further and provide greater protection than the ECHR – see below).

The Conservatives argue that countries with their own national bill of rights are given greater latitude by the ECtHR. They rely on the German Basic Law (bill of rights) to argue that 'the existence of a clear and codified British Bill of Rights will tend to lead the European Court of Human Rights to apply the "margin of appreciation"'.[57] The doctrine of the 'margin of appreciation' is part of the jurisprudence of the ECtHR. The Court acknowledges that, by reason of their direct and continuous contact with the 'vital forces of their countries', the national authorities (including the courts) are better placed to evaluate local

the following in the preamble: 'human rights come with responsibilities and must be exercised in a way that respects the human rights of others'.
[54] As the government have acknowledged. See n 49.
[55] 'Liberty and Community in Britain', Speech for Conservative Liberty Forum, 2 October 2006. http://www.dominicgrieve.org.uk/record.jsp?type=speech&ID=67 (Last visited 30th October 2009).
[56] *Ibid.*
[57] n 35.

needs and conditions than an international court.[58] As Professor Klug has pointed out, the application of this doctrine depends on the context and a range of factors (not *only* one factor, as she was cited as saying in an earlier edition of this journal[59]). The doctrine is particularly likely to be applied where there is no European-wide common standard or where the courts are required to determine the necessary limitations on rights, particularly in relation to social, economic or moral issues.[60]

The JCHR concluded in its report 'A Bill of Rights for the UK?', 'it is both legally and empirically incorrect to suggest that a Bill of Rights would lead the European Court of Human Rights to give a greater margin of appreciation to the UK than is currently the case.'[61] As pointed out in an earlier edition of this journal, there is some case law which demonstrates that the ECtHR gives no specific weight to German Basic Law so as to increase the normal margin of appreciation allowed by the ECtHR to states. In *Von Hannover*, a case about privacy and freedom of press, the ECtHR appear to give no weight in applying the margin of appreciation to the fact that the German Constitutional Court had interpreted its Basic Law to dismiss the appeal of the applicant. The ECtHR held that Germany had breached the applicants rights under Article 8 (right to private and family life).[62]

The crucial point is that the British courts can anyway develop their own interpretation of the rights in the HRA, provided that this does not weaken the protection afforded by the ECHR. The ECHR acts as a floor, *not* as a ceiling. Under section 2 of the HRA judges are required to 'take into account' Strasbourg case law but they are *not bound by it*. A Conservative amendment during the passage of the HRA aimed at binding our courts to ECtHR jurisprudence was rejected on the grounds that there may be occasions when it would be right for the UK courts to depart from Strasbourg decisions and the hope that our

---

[58] *Buckley v UK* (1996) 23 EHRR 101 at para [75].

[59] T Rycroft, 'The Rationality of the Conservatives Party's Proposal for a British Bill of Rights' (2008) 1(1) *UCL Human Rights Review* 51.

[60] F Klug, 'Report on the Working Practices of the JCHR', published in 'The Committee's Future Working Practices', JCHR, Twenty-third report of session 2005-06.

[61] 'A Bill of Rights for the UK?', JCHR, Twenty-ninth report of session 2007-08, para [42]. See also 'Public protection, proportionality, and the search for balance', Benjamin Goold, Liora Lazarus and Gabriel Swiney, University of Oxford, 2007.

[62] *Van Hannover v Germany* (2005) 40 EHRR 1. See n 59.

courts would give lead to Europe as well as be led.[63] Although, the courts have begun to interpret section 2 HRA as if it required them to stay within the confines of the ECtHR case law,[64] which was not the original intention behind the HRA, our courts can and do develop their own case law and go further than ECtHR.[65]

A better Bill of Rights or a 'British' Bill of Rights?
As Professor Klug has argued, it is, of course, possible to have a stronger, better bill of rights which includes additional rights to supplement those in the HRA.[66] The Conservatives have suggested that a British Bill of Rights could include the right to trial by jury,[67] which is absent from the HRA, and 'rights to government information'.[68] Although the HRA already protects the standard rights included in bills of rights across the globe, a 'wish list' of rights to supplement the HRA might include a stronger equality clause, specific rights for children and asylum seekers, economic and social rights and maybe stronger administrative justice provisions.[69]

However, David Cameron gives a different message when he promises a 'new solution that protects liberties in this country that is home-grown and sensitive to Britain's legal inheritance'.[70] It suggests that 'British liberties' are fundamentally different to the human rights in the HRA, rather than an integral part of them. Henry Porter, the editor of the UCL report, has also called for a new bill of rights 'that is clearly

---

[63] See *Hansard*, House of Lords, 18 November 1997, column 515 and 19 January 1998, column 1271.
[64] See R *(Ullah) v Secretary of State for the Home Department* [2004] UKHL 26.
[65] See for example, *Mendoza v Ghaidan* [2002] EWCA Civ 1533; *EM (Lebanon) v Secretary of State for the Home Department* [2008] UKHL 64.
[66] See F Klug, evidence to the JCHR Inquiry on a British Bill of Rights, 3 December 2007; F Klug (n 52).
[67] See n 55.
[68] Nick Herbert, 'Rights without responsibilities: a decade of the Human Rights Act', British Library lecture, 24 November 2008.
[69] Economic and social rights, like the right to health, consistently come out on top when the public are polled on which rights should be included in a bill of rights. Concerns about excessive litigation and the justiciability of these rights would have to be addressed when framing them. See also 'A Bill of Rights for Northern Ireland: Advice to the Secretary of State for Northern Ireland', Northern Ireland Human Rights Commission, 10 December 2008.
[70] n 35.

British in origin and that draws its potency from our traditions and culture, and from the settlements of 1689 and Magna Carta.'[71]

But this discourse – even if it is no more than that – would suggest that the global dialogue on human rights does not sit comfortably on these islands, just as President Obama is taking the US in the opposite direction and rolling back from former President Bush's arguments for exceptionalism.[72] Most modern bills of rights are based on international human rights principles and President Obama has sought to link the US Bill of Rights to these values, to which many countries and cultures have contributed.[73] Chris Huhne warned against calling rights 'British' at the Convention on Modern Liberty:

> 'It is essential that we don't abolish the Human Rights Act… we must remember why the Human Rights Act is so important, as opposed to British rights…. Any society at some point in the future can decide who its citizens are and who they are not. That is what happened in Nazi Germany…If we define rights as British, that is the risk that we run again and we must not allow that to happen.'[74]

Of course, we can argue for a stronger or more comprehensive bill of rights. But would we be doing so if the HRA was called 'Bill of Rights' as it might well have been, or would we think our main priority in the current political climate must be to defend it until it has bedded down? Sir Alan Beith, Liberal Democrat MP and Chairman of the Justice Committee of the House of Commons, made a similar point in a House of Commons debate on a Bill of Rights:

> 'Should we go through the process of creating a new Bill of Rights, or should we do more to make the one that we have work more

---

[71] H Porter, 'Why I told Parliament: you've failed us on liberty', *The Observer*, 9 March 2008.
[72] 'When the United States stands up for human rights, by example at home and by effort abroad, we align ourselves with men and women around the world who struggle for the right to speak their minds, to choose their leaders, and to be treated with dignity and respect.' Statement of President-elect Obama on Human Rights Day, 10 December 2008.
[73] 'The United States was founded on the idea that all people are endowed with inalienable rights, and that principle has allowed us to work to perfect our union at home while standing as a beacon of hope to the world. Today, that principle is embodied in agreements Americans helped forge - the Universal Declaration of Human Rights, the Geneva Conventions, and treaties against torture and genocide - and it unites us with people from every country and culture.' Statement of President-elect Obama on Human Rights Day, 10 December 2008.
[74] Speech at the Convention on Modern Liberty, 28 February 2009.

effectively? One of the more worrying things is that several important rights have been damaged or abrogated under the present regime, and there is no particular evidence that the creation of an additional Bill of Rights would put a stop to that. Indeed, if anything, some of its advocates seem to hope that it would cause the Human Rights Act 1998 to have less impact than it does now…We should be concentrating our effort on making sure that the existing system works, and that on the occasions when we must consider derogating from it we do so by a process that involves Parliament more fully and effectively.'[75]

5. How the HRA has protected rights and freedoms

There are numerous examples of how the HRA has helped to protect traditional civil liberties, including some of those issues addressed in the UCL report. A few examples are given below.

Freedom of assembly

This is protected by Article 11, the right to freedom of assembly and association.[76] An example of how the HRA has been used to protect the right to free assembly is the *Laporte* case.[77] It concerned the decision by the police to stop a coach of demonstrators reaching a demonstration, which was challenged under the HRA. The police concluded that a breach of the peace was not imminent but decided to send the coaches home with a police escort to prevent a breach of the peace occurring at the demonstration when the passengers arrived. The House of Lords ruled that the police must take no more intrusive action than appeared necessary to prevent the breach of the peace. The police had failed to discharge the burden of establishing that the actions they took were proportionate and constituted the least restriction necessary to the rights of freedom of speech (protected under Article

---

[75] Bill of Rights debate, House of Commons, Hansard, 25 June 2009, column 321 WH.

[76] '1) Everyone has the right to freedom of peaceful assembly and to freedom of association with others, including the right to form and to join trade unions for the protection of his interests. 2) No restrictions shall be placed on the exercise of these rights other than such as are prescribed by law and are necessary in a democratic society in the interests of national security or public safety, for the prevention of disorder or crime, for the protection of health or morals or for the protection of the rights and freedoms of others. This Article shall not prevent the imposition of lawful restrictions on the exercise of these rights by members of the armed forces, of the police or of the administration of the State.'

[77] *R (Laporte) v Chief Constable of Gloucestershire* [2006] UKHL 55.

10) and freedom of peaceful assembly. It was wholly disproportionate to restrict a person's exercise of her rights under Articles 10 and 11 because she was in the company of others, some of whom might, at some time in the future, breach the peace.

The House of Lords referred to the 'constitutional shift' brought about by the HRA, so that it is no longer necessary to debate whether we have a right to freedom of assembly. Lord Carswell stated:

> 'Dicey famously observed that it can hardly be said that our constitution knows of such a thing as any specific right of public meeting, a statement which engaged the attention of generations of law students. It is no longer necessary in this sphere of the law to debate the extent to which citizens are at liberty to engage in any activity which has not been made lawful. It has been overtaken by the provisions of the Human Rights Act 1998, under which the rights contained in articles 10 and 11 of the [ECHR] are now part of domestic law – termed by Sedley LJ in *Redmond-Bate v Director of Public Prosecutions* (1999) a "constitutional shift".'[78]

Detention without charge/control orders

A group of foreign nationals who had been certified by the Secretary of State as suspected international terrorists under the Anti-terrorism, Crime and Security Act 2001, and detained without charge or trial under section 23 of that Act, challenged their detention using the HRA.[79] The 2001 Act passed through Parliament in less than a month, with little time for debate. There are parallels here with legislation passed in the US, discussed above. Just as the US Bill of Rights could not stop the USA Patriot Act 2001 and a raft of other measures being passed in the wake of the September 11th terrorist attack, the HRA likewise could not prevent Parliament passing the 2001 Act. However, when detention without charge was challenged using the HRA, the House of Lords formally declared that section 23 of the 2001 Act was incompatible with the right to liberty (Article 5) and the prohibition of discrimination (Article 14) as the detention provisions were disproportionate and discriminated on the grounds of nationality or immigration status.

---

[78] *Ibid.*, at para [93]. See also Lord Bingham at para [34].
[79] *A and others v Secretary of State for the Home Department* [2004] UKHL 56.

As we have seen, unlike in the US, the UK courts do not have the power to strike down legislation they find to be incompatible with rights. To preserve Parliamentary sovereignty, the courts can only formally declare primary legislation incompatible. However, this case is an example of the dialogue under the HRA in action and working successfully. Parliament passed the provision in the 2001 Act. The victims were able to challenge the provision in the courts using the HRA. Civil society groups, such as Liberty and Amnesty International, made written and oral submissions to the court to highlight their concerns. The court was able to declare that the provision was incompatible with rights. It was then for Parliament to decide how to proceed, which they did within 3 months of the judgment. The provisions were repealed by the Prevention of Terrorism Act 2005, which put in place a new regime of control orders. The claimants were still free to take their case further, to the ECtHR, where they received (minimal) damages for the violation of their right to liberty.[80]

Although the courts were not able to strike down the offending legislation, the ultimate result here was the same – the provision was repealed – but, crucially, Parliament was involved in the process. It could be argued that the fact that the courts did not have the power to strike down the legislation actually led to a stronger judgment in the case. Had the courts been able to strike down section 23 instead of making a declaration of incompatibility, would they have been so staunch in their attack on the provision, or would they have shown deference to Parliament on this important issue of national security? When giving evidence to the JCHR inquiry into a Bill of Rights for the UK, Baroness Hale, a member of the House of Lords who sat on the *A* case, responded to a question on whether our courts would be comfortable with a power to strike down legislation as follows:

'I think we would find it extremely novel, quite alarming and would hesitate to use it.'[81]

The dialogue continued once the 2005 Act was passed, which put in place the 'control order' regime. Under the 2005 Act the Home

---

[80] *A and others v UK*, ECtHR Grand Chamber, 19 February 2009.
[81] Oral evidence to the JCHR, 4 March 2008.

Secretary may make a 'non-derogating' control order against a person he suspects of being involved in terrorist activity.[82] The HRA has been used to challenge control orders, under both Article 5 (the right to liberty) and Article 6 (the right to a fair trial). Under Article 5, the House of Lords ruled that the non-derogating control orders imposed on a group of Iraqi and Iranian asylum seekers, which, among other things, imposed an 18-hour curfew and prohibited social contact with anybody who was not authorised by the Home Office, amounted to a deprivation of liberty contrary to Article 5.[83] Under the 2005 Act the Secretary of State had no power to make an order that was incompatible with Article 5 and any such order was a nullity. Therefore the lower court had quashed the order.[84] The government responded by issuing new orders, subjecting the men to less restrictive conditions.

Under Article 6, it was argued that control orders violated the right to a fair trial because of the reliance by the judges making the orders on material received in closed hearing, the nature of which was not disclosed to the appellants. The House of Lords ruled that the right to a fair hearing under Article 6 meant that a defendant must be given sufficient information about the allegations against him to enable him to give effective instructions to the special advocate representing him.[85] Where the open material consists purely of general assertions and the case against the 'controlled person' is based solely or to a decisive degree on closed materials, the requirements of a fair trial will not be satisfied, however cogent the case based on the closed materials may be. The House of Lords ordered the cases to be remitted back to judges for reconsideration in accordance with the Law Lords' judgment.

It has been argued that, because the courts have not outlawed the entire control order regime, the control order rulings are more important for what they appeared to permit, rather than what they purported to prohibit.[86] But the point is that without the HRA, these

---

[82] The 2005 Act also allows for 'derogating' control orders which can only be made where the government has derogated from Article 5 and must be made by a court. No derogating control orders have been made. See *Secret Evidence*, Justice, June 2009.

[83] *Secretary of State for the Home Department v JJ and others* [2007] UKHL 45.

[84] *Secretary of State for the Home Department v JJ and others* [2006] EWHC 1623 (Admin).

[85] *Secretary of State for the Home Department v AF and others* [2009] UKHL 28.

[86] See K Ewing and J-C Tham, 'The Continuing Futility of the Human Rights Act' [2008] *Public Law* 668.

challenges could almost certainly not have been brought in domestic courts. As argued above, a bill of rights does not end debate about the boundaries of rights and freedoms and it is possible for the courts to go further than the ECtHR and provide more protection. But without the HRA, those detained under the 2001 Act could only have filed an application at the ECtHR to challenge their detention. The road to Strasbourg is indeed a long one, with cases taking years to reach the court, a situation which is not helped by the backlog of cases awaiting the court's attention.

Torture evidence

The prohibition of torture under Article 3 is absolute. The right cannot be limited or qualified. The right also covers the admission of evidence in court that might have been procured by torture. The Special Immigration Appeals Commission (Procedure) Rules 2003, which said the Commission could receive evidence that would not be admissible in a court of law, was challenged and the court ruled that it did not extend to statements procured by torture.[87] The Commission could not receive evidence that had or might have been procured by torture inflicted by officials of a foreign state even without the complicity of the British authorities. This conclusion was based on the common law rule excluding evidence procured by torture and gave effect to the absolute prohibition against torture in Article 3. The Commission should refuse to admit evidence if it concluded on a balance of probabilities that the evidence had been obtained by torture. If the Commission was left in doubt as to whether the evidence had been obtained by torture, then it should admit it, but it had to bear its doubt in mind when evaluating the evidence.

Protection for asylum seekers

The *Limbuela* case concerned a group of asylum seekers who were excluded from support for accommodation and essential living needs under the Immigration and Asylum Act 1999 Part VI by the Nationality, Immigration and Asylum Act 2002 section 55(1) as the Secretary of State had decided that they had not made their claims for

---

[87] *A and others v Secretary of State for the Home Department* [2005] UKHL 71.

asylum as soon as reasonably practicable after their arrival in the UK. The House of Lords ruled that as soon as an asylum seeker makes it clear that there is an imminent prospect of his treatment reaching inhuman and degrading levels (such as sleeping in street, being seriously hungry and being unable to satisfy basic hygiene requirements), the Secretary of State had a power under asylum legislation and a duty under the HRA to act to avoid it.[88] Following the earlier Court of Appeal decision (which was upheld by the House of Lords), the Immigration and Nationality Directorate adopted a new approach to section 55 to comply with the judgment which stated that 'no claimant who does not have alternative sources of support, including adequate food and basic amenities, such as washing facilities and night shelter, is refused support.'[89]

The UCL report refers to the legislation at issue in this case and lists it in its 'inventory of losses', quoting Lord Bingham from the House of Lords judgment, without acknowledging the fact that the legislation was challenged under the HRA and that the case was successful and brought about a change in policy.

Restraint of young people

The Secure Training Centre (Amendment) Rules 2007 allowed officers working in such institutions for young offenders to physically restrain and seclude a young person to ensure 'good order and discipline'. These amendments were passed with very limited consultation and with no race equality impact assessment. The Court of Appeal ruled that any system of restraint that involves physical intervention against another's will and carries the threat of injury or death, engages the Article 3 prohibition on inhuman and degrading treatment. This is particularly so when it applies to a child who is in the custody of the state. The

---

[88] *R (Limbuela and others) v Secretary of State for the Home Department* [2005] UKHL 66

[89] Home Office, 'Asylum Statistics: 4th quarter 2005 UK', 2005. However, concern remains about the use of section 55 to refuse some subsistence-only support claims from applicants with accommodation and the destitution of failed asylum seekers due to the narrow interpretation of the case by the government. See 'The Treatment of Asylum Seekers', JCHR, Tenth Report of Session 2006-07; 'Government Response to the Committee's Tenth Report of this Session: The Treatment of Asylum Seekers', JCHR, Seventeenth Report of Session 2006-07; Alice Donald, Elizabeth Mottershaw, Philip Leach and Jenny Watson, 'Evaluating the impact of selected cases under the Human Rights Act on public services provision', Equality and Human Rights Commission, June 2009.

Secretary of State could not establish that the system was necessary for ensuring 'good order and discipline' and the Rules breached Article 3. The Rules were quashed by the court.[90]

These cases are just a few examples of how the HRA has protected rights and freedoms in the sort of areas outlined in the UCL report. There are numerous others.[91]

6. Development of rights and positive obligations

The approach taken in the UCL report is one of individual freedom from state interference. It focuses on *freedom* and *liberty* and talks about the rights set down 'nearly 800 years ago in Magna Carta'. However, human rights consciousness and law have evolved considerably since then to include values like dignity and equality (not just equality before the law, but equal protection of the law and the right to be free from discrimination). Modern human rights documents also embrace the values of community and mutual respect, by including limitations on most rights, as is necessary in a democratic society to protect the rights and freedoms of others and the interests of the wider community. This 'second wave' of human rights thinking[92] did not turn its back on the 'first wave' values of liberty and justice and continues to protect the individual from abuses by the state, as the examples above demonstrate. But in order to uphold dignity and equality, the role of the state has developed from an obligation to refrain from interfering with basic liberties to an evolving duty on states to protect fundamental rights, including 'positive obligations' to do so even, in some circumstances, where private individuals are the only protagonists (see below).[93]

As Andrew Dismore, the Chair of the JCHR, points out 'the Convention on Modern Liberty…has done an excellent job in raising public awareness of the need to protect the vital traditional liberties…but that is only half the story. A modern Bill of Rights must provide such protection but, equally, it cannot confine itself to purely

---

[90] *R (C) v Secretary of State for Justice* [2008] EWCA 882.
[91] See F Klug and H Wildbore, 'Protecting rights: how do we stop rights and freedoms being a political football?', Unlock Democracy, 2009, Appendix 2, which lists further examples.
[92] See F Klug, *Values for a Godless Age: the story of the United Kingdom's new bill of rights* (Harmondsworth, Penguin, 2000).
[93] For example, see *A v UK* (1998) 27 EHRR 611 and *Osman v UK* (1998) 29 EHRR 245.

libertarian concerns if it is to be relevant to our 21st century society and all its citizens…the human rights obligations of today require the state to take action to protect human rights, whether that means providing public services such as health and education, protecting against the insecurity of destitution by providing welfare benefits, or protecting the vulnerable against the powerful, including those with private power.'[94]

Like other post-war human rights documents, the HRA embodies the 'second wave' of human rights thinking. There are numerous examples of how the HRA has protected the rights of people by upholding values like dignity, equality and community. A few examples are listed below, beginning with the landmark ECtHR decision on the positive obligations on States in relation to the right to life. (Further examples are listed in the footnote.[95])

Obligation to protect life

The ECtHR held that the right to life under Article 2 not only prevents the State from intentionally taking life, it also requires States to take appropriate steps to safeguard life. The State's duty includes putting in place effective criminal law provisions to deter the commission of offences and law-enforcement machinery. Article 2 may also go beyond that to imply in certain well-defined circumstances a positive obligation on authorities to take preventative operational measures to protect an individual whose life is at risk from the criminal acts of another individual, for example from hate crime or domestic violence. This duty will be breached where it can be shown that the authorities failed to do all that could reasonably be expected of them to avoid a 'real and immediate' risk to the life of an identified individual about which they knew, or ought to have known.[96] As a result of this case the majority of the 43 police forces in England and Wales have specific policies on

---

[94] Bill of Rights debate, House of Commons, Hansard, 25 June 2009, column 309 WH.
[95] See for example R *(A and B) v East Sussex County Council* [2003] EWHC 167 (Admin); *Ahmad Raja Ghaidan v Antonio Mendoza* [2004] UKHL 30; *Bellinger v Bellinger* [2003] UKHL 21; *Secretary of State for Defence v R (Smith)* [2009] EWCA Civ 441 and *Secretary of State for Defence v R (Smith)* [2009] EWCA Civ 441; *Cowl et al v Plymouth City Council* [2001] EWCA Civ 1935; R *(SG) v Liverpool City Council* October 2002 (unreported).
[96] *Osman v UK* (1998) 29 EHRR 245.

handling threats to life and the Association of Chief Police Officers has produced a set of minimum standards relevant to 'protective services'.[97]

Duty to investigate death in custody
Following the murder of a prisoner by his racist cell-mate, the family brought a successful challenge under the HRA for a public inquiry. The court said where a death has occurred in custody the state is under a duty to publicly investigate before an independent judicial tribunal with an opportunity for relatives of the deceased to participate. Following the case the Prison Service introduced changes to its policy and procedures relating to cell-sharing risks, allowing information-sharing to identify high risk factors.[98]

Duty to take positive action to secure physical integrity and dignity
Where a local authority knew that a disabled tenant's housing was inappropriate but did not move her to suitably adapted accommodation, the court ruled that they failed in their duty to take positive steps to enable her and her family to lead as normal a family life as possible and secure her physical integrity and dignity under Article 8 of the ECHR (the right to private and family life). The court awarded damages to the tenant for this breach.[99]

Conclusion
This article set out to argue that the HRA was not to 'blame' for the erosion of liberty outlined in the UCL report, that on the contrary, the Act has helped to protect fundamental rights and freedoms and that the situation would have been far worse without it. The Act is predicated on the assumption that the protection of human rights is not something which should be removed to the court room but that we all have our part to play in protecting ourselves from the draconian powers of the state. A bill of rights cannot *alone* hold back the power of a state intent on passing such measures (as the USA demonstrates). Replacing the HRA with a new bill of rights will not solve the problem of the state passing legislation which curtails our rights. What is needed is a strong

---

[97] 'Human Rights Inquiry', Equality and Human Rights Commission, June 2009.
[98] *R (Amin) v Secretary of State for the Home Department* [2003] UKHL 51.
[99] *R (Bernard) v Enfield* [2002] EWHC 2282 Admin.

Parliament which has healthy debates on rights and their limitations and takes decisions on issues like proportionality and balancing competing rights. We need a strong civil society and an engaged public to contribute to these debates. We need vigilant courts to act as a guardian for rights when such measures are passed. Crucially, we need to bed down the HRA. This includes ensuring there is sufficient human rights training for staff in public authorities and beyond, educating the public on the Act and the human rights principles it enshrines and promoting the HRA and its positive effects to address public and media concerns. We need to use our bill of rights as a tool to stand up to the state and to resist rights-curtailing measures.

All members of the Council of Europe have incorporated the ECHR into their law and many of those countries also have their own national bill of rights or a constitution containing fundamental rights. It is not a question of *either* incorporate the ECHR *or* have a domestic bill of rights, so why is the debate in the UK being framed in this way? If we were to de-incorporate from the ECHR and introduce a national bill of rights on the back of repealing a bill of rights that enshrines universal human rights norms, what message would we be sending to rest of the world?

Human Rights, Horizontality and the Public/Private Divide: Towards a Holistic Approach

ALISON L YOUNG[*]

The protection of human rights is often regarded as an aspect of public law, where an individual protects her human rights from interference by the State. This focus has perhaps been reinforced by the use of International Treaties designed to protect human rights, particularly the European Convention on Human Rights (ECHR) in the United Kingdom. The enactment of sections 6(1) and 6(3)(a) of the Human Rights Act 1998 challenged this perception that human rights are properly regarded as an aspect of public law, imposing obligations on state bodies. Section 6(1) states that it is unlawful for a public authority to act contrary to Convention rights. Section 6(3)(a) expressly includes courts and tribunals within the definition of a public authority. Following their enactment, academic commentary was divided as to the precise manner in which the Act would require courts to act in a manner compatible with Convention rights, focusing in particular upon the extent to which courts would be required to modify provisions of the common law in order to ensure their compatibility with Convention rights. The courts appear to have adopted a form of indirect horizontal effect, where Convention rights, or the values underpinning those Convention rights, become part of the content of existing common law causes of action.[1] However, despite general agreement that English law has adopted a form of indirect horizontal effect, there is both a plethora of possible models of the form of indirect effect[2] and indecision as to the precise model adopted by the court.[3]

---

[*] Hertford College, University of Oxford.

[1] *Campbell v MGN Ltd* [2004] UKHL 22; [2004] 2 AC 457 and *Douglas v Hello Ltd (3)* [2005] EWCA Civ 595; [2006] QB 125. This case was subsequently appealed to the House of Lords, but the issues of privacy and the horizontal impact of the Human Rights Act 1998 were not raised at appeal.

[2] See, for example, K Ewing 'The Human Rights Act and Parliamentary Democracy' (1999) 62 *Modern Law Review* 79; M Hunt 'The Horizontal Effect of the Human Rights Act' (1998) *Public Law* 423; I Leigh 'Horizontal Rights, the Human Rights Act and Privacy: Lessons from the

What has generated less comment are the different ways in which the Act provides for horizontal effect, both as regards obligations placed upon the court through sections 6(1) and 6(3)(a) other than the development of substantive principles of the common law, as well as that created by other sections of the Act. It is by examining these other means of creating horizontal effect that we recognise an emerging paradox in English law: human rights appear to be receiving greater protection through the operation of private law, particularly when this occurs through a modification of the common law, than through the operation of public law. This paradox emerges for two reasons. First, there is a greater propensity to rely on arguments against horizontal effect with regard to horizontal effect created through public law than through private law. Second, courts are more willing to develop human rights beyond the interpretation of the rights provided for by the ECtHR when modifying the common law than when interpreting statutory provisions or when adjudicating upon actions for judicial review.

An examination of this paradox is useful for two purposes. First, it casts doubt upon interpretations of the division between public and private law. This suggests either that our analysis of the distinction is insufficiently sophisticated, or that English law is developing in the wrong direction. Second, it provides a means through which to approach the horizontal effect of human rights in a new manner, recognising that different rights are more suited to different types of protection. This is based in particular upon the different forms of constitutionalisation that occur when human rights are protected through the common law than through the application of principles of

---

Commonwealth?' (1999) 48 *International and Comparative Law Quarterly* 57; B Markesenis 'Privacy, Freedom of Expression and the Horizontal Effect of the Human Rights Bill: Lessons from Germany' (1999) 115 *Law Quarterly Review* 47; G Phillipson 'The Human Rights Act, "Horizontal Effect" and the Common Law: a Bang or a Whimper?' (1999) 62 *Modern Law Review* 824; T Raphael 'The Problem of Horizontal Effect' [2000] *European Human Rights Law Review* 493; R Singh 'Privacy and the Media after the Human Rights Act' (1998) *European Human Rights Law Review* 722; Sir William Wade 'The United Kingdom's Bill of Rights' in Hare and Forsyth (eds.) *Constitutional Reform in the United Kingdom: Practice and Principles* (Hart Publishing, Oxford 1998) 62 and AL Young 'Horizontality and the Human Rights Act 1998' in Katja S Ziegler (ed) *Human Rights and Private Law: Privacy as Autonomy* (Hart Publishing, Oxford 2007).
[3] G Phillipson 'Clarity Postponed: Horizontal Effect after *Campbell*' in H Fenwick, R Masterman and G Phillipson (eds) *Judicial Reasoning under the UK Human Rights Act* (Cambridge University Press, Cambridge 2007) 143.

public law. This article will conclude that English law would benefit from taking a holistic approach to horizontality, recognising the extent to which human rights should be horizontally applicable[4] and being sensitive to institutional and constitutional considerations when determining whether horizontal effect is best achieved through the mechanisms of public or private law.

1. Horizontal Effect and the Human Rights Act

There are three sections of the Human Rights 1998 other than sections 6(1) and 6(3)(a) that can create horizontal effect: section 3(1); section 12(4) and the combination of sections 6(1) and 6(3)(b). In addition, section 6(1) and 6(3)(a) may give rise to horizontal effect other than through the modification of the common law. Not only does the Human Rights Act create horizontal effect in a variety of ways, but also the Act creates different forms of horizontal effect.

First, a distinction can be drawn between horizontal effect that occurs in private law through the modification of the common law and that which occurs through a Convention-compatible reading of legislative provisions. Horizontal effect is achieved predominantly in private law through the operation of sections 6(1) and 6(3)(a) when courts modify substantive provisions of the common law to ensure its compatibility with Convention rights or the values underpinning these rights. Section 3(1) requires that primary and secondary legislation be read and given effect in a manner compatible with Convention rights, so far as it is possible to do so. To date, there has been no restriction upon the ability of the court to interpret statutory provisions in a manner compatible with Convention rights where to do so would require the creation of an obligation for an individual.[5] In *Ghaidan v Godin-Mendoza*,[6] for example, a Convention-compatible reading of paragraph 2 of Schedule 1 to the Rent Act 1977 created an obligation on a private landlord to treat the

---

[4] On the distinction between horizontal effect and horizontal applicability, see D Beyleveld and S Pattinson 'Horizontal Applicability and Horizontal Effect' (2002) 118 *Law Quarterly Review* 623.

[5] This contrasts with the position in European Community law, where the obligation to interpret national law in a manner compatible with European Community law does reach a limit when this requires the creation of an obligation in criminal law, or a heightening of a criminal penalty, C-80/86 *Kolpinghuis Nijmegen* [1987] ECR 3969 and C-387/02 *Silvio Berlusconi* [2005] ECR I-3565.

[6] [2004] UKHL 30; [2004] 2 AC 557.

surviving homosexual partner of a statutory tenant as a 'spouse' and, therefore, a statutory tenant. As such, Mr Ghaidan was unable to obtain an order for possession of the flat, thereby protecting the Article 8 right to the family home of Mr Godin-Mendoza. This example of horizontal effect occurs in private law – it arises in a property dispute between two private individuals and requires courts to re-interpret statutory provisions protecting private rights.

A second distinction arises between horizontal effect that applies to substantive provisions of private law and that which occurs through the modification of private law remedies and procedures. A modification of private law procedures may occur through the operation of sections 6(1) and 6(3)(a), which require courts to act in a manner compatible with Convention rights as regards all of their functions, not merely the adjudication of disputes in common law. This may apply, for example, to the inherent jurisdiction of the court to grant court orders. In *In re S (A Child)(Identification: Restrictions on Publication)*[7] an application was made by S, whose mother was to stand trial for the murder of his brother, to restrain the publication of information that could be used to identify S when media institutions reported on the trial of S's mother. At first instance and in the Court of Appeal, the court examined whether the court enjoyed an inherent jurisdiction to grant an order to restrain publication in these circumstances, using the Convention rights of Article 8 and Article 10 ECHR to determine the existence of such jurisdiction and the way in which it should be exercised. The House of Lords concluded that the jurisdiction to grant a court order would derive directly from Articles 8 and 10, with decisions as to whether the court order should be granted being based upon the relative merits of the right to privacy and the right to freedom of expression before the court. Given the importance of justice, requiring the reporting of criminal trials, the House of Lords concluded that no court order should be granted. As such, S was unable to act in a manner so as to prevent newspapers from publishing his identity when reporting on the trial. If the court had reached the opposite conclusion –as was the case in the Court of Appeal – then the newspaper would be prevented from acting in a manner that harmed S's convention right to privacy.

---

[7] [2004] UKHL 47; [2005] 1 AC 593.

A more specific form of horizontal effect through a modification of private law procedures is found in section 12(4) of the Act. This requires that, when granting an interim injunction, the court 'must have particular regard to the Convention right to freedom of expression'. This section is often applied in private situations, where an individual wishes to restrain publication. For example, in *Douglas v Hello! Ltd*,[8] Catherine Zeta-Jones and Michael Douglas wished to restrain the publication of photographs of their wedding in *Hello!* magazine in order to protect their right to privacy. When determining whether to grant an injunction to restrain publication, the court paid attention to the right to freedom of expression of *Hello!* magazine and the right to privacy of Mr Douglas and Miss Zeta-Jones. As the right to freedom of privacy was deemed insufficiently strong to override the right to freedom of expression, the court refused to grant an injunction, effectively preventing Mr Douglas and Miss Zeta-Jones from acting in a manner that would restrict the right to freedom of expression of *Hello!* magazine. In *Cream Holdings Ltd v Banerjee*,[9] Cream Holdings wished to stop their former accountant, Miss Banerjee, from publishing confidential information that might harm their business interests. The court refused to grant an interim injunction, considering the material to be a serious matter of public interest. As such, Cream Holdings Ltd was prevented from acting in a manner that would harm the right to freedom of expression of Miss Banerjee. In both these examples, an obligation is placed upon a private individual to refrain from acting in a manner that would harm the Convention rights of others. Both forms of horizontal effect occurred through a modification of provisions of private law procedural rules.

Third, a distinction can be drawn between horizontal effect arising in private law and that arising in public law. Horizontal effect can arise in public law through the application of sections 6(1) and 6(3)(b) of the Act. Section 6(3)(b) includes 'any person certain of whose functions are functions of a public nature' within the definition of a public authority, making it unlawful for that body to contravene Convention rights when performing a public function. This section can create horizontal effect as it expressly includes hybrid public authorities

---

[8] [2001] QB 967.
[9] [2004] UKHL 44; [2005] 1 AC 253.

– private institutions that perform public functions. This is illustrated by the decision of *Poplar Housing v Donoghue*.[10] Poplar Housing was a housing association - a private institution. Yet, the court determined that it was performing a public function. Consequently, its social housing activities had to comply with Articles 8 and 6 ECHR.

Divergence emerges in particular between the extent to which horizontal effect arises in public law and in private law. Not only is there evidence of a broader form of horizontal effect in private law, but also private law appears to grant a stronger protection of the Convention rights to which they grant horizontal effect – with the possible exception of horizontal effect occurring through the modification of statutory as opposed to common law provisions.

2. The Paradox of Horizontal Effect

I. A stronger form of horizontal effect in private law.

Whilst the definition of a public authority for the purposes of section 6(3)(b) has been interpreted more narrowly than expected, the scope of horizontal effect through the modification of the common law has been interpreted more broadly than an acceptance of indirect effect would appear to support.

The most recent House of Lord's decision to consider the definition of a public authority for the purposes of section 6(3)(b) is *YL v Birmingham City Council (YL)*.[11] YL was an 84 year old women suffering from Alzheimer's disease who lived in a care home run by Southern Cross, a private company. Her accommodation had been arranged by Birmingham City Council, according to their duty under sections 21 and 26 of the National Assistance Act 1948. The council also paid the greater portion of the fees of the care home, with a supplement being paid by YL's family. The issue of whether a care home providing accommodation to those whom a public authority had a duty to house/arrange accommodation had already been decided by the Court of Appeal in *R (Heather) v Leonard Cheshire Foundation (Leonard Cheshire)*,[12] which concluded that a private care home run by the Leonard Cheshire Foundation was not a public authority for the purposes of section

10 [2001] EWCA Civ 595.
11 [2007] UKHL 27; [2007] 3 WLR 112.
12 [2002] EWCA Civ 366; [2002] 2 All ER 936.

6(3)(b). This judgment had been subjected to two main lines of criticism. First, it was argued that *Leonard Cheshire* had taken an institutional as opposed to a functional approach when determining the meaning of a public authority, focusing upon how far the private body was enmeshed with the public authority with whom it contracted to provide services.[13] The Leonard Cheshire Foundation provided accommodation and care to individuals with disabilities, but was not deemed to be standing in the shoes of the public authority, exercising statutory powers. This is contrasted to the outcome in the earlier decision of *Poplar Housing and Regeneration Community Association Limited v Donoghue (Poplar Housing)*,[14] where Poplar Housing, which provided houses to homeless individuals that the local authority had an obligation to house, was found to be a public authority for the purposes of section 6(3)(b). Poplar Housing was enmeshed with the local authority: it had been created by the local authority to take over the housing stock of the local authority; five board members of Poplar Housing were members of the council and the local authority provided guidance as to how Poplar Housing was to act towards its tenants. Second, the narrow reading of section 6(3)(b) was criticised for failing to provide an adequate protection of the Convention rights of vulnerable groups in society, whose rights would have been protected had they been placed in care homes run by the local authority.[15] However, despite this pressure to broaden the interpretation of section 6(3)(b), the House of Lords held by a majority of 3 votes to 2 that the care home in *YL* was not a public authority.

   YL does provide for a potentially broader definition of a public authority - and thus a broader form of horizontal effect - than that emerging through earlier case law, as it adopts a predominantly

---

[13] See, for example, P Craig 'Contracting Out, the Human Rights Act and the Scope of Judicial Review' (2002) 118 *Law Quarterly Review* 551; D Oliver 'Functions of a Public Nature under the Human Rights Act [2004] *Public Law* 329; C Donnelly '*Leonard Cheshire* Again and Beyond: Private Contractors, Contract and section 6(3)(b) Human Rights Act 1998' [2005] *Public Law* 785 and S Palmer 'Public, Private and the Human Rights Act 1998: an Ideological Divide' (2008) 66 *Cambridge Law Journal* 559. 'The Meaning of a Public Authority under the Human Rights Act' 7th report of the 2003-4 session of the Joint Committee of Human Rights HL 39/HC 382 and 'The Meaning of Public Authority under the Human Rights Act' 9th report of the 2006-7 session of the Joint Committee of Human Rights, HL 77/HC 410.

[14] [2002] QB 48.

[15] See, in particular, Donnelly (n 13), and two reports of the Joint Committee of Human Rights, (n 13).

functionalist approach to the definition of section 6(3)(b).[16] However, the majority defined a public function more narrowly than the minority, influenced, at least in part, by a different account of the purpose of section 6(3)(b). Whilst the minority regarded the purpose of section 6(3)(b) as being to ensure a broad protection of human rights,[17] the majority regarding the purpose of the section was to ensure that bodies who would be liable for breaches of the Convention before the Strasbourg court would also be liable for breaches of Convention rights in English law.[18] The majority judgment drew a distinction between the scope of a public function, and a function that a public authority was under a duty to provide. The mere fact that a private body was contractually obliged by a public authority to provide a service that the public authority would otherwise have been required to provide did not mean that the private body in question was performing a public function.[19] A private body would be regarded as performing a public function were it to exercise a governmental function, wielding coercive powers.[20] Nor was it sufficient that the local authority was paying for the service provided by the private body,[21] (although this would indicate the existence of a public function were the local authority to pay for the service as a whole, or to subsidise the provision of this service)[22] or that the function in question was subject to regulation by the government.[23] The service provided by the care home was that of accommodation, carried out for commercial purposes and subject to commercial regulation through private law, as opposed to the public function of arranging accommodation according to a statutory duty.[24] The minority judgment focused more broadly on the function of the state to provide care for the vulnerable, regarding the legislation as illustrating an

---

[16] n 11, paras [5]-[13](Lord Bingham), [30]-[31](Lord Scott), [61]-[72](Baroness Hale), [86]-[91] and [100]-[106](Lord Mance) and [124]-[132](Lord Neuberger).

[17] *Ibid.,* paras [4](Lord Bingham) and [54]-[55](Baroness Hale).

[18] This is particularly true of the judgment of Lord Mance, *ibid.,* paras [87]-[88] and [102].

[19] *Ibid.,* paras [29]-[31](Lord Scott), [104]-[106] and [117](Lord Mance) and [144](Lord Neuberger).

[20] *Ibid.,* paras [28] (Lord Scott), [100](Lord Mance) and [150], [158]-[159] and [166] (Lord Neuberger).

[21] *Ibid.,* paras [117]-[120](Lord Mance) and [141](Lord Neuberger).

[22] *Ibid.,* paras [27](Lord Scott) and [148] (Lord Neuberger).

[23] *Ibid.,* paras [103](Lord Mance) and [134] (Lord Neuberger).

[24] *Ibid.,* paras [29-34] (Lord Scott), [107]-[117](Lord Mance) and [147](Lord Neuberger).

assumption of responsibility by the State for the care of the elderly.[25] The fact that Birmingham City Council paid for this service reinforced this assumption of responsibility, the local authority being required to pay for the care services of those who were unable to provide for themselves.[26] Given this assumption of responsibility for the vulnerable, the definition of a public function needed to be defined broadly, to ensure that those in private care homes were able to effectively protect their Convention rights.[27] The subsequent reversal of this classification of care homes as private bodies by the legislature adds weight to the perception that majority adopted an overly narrow interpretation of the definition of a public body.[28]

YL was recently applied in the Court of Appeal decision of *London and Quadrant Housing Trust v R (on the application of Weaver)(Weaver)*[29] which discussed whether the decision by a Housing Trust to terminate a tenancy was a public act, as part of a public function performed by a hybrid public authority. Although the majority determined that the act in question formed part of the public functions of the housing trust, the case confirms the narrower approach to a definition of a hybrid public authority found in *YL*.

Moreover, *Weaver* provides a further narrowing of the definition of a public authority for the purposes of section 6(3)(b), further restricting horizontal effect occurring through public law. The decision focused on the relationship between sections 6(3)(b) and 6(5) of the Human Rights Act 1998, which restricts the liability of hybrid public authorities to comply with Convention rights so as not to apply to acts the nature of which is private. Consequently, even if a function is classed as a public function in general, it may be that specific acts that fall within the mantle of performing this public function are nevertheless classified as private acts and are thus not subject to Convention obligations. When determining whether the act in question is public or private, Elias LJ relied on three factors: the source of the power under which the act is performed; the nature of the activities of which the act was a part and the close connection between the act and

---

[25] *Ibid.,* paras [7] and [15](Lord Bingham) [65]-[67](Baroness Hale).
[26] *Ibid.,* paras [18](Lord Bingham) and [65]-[68] (Baroness Hale).
[27] *Ibid.,* paras [19](Lord Bingham) and [60] and [71](Baroness Hale).
[28] Health and Social Care Act 2008, section 145(1).
[29] [2009] EWCA Civ 587; [2009] All ER (D) 179 (Jun).

the function of which the act formed a part.[30] Lord Collins agreed with these factors, placing particular importance upon the connection between whether the act was public or private and whether the function of which it formed a part was public or private.[31] For Elias LJ, the termination of the tenancy agreement was a public act because it was part of the public function of the housing association to provide social housing – which he classified as a governmental function - with a significant reliance on public finance and subject to statutory regulation to ensure that the housing association performed this social function.[32] Rix LJ, dissenting, focused predominantly upon the purely private and contractual nature of a tenancy agreement, failing to see how such a standard contractual agreement could be subject to public law.[33] In reaching his conclusion, he stressed the need to distinguish clearly between the general functions of a hybrid public body and the nature of the specific act that formed the subject of the legal action in question.[34] If followed, his approach to section 6 would restrict its possibility to create horizontal effect even further.

The narrow scope of horizontal effect through the operation of public law stands in stark contrast to the development of horizontal effect through the common law, in particular when we analyse the role of section 6(3)(a) in the development of the tort of breach of confidence to protect the Convention right to privacy found in Article 8 ECHR. Although sections 6(1) and 6(3)(a) have not required the courts to create a free standing tort of privacy,[35] the modification to the tort of breach of confidential information is such as to give rise to a tort of privacy in all but name. Prior to the enactment of the Human Rights Act, the tort of breach of confidential information rested predominantly upon the establishment of a duty of confidence, that duty being breached by the individual who disclosed the confidential information to the detriment of the owner of that information. As confirmed in *Campbell v MGN,* the tort can now occur even when there is no duty of confidence, resting upon the classification of the

---

[30] *Ibid.,* para [41] .
[31] *Ibid.,* para[100].
[32] *Ibid.,* paras [68]-[76].
[33] *Ibid.,* para [153].
[34] *Ibid.,* paras [150]-[152].
[35] *Wainwright v Home Office* [2003] UKHL 53; [2004] 2 AC 406.

published information as confidential; so much so that Lord Nicholls re-christened the tort as the 'misuse of private information'.[36] More importantly the tort has effectively become the means through which Articles 8 and 10 ECHR are incorporated into English law.

The extent to which sections 6(1) and 6(3)(a) require the common law to be modified in order to protect Convention rights is best illustrated by the Court of Appeal decision of *McKennitt v Ash*.[37] Loreena McKennitt was a well-known Canadian folk singer, who had striven to ensure that her private life was guarded from public scrutiny. Ash was a close former friend of McKennitt, who wrote a book detailing aspects of McKennitt's private life. McKennitt sought an injunction to prevent further publication of the book, in reliance on a breach of privacy and breach of confidence. Buxton LJ, giving the leading judgment, made it clear that the content of the tort of breach of confidence was entirely dictated by the content of Articles 8 and 10, the content of these provisions being 'shoe-horned' into the tort of breach of confidence.[38] This approach was confirmed in the later Court of Appeal decision of *Murray v Express Newspapers Plc*.[39] Although Buxton LJ clearly explained that there still remains no common law tort of privacy and never expressly stated that Convention rights had direct substantive horizontal effect, the impact of indirect horizontal effect is closer to that of direct effect.[40] There appear to be little, if any, limits placed upon the obligation of the court to develop existing common law principles in a manner to ensure that that mirror the content of Convention rights, save that the court is not required to create new causes of action.

II. A stronger protection of Convention rights in private law?

Paradoxically, Convention rights appear to receive a stronger protection in private law than in public law. This is for two main reasons. First, in public law cases, the court has relied upon section 2(1) in a restrictive manner, viewing Convention rights as providing a ceiling as opposed to

[36] [2004] UKHL 22, [2004] 2 AC 457 [15].
[37] [2006] EWCA Civ 1714; [2007] 3 WLR 194.
[38] *Ibid.*, para [8].
[39] [2008] EWCA Civ 446, [27];[2008] 3 WLR 1360.
[40] See N Moreham, 'Privacy and Horizontality: Relegating the Common Law' (2007) 123 *Law Quarterly Review* 373, 374-375.

a floor of human rights protections. Although this constraint appears to have been relaxed slightly in the recent House of Lord's decision in *Re P (Adoption: Unmarried couple)*,[41] the restriction is still in place, in a way that is not present in private law cases. Second, courts are concerned with issues of deference in public law cases. Although Lord Bingham appeared to dismiss a concept of deference in *Huang v Secretary of State for the Home Department*,[42] there is still evidence of courts providing a weaker definition of rights in public law than in private law cases, where deference does not appear to be an issue.

a) Section 2(1) Human Rights Act 1998
Section 2(1) of the Human Rights Act 1998 requires that courts 'must take into account' decisions of the ECtHR when adjudicating upon issues that concern Convention rights. In a consistent line of case law, courts deciding judicial review cases that concern Convention rights have interpreted section 2(1) to require courts to ensure that English law matches the definition of Convention rights provided by the ECtHR, but goes no further. Lewis refers to this as the 'mirror principle' – as English law must mirror Convention rights as interpreted by the ECtHR.[43] The mirror principle has its origins in the dicta of Lord Bingham in *R (on the application of Ullah) v Special Adjudicator*,[44] which stated that, although decisions of the ECtHR were not strictly binding, 'courts should, in the absence of some special circumstances, follow any clear and constant jurisprudence of the European Court of Human Rights'.[45] As such, '[t]he duty of national courts is to keep pace with the Strasbourg jurisprudence as it evolves over time: no more, but certainly no less'.[46] This obligation appeared to be strengthened in *R (on the application of Al Skeini and others) v Secretary of State for Defence*,[47] where Lord Brown cited Lord Bingham's dicta, narrowing it by adding: 'I

---

[41] [2008] UKHL 38; [2009] 1 AC 173.
[42] [2007] UKHL 11; [2007] 2 AC 167.
[43] J Lewis, 'The European ceiling on Human Rights' [2007] *Public Law* 720 and 'In re P and others: an exception to the 'no more and certainly no less' rule' [2009] *Public Law* 43.
[44] [2004] UKHL 26, [2004] 2 AC 323.
[45] *Ibid.*, para [20]. For a detailed analysis and criticism of the case law leading up to this decision, see R Masterman, 'Section 2(1) of the Human Rights Act 1998: binding domestic courts to Strasbourg' [2004] *Public Law* 725.
[46] *Ibid.*, para[20].
[47] [2007] UKHL 26; [2008] 1 AC 153.

would respectfully suggest that last sentence could as well have ended "no less, but certainly no more"'.[48]

Re P appears to weaken this requirement. The case concerned a challenge to adoption regulations in Northern Ireland, which did not permit unmarried couples to adopt. Although there was no clear decision of the ECtHR requiring unmarried couples to adopt, the House of Lords concluded that the adoption regulations were contrary to Articles 8 and 14 ECHR, effectively developing English law beyond the requirements of the ECHR, as set down by the ECtHR. The case is an example of the special circumstances in which courts are prepared to go beyond ECtHR decisions – where there is a clear line of developing case law before the Strasbourg court which suggests that, if the ECtHR were to hear the decision, it would conclude that it was contrary to Convention rights.[49] In addition, there was agreement that the 'straight jacket'[50] of decisions of the ECtHR did not apply in those circumstances where the Strasbourg court had granted a margin of appreciation.[51]

Even this more relaxed approach is more restrictive than the approach of the courts in private law cases,[52] particularly given the example of *Campbell v MGN*.[53] What is remarkable about the case is that the House of Lords were willing to apply Article 8 to horizontal situations, requiring a private media organisation to protect Miss Campbell's right to privacy, even though there was no clear case law of the ECtHR requiring that Article 8 should have horizontal application in such situations. Nor was there a clear line of case law indicating that the ECtHR was prepared to move in this direction. The court did, later, extend Article 8 to apply in horizontal situations in *Von Hannover v*

---

[48] *Ibid.*, para [106]. Lord Brown's interpretation was also affirmed by Baroness Hale, *ibid.*, para [90]. For a detailed analysis of the mirror principle and its refinement, see Lewis (n43) above and J Wright, 'Interpreting section 2(1) of the Human Rights Act 1998: towards an indigenous jurisprudence of Human Rights' [2009] *Public Law* 595.

[49] *Ibid.*, paras [21]-[29](Lord Hoffmann);[53] (Lord Hope); [136]-[142] (Lord Mance). Baroness Hale was unsure whether the European Court of Human Rights case law would develop in this manner and Lord Walker disagreed. See Lewis n 43 above.

[50] *Ibid.*, para [50](Lord Hope).

[51] *Ibid.*, paras [31]-[37] (Lord Hoffmann); [50] (Lord Hope); [120] (Baroness Hale); [127]-[130] (Lord Mance).

[52] This divergence is remarked upon by Wright (n 48) 599-600 and n 43, 742.

[53] n 1.

Germany,[54] a case which has been regarded as anything but uncontroversial.[55]

Although three of their Lordships in *Campbell v MGN* referred to decisions of the ECtHR in their judgments, none of them discussed section 2(1), nor appeared to regard the decisions of the Strasbourg court as constraining their development of Convention rights.[56] Lord Hoffmann even noted that the ECtHR did not require Article 8 to be interpreted so as to apply to horizontal situations, arguing instead that section 6(3)(a) required the court to recognise the values underpinning Convention rights, which then influence the development of the common law. Lord Hoffmann did not see why the values of autonomy and dignity which underpinned Article 8 would apply so as to restrain actions of the State, but not so as to restrain actions of private individuals.[57]

b) Deference

The extent to which concerns over deference in public law cases can lead to a stronger protection of Convention rights in private law can be best illustrated by divergent developments in the law relating to the protection of the Article 10 ECHR right to freedom of expression. Two recent House of Lords decisions, R *(ProLife Alliance) v British Broadcasting Corporation (ProLife)*[58] and *(Animal Defenders International) v Secretary of State for Culture, Media and Sport (ADI)*[59] have been criticised for providing a weak protection of the right to freedom of expression, especially given that the cases concerned political expression, which receives a stronger protection in decisions of the ECtHR.[60] In *ProLife*, a challenge was

---

[54] [2004] ECHR 59320/00; (2004) 16 BHRC 545.
[55] N Moreham, 'Privacy in Public Places' (2006) 65 *Cambridge Law Journal* 606, B Rudolf 'Case Comment: Von Hannover v Germany' (2006) 4 *International Journal of Constitutional Law* 533 and N Hatziz, 'Giving Privacy its due: private activities of public figures in *Von Hannover v Germany*' (2005) 16 *King's College Law Journal* 143.
[56] *Campbell* (n 1) paras [49]-[50] (Lord Hoffmann); [86], [107]-[110], [117]-[120] (Lord Hope); [145] (Baroness Hale).
[57] *Ibid.*, paras [49]-[50].
[58] [2003] UKHL 23; [2004] 1 AC 185.
[59] [2008] UKHL 15; [2008] 1 AC 1312.
[60] For criticism of *ProLife* see E Barendt, 'Free Speech and Abortion' [2003] *Public Law* 580. For criticism of *ADI* see T Lewis and P Cumper, 'Balancing freedom of political expression against equality of political opportunity: the courts and the UK's broadcasting ban on political advertising' [2009] *Public Law* 89, CJS Knight, 'Monkeying around with Free Speech' [2008] *Law*

made to the decision of the BBC to refuse to broadcast a party political broadcast by ProLife Alliance which included pictures of aborted foetuses. In contrast to the Court of Appeal, which had stressed the importance of political speech, the House of Lords, by a majority, concluded that there had been no breach of Article 8 ECHR. In doing so, the court deferred to the opinion of the BBC to refuse to show the pictures on the grounds of taste and decency. Two reasons emerged for paying deference to the BBC. First, matters of taste and decency are regarded as within the ambit of expertise of the BBC as opposed to the courts.[61] Second, regulations created by Parliament required the BBC to restrict broadcasts on the grounds of taste and decency. It was clear that restricting freedom of expression on the grounds of taste and decency was compatible with Article 10 ECHR. As such, the court should be reluctant to overturn a decision of the BBC applying the general regulations established by Parliament.[62]

ADI concerned a challenge to section 321(2) of the Communications Act 2003, which prohibited political advertising on television and radio. When passing the Act, the Government had made a section 19(1)(b) statement – i.e. that the Government wished to pass the legislation even though it was not able to state that it was compatible with Convention rights. Lord Bingham, giving the leading judgment, gave three reasons for deferring to the opinion of Parliament: that MPs are experts in democracy and therefore better able to determine whether a ban on political advertising best serves democracy;[63] that courts should be reluctant to challenge a section 19(1)(b) statement[64] and that the case concerned an area where states were granted a wide margin of appreciation by the ECtHR, particularly where the legislation in question provided for general as opposed to particular rules.[65] Lord Bingham's comments are given after the

---

Quarterly Review 557, J Rowbottom, 'Political Advertising and the broadcast media' [2008] *Cambridge Law Journal* 450 and N McCormick, 'Right to freedom of political expression – prohibition on political advertising on television' (2009) *Entertainment Law Review* 190.
[61] n 58, paras [15]-[16] (Lord Nicholls), [62] and [80](Lord Hoffmann), [132]-[145](Lord Walker).
[62] *Ibid.*, para [77] (Lord Hoffmann).
[63] *Ibid.*, para [33].
[64] *Ibid.*
[65] *Ibid.*, para [34]-[36].

decision in *Huang v Secretary of State for the Home Department*,[66] where he criticised the concept of deference, referring instead to the 'performance of the ordinary judicial task of weighing up the competing considerations on each side and according appropriate weight to the judgment of a person with responsibility for a given subject matter and access to special sources of knowledge and advice'.[67] In this particular case, it would appear that the courts were willing to give a large degree of weight to the opinion of Parliament.

Deference is not discussed, however, when courts apply Convention rights in private law cases. In addition, the reluctance to provide a strong protection of the right to freedom of expression can be contrasted with recent developments in defamation law, particularly concerning political libels. The recognition of the need to protect freedom of expression has led the courts to modify the content of private law: by prohibiting local authorities from bringing defamation actions to protect their reputation[68] and through adapting the defence of qualified privilege to include circumstances in which the media communicates information to the public at large, provided that, in doing so, it complies with the standards of responsible journalism (the *Reynolds* privilege).[69] In applying the *Reynolds* privilege, the court has developed the defence of reportage. In order to satisfy the requirements of the *Reynolds* privilege, publishers normally need to demonstrate that they have taken reasonable steps to verify the truth of the information contained in the defamatory article. However, the reportage defence allows a publisher to benefit from the *Reynolds* privilege without the need to verify the truth of the allegations that it is reporting.[70] The defence applies when publishers provide an accurate report, on a matter of pressing public interest, of the fact that allegations have been made and may even include a unilateral report of one side of a particular argument.[71] This protection of freedom of expression goes beyond the

---

[66] n 42.
[67] *Ibid.*, para [16].
[68] *Derbyshire County Council v Times* [1993] AC 534.
[69] *Reynolds v Times* [2001] 2 AC 127.
[70] *Al-Fagih v HH Saudi Research and Marketing (UK) Ltd* [2001] EWCA Civ 1634; [2002] EMLR 13.
[71] *Roberts v Gable* [2007] EWCA Civ 721; [2008] QB 502 and *Charman v Orion Publishing Group Ltd* [2007] EWCA Civ 972; [2008] 1 All ER 750.

requirements of Article 10 ECHR.[72] Moreover, it seems to contradict established principles of defamation law, most notably the repetition rule, which treats an accurate repetition of a defamatory statement in the same way as the original publication of the statement.[73] This contradiction could have been used as a reason for failing to develop the law in this direction, in a sense deferring to established principles of English tort law in a manner similar to the way in which the court defers to the opinion of Parliament or the administration in public law cases.

III. Consequences

a) The public/private divide

The emerging divergent protection of Convention rights has consequences both for the division between public and private law, as well as for horizontal effect. If public law provides for a weaker protection of Convention rights than that found in private law, then this would add weight to Dawn Oliver's arguments rejecting the call to broaden the definition of public authorities for the purposes of the Human Rights Act 1998.[74] One of the main criticisms of the narrow definition of a public authority is the fear that this will lead to a lower protection of human rights. By contracting with private companies to provide public services, both local authorities and the private company now providing these services would appear to escape liability for a breach of Convention rights under section 6(1) of the Act. This problem is exacerbated as often the services contracted out to private companies are provided to vulnerable groups in society - the very people whose human rights are arguably more in need of protection.[75] However, a narrow definition of a public authority may not provide a

---

[72] G Busuttil, 'Reportage: a not entirely neutral report' [2009] 20 *Entertainment Law Review* 44, 49-50.

[73] *Ibid.*, 48.

[74] See D Oliver 'The frontiers of the State... (n 13); 'Functions of a public nature...(n 13) and 'Chancel repairs and the Human Rights Act' [2001] *Public Law* 651.

[75] See the academic commentary listed at n 13. The 9th report of the Joint Committee of Human Rights for 2006-7 provides particularly graphic examples of breaches of the human rights of the elderly by private care homes.

weaker protection of Convention rights if this is accompanied by a strong protection of human rights in private law.[76]

Moreover, Oliver argues that a protection of human rights through private law is less likely to stifle pluralism, tolerance and diversity in the law, as private bodies would be able to operate without a restriction of their rights by the regulations that would be placed upon them if they were deemed to be part of the state.[77] In addition, Oliver argues that imposing obligations on private bodies through public law further restricts the rights of individuals, as the scope of the obligation placed upon the private individual is purely determined by an application of the ECHR. However, the Convention, being devised for application to state bodies, does not pay adequate attention to the Convention rights of the private body whose actions could potentially harm the Convention rights of others. In addition, its provisions are too vague to provide an adequate mechanism through which to balance competing rights claims.[78] These difficulties are exacerbated by the uncertainty surrounding the scope of a broader definition of a public authority. This makes it difficult for private bodies to take necessary managerial decisions, as the private body is not sure whether by doing so they will be classed as a public authority and therefore subject to human rights obligations and, if this is the case, what the scope of these human rights obligations will be. This in turn has the practical consequence of dissuading private bodies from providing services that could be classed as a social right or from contracting to provide services for public authorities.[79] In contrast, horizontal effect in private law occurs through the modification of current doctrines of the common law, which both recognises and protects the human rights of private individuals and also provides clearer guidelines as to how competing rights should be balanced through established precedents.[80] For Oliver, indirect horizontal effect in private law provides a better means through

---

[76] 'The frontiers of the State...' (n 13) 476-7.
[77] Oliver has other supplementary reasons for a narrow definition of the state. The discussion focuses on this justification both because it appears to be her primary reason for proscribing a narrow definition of the state and also because it is most relevant to determining a justification of the current legal position.
[78] 'Functions of a public nature (n 13) 344.
[79] 'The frontiers of the State...' (n 13) 488-90; and 'Functions of a public nature...' (n 13) 342-3.
[80] 'The frontiers of the State...' (*ibid.*) 490-92; and 'Functions of a public nature...' (*ibid.*) 340-2.

which to ensure that the human rights of the vulnerable are protected without harming the human rights and commercial freedom of private bodies performing services on behalf of public authorities.

However, Oliver's arguments rest upon a contrast between public and private law that is different from that currently found in English law. It is not clear that public law would be less able to balance competing rights than private law. In *YL*, the fear was that human rights obligations would be imposed upon a private care home, meaning that it was unable to terminate a residency agreement if it could be demonstrated that the relatives of the resident had been abusive to the staff of the care home. However, it is not clear that Article 8 of the ECHR would have required the care home to have continued to provide YL with a home in these circumstances. Recent decisions of the ECtHR and the House of Lords confirm that lawful termination of a residency agreement – for example through non payment of rent – would normally not breach Article 8 rights.[81] Nor is it clearly the case that private law is better able to balance rights, particularly following the developments in *McKennitt v Ash*, where, instead of Convention rights being used to develop existing rules of the common law, with common law precedents providing necessary guidance as to how rights should be balanced, Articles 8 and 10 ECHR have become the very content of the law. As such, the same problems of a lack of guidance from the ECtHR and the difficulty of balancing broadly phrased rights provisions can occur in private as well as public law. The common law may be developed in a manner that fails to adequately take account of competing private rights, as illustrated by the development of the reportage defence. Although the defence of reportage has been praised for providing a stronger protection of freedom of expression, going beyond the requirements of Article 10 ECHR, it has also been criticised for potentially breaching Convention rights by failing to provide a sufficient protection of reputation and privacy, effectively failing to balance Article 10 with Article 8 ECHR.[82]

---

[81] See I Loveland, 'A tale of two trespassers: reconsidering the impact of the Human Rights Act on rights of residence in rented housing: part 1' [2009] *European Human Rights Law Review* 148 and 'A tale of two trespassers: reconsidering the impact of the Human Rights Act on rights of residence in rented housing: part 2' [2009] *European Human Rights Law Review* 495 for a discussion of the relevant case law.

[82] n 72, 49-50.

a) Classification of horizontal effect

In addition, the strength with which Convention rights are protected by private law calls into question the manner in which we classify forms of horizontal effect. First, a distinction is drawn between direct and indirect effect. Convention rights would have direct effect in English law if an individual could automatically rely upon Convention rights in English courts, effectively creating a generic tort of a beach of Convention rights. Convention rights have indirect effect when it is not possible to rely on Convention rights in this manner. Instead, existing provisions of English law are interpreted in a manner compatible with Convention rights, or with the values underpinning Convention rights. Direct effect is regarded as providing for a stronger protection of Convention rights, given that direct effect always ensures that Convention rights are protected, whereas, in a system of indirect effect, it is possible that current provisions of English law cannot be developed so as to protect Convention rights. However, when current provisions of English private law are merely seen as the means through which Convention rights enter into English law, as would appear to be the case as regards the right to privacy, then this distinction is obliterated in all but name. Convention rights are protected in the same manner as if they had direct effect.[83]

A further distinction is drawn between two forms of indirect effect. Strong indirect effect occurs when Courts are faced with an obligation or a power to develop the law in line with Convention rights. Weak indirect effect occurs when courts are obliged or empowered to develop the law in line with the values underpinning Convention rights.[84] As the distinction suggests, strong indirect effect would appear to provide a stronger protection of rights, given the aim to ensure that English law incorporates Convention rights, as opposed to the values underpinning these rights. However, the judgment of Lord Hoffmann in *Campbell v MGN*[85] would suggest the contrary. Lord Hoffmann refers to the way in which, following the enactment of the Human Rights Act

---

[83] N Moreham, 'Privacy and Horizontality: Relegating the Common Law' (2007) 123 *Law Quarterly Review* 373, 375.

[84] G Phillipson, 'The Human Rights Act, "Horizontal Effect" and the Common Law: a Bang or a Whimper?' (1999) 62 *Modern Law Review* 824, 829-33.

[85] n 1.

1998, the court is required to develop the common law in line with values underpinning Convention rights. As such, when incorporating these values into the tort of breach of confidential information, Lord Hoffmann was able to conclude that the values underpinning Convention rights applied equally to protect privacy from being invaded by other individuals as it did to protect privacy from being invaded by the State, even though this meant that the common law developed beyond the requirements of the ECHR as then interpreted by the ECtHR.[86] However, when faced with a requirement to ensure that legislation, or actions of public authorities, does not contravene Convention rights, the courts have been much more reluctant to develop the law beyond Convention rights as interpreted by the European Court of Human Rights. There is the possibility, therefore, that weak indirect effect could provide for a stronger protection of human rights than strong indirect effect.

3. Paradox or Perception?

The previous section presented a possible paradox in English law – that private law provides a greater protection of human rights than that achieved through public law. However, this conclusion was reached through a discussion of certain specific areas of the law. To determine more conclusively both the existence and extent of this paradox would require a comprehensive analysis of every case decided since the coming into force of the Human Rights Act 1998 – a task far beyond this article. It could be argued, therefore, that evidence has only been provided of a perceived divergence in protection, calling into question the evidence in support of the paradox and its consequences.

A closer examination of the divergent case law presented above reveals two main factors that influence the development of a more restrictive approach to rights in public law cases: the separation of powers between the judiciary and the legislature and the debate surrounding the purpose of the Human Rights Act. These issues are not as prevalent in private law cases. Although concerns as to the separation of powers do arise in private law cases, they are different in nature. The question as to the purpose of the Human Rights Act does not arise in private law cases. These differences explain the divergence

---

[86] *Ibid.*, paras [49]-[50].

between the protection of Convention rights through private and public law, suggesting that there is some substance to the paradox presented above. It also illustrates that the divergence identified is not merely related to the differences between the protection of human rights in public and private law cases, but is based upon a more complex interplay between judicial review, the role of statutes and the development of the common law. These concerns, coupled with an account of the different features of public and private law, undermine the drawing of any stark conclusions as regards the preference for a protection of rights through public law, or through the development of horizontal effect in private law. Rather, it calls for the law to take a more holistic approach, recognising that different mechanisms are more suited to different rights.

I. The Separation of Powers

Concerns as to the separation of powers arise in three main ways in public law cases, influencing the adoption of a narrower definition of a public authority for the purposes of section 6(3)(b), the interpretation of section 2(1) and the way in which deference can restrict the scope and application of Convention rights. Only one of these concerns is relevant to private law cases.

First, courts in public law cases and those involving statutory interpretation are concerned to delineate between issues that are more suitable for resolution by Parliament than for resolution by the court. When the court determines that an issue is more suited to resolution by Parliament, courts defer to the opinion of Parliament concerning the definition of the Convention right in question, leading to the perception that rights are protected to a lesser extent in public law than in private law. In *ProLife*, Lord Hoffmann drew a distinction between legal matters, concerning the application of rights, and issues of social policy and the allocation of resources. The determination of matters of taste and decency was a matter of social policy, best suited to the assessment of Parliament and the BBC. As such, Lord Hoffmann was reluctant to regard the BBC as having contravened Convention rights, essentially providing a narrower definition of the right to freedom of expression than that provided by the Court of Appeal.[87] Lord Bingham in *ADI* was

---

[87] n 58, paras [76]-[80].

reluctant to declare section 302 of the Communications Act 2003 incompatible with Convention rights, in part, because he saw Parliament as better suited to determining the requirements of a proper protection of political speech so as to facilitate a healthy democracy than the courts.[88]

These concerns do not arise in private law cases discussing the modification of common law doctrines so as to accommodate Convention rights. There are two possible reasons for this divergence. First, tensions do not arise as the development of the common law is regarded as a quintessential function of the courts as opposed to Parliament. As such, there is no need for courts to be concerned as to whether the development of the provision of the common law is, by nature of its subject matter alone, more suited to development by the judiciary or the legislature. Second, the function of the court is different. In judicial review cases, courts are asked either to strike down an action of a public authority as unlawful through having contravened Convention rights. When applying a statute in either a public or a private law case, courts are obliged to read and give effect to legislation so as to render it Convention-compatible, or to declare provisions of legislation to be incompatible with Convention rights. In cases of indirect horizontal effect, the court is asked to develop the common law so as to reflect either Convention rights or the values underpinning these rights. This latter function is more clearly recognised as a long-standing aspect of the judicial function as it is understood in English law.

Courts are also influenced in public law cases and when interpreting statutory provisions by the need to defer to Parliament for reasons of Parliamentary legislative supremacy; an issue which, again, does not arise in the classic example of indirect horizontal effect in private law where the court is merely modifying provisions of the common law. A concern to maintain Parliamentary sovereignty can be illustrated by the reluctance of the court in public law cases to develop Convention rights beyond the definition provided by the European Court of Human Rights. Lord Bingham in R *(on the application of Ullah) v Special Adjudicator,*[89] Lord Brown in R *(on the application of Al Skeini and*

---

[88] n 59, para [33].
[89] n 44, para [20].

others) v Secretary of State for Defence[90] and Baroness Hale in *Al Skeini*[91] and
R *(Animal Defenders International) v Secretary of State for Culture, Media and
Sport (ADI)*[92] all refer to the ability of both Parliament and the courts,
through the development of the common law, to develop a protection
of rights that is stronger than that provided by the Convention.
However, they regard the role of the courts in public law cases as
restricted to following the definition of Convention rights as provided
by the ECtHR, ensuring that legislation or the actions of public
authorities has not contravened the ECHR.

Wright notes this distinction between the approach of the
courts to section 2(1) in public law and private law cases and attributes
it to a divergence between the duty of the court to ensure that statutes
do not contravene Convention rights and the power of the courts to
develop human rights further than that provided by the Convention
through developing the common law.[93] The distinction also appears to
be influenced by concerns to preserve Parliamentary sovereignty and
the need to delineate between the functions of the legislature and the
court, given the different function of the court in public and private
law. In addition, the distinction illustrates the tension between two
different forms of constitutionalisation, one occurring through the
operation of public law and the other through the operation of private
law.[94] In public law there is a move towards constitutionalistion through
the establishment of a hierarchical relationship between constitutional
principles – here found in the content of Convention rights – and
statutory provisions. Although the court cannot overturn statutory
provisions that contravene Convention rights, the greater ability to read
these provisions so as to ensure their compatibility with Convention
rights[95] and the ability to make a declaration of incompatibility[96]
establishes Convention rights as having greater importance than other
rights. In private law, constitutionalisation takes a different form,
relying upon the development of fundamental principles and values that

---

[90] n 47, paras [105]-[106].
[91] *Ibid.*, para [90].
[92] n 59, para [53].
[93] Wright (n 48).
[94] This distinction is derived from that developed by M Loughlin, 'Constitutionalisation: a
Twenty-Fifth Anniversary Essay' (2005) 25 *Oxford Journal of Legal Studies* 183, 183-4.
[95] Human Rights Act 1998, section 3(1).
[96] Human Rights Act 1998, section 4.

run through and influence the development of the common law. These principles are not hierarchical in the same sense. Although regarded as fundamental, they are fundamental in the sense that they underpin and influence the content of the common law, as opposed to overriding principles of the common law with which they conflict. The development of these principles is an established judicial function. In addition, as the common law is developed in line with Convention rights and values, there is an enmeshment of the content of the ECHR with the common law. This is clearly a task more suited to the English courts than to the European Court of Human Rights, thus reducing the requirement of the need to follow decisions of the ECtHR.

Third, the separation of powers plays a role in the extent to which the legislature or the judiciary is better suited to providing a remedy for a perceived divergence between English law and the content of Convention rights. In public law cases, courts use such concerns to issue a declaration of incompatibility as opposed to providing for a Convention-compatible interpretation of legislation. In particular, courts are concerned about providing Convention-compatible interpretations where to do so would require courts to take account of complex social and practical ramifications, or where it would require the development of administrative measures. This is illustrated by the judgment of Lord Nicholls in *Bellinger v Bellinger*,[97] which was referred to in *In re P* by Lord Hope,[98] who concluded that the issue was suitable for remedy by the court, and Lord Walker, who reached the opposite conclusion.[99]

A similar concern is present in common law cases, where courts are concerned to ensure that developments of the common law to ensure compatibility with either Convention rights or the values underpinning Convention rights, do not require the creation of a new tort[100] and can be seen as an incremental development of the common law.[101] In addition, even in those areas where the courts have modified the common law to a great extent, protecting rights beyond the decisions of the ECtHR, these developments are the culmination of a

---

[97] [2003] UKHL 21; [2003] 2 AC 467, paras [37]-[41].
[98] n 41, para [55], which concluded that the matter was suitable for resolution by the Courts.
[99] *Ibid.*, paras [81]-[83].
[100] n 35.
[101] *Douglas v Hello! Ltd* [2001] 2 WLR 992, 1017, para [91] (Sedley LJ).

series of incremental developments of the common law. As regards the protection of privacy, judicial statements supporting the extension of the tort of breach of confidence to include disclosures of private information, regardless of whether that information was disclosed in breach of confidence or otherwise, can be found in case law predating the enactment of the Human Rights Act.[102] The development of the reportage defence builds on the protection of freedom of expression found in *Reynolds v Times*[103] which itself built upon modifications of the tort of defamation in *Derbyshire County Council v Times*.[104] Although ultimately the influence of Convention rights arguably provided the catalyst for a final and more dramatic alteration to the common law, this was produced through a series of incremental measures – a task more suited to judicial as opposed to legislative law-making.[105]

II. The purpose of the Human Rights Act

A tension is evident in public law cases as to whether the purpose of the Human Rights Act is to give rise to a protection of domestic rights, influenced by the content of the ECHR, or as to whether the purpose of the Act is to ensure that the UK avoids future findings by the ECtHR that it has acted contrary to the ECHR. This tension is evident in the decision of *YL*, where Baroness Hale and Lord Bingham preferred a broad interpretation of a public authority, influenced, in part, by the need to take a domestic approach to the interpretation of section 6(3)(b). This is in contrast to the narrow definition of a public authority provided by Lord Mance, who focused upon the purpose of the Human Rights Act as a means of avoiding future liability in Strasbourg.[106] The same tension is evident in cases regarding the extent to which section 2(1) requires English courts to treat decisions of the ECtHR as binding precedents as to the definition of Convention rights. The ECHR is regarded as an international document, meaning that the responsibility for interpreting definitions of Convention rights rests

---

[102] See, most notably, *AG v Guardian (2)* [1990] 1 AC 109, 281 and Laws LJ in *Hellewell v CC of Derbyshire* [1995] 1 WLR 804, 807.
[103] [2001] 2 AC 127.
[104] [1993] AC 534.
[105] See A Kavanagh, 'The elusive Divide between Interpretation and Legislation under the Human Rights Act 1998' (2004) 24 *Oxford Journal of Legal Studies* 259.
[106] n 11, paras [4] (Lord Bingham), [54]-[55] and [61] (Baroness Hale) and [88] and [102] (Lord Mance).

with the European Court of Human Rights. As the obligation of the court is to ensure that it reads and gives effect to legislation in a manner compatible with Convention rights, so the obligation of the court is to follow the decisions of the European Court of Human Rights as to the definition of these Convention rights.[107] Lord Scott, who dissented in *Al Skeini*, was influenced at least in part by distinguishing between domestic rights and Convention rights, with English courts having the ability to develop domestic rights beyond the scope of Convention rights as defined by the European Court of Human Rights.[108]

This tension is not present in private law cases which do not require statutory interpretation, even in privacy cases where the court uses the content of Articles 8 and 10 ECHR to provide the substance of the tort of breach of confidential information. The explanation lies in an understanding of the different function of the court when developing the common law, with its different process of constitutionalisation. The courts are not required to overturn provisions of the common law that contravene Convention rights, or to ensure that provisions of the common law in its entirety mirror Convention rights. Rather, when developing the common law, courts see their role as incorporating Convention rights and values into provisions of the common law, building on prior incremental developments of the common law to protect fundamental constitutional rights. These rights are influenced to a greater or lesser degree by the content of Convention rights, depending upon the extent to which these rights were previously protected as fundamental constitutional rights in English law and the existing provisions of the common law into which Convention rights are interpreted.

4. Conclusion: Towards a Holistic Approach to Horizontality.

Academic discussion of horizontal effect in English law has focused predominantly upon the way in which courts are required to modify the common law in order to ensure that they do not breach their obligation, as public authorities, to act in a manner compatible with Convention rights. However, horizontal effect can be achieved in a variety of ways, using provisions of public as well as private law. In

---

[107] See the text relating to n 89 - 92.
[108] n 47.

analysing these different mechanisms an apparent paradox has emerged: that horizontal effect is more extensive in private law as opposed to public law and that Convention rights appear to be protected to a greater extent by provisions of private law as opposed to public law. If true, this paradox casts doubt upon the nature of the distinction between public and private law.

However, a closer analysis reveals that the paradox is best explained by the different operation of the doctrine of the separation of powers in public and private law, as well as a different approach to the process of constitutionalisation. Concerns as to the separation of power between the judiciary and the legislature arise when courts create horizontal effect through section 3(1) of the Human Rights Act, as well as when horizontal effect arises through a combination of section 6(1) and section 6(3)(b) of the Act. Such concerns do not arise in the same manner when courts develop the common law in order to reflect Convention rights or the values underpinning these rights. It is accepted that courts have the inherent jurisdiction to develop principles of the common law, any form of deference shown being akin to the remedial deference found in public law, with courts being careful to ensure that they only engage in incremental law-making, developing the common law through a series of steps. Nor are common law judgments concerned to ensure that their decisions reflect the definition of rights found in the Convention. This distinction derives from the different forms of constitutionalisation found in public law and private law cases. Whilst decisions in public law appear to be moving towards a hierarchical relationship between the Convention and English law, with is focused on ensuring the UK avoids future liability for breaching Convention rights before the ECtHR, the process of constitutionalisation in private law is more organic, where Convention rights and values are enmeshed with fundamental rights of the common law.

The divergence between horizontal effect in private and public law suggests the need to take a holistic approach to horizontal effect, based not upon assumptions as to whether private law or public law is better able to balance the respective rights of two private individuals, but upon the type of constitutionalisation required to protect these rights, as well as upon an understanding of whether the legislature or the courts are best-suited to balancing the particular competing Convention rights of two private individuals.

Will Permitting Judicial Enforcement of a Bill of Rights Ensure That Political Debate Will Be Impoverished and Reduce the Scope of Democratic Debate and Dialogue?

KATHERINE HODSON[*]

The above question is underpinned by the longstanding tension thought to exist between democracy and judicial enforcement of a bill of rights. Such enforcement is thought to create a democratic dilemma. However, the truth of the statement could be affected by a number of factors. Where formal bills of rights exist, their content and status vary widely. [1] Furthermore, there are numerous models for judicial enforcement of such bills. [2] It is beyond the scope of this essay to discuss all of these variables. As such, I will confine my consideration to a 'core case'[3] and focus on the US model of judicial review whereby judges enforce an entrenched bill of rights in concrete cases and ultimately have the power to strike down legislation. [4] Shapiro and Stone describe this as the power whereby 'any judge in any court, in any case, at any time, at the behest of any litigating party has the power to declare a law unconstitutional.'[5]

I have chosen not to discuss what have been described as 'dialogic' forms of judicial review such as that found in Canada. While

---

[*] Katherine Hodson completed her LLM at UCL Laws and is now a barrister at Goldsmiths Chambers.

[1] For a discussion of the various models see M Darrow and P Alston 'Bills of Rights in Comparative Perspective' in P Alston (ed.) *Promoting Human Rights Through Bills of Rights: Comparative Perspectives* (Oxford University Press, Oxford 1999) 471.

[2] Jeremy Waldron discusses these in 'The Core of the Case Against Judicial Review' (2006) 115 *Yale Law Journal* 1346, 1353-1359. See also, S Gardbaum 'The New Commonwealth Model of Constitutionalism' (2001) 49 *American Journal of Comparative Law* 707 for a discussion of the growth of constitutionalism and the various models that have developed throughout the world.

[3] Here I am borrowing from Waldron, *ibid.*

[4] It is recognised that the term judicial review can encompass the constitutional review of administrative acts as well as legislation. Here the term is confined to the latter type of review whereby constitutionally granted rights are enforced.

[5] M Shapiro and A Stone 'The New Constitutional Politics of Europe' (1994) 26(4) *Comparative Political Studies* 397, 400.

such models have been said to provide a solution to the democratic dilemma,[6] they undoubtedly represent a weaker form of judicial review than the US model.[7] Thus, they could be said to represent a compromise position. I will argue that such compromise is unnecessary.

Therefore, I focus on the US model not only due its adoption in many countries throughout the world,[8] but also because, as one of the strongest forms of judicial review, it brings into sharp focus the issues underpinned by the statement I am asked to consider. In a democratic society, legislation is the product of political debate and democratic dialogue. As such, when judges are permitted to strike down legislation one can argue that the democratic debate and dialogue leading to the creation of that law has been impoverished. Furthermore, when the judiciary has the final say on such matters, it can be said that the scope of democratic debate is reduced as those matters are effectively placed outside of the realm of that debate.

Like Waldron, I will consider the issues in two parts.[9] Firstly, I will discuss 'process-related' arguments and secondly, I will analyse the 'outcome-related' considerations. By reconsidering what democracy entails, I conclude that Waldron was wrong to say that the process-related arguments weigh in favour of the legislators.[10] Moreover, unlike Waldron, I will argue that the outcome related reasons, weigh unequivocally in favour of the courts. Thus I will show that judicial enforcement of a bill of rights does not impoverish political debate or reduce the scope of democratic dialogue.

---

[6] For example, Hogg and Bushell have argued that the design of the Canadian Charter actually creates institutional dialogue between the court and legislature. PW Hogg and A Bushell 'The Charter Dialogue Between Courts and Legislatures' (1997) 35 *Osgoode Hall Law Journal* 75. See also LE Weinrib 'Learning to Live with the Override' (1989-90) 15 *McGill Law Journal* 541.

[7] Waldron also distinguishes between strong and weak forms of judicial review and likewise 'targets' strong judicial review (n 2) 1354-7.

[8] Indeed, Gardbaum has argued that the growth of world constitutionalism has involved the growth of the model of constitutionalism invented in the United States (n 2) 708 and 718. Likewise, see A Lester QC, 'The Overseas Trade in the American Bill of Rights' (1988) 88 *Columbia Law Review* 537.

[9] n 2.

[10] *Ibid.*, 1386.

1. Process Related Arguments

Arguments that Judicial Review is Undemocratic

'Process-related' arguments are concerned with who should make or participate in a given decision rather than considerations about the appropriate outcomes.[11] Thus, judicial review is criticised because it places final decision making power in the hands of a small number of unelected[12] and unaccountable individuals. Once appointed, judges serve for life and are therefore shielded from the need to please the public. Furthermore, as bills of rights are often framed in broad terms, judges have great interpretive freedom such that rather than applying the law, they can create it.[13] Thus judicial review is criticised for being undemocratic and breaching the doctrine of separation of powers. Nonetheless, it is apparent that if these criticisms are to be properly addressed, it is essential to consider how democracy is understood.

At its simplest, democracy is defined as 'government by the people.'[14] This idea of self government is 'the degree to which the decision making process allows individuals the capacity to understand themselves as collective authors of the law that each is subject to.'[15] A similar, although different, definition of democracy holds that it is a form of majority rule[16] so that on important matters, 'the decision that is reached is the decision that a majority or plurality of citizens favors.'[17]

Based on such constructions, one can immediately see the tension between judicial review and democracy. When a small group of unelected judges strike down laws, the 'will of the people' can be said to

---

[11] Waldron (n 2) 1372-3.

[12] It should be noted that in some US states, judges are elected. However, Supreme Court Judges, Circuit Court Judges and District Court Justices are all appointed through the political branch in accordance with Article 2 of the Constitution.

[13] For a discussion of this particular criticism, see T Campbell 'Democratic Aspects of Ethical Positivism' in T Campbell and J Goldsworthy (eds.) *Judicial Power, Democracy and Legal Positivism* (Ashgate, London 2000) 28.

[14] R Dworkin 'The Moral Reading and the Majoritarian Premise' in HH Koh and RC Slye (eds.) *Deliberative Democracy and Human Rights* (Yale University Press, New Haven 1999).

[15] CF Zurn *Deliberative Democracy and the Institutions of Judicial Review* (Cambridge University Press, Cambridge 2007) 5.

[16] For a discussion of the subtle differences between these two notions of democracy see Zurn, *ibid.*, 2-6.

[17] Dworkin (n 14) 95.

be thwarted and a counter-majoritarian difficulty arises.[18] However, modern critics of judicial review base their arguments on more complex notions of democracy. Democracy is not seen as mere majority rule but *legitimate* majority rule.[19]

For Ewing, democracy is a process through which political equality is achieved. He argues that when citizens have the equal right to participate in the election of representatives, who in turn are properly accountable on a regular basis, they are guaranteed an equal part and equal respect in the political process.[20] Parliamentary sovereignty achieved through such processes is the legal and constitutional expression of the popular sovereignty of the people and is a condition of social democracy.[21]

Democracy therefore has conditions of participation, representation and accountability. Writing with Gearty, Ewing argues that judicial review detracts from each of these conditions.[22] Firstly, it lacks the criteria of participation because power is placed in the hands of a 'small privileged elite' and 'community participation is confined to the role of the litigant.'[23] In turn, access as a litigant is limited because entry to the system requires money and power[24] giving the rich and powerful a disproportionate ability to participate.[25] Secondly, judicial review lacks the condition of being representative. Judges are both unrepresentative in the sense of being unelected, but also in the sense of failing to reflect the community they represent.[26] Finally, judges are not accountable to the community on whose behalf they exercise power because for all practical purposes they cannot be removed from office

---

[18] AM Bickel *The Least Dangerous Branch: The Supreme Court at the Bar of Politics* (2nd ed. Yale University Press, New Haven 1986) 16 – 18.

[19] C Schneider 'The Constitutional Protection of Rights in Dworkin's and Habermas' Theories of Democracy' (2000) *UCL Jurisprudence Review* 101, 103.

[20] K Ewing 'Human Rights, Social Democracy and Constitutional Reform' in C Gearty and A Tomkins (eds.) *Understanding Human Rights* (Mansell Publishing, London 1996) 43.

[21] *Ibid.*, 43 – 44.

[22] K Ewing and C Gearty *Democracy or a Bill of Rights* (Society of Labour Lawyers, London).

[23] n 20, 43 – 44.

[24] n 22, 4.

[25] n 20, 44. Noting that multinational companies can also access the courts Ewing, describes it as 'grotesque' that they can 'cause to be determined in the name of human rights what the elected and accountable representatives can or cannot do.'

[26] n 22, 5. Using the example of the United Kingdom, Gearty and Ewing comment that Judges are homogenous in terms of their social background, age, race and sex.

until death or retirement. Therefore, when sovereign power is handed over to a small group of public officials, political equality is not preserved.[27]

For Waldron, democracy is the 'right to participate on equal terms in social decisions on issues of high principle.'[28] The starting point for his argument is that disagreement about rights is inevitable and intractable. That is not to say that people do not take rights seriously, but that in most cases, reasonable and good faith disagreement will persist.[29] As such, it is necessary to answer the question of *authority* and to decide who should resolve these disagreements and how.[30] In this context, Waldron says that the right of participation is the 'right of rights' because it resolves the question of authority.[31] It respects each person as a 'rights bearer' and therefore as someone who is entitled, as the subject of the conversation, to have a considered view on the matter.[32] It also 'respects human plurality,' as it is a process which assembles diverse perspectives and experiences when public decisions are taken.[33]

In the realm of modern democracies, Waldron therefore argues that a representative legislature using principles of majority decision making is the body that should make decisions about rights. Each person in society has an equal right to participate in fair elections to the legislature and majority decision making, better than any other rule, treats participants equally giving equal weight to all opinions.[34] Thus, 'our respect for such democratic rights is called seriously into question when proposals are made to shift decisions about the conception and revision of basic rights from the legislature to the courtroom,'[35] and, the

---

[27] n 20.
[28] J Waldron 'A Right-Based Critique of Constitutional Rights' (1993) 13 *Oxford Journal of Legal Studies* 18, 20. See also, J Waldron *Law and Disagreement* (Oxford University Press, Oxford 1999) 283.
[29] Waldron (n 2) 1367 – 8. *Ibid.* ('A Right-Based Critique...'), 28 – 31. *Ibid.* (*Law and Disagreement*), 246 and 311.
[30] 'A Right Based Critique...' (*ibid.*), 31-34. *Law and Disagreement* (*ibid.*), 244 – 245.
[31] 'A Right Based Critique...' (*ibid.*), 36 – 39. *Law and Disagreement* (*ibid.*), 249 and 254.
[32] 'A Right Based Critique...' (*ibid.*), 37. *Law and Disagreement* (*ibid.*), 251.
[33] 'A Right Based Critique...' (*ibid.*), 37.
[34] Waldron (n 2) 1387 – 1388.
[35] 'A Right Based Critique...' (n 28), 20.

'preponderance of process related reasons weigh unequivocally against judicial review.'[36]

In my opinion, when democracy is characterised in the above ways, it is impossible to resist the conclusion that there are a number of valid concerns about the legitimacy of judicial review. This undoubtedly explains why debates as to its legitimacy continue to rage despite increased globalisation of the practice.[37] The fact that judges are not representative, in the sense of being unelected, is true of most judges.[38] Furthermore, empirical evidence from the U.S. supports the contention that judges generally do not reflect all of the groups they serve in society.[39] Strictly, one must also concede that judges are unaccountable in that they cannot be removed from office. However, judges are not completely immune from the pressures of politics and public opinion. Indeed, the famous 'switch in time that saved nine' and brought to an end the '*Lochner* era'[40] of the US Supreme Court is one example of how judges can in fact be forced to account.[41]

There is also credibility in the suggestion that there is some loss to participation, when judicial review occurs. It perhaps overstates the case to suggest that money and power disproportionately affect participation; such criticisms leave out of account the availability of legal aid, pro-bono work and the involvement of non-governmental organisations.[42] However, this point aside, judicial review in individual concrete cases inevitably places limits on the extent of public participation. Although pressure groups may be permitted to intervene,

---

[36] Waldron (n 2) 1386.

[37] Gaudbaum (n 2).

[38] n 12.

[39] Lawyers Committee for Civil Rights Under Law 'Answering the Call For a More Diverse Judiciary: A Review of State Judicial Selection Models and their Impact on Diversity', (2005). The report speaks of an 'overabundance of white male judges' (page 8) and points out that only 10.1% of state judges are from minorities compared with 35.3% in the population overall (page 9).

[40] *Lochner v New York* 198 US 45 (1905).

[41] In response to the Court's persistent invalidation of various forms of 'New Deal' legislation, in 1937 President Roosevelt proposed his famous 'Court-packing bill', designed to make sweeping changes to the judiciary. During the period when the bill was being considered, the Court made its famous 'switch in time that saved nine' by abandoning opposition to the New Deal. See M Shapiro and RJ Tresolini *American Constitutional Law* (6th edn. Prentice Hall, New York 1983) 20 – 21.

[42] Michael Zander *A Bill of Rights?* (4th edn. Sweet and Maxwell, London 1997) 79 – 80.

not everyone who ultimately may be affected by the decision can have their say. In the case of *Roe v Wade*[43] the rights of many women were affected by the hugely controversial decision and yet the overwhelming majority had no right to a say before the Court.

Thus, applying the above characterisations of democracy, one could conclude that there is force in the statement I am asked to discuss. Indeed, many supporters of judicial review have thus felt compelled to concede that it is an undemocratic institution.[44] However, a number of supporters of judicial review argue that a solution can be found by reconsidering what democracy entails.

Framing Judicial Review within Democracy
One rather unsophisticated attempt to resolve the dilemma is to argue that when judicial review is created through democratic processes and with the support of the statistical majority of the public, it is a product of, not antithetical to, democracy.[45] While the power of judicial review in the US was created by the judiciary rather than the legislature,[46] many countries have created this power following democratic discussion and consultation.[47] However, as Waldron points out, were a nation to decide to vote for a dictatorship, this would hardly amount to democracy[48] and, as already discussed, democratic critiques of judicial review are based on far more than such 'a crude statistical view' of democracy.[49]

A similar argument propounded by Freeman, posits that when judges enforce a bill of rights, they are simply enforcing societies' own 'pre-commitment to rights' and thus they do not thwart the will of the people.[50] However, Waldron argues that because disagreement persists as to what exactly people have pre-committed to, the question of

---

[43] 410 US 113 (1973).
[44] For example Bickel (n 18).
[45] For example, in the run up to the adoption of the UK Human Rights Act, Dworkin pointed out that 71% of the UK thought that a Constitutional Bill of Rights would improve democracy. R Dworkin *A Bill of Rights for Britain* (Chatto and Windus, London 1990) 37.
[46] *Marbury v Madison* 5 US 137 (1803).
[47] For example s167 of the South African Constitution specifically empowers the South African Constitutional Court to decide on the constitutionality of parliamentary or provincial bills.
[48] n 28 ('A Right Based Critique...') 46.
[49] *Ibid.*, 47.
[50] S Freeman, 'Constitutional Democracy and the Legitimacy of Judicial Review' (1990) *Law and Philosophy* 9.

authority is not resolved.[51] Furthermore, the notion of pre-commitment fails to take into account the 'plurality of politics, the reasonableness of disagreement and the dynamic of debate.'[52]

Ely provides a more compelling solution to the problem. Like Waldron, he accepts the difficulty of disagreement about rights. However, Ely does not accept that this precludes judicial review. For him, the US Constitution is primarily concerned with ensuring procedural fairness and broad participation in the processes and distribution of government.[53] Even provisions that on first glance appear to guarantee 'substantive' results are actually concerned with process.[54] Thus, judicial review is not undemocratic provided that it is used to ensure that the structures and procedures necessary for democracy are preserved. The courts should only be concerned with 'disabling rights'[55] in so far as they are 'functionally structural' as well. In these circumstances, judicial review is a 'representation-reinforcing' rather than a 'value-protecting' process and is entirely supportive of the underlying concept of representative democracy.[56] For Ely, the institutional independence of the courts makes them well suited to this role.[57]

Ely's account of judicial review is therefore entirely process related and he does not rely upon the idea that judges might have superior abilities to make judgments about matters of morality or principle. Courts are simply the referees of the rules of the 'democratic game'[58] and therefore, the difficulty of disagreement about rights is avoided. Consequently, he offers a solution to the democratic dilemma.

However, Ely is criticised for relying only on majoritarian theory of democracy.[59] Furthermore, his account only supports judicial review of a limited number of structural or procedural rights. Thus, although

---

[51] Waldron (n 2) 1393.
[52] *Law and Disagreement* (n 28) 271.
[53] J Ely *Democracy and Distrust* (Harvard University Press, Cambridge 1980) 87.
[54] *Ibid.*, 90 - 101.
[55] The term 'disabling rights' is taken from R Dworkin 'Equality, Democracy and Constitution: We the People in Court' (1990) 28 *Alberta Law Review* 324, 326.
[56] n 53, 88 and 102.
[57] *Ibid.*, 103.
[58] n 15, 64.
[59] *Ibid.*, 53 and 106. n 55, 342.

Ely's approach would commend decisions such as *Wesberry v Sanders*,[60] it would not support decisions such as *Roe v Wade*.[61] It is also argued that Ely's account would not support judicial review of freedom of religion[62] and could lead to arbitrary results in an attempt to divorce matters of procedure from matters of substance.[63] Additionally it is said that his model does not enable account to be taken of 'ends' of democracy and the need for 'responsiveness to public reason.'[64]

Thus, Ely's rescue of democracy from the constitution 'is only a partial success'[65] and fails to afford judicial protection to many rights not deemed essential representative democracy. Furthermore, Dworkin posits that once democracy is defined as something more than 'majority rule', political and moral notions are introduced making it is impossible for judges to divorce matters of substance and morals from their decisions.[66] As such, Dworkin advances an alternative solution.

For Dworkin, the purely statistical or majoritarian view of democracy recommends a political system in which the majority is free to deprive the minority of an equal part and equal stake in government.[67] Crucially, it fails to treat all members of a community as 'moral members.'[68] This requires that each person is treated with equal moral concern[69] and is granted the right to participate[70] as a free and

---

[60] 376 US 1 (1964), to ensure that representatives be chosen 'by the people' it was held each person's vote must be equal and therefore, that, unfair districting patterns set up to elect congressional representatives had to be re-apportioned. For a discussion, see J Arthur 'Judicial Review, Democracy and the Special Competency of Judges' in R Bellamy (ed.) *Constitutionalism, Democracy and Sovereignty: American and European Perspectives* (Avebury, Aldershot 1996).

[61] n 43.

[62] n 55, 343.

[63] DJ Galligan 'Judicial Review and Democratic Principles: Two Theories' 57 *Australian Law Journal* 69, 78. Galligan argues that by applying Ely's theory, a law adversely affecting blacks might be struck down while one adversely affecting homosexuals might not be. A similar argument is made by R Dworkin *A Matter of Principle* (Harvard University Press, Cambridge 1986) 66.

[64] Zurn argues that these principles are ideally a part of democratic self rule (n 15) 53.

[65] n 55, 328.

[66] *A Matter of Principle* (n 63) 64. See also 'Judicial Review and Democratic Principles' (n 63) 77-78.

[67] n 55, 331.

[68] n 14, 102. And Ronald Dworkin *Freedom's Law: The Moral Reading of the American Constitution* (Harvard University Press, Cambridge 1996) 23.

[69] Dworkin defines this as a condition of 'reciprocity', a person is not a member unless he is treated as such by others. R Dworkin 'Constitutionalism and Democracy' (1995) *European Journal of Philosophy* 2, 5. See also *ibid.*, 24 – 26.

independent moral agent. Thus, a political community must give each citizen a *part* in the collective, a *stake* in it and *independence* from it.[71] Political equality does not mean that people should have equal power but that they should have equal status [72] and the overall aim of democracy should be that collective decisions are made by political institutions that treat all members as individuals with equal concern and respect.[73] Dworkin argues that the 'communal model' of majoritarian democracy satisfies these conditions[74] and that within this model, a bill of rights is a way of structuring democracy and ensuring equal status.[75] Therefore, 'democracy and constitutional constraint are not antagonists, but partners in crime.'[76]

Dworkin's account of democracy incorporates substantive values of morality and principle.[77] As such, he justifies constitutional protection of many more 'disabling provisions' than Ely's account.[78] However, as Dworkin himself concedes,[79] the above account does not, by itself, create a positive case for judicial review. It does not explain why the Court, rather than any other body, should protect these rights. To answer this question, Dworkin sees 'no alternative'[80] but to use a results-driven standard. Thus, the best institutional structure is one which produces the best answers to the moral question of what the democratic conditions are.[81] Ultimately, if a court makes a right decision in line with the substantive aims of democracy, nothing is lost to democracy.[82]

Therefore, Dworkin's redefinition of democracy succeeds in showing that judicial review is *not necessarily* undemocratic but can take us no further than that. This is because for Dworkin, democracy is achieved whenever its substantive outcomes are secured '*whatever* those

---

[70] n 68, 24 – 26.
[71] n 69, 9. And n 55, 337 -342.
[72] n 68, 26 – 29.
[73] n 14, 96.
[74] n 55, 330 – 336.
[75] *Ibid.*, 330.
[76] *Ibid.*, 346.
[77] Substantialist argument for judicial review are discussed further by Zurn (n 15) 35 – 38.
[78] n 55, 337 – 346.
[79] n 68, 33.
[80] *Ibid.*, 34.
[81] n 14, 112.
[82] *Ibid.*, 111.

processes happen to be and *however* they are institutionalized.'[83] Furthermore, by testing whether an institution is democratic according to its substantive results, Dworkin undoubtedly re-awakens the difficulty that Ely sought to avoid, that of disagreement. He concedes that citizens may require a structure for deciding the best institutional design, but accepts that this is what a theory of democracy cannot provide, and that this is why 'the initial making of a constitution is such a mysterious matter.'[84] As such, Dworkin's account does not create a positive case for judicial review *only* on process related grounds.

Thus we have a dilemma. Process related arguments for judicial review, of the kind propounded by Ely, avoid disagreement but omit the protection of many non political rights,[85] whereas, substantive accounts escape these limitations but re-introduce the difficulty of disagreement. Zurn argues that a solution to this dilemma can be found in Habermas' account of deliberative democracy.[86] Deliberative democrats believe that actual debate is a pre-requisite of legitimate democratic processes[87] and political decisions should arise from the reasoned deliberations of free and equal citizens concerned to solve collectively shared problems.[88]

Habermas criticises Ely for having left in the background a theory of democracy.[89] Accepting that modern societies preclude a unitary common consciousness he argues that society can develop norms through a process of deliberative democracy which facilitates the achievement of a 'we perspective from which all can test in common whether they wish to make a controversial norm the basis of their shared practice.'[90] Laws are tested not according to their substantive content but according to whether procedurally they are legitimate, that is, created through the correct processes.[91]

---

[83] n 15, 117.
[84] n 68, 34.
[85] n 14, 106.
[86] *Ibid.*, Chapter 7.
[87] n 13, 9.
[88] n 15, 165.
[89] J Habermas *Between Facts and Norms* (The MIT Press, Cambridge 1996) 266.
[90] J Habermas 'Reconciliation through the Public Use of Reason: Remarks on John Rawls' Political Liberalism' (1995) *Journal of Philosophy* 109, 117.
[91] n 15, 228 – 229.

In turn, Habermas argues that an effective deliberative democracy requires the constitutional protection of a number of rights that individuals would grant each other if they wished to legitimately regulate their interactions through the medium of law. According to this model, many more rights than Ely's model would be necessary to ensure the system of deliberative democracy including rights to equal subjective liberties, equal membership and basic provision of living conditions.[92]

Thus Habermas appears to bridge the gap between Dworkin and Ely. His account of democracy is procedural and he therefore removes the need to have recourse to 'substantivist checks.'[93] Furthermore, his more developed account of democracy justifies the protection of many more 'disabling rights' than Ely's account.[94] Turning to judicial review, Habermas argues that it fits within the framework of democracy because it is necessary to 'keep watch' over the system of rights so that procedural fairness and the openness of democratic process is guaranteed. However, Habermas' account of democracy also requires that judges are far more than the referees of the game and that they take an active part in 'ensuring the equal opportunity of all citizens to actualize their legally ensured private and public autonomy.'[95] Thus he recommends an activist judicial review.[96]

Ultimately, Zurn criticises Habermas for taking insufficient account of why it should be the *judiciary* rather than any other institution that should adjudicate upon the constitution. Habermas briefly considers other models, but thereafter 'presupposes' that the institutional question is settled.[97] As such, Zurn ultimately finds it necessary to consider outcome related considerations related to institutional design.[98]

---

[92] *Ibid.*, 232. And n 89, 122.
[93] n 15, 225.
[94] *Ibid.*, 235.
[95] *Ibid.*, 239.
[96] *Ibid.*
[97] *Ibid.*, 243-4.
[98] *Ibid.*

Conclusion on the Process Related Arguments

In this part, I have analysed how democracy is understood by both the critics and supporters of judicial review. It was not my purpose to arrive at a settled account of democracy, that is beyond the scope of this essay. Instead I have sought to demonstrate that, in the light of the competing conceptions of democracy, Waldron was wrong to conclude that there is *necessarily* a loss to democracy 'when an unelected or unaccountable individual or institution makes a binding decision about what democracy requires.'[99] In this context, Habermas' deliberative account of democracy provides the most compelling support for judicial review, avoiding the disagreement surrounding Dworkin's substantivist account, but, evading the limitations of Ely's theory. Ultimately however, it appears that if a positive case for judicial review is to be made out, one must also address the question of institutional design and the 'outcome related' considerations. Indeed, having cast doubt on the 'procedural' objections to judicial review, in the second part I will show that the 'outcome related' arguments provide a compelling and positive case for judicial review.

2. Outcome Related Arguments

Outcome related arguments 'are reasons for designing the decision-procedure in a way that will ensure the appropriate outcome.'[100] For Kavanagh, the justice of the outcomes of political decisions is the fundamental criterion because even when political decisions are taken by representative elected bodies, an injustice can be done when the outcomes of those decisions are wrong, unfair or unjust.[101] Likewise, Rawls posits that we should test constitutional arrangements according to the overall balance of justice. We should weigh the loss to liberty of less participation against the type of liberty that is gained by other constitutional mechanisms.[102]

In the face of disagreement about rights the above approach might seem problematic. However, it is possible to assess general institutional considerations about the way the respective institutions

---

[99] *Law and Disagreement* (n 28) 293.
[100] 'The Core of the Case…' (n 2) 1373.
[101] A Kavanagh 'Participation and Judicial Review: A Reply to Jeremy Waldron' (2003) 22 *Law and Philosophy* 451, 462.
[102] J Rawls *A Theory of Justice* (Revised edn. Oxford University Press, Oxford 1999) 203.

perform their job.[103] Furthermore, just because we disagree about rights, does not mean that the solution is necessarily the democratically elected legislature; such disagreement might equally be said to impugn participatory majoritarianism. [104] Thus if we are to prefer one mechanism above another, we must question why that arrangement has a special claim.[105] Indeed, even Waldron endorses such an approach, pointing out that we can choose a set of procedures that are *most likely* to get at the truth, whatever that truth turns out to be.[106]

Special Qualities of the Judiciary

One strong outcome related argument in favour of judicial review stems from the independence of the judiciary. Because of this it is said that judges are best placed to make decision without being influenced by political considerations[107] or fear of popular dissatisfaction with their performance.[108] This consideration underpins Ely's theory that judges can be seen as 'referees of the democratic game.' An accountable politician might 'trim on principle' due to concerns about what the electorate might think[109] and may be vulnerable to financial or political pressure.[110] Therefore, the fact of their being unaccountable, rather than being a weakness, places them at an advantage over the legislature. Indeed, Kavanagh points out that the fact that we are affected by a decision may be precisely the reason why we should not take it. [111]

It is also argued that judges are better than the legislature in deciding rights based disputes. Dworkin argues that they are far more developed than legislatures at making claims for 'moral consistency' whereby they have to imagine the circumstances in which the claimed right might provide unacceptable results.[112] Furthermore, the reasoned decisions provided by judges is said to make them well suited to

---

[103] n 101, 466.
[104] *Ibid.*, 467.
[105] *Ibid.*, 469.
[106] Waldron (n 2) 1373.
[107] n 42, 81. And n 101, 471.
[108] Dworkin (n 63) 25.
[109] n 42, 81.
[110] Dworkin (n 63) 112-113.
[111] n 101, 470.
[112] Dworkin (n 63) 24.

resolving issues about individual rights.[113] Rawls argues that juristic discourse is the paradigmatic idiom for public deliberation.[114]

The above arguments are strongly countered by opponents of judicial review. It is said that sectarian pressures also explain judicial neglect of rights[115] and the judiciary may face the same bureaucratic pressures as the government.[116] Indeed, I have already noted that public pressure may influence the work of the court.[117] Furthermore, members of the Critical Legal Studies Movement question the claim that judges can be free of bias, because interpreting and settling the law is very subjective and creative. As such, judges' personal views will effectively control how much sovereignty people will enjoy[118] and 'because judges like legislators are morally fallible, we would still face the danger of occasional, possibly egregious injustice.'[119] Furthermore, the flexibility created by bills of rights may cause judges to stray into the political arena, an arena which is best served by politicians.[120]

Kramer questions the romanticised accounts of 'lawyers-cum-philosophers/political scientists, studiously pondering weighty questions of principle before crafting careful explanations that reflect deeply on the theoretical dilemmas they have faced.'[121] In fact, the business of courts may be left to staff behind court doors.[122] Likewise, it is said that decisions of the courts are more concerned with the technicalia of legal argument, jurisdiction, precedent, consistency,

---

[113] This is an argument recognised by Waldron (n 2) 1382.

[114] n 15, 167.

[115] Waldron (n 2) 1377.

[116] L Kramer *The People Themselves: Popular Constitutionalism and Judicial Review* (Oxford University Press, Oxford 2004) 240.

[117] I have argued that the end of the '*Lochner* era' was brought to an end partly as a result of the judiciary's responsiveness to public pressure.

[118] D Beatty 'Human Rights and the Rule of Law' in David Beatty (ed.) *Human Rights and Judicial Review: A Comparative Perspective* (Martinus Nijhoff, London 1994) 6 – 7.

[119] F Schauer 'Legal Positivism and the Contingent Autonomy of Law' in T Campbell and J Goldsworthy (n 13) 242.

[120] JA Griffith 'The Political Constitution' (1979) 42 *Modern Law Review* 1, 16. Dworkin also acknowledges that Judges may stray into the political arena, but suggests that we should distinguish between arguments of political principle and political policy. Judges should rest their judgments on the former, but not on the latter (n 63) 11.

[121] n 116, 240.

[122] *Ibid.*, 239 – 240.

authorisation and canons of construction than with moral principle.[123] Finally, the point is made that congressional decisions, no less than judicial decisions, also depend on appropriate and persuasive justifications being found for a vote.[124] Indeed, Waldron argues that legislative debates can be rich with reasoning.[125]

Many of the above criticisms in turn are disputed by the supporters of judicial review[126] and it is difficult to untangle the competing arguments about which institution is *superior*. Whilst judges are *expected* to be independent and have excellent reasoning skills, what is disputed is whether they do so in practice and whether they do so better than the legislatures. Furthermore, in the face of disagreement about rights, it is difficult to build a convincing case for either institution on 'empirical grounds.' For every *Brown v Board of Education*,[127] one can find a *Plessy v Ferguson*.[128] Therefore I conclude that claims as to superiority do not provide a convincing solution.

Protection Against the Failings and Excesses of the Legislature
An alternative outcome related approach is to view judicial review as a means of protecting individuals against the will of the majority. Calsamiglia describes this approach as pre-supposing shortcomings in the system of democracy such that the 'boat of democracy must be directed by a captain that knows right from wrong.'[129] Furthermore, Beatty suggests that following the horrors of fascism and militaristic rule and the tyranny of communist cliques, the 'conventional wisdom of ordinary people has been to subject the principle of democratic rule to a more demanding definition of the rule of law and human rights protection.'[130]

Calsamiglia argues that the relationship between the people and those who represent them is in fact weak. He challenges the claim that

---

[123] Zurn makes this observation having reviewed a number of decisions of the U.S. Supreme Court (n 15) 187. Waldron makes a similar point (n 2) 1383.

[124] n 116, 240.

[125] Waldron (n 2) 1384.

[126] For example, Zander disputes the claims that judges are necessarily politicised by exercising control over a bill of rights (n 42) 107 – 108.

[127] 347 US 483 (1954).

[128] 163 US 537 (1896).

[129] Calsamiglia 'Constitutionalism and Democracy' in HH Koh and RC Slye (n 14) 139.

[130] n 118, 1.

legislatures are representative pointing out that elections take place in finite political divisions which have many consequences for the role of the representative.[131] Zander also argues that voting often has little to do with governing. Using the example of the UK he points out that often non-elected civil servants have more power than elected back bench MPs.[132]

Concerning participation, Dworkin points out that there are many citizens who are disenfranchised entirely.[133] Similarly, Kavanagh argues that those who lack political organisation or whose rights are thought to place an excessive burden on the system are effectively excluded from the political process.[134] Indeed, it is these inequalities that lead many commentators to observe that democratic majoritarianism, carries with it a danger of 'tyranny of the majority.'

On the basis of the above, it is argued that judicial review enhances participation and political equality as individual citizens are more able to access judicial than legislative processes.[135] Furthermore, it protects individual citizens by placing power in the hands of the aggrieved[136] and by providing a means of ensuring that governments do not act arbitrarily or unfairly.[137] For Dworkin, minorities therefore have most to gain from the transfer of power than any other group because the majoritarian bias of the legislature works most harshly against them.[138] In a similar vein, Kavanagh argues that judicial review can provide a means of participation that is more effective than simply having one vote in a million. Indeed, Calsamiglia posits that one of the great achievements of contemporary political theory has been to design mechanisms to address the tyranny of the majority.[139]

Furthermore, it is said that the democratic process cannot legislate for all possible situations. Indeed, governments may be resistant to change[140] or may deliberately choose not to legislate on

---

[131] n 129, 138 -139
[132] n 42, 79.
[133] Dworkin (n 63) 27.
[134] n 101, 479.
[135] n 42, 79.
[136] *Ibid.*, 68.
[137] n 118, 25.
[138] Dworkin (n 63) 28.
[139] n 129, 138.
[140] n 42, 64 – 65.

controversial matters.[141] Thus judicial review can ensure that such holes can be plugged and avoid injustice to individuals. It provides flexibility so that, in the light of the facts of the individual cases, the law can move with the times and fashion appropriate remedies.[142]

The premise of the above arguments is not that the courts are superior to the legislature. Rather, it is that the courts can protect against recognised defects in the political system. Indeed, it is interesting to note that Waldron does not dismiss these arguments. He accepts that 'some sort of power of judicial review' might be justified by the fact that legislators may not always anticipate the issues arising from subsequent application of legislation. However, he argues that this is a case for weak, rather than strong judicial review.[143] Furthermore, he accepts the danger of tyranny of the majority, but prefers to place this danger outside the core of his case.[144]

Waldron's side-stepping is telling. Furthermore, he fails to tell us when it is that the danger of tyranny of the majority, would justify recourse to judicial review. At the outset of 'The Core of the Case' Waldron accepts that judicial review may be 'necessary as a protective measure'[145] against legislative pathologies in particular countries. He also accepts that the political process cannot be perfect.[146] However, he never tells us what criteria should determine when resort to judicial review becomes necessary. Given that Waldron accepts the danger of 'tyranny of the majority,' rather than placing this outside the 'core case,' I conclude that this danger ought by itself to be accepted as a good reason for the institution of judicial review.

Two final points should be noted in response to the above. Waldron criticises supporters of judicial review, for failing to note that decisions in the courts are also made by 'majority voting.' In the end, five votes can defeat four in the Supreme Court.[147] Thus, size matters to Waldron. Elsewhere he points out that if majority voting is to be used, it is preferable that a *large* legislature should have the final say, rather

---

[141] n 13, 28.
[142] n 42, 64 – 65.
[143] Waldron (n 2) 1370.
[144] *Ibid.,* 1398.
[145] *Ibid.,* 1352.
[146] *Ibid.,* 1372.
[147] *Ibid.,* 1391.

than a group of nine individuals.[148] However, this appears to miss the point. The advantage of the courts is not their size or method of voting but that any lone individual can access the system and force a debate about his rights.

A final point made by critics of judicial review is that the above argument is premised on a 'distrust' of our fellow citizens such that supporters of judicial review are today's Aristocrats. [149] This point however, can easily be countered by reminding ourselves of why many bills of rights came into being in the first place. Lessons from the past, have taught many nations of the need to protect individuals from the tyrannies of governmental power. [150] That is not to say that judicial review is *necessary* to protect rights. [151] However, it underlines that reliance on judicial review is not based on arrogance, but upon humbly learning lessons from history. 'Guarding against risk should be a stronger motivating factor in setting up institutions, than any optimism we may have about people's willingness to do the right thing.'[152]

Conclusion on Outcome Relate Arguments

Overall, I have concluded that the competing claims made as to the superiority of each institution do not assist in resolving the debate. However, a strong case for judicial review can be made by pointing out the potential shortcomings in the legislature. The danger of tyranny of the majority and the fact that the legislature may not anticipate all situations are arguments that even Waldron accepts. His only answer is an attempt to confine these arguments to the sidelines. I argue that such evasion is to ignore the real value of judicial review, supported by its spread around the globe. History tells us the importance of protecting these rights. The outcome related reasons unequivocally weigh in favour of judicial review.

---

[148] *Law and Disagreement* (n 28) 50.

[149] n 116, 247.

[150] n 42, 40 – 41.

[151] Strong protection of rights can be achieved even in the absence of a strong judicial review. See Darrow and Alston (n 1) 476 where the example of Norway, Sweden and Switzerland are discussed. See also n 13, 247.

[152] n 101, 477.

Conclusion

I have sought to answer in the negative the question I have considered. Judicial review does not impoverish political debate or reduce the scope of democratic dialogue. In the first part, I have demonstrated, on process related grounds, how judicial review might in fact be framed within a democratic construct so that it enriches, rather than impoverishes, the process. However, ultimately I conclude that the 'outcome related considerations' provide the strongest arguments in favour of judicial review. In this context, I argue that the overall value of judicial review lies in its ability to protect every individual, no matter how small his case, from the ignorance or excesses of the majority. In turn, rather than inhibiting debate, it creates it. As Bickel says 'virtually all decisions of the Supreme Court are the beginnings of conversations between the Court and the people and their representatives.'[153]

The above advantage is exemplified by the recent case law of the US Supreme Court concerning the detention of terrorists at Guantanamo Bay. Perhaps it is difficult to imagine individuals who have less voice politically and yet, the courts have repeatedly sought to find ways of protecting their rights.[154] In so doing, democratic dialogue has been enhanced:

> 'The political branches, consistent with their independent obligations to interpret and uphold the Constitution, can engage in a genuine debate about how best to preserve constitutional values while protecting the Nation from terrorism… ("[J]udicial insistence upon that consultation does not weaken our Nation's ability to deal with danger. To the contrary, that insistence strengthens the Nation's ability to determine—through democratic means—how best to do so").'[155]

---

[153] AM Bickel, *The Supreme Court and the Idea of Progress*, (1st edn. Yale University Press, New York 1978) 91.
[154] *Boumediene v Bush* 553 US (2008), *Rasul v Bush* 542 US 446 and *Hamdan v Rumsfeld* 548 US 557.
[155] *Boumediene* (*ibid.*) 69, quoting from *Hamdan* (*ibid.*) 636.

The Racial and Religious Hatred Act 2006 and Offensive Speech: Has the Sensitivity of the ECtHR Overly-Influenced UK law?

RAFFAELLA GUINANE[*]

> 'If all mankind minus one were of one opinion, and only one person were of the contrary opinion, mankind would be no more justified in silencing that one person than he, if he had the power, would be justified in silencing mankind.'[1]

Introduction

To what extent should legal protection be given to those whose opinions or beliefs are ridiculed or 'threatened'? Should the interests of those wishing to express their views, regardless of detriment to some other individual or group, be protected also? How are these conflicting rights and liberties to be balanced? The essence of these questions is to consider consequentialism versus deontology; liberalism versus communitarianism. Has Parliament's attempt to remedy what it sees as a lingering 'inequality' between various racial and religious groups been successful, and how has it been influenced by the jurisprudence of the ECtHR?

The purpose of this essay is to consider whether the Racial and Religious Hatred Act 2006 has destabilized the delicate balance between freedom of speech and religious sensibilities. The first part will outline arguments against the proposition that the legislation is 'overly sensitive' to those susceptible to 'offence' or vulnerable to attacks caused by 'hate' speech. The second part will examine the relevant European case-law and analyse the issue of whether there has been a lack of legal sensitivity toward those exercising their right to freedom of speech, and by extension the freedom to offend, considering the reasoning which has given rise to assertions that lack of judicial clarity has come dangerously close to creating a 'right not to be offended'.[2] The third

---

[*] Raffaella Guinane studied for an MA in Legal and Political Theory at UCL.

[1] JS Mill, *On Liberty* (2nd ed, Longmans, Green, Reader & Dyer; London 1863) 35.
[2] This argument, as put forth by Ian Cram, will be considered in more detail below.

part will offer a broad outline of the freedom of speech principles brought into play. In the final part, we will consider the impact and efficacy of this legislation in light of whether it constitutes 'over-sensitivity' to those who wish not to be offended or whether the argument that freedom of speech has been inherently restricted is over-emphasised.

1. Legislative sensitivity to 'offensiveness': a proportionate response to 9/11 and societal tensions?

In the wake of 9/11 and the London bombings in July 2005, Britain has become a hotbed of racial and religious tension so acute that it has been suggested that society is undergoing fragmentation along racial and religious lines.[3] Examples of recent racial and religious tension are exemplified by the Oldham riots, and the outcry at a controversial play depicting the Sikh community, *Behzti*. This tension is not limited to the domestic sphere however. In 2004, Dutch filmmaker Van Gogh was murdered for producing a film about the mistreatment of women in Islam, named *Submission*. An international wave of outcry by the Muslim community in 2006 followed from the publication of the 'Danish Cartoons' Embassies and churches were burned down in protest, resulting in the death of 16 people.[4]

Britain has a long history of ethnic diversity, protection for which was first codified in the Race Relations Act 1965 with the creation of the offence of 'incitement to racial hatred'.[5] There have since been numerous attempts to extend the offence to 'incitement to *religious* hatred': the Public Order Act 1986; the Criminal Justice and Public Order Bill 1994; the Religious Offences Bill 2000; the Anti-Terrorism, Crime and Security Act 2001; and more recently the Serious and Organised Crime Bill 2004. In the aftermath of the terrorist attacks by Al-Qaida, the British Muslim community became the target of acute

---

[3] K Malik, 'What should integration mean in Britain today?'
http://www.kenanmalik.com/debates/crick_jcwi.html (Last visited 29th October 2009).
[4] A Hill and A Asthana, 'Nigeria cartoon riots kill 16'
www.guardian.co.uk/world/2006/feb/19/muhammadcartoons.ameliahill (Last visited 29th October 2009).
[5] For a more detailed account of the history of the offence of 'Incitement to Racial Hatred' please see I Hare, 'Crosses, Crescents and Sacred Cows: Criminalising Incitement to Religious Hatred' [2006] *Public Law* 520-537; P Leopald, 'Incitement to Hatred- The History of a Controversial Criminal Offence' [1977] *Public Law* 389.

hostility. The Forum Against Islamophobia and Racism (FAIR) stated that the 'shifting focus of bigotry' post 9/11 exclusively targeted the Muslim community.[6] The European Union Monitoring Centre for Racism and Xenophobia commissioned a study which found that, 'a greater receptivity towards anti-Muslim and other xenophobic ideas and sentiments has, and may well continue to, become tolerated'.[7] In a speech to the Institute of Public Policy Research in 2004, the then Home Secretary David Blunkett set out the case for criminalisation of incitement to religious hatred, concluding: the 'arguments for this extension of the law have grown stronger since 2001'.[8]

Political Justifications for the Racial and Religious Hatred Act 2006
The Government's position was that the Racial and Religious Hatred Act pursued a legitimate aim and was a proportionate response to the problems faced by minority communities. Incitement to religious hatred, although not rife, is considered to be destructive and divisive, leading to mistrust, hostility and a breakdown in social cohesion.[9] The legislation was a consequentialist approach to tackling the problem: 'the end justifies the means'. The argument put forward by the Muslim Community was that existing legislation did not protect them from incitement to hatred. Their view was that they had been denied legal protection due to the fact that they could not be defined as a 'racial' group, whereas other minority groups such as Jews and Sikhs were covered by the Race Relations provisions[10]. Furthermore, that Anglicans were disproportionately favoured under the Blasphemy laws[11] only increased a sense of discrimination and victimisation.

---

[6] 'The Religious Offences Bill 2002- A Response', www.fairuk.org/docs/rof2002.pdf (Last visited 29th October 2009).
[7] Allen & Nielsen, *Summary Report on Islamophobia in the EU after 11th September 2001,* Vienna: European Monitoring Centre for Racism and Xenophobia, 2002, 43.
[8] 'New Challenges for Race Equality and Community Cohesion in the 21st Century' www.ippr.org/uploadedFiles/events/Blunkettspeech.pdf (Last visited 29th October 2009).
[9] Letter from Caroline Flint MP, Parliamentary Under Secretary of State for the Home Office (February 3, 2005) in response to the Joint Committee on Human Rights' Fourth Report, *First Progress Report* (2004-05 HL 26/HC 224).
[10] *Mandala v Dowell Lee* (1983) 1All ER 1062.
[11] As of the implementation of the Criminal Justice and Immigration Act 2008 on 8 May, the law of Blasphemy has now been abolished in the UK, see s79 of the Criminal Justice and Immigration Act 2008.

The underlying rationale

It is submitted that the rationale for the enactment of the Religious Hatred Act can be split into three distinct lines of argument: philosophical, legal, and political. The philosophical argument, that is, Mill's 'harm principle'[12] is the most persuasive of the three. Critical Race theorists such as Matsuda argue in favour of criminalising racist or 'hate' speech on the basis that it has been shown to cause psychological harm to those targeted and, furthermore, reinforces racist ideas in the minds of the majority. This, Matsuda argues, leads to an entrenchment of racist attitudes which spawn discriminatory or violent acts.[13] Barendt also concurs with this line of argument: 'In these circumstances, respect for human dignity perhaps legitimizes the proscription of racist speech, rather than amounting to an argument for its tolerance.'[14]

The legal argument holds less sway. Under the ECHR, the UK is under an obligation to ensure that the rights of citizens to freedom of thought, conscience and religion[15] are upheld, and is also obligated under the IPCCR to ensure that 'any advocacy of national, racial or religious hatred that constitutes incitement to discrimination, hostility or violence shall be prohibited by law.'[16] Hare comments that this justification is 'not persuasive'.[17]

The political argument necessarily draws upon the philosophical and legal justifications, with one added element. This Act served also as political currency in the face of dwindling popular support over the Iraq war, an assertion the Government would undoubtedly deny. This was indeed the perception in significant quarters, who voiced concern: 'this piece of legislation is driven by political motives to stem the haemorrhaging of Labour support amongst the Muslim community'.[18]

---

[12] n 1, 23: 'The only purpose for which power can be rightfully exercised over any member of a civilized community, against his will, is to prevent harm to others.'
[13] MJ Matsuda, *Words that wound: Critical Race Theory, Assaultive Speech and the First Amendment* (Westview Press, Boulder 1993).
[14] E Barendt, *Freedom of Speech* (Oxford University Press, Oxford 2005) 33.
[15] Article 9, ECHR.
[16] Article 20, United Nations International Covenant on Civil and Political Rights.
[17] n 5.
[18] Dr Ghayasuddin Siddiqui of the Muslim Parliament quoted in *'Racial and Religious Hatred Bill: Liberty's Briefing for Second Reading in the House of Commons'* June 2005.

Arguments against cries of 'over-sensitivity': a summary

For the reasons set out above, it may be argued that the new legislation is not entirely 'overly sensitive' to the wishes of people not to be offended. The Government's intention was to redress the imbalance of legal protection afforded to some groups rather than others. From the perspective of the Muslim community, the fact that they as a whole were being targeted as a result of the horrific acts of a minority of Islamic fundamentalists was openly discriminatory. The lack of legal protection for one group against this potentially damaging form of discrimination, in contrast with protection in various forms for others was unjust and untenable. The Government fully supported this proposition, which went through extensive stages of development and amendment at the behest of the House of Lords. As stated, the act is a consequentialist response: that in order to promote peace and tolerance within the wider community, 'democratic freedom sometimes requires the truncation of these rights....'[19] But has the truncation of this most fundamental right now gone too far? And what role does the EctHR have to play in this shift in politico-legal attitudes?

2. The judicial approach of the ECtHR: a conflict of philosophy?

It has been argued that European judicial reasoning concerning freedom of speech issues is distinctly 'under-theorised'.[20] As will be illustrated by analysis of the cases below, it is reasonable to infer that while the Court is entrusted to protect the 'liberalistic' ideal of 'freedom of speech', its methodology places it in a firmly in a consequentialist, communitarian realm.

In *Handyside v UK* the ECtHR held that freedom of speech was a *'fundamental* freedom of democratic society...[which extends] to ideas that offend, shock or disturb the State or any sector of the population.'[21] It is perplexing, then, that this broadmindedness seems to have escaped the Court (but not the Commission) in subsequent decisions involving conflicts between freedom of expression and religious beliefs, where the Court has demonstrated an increasingly

---

[19] Conor Gearty, 'Rethinking Civil Liberties in a Counter-Terrorism' *World Field Day Review* (2007).
[20] See I Hare (n 5); also Fenwick and Phillipson, *Media Freedom under the Human Rights Act* (Oxford University Press, Oxford 2006) 6.
[21] (1976) 1 EHRR 737, (emphasis added).

irrational reluctance to interfere with the decisions of Member States under the doctrine of the margin of appreciation.[22] The most obvious example of this *volte-face* in opinion is to be found in the case of *Otto-Preminger v Austria*.[23] The Court ruled that there had been no breach of Article 10 in the seizure and forfeiture by the State of a film which denigrated Christ, the Virgin Mary, and the Eucharist.[24] The most startling element of the judgment asserted that those who claim a right under Article 10 are under,

> 'an obligation to avoid as far as possible expressions that are gratuitously offensive to others and thus an *infringement of their rights* and which therefore do not contribute to any form of debate capable of furthering progress in human affairs...'[25]

This is an incredible statement, both for its assertion and lack of reasoning, but fortunately it was not without criticism. In an ardent joint dissenting judgement, Judges Palm, Pekkanen and Makarczyk opposed the ruling thus: 'there is no point guaranteeing this freedom only as long as it is used in accordance with accepted opinion'.[26] In barely-contained indignation, Fenwick and Phillipson contend that the fallacious reasoning of the Court descended into 'downright intellectual dishonesty'.[27]

It is this passage which provides the basis for examination as to whether the ruling in *Otto Preminger* gives rise to a free-standing 'right' not to be offended. If this is the case, it follows that the scope left in respect of criminalising the dissemination of racially or religiously offensive material (the ECtHR being the impetus for the legislative action of the UK) is indeed 'overly sensitive' in favour of those wishing not to be offended. Any implications arising from the right to freedom

---

[22] For further discussion on the subject of the impact of the margin of appreciation on this area of the jurisprudence of the ECtHR, see I Cram 'The Danish Cartoons, Offensive Expression and Democratic Legitimacy' in I Hare and J Weinstein (eds.), *Extreme Speech and Democracy* (Oxford University Press, Oxford 2009).

[23] (1994) 19 EHRR 34.

[24] The Commission, on the other hand, found a breach of Article 10 in a forcefully worded argument for artistic licence: 'A complete prohibition...must be seen as a disproportionate measure, except where there are very stringent reasons...' No. 13470/87 (1993).

[25] n 23, 49 (emphasis added).

[26] *Ibid.*, 61.

[27] n 20, 493.

of speech are hardly touched upon, which is clearly contrary to the emphasis placed on it in *Handyside*.

In *Wingrove v UK*,[28] the issue in dispute was the BBFC's refusal to classify the video, 'Visions of Ecstasy'[29] which had the consequence that the film could not be lawfully distributed in the UK. This amounted to a prior restraint, but the Court was not persuaded that the State had overstepped its margin of appreciation, and did not accept argument that the State's action had been 'unreasonable'. Therefore, there could be no breach of Article 10. In weighing up the countervailing interests contained within Article 10(1) and (2), Judge Pettiti expressed concern at the 'difficult balancing exercise that has to be carried out...where religious sensibilities are confronted by freedom of expression...' The immediate problem posed by the use of the phrase 'balancing exercise' is one of distortion of the nature of the right to freedom of speech. Even with the qualifications prescribed in Article 10(2) (Barendt argues that on a superficial reading the qualification more or less negates the offence altogether),[30] there is a presumption that where a right and a *civil liberty* are in conflict, there is a presumption in favour of the right, which will take precedence unless the following can be shown:

- That the restriction is prescribed by law; and
- That such restriction is *necessary in a democratic society*.

Furthermore, the ECtHR has refined these conditions so that 'necessary' is defined as:

- A 'pressing social need';
- Proportionate to the aim pursued; and
- For 'relevant and sufficient' reasons.[31]

The approach taken in *Wingrove*, once again contrary to that of the Commission, could reasonably be seen as adding further weight to

---

[28] (1997) 24 EHRR 1.
[29] The film depicted Christ featuring in the fictional erotic fantasies of a 16th century nun.
[30] n 14, 65.
[31] *Sunday Times v UK* (1979) 2 EHRR 254, 270.

the possibility that a 'right' not to be offended on the basis of religion was emerging from the ECtHR. The Court was certainly treading on dangerous ground. *Otto Preminger* implied that the 'rights of others' in Article 10(2) was brought into play by reference to the 'religious freedom' afforded by Article 9. As well as eroding the reach of Article 10, this reasoning was unsound, something which was recognised by Judge Pettiti in *Wingrove* when he declared that Article 9 was 'not in issue'. If these cases *did* confer a right not to be offended then the analysis that Article 10 would be the relevant vehicle must be correct.

These cases showed a Court teetering on the edge of absurdity, and further conflation of these two fundamental Convention principles would have been disastrous. The differences between the Court and the Commission, the latter expressly denying a 'right' of protection from religious offence in *Choudhury*[32] only served to confuse matters further. One theory for the inconsistency in the Court's approach is that a lack of consensus amongst Member States in respect of moral principles necessitates that a wider margin of appreciation be given.[33]

This author would argue that this represents a deeper conflict of ideology: communitarianism prevailing over individualism; consequentialism over deontology. This argument can be supported by the stance taken by the court in respect of 'gratuitous offence'[34]. In the cases cited above, The Court plainly took the view that this category of speech was undeserving of protection under Article 10. In *Norwood v UK*[35] the Court held that "such a...vehement attack...is incompatible with the values proclaimed and guaranteed by the convention", and by virtue of Article 17 found Norwood's application under Article 10 to be inadmissible. This standpoint was consolidated recently in *IA v Turkey*[36] where the Court stated that there was a 'duty on speakers to avoid expressions that are gratuitously offensive'. This position has the result that the ECtHR, by affording protection of speech according to content, has become the arbiter on European 'taste and decency', a role

---

[32] *Choudhury v UK* (1991) No 17349/1990.
[33] See E Benventisti, 'Margin of Appreciation, Consensus and Universal Standards' (1999) 31 *New York University Journal of International Law & Politics* 843.
[34] For more detailed consideration on the merits of 'gratuitous offence', see I Cram, *Contested Words: Legal Restrictions on Freedom of Speech in Liberal Democracies* (Ashgate, Farnham 2002).
[35] (2004) 40 EHRR SE 111.
[36] (2007) 45 EHRR 30.

which it shied away from in earlier cases with the justification that Member States were better placed to decide this issue. This is a most undesirable state of affairs, and gives rise to the very real possibility that in following this approach, Member States may seek to further restrict other categories of speech. Robert Post argues that 'the cost to public discourse may be high'.[37]

It is clear beyond doubt that the Court has indeed taken a favourable stance toward those who wish to avoid being offended, at great cost to free speech principles, and by extension those who wish to be 'offensive'. We will consider below what impact this has had on the UK's attitudes to criminalisation of racially or religiously offensive material.

3. The Free Speech Principle

> "'Freedom of expression is a liberal puzzle"...it is prized by liberals for reasons they may not understand.'[38]

Philosophical opinion on the nature of freedom of speech as a basic human right is starkly divided. While there are those who would suggest that the discovery of truth holds the highest social value, there are other voices who argue that freedom of speech is a 'universal human right...constitutive of [democracy].'[39] It can be said that   judicial interpretation on the subject shows similar division as to the conceptual nature of speech and subsequently tension between philosophical and statutory considerations. The case-law that emerges makes it difficult to say with any certainty why certain jurisdictions take an individualist, absolutist view, such as America, and why others prefer a more deontological approach. This lack of coherence makes it more challenging to understand judicial perspectives behind the balancing exercise the State and the ECtHR must necessarily strike in the interests of fairness, respect and equality which are essential to promote a harmonious democracy.

---

[37] See 'The Constitutional Concept of Public Discourse: Outrageous Opinion, Democratic Deliberation and *Hustler Magazine v Falwell*' (1990) 103 *Harvard Law Review* 605.
[38] J Raz, 'Free Speech Expression and Personal Identification' (1991) 11 *Oxford Journal of Legal Studies* 303.
[39] See Dworkin's Foreword in I Hare and J Weinstein (n 22).

The Argument from Autonomy
This major theory of free speech sees speech as an integral part of autonomous self-development. There is a similarity with the argument from truth in that the concept of autonomy may be of fundamental benefit to the individual, or that its exercise may lead to similar positive development in others, thereby benefiting society as a whole. This theory, which is forcefully argued by Dworkin[40] and from the perspective of moral autonomy, Scanlon,[41] has deontological roots. Barendt argues that it is reasonable to pose the question of, 'why is freedom of speech particularly important to individual autonomy'? 'It is far from clear that unlimited free speech is necessarily conducive to personal happiness...unless some reasons can be given for treating expression as particularly significant...[it] becomes hard to distinguish from general libertarian claims.' There is force in this argument in that it requires extra qualification if it is to be the justification for a basic human right to freedom of speech. Rawls argues that a consequentialist justification is not necessarily more desirable however: 'To be sure, in any kind of well-ordered society the strength of the sense of social justice will not be the same in all social groups...it is characteristic of the morality of authority when conceived as a morality for the social order as a whole to demand self-sacrifice for the sake of a higher good and to deprecate the worth of the individual.'[42] It is perhaps necessary to combine elements of both the consequentialist and the deontological to come to a morally acceptable balance between freedom of speech and countervailing interests.

The Argument from Truth
This orthodox free speech theory posits that robust debate and argument enables us to come to the 'truth' of any given subject. Cram argues that this promotes a more knowledgeable society: 'The discovery of truth adds to knowledge and the more knowledgeable society is surely better off than the less knowledgeable.'[43] This is argument has roots in the Millian concept of truth: that truth in itself is a valuable

---

[40] R Dworkin *The Coming Battles over Free Speech* (1992) New York Review of Books
[41] T Scanlon 'A Theory of Freedom of Expression' (1972) 1 *Philosophy and Public Affairs* 204.
[42] J Rawls, *A Theory of Justice* (Harvard University Press, Cambridge 2005) 500.
[43] I Cram, 'Minors' Privacy, Free Speech and the Courts' (1997) *Public Law* 410.

fundamental, or that its value can be derived from its impact on the positive development on society.   But is this sufficient justification towards the fundamental importance of free speech as a whole? The Millian argument is flawed in that it assumes that robust debate will necessarily lead to the discovery of the truth.   The true fallacy of this theory is that of the assumption that publication of truth is necessarily in the best interests of society. However, this argument is not without redeeming features: extending the reasoning brings us to the theory of a 'marketplace of ideas'.[44]

The Argument from Democracy

This could be deemed as the most fashionable[45] or even most prevalent free speech theory in Western jurisdictions. It is a simple one: individuals must have a reasonable understanding of political issues to fully participate in a democracy. There are two forms of this argument, consequentialist and constitutional. The problem with the assertion that democracy underpins freedom of speech, is that it cannot apply where a democracy chooses to limit one form of speech or another. Dworkin's alternative form of a constitutional concept, is that every individual has an entitlement to participation in democracy which is so fundamental that it 'cannot be surrendered to the powers of the elected majority.'[46] This theory echoes this work's opening quote.

It is submitted that these theories on free speech, while being unable provide a consensus, provide powerful argument not just for its fundamental value but also justification against arbitrary restriction. It is these arguments the UK courts and Parliament have borne in mind with regard to the creation of the Racial and Religious Hatred Act 2006.

4. Criminalisation of racially and religiously offensive material: insufficient sensitivity towards free speech principles?

> '...Linguistic expression serves a dual communicative function: it conveys not only ideas capable of relatively precise, detached

---

[44] *Abrams v US* 250 US 616 (1919).
[45] n 13, 18.
[46] R Dworkin, *The Philosophy of Law* (Oxford University Press, Oxford 1977) 15.

explication, but otherwise inexpressible emotions as well...words are chosen as much for their emotive as their cognitive force...'[47]

It is for precisely this reason that 'speech' is so difficult to interpret from a legalistic point of view. What offends one person will not offend another, and how is the court to be the objective arbiter on offence in such a diverse society? Lord Steyn said in *Alconbury*[48] that the UK courts should follow any 'clear and constant jurisprudence of the ECtHR'. As argued above, it is evident that there is neither a 'clear' nor 'constant' rational to be derived from Strasbourg.

What is clear, however, is that the scope left by the ECtHR in respect of the UK's criminalisation of religiously offensive material is so overly sensitive that it gives rise to a 'quasi-right' to protection of offence against religious sensibilities. While there has been deep anxiety in the UK that the new offence will encroach upon (or even erode) free speech principles, it is submitted that this fear is unwarranted when the legislation is properly analysed. However, it is not evident that the UK Parliament or Courts have blindly followed European influence. In terms of the abolition of Blasphemy, it is clear that European approval, despite obvious incompatibility with the convention, exacerbated the procrastination of the UK government. In relation to free speech and religious sensibilities however, the UK has sought to take a more considered approach than can be said of Strasbourg.

Fenwick and Phillipson argue convincingly that the aim of the Act is not to prevent offence being given, but 'to prevent hatred being stirred up against those who subscribe to the belief.'[49] Therefore, offence is irrelevant; it is the act of the non-believer that the law is seeking to regulate. Lord Falconer expressed the government's view that the legislation 'is not about beliefs'.[50] The abolition of Blasphemy law shows governmental motive to be well-intentioned towards achieving a balance of interests. Previous case law under blasphemy law could be said to be restrictive of free speech.[51] As of the attempted

---

[47] *Cohen v California* 403 US 15 (1971).
[48] R *(on the application of Alconbury Development Ltd) v Secretary of State for the Environment, Transport and the Regions* [2003] 2 AC 295
[49] *Ibid.*, 517
[50] HL Deb col 163 (11 Oct 2005).
[51] See *R v Lemon* [1979] AC 617.

prosecution in relation to *Jerry Springer the Opera*, this could not be said to be the case. The courts have also used public order legislation in order to penalise hate speech by those in the minority.[52]

Hare argues, however, that this is irrelevant: 'The UK already has ample general criminal law provisions to deal with incitement to hatred and any public order consequences which may follow from it and therefore has no need of further restrictions which are certain to make us less free and are likely to prove counter-productive'.[53] This author would concur with this view, especially in light of the worrying counter terrorism legislation which has had a great impact on the right to protest freely, and other restrictive measures which also have free speech implications, such as a compulsory police register of musical and live events.

Section 29 B(1) of the Act provides:

> 'A person who uses threatening words or behaviour, or displays any written material which is threatening, is guilty if an offence if he intends thereby to stir up religious hatred.'

This is significantly narrower that the offences of the OAPA 1861 due to the amendment by the Lords:

> 'Nothing in this part shall be read or given effect in a way which prohibits or restricts discussion, criticism or expressions of antipathy, dislike, ridicule, insult or abuse of particular religions or the beliefs or practices of their adherents, or of any other belief system or the beliefs of its adherents, or proselytising or urging adherents of a different religion or belief system to cease practising their religion or belief system.'

This provision appears to narrow the scope of the offence so far as to make it almost completely ineffectual. It cannot be said that the UK Parliament's intention for this Act was to render free speech principles unimportant. Instead, it indicates a clear desire to attempt to balance what may be deemed as impossible to balance.

---

[52] *R v Abu Hamza* [2006] EWCA Crim 2918.
[53] n 5.

Legislative intention aside, there are still worrying implications that arise in respect of the encroachment upon free speech. These implications are totally dependent on judicial interpretation: a highly subjective and labile beast.

> 'If government proscribes hate speech, or other speech of which is disapproves, it takes sides on issues of controversy and so abandons the neutrality it must show if it is to honour equality...to all members of the community...but the argument does not mean that hate speech laws are necessarily incompatible with freedom of speech; it means that the courts should interpret and apply them with regard for the values of free speech and not allow them to be abused. Hate speech laws only lead to the suppression of radical political speech if the courts allow that to happen.'[54]

Conclusion

The UK has been cautious to strike a legal (and arguably moral) balance between the offensive and the offended. This has been successful in as far as it assuages the inequality felt by minorities without overly restricting the free speech rights of the majority. That said, there are still major free speech issues which will only be addressed once there is any case law on the subject. The decisions of the ECtHR can often be the catalyst which sways general UK jurisprudence, but they are by no means always the decisive factor. The European institutions themselves are sometimes deeply conflicted, often with the Commission and the Court airing their dirty linen in public. While this could indicate structural and ideological disharmony in Europe, it is also indicative of how arduous it is to interpret and give effect to this area of the law in a way which is not just fashionable or morally acceptable, but legitimate. Ideas and beliefs may be deeply held, but their very nature dictates that they are unequal. In the current political climate, the problems posed by cultural and religious diversity and concepts of 'what is offensive' threaten to tear the very fabric of British society. The debate as to whether the act is too sensitive to one side or another is largely trumped by the fact that it is practicably unworkable. The UK has taken a more measured approach than Strasbourg to the problems posed by this question. However, the question of whether this approach will be

---

[54] n 14, 161

exploited by the prevailing political wind is a very real possibility, and one which must be reconsidered urgently if that situation arises.

Pornography as Protected Speech?
The Margins of Constitutional Protection

HIN-YAN LIU[*]

Introduction

The regulation of pornography is a particularly problematic area of freedom of speech law and its complexities are highlighted by the widely varying approaches adopted in different jurisdictions. The initial question of whether sexually explicit material can be considered as speech will be addressed in a theoretical context. Then, the focus will move to the theoretically justifiable boundaries of the protection within the spectrum of sexually explicit material, with emphasis upon the distinction between pornography and obscenity. Finally, assuming that such material is protected by constitutional speech clauses, justifications for limited protection will be explored with reference to specific and potential harms. These theoretical intricacies will be analysed through the jurisprudence from the United States, Canada, and the European Court of Human Rights (ECtHR), which represent the application of different theoretical positions. The relative strengths and weaknesses of these positions will then be considered with a view to forming a more coherent policy for the regulation of sexually explicit material.

Pornography as Speech

A broad, single-tier conception of speech would deny any difficulty in finding that sexually explicit material is protected by constitutional free speech provisions which cover all forms of representation.[1] The ECtHR has a broad conception of the freedom of expression, as shown in *Handyside v UK*[2] where Article 10 'is applicable not only to "information" or "ideas" that are favourably received...but also those

---

[*] PhD Candidate, King's College London and Visiting Lecturer, University of Westminster. This piece was written for the LLM at UCL Laws.

[1] E Barendt, *Freedom of Speech* (2nd ed. Oxford University Press, Oxford 2007) 355.
[2] [1979-80] 1 EHRR 737.

that offend, shock, or disturb the State or any sector of the population.'[3] The Court held that blasphemous pornography was included within Article 10 in *Wingrove v UK*,[4] but granted a wide margin of appreciation to the UK, accepting that the restrictions were justified under Article 10(2).[5]

Similarly, the Supreme Court of Canada has consistently held that s2(b) of the Charter of Fundamental Rights and Freedoms 1982 encompasses all forms of expression, and as a result, all limitations have to be justified under s1 and satisfy the three limbs of the test in *R v Oakes*.[6] This breadth is best illuminated by the inclusion of obscenity in *R v Butler*[7] and hate speech, per *R v Keegstra*,[8] within Charter protection; areas that are held to be outside the scope of constitutional protection in other jurisdictions. The parallel US cases of *Miller v California*[9] and *Chaplinsky v New Hampshire*,[10] for these categories respectively, show the two-tier system of the First Amendment excluding these categories from constitutional protection. Murphy J, for a unanimous Supreme Court in the latter case, said that 'there are certain well-defined and narrowly-limited classes of speech, the prevention and punishment of which have never been thought to raise a constitutional problem. These include the lewd and obscene.'[11]

The initial categorisation of expressive material in jurisdictions adhering to the two-tier system is therefore of utmost importance as it determines the limits of constitutional safeguards. An analysis of First Amendment jurisprudence of this distinction highlights the extreme difficulties in establishing a clear and coherent boundary for the exclusion of obscenity and suggests that this position is untenable.

The original common law test for obscenity which set it off as a separate and distinct category excluded from protection was originally

---

[3] *Ibid.*, para [48].

[4] [1997] 24 EHRR 1.

[5] C Ovey and R White, *Jacobs & White: The European Convention on Human Rights* (4th ed. Oxford University Press, New York 2006) 332-333.

[6] [1986] 1 SCR 103.

[7] [1992] 1 SCR 452.

[8] [1990] 3 SCR 697.

[9] [1973] 413 US 15.

[10] [1942] 315 US 568.

[11] *Ibid.*, 572-573.

formulated in the United Kingdom by Cockburn CJ in *R v Hicklin*,[12] but this was superceded by *Roth v US*.[13] In that case, Brennan J approvingly cited Murphy J, above, and held that obscenity was outside the ambit of the First Amendment.[14] However, in *Paris Adult Theatre v Slaton*,[15] he abandoned this position in dissent (joined by Stewart and Marshall JJ) saying that the First Amendment 'prohibit[s] the State and Federal Governments from attempting wholly to suppress sexually orientated materials on the basis of their allegedly "obscene" contents.'[16] This conclusion is due to his opinion that 'no one definition, no matter how precisely or narrowly drawn, can possibly suffice for all situations...without also creating a substantial risk of encroachment upon the guarantees of the...First Amendment.'[17]

In *Miller*, the companion and leading case to *Paris*, Burger CJ for a five-judge majority stated the definitive test, reaffirmed *Roth* and excluded obscenity from constitutional protection as a matter of law. All the limbs of the tripartite test must be passed for material to be classified as obscene: whether the average person, applying contemporary community standards, would find that the work, taken as a whole, appeals to the prurient interest; whether the work depicts or describes, in a patently offensive way, sexual conduct or excretory functions specifically defined by applicable state law; and whether the work, taken as a whole, lacks serious literary, artistic, political, or scientific value.[18] Dissenting, Douglas J noted the failed attempts at defining obscenity and the difficulty of its application, concluding that the Supreme Court had written these standards into the Constitution itself as it is neither explicitly in the text, or implied by it.[19]

In the US, the exclusion of obscenity from First Amendment protection is still good law, albeit one on increasingly infirm theoretical ground. It must be remembered that 'sex and obscenity are not synonymous. Obscene material is material which deals with sex in a

---

[12] [1868] LR 3 QB 360, 371.
[13] [1957] 354 US 476, 487.
[14] *Ibid.,* 485.
[15] [1973] 413 US 49.
[16] *Ibid.,* 113.
[17] *Ibid.,* 84.
[18] n 9, 24.
[19] *Ibid.,* 38-40.

manner appealing to prurient interest,'[20] and constitutional protection will be extended to pornography which does not reach that threshold.

The more fundamental question of whether such material should be considered as speech has to be addressed, since *prima facie*, sexually explicit materials do not serve the purposes which merit the high levels of protection extended to the freedom of speech.

There are difficulties in applying Mill's truth argument to sexually explicit material as it is hard to see how it can reveal or reaffirm a claim to truth when its portrayal is essentially non-cognitive.[21] This presumption can, however, be challenged by the medical use of such material, which is safeguarded in Canada, since a communicative function of useful information can be implied; a message is capable of being understood by a proportion of the recipients and such material is protected under Charter s2(b). The third limb of the *Miller* test, used to distinguish obscenity from other material, provides for the defence of 'serious literary, artistic, political or scientific value'[22] which further supports the idea that such depictions are potentially relevant for the furtherance of truth and human knowledge. It is arguable that the communicative capacity of these materials at least partially provides the basis for its legal status as protected speech due to its contribution to the search and defence of truth.

The legal threshold for constitutional protection does not depend upon the speech being cognitive in nature as shown in *Cohen v California*,[23] where a profane slogan was found to be within the First Amendment. If such an emotive explicative which has no claim to truth is protected, it is difficult to justifiably exclude pornography.[24] Similarly, that serious literary and artistic work is covered alongside truth-orientated justifications under the last limb of the *Miller* test supports the wider ambit of legal speech. The ambiguous concept of obscenity in the two-tiered system potentially creates a 'chilling effect' upon serious works of literature or art. The Williams Committee,[25] conceded

---

[20] n 13, 487.
[21] n 1, 356.
[22] n 9, 24.
[23] [1971] 403 US 15.
[24] n 1, 357.
[25] Report of the Committee on Obscenity and Film Censorship. (1979) Cmnd 7772, paras [5.15]-[5.25].

difficulties in applying the truth argument to pornography, but in face of the likelihood that serious literature would be caught by obscenity laws in the UK, concluded in favour of a presumption for free speech.[26]

The further distinction between written and pictorial material in the obscenity context is best illustrated by *Kaplan v California*,[27] where Burger CJ held that written material occupied 'a preferred place in our hierarchy of values' due to the importance of protecting the communication of ideas.[28] Whilst this decision is laudable for its presumptive exclusion of literary work from the ambit of obscenity, the distinction drawn between different media of expression is arguably incoherent and threatens pictorial or other forms of expression disproportionately. An arguably better position is adopted by Sopinka J in *Butler* where first the premise that physical activity cannot be expression is rejected, and secondly that the creator of a film, through the act of choosing the images, is attempting to communicate meaning.[29]

Post-modern art provides the best challenge to this division.[30] The movement redefined the very concept of art, rejecting the requirements of seriousness and value, which further challenged the *Miller* decision.[31] These artists even attacked the idea that there is a distinction between art and obscenity, creating expressive works likely to be legally within the latter category, potentially creating an incalculable chilling effect.[32] Adler concludes with a choice, 'either we protect art as a whole or we protect ourselves from obscenity. But we choose one at the sacrifice of the other. It is impossible to do both.'[33] Accordingly, a societal choice is made; in two-tier jurisdictions the law protects against obscenity, whereas single-tier systems prefer to err on the side of free speech.

---

[26] n 1, 357.
[27] [1973] 413 US 115.
[28] *Ibid.,* 119.
[29] n.. 7, para [74].
[30] A Adler, 'Post-Modern Art and the Death of Obscenity Law' (1989-1990) 99 *Yale Law Journal* 1359.
[31] *Ibid.,* 1362-1364.
[32] *Ibid.,* 1369-1375.
[33] *Ibid.,* 1359.

In addition to artistic expression, another self-expression argument needs to be explored - that of personal identification.[34] The contention is that public expression should be protected as it serves to validate ways of life, and conversely, that censorship insults and marginalises those lifestyles.[35] At first glance, these arguments appear not to be applicable in this context, but it is conceivable that explicit materials serve vulnerable minority group interests, such as those of the homosexual community. The Canadian *Little Sisters* [36] case can be applauded in this respect, since although the violation of Charter s2(b) was justified under s1, Binnie J found that explicit homosexual material is presumptively outside the ambit of obscenity per *Butler*.[37] The *Butler* test, in emphasising depictions of violence as the dominant criteria of obscenity, impliedly rejected the old conservative 'hierarchy of sexual value: straight sex good; queer sex bad,' resulting in a more enlightened obscenity law shown by a decrease in detention of non-violent queer sexual material at the border.[38] Indeed, insofar as homosexuality is a live or latent political issue in a jurisdiction, such material may be considered as political expression, providing further support for its inclusion within free speech protection clauses.

That pornography could qualify as a form of political expression is embodied in the feminist argument expounded by MacKinnon grounding prohibition upon its occasioning actual and severe harm. 'Pornography...is a political practice, a practice of power and powerless.' [39] In the *American Booksellers v Hudnut* [40] case, an Indianapolis ordinance based upon this account of pornography was challenged. Not only did Judge Easterbrook remark that '[a]ll of [pornography's] unhappy effects depend upon mental intermediation,'[41]

---

[34] J Raz, 'Free Expression and Personal Identification' (1991) 11 *Oxford Journal of Legal Studies* 303.

[35] *Ibid.,* 312-316.

[36] [2000] 2 SCR 1120.

[37] *Ibid.,* 1162.

[38] B Ryder, 'The *Little Sisters* Case, Administrative Censorship, and Obscenity Law' (2001) 39 *Osgoode Hall Law Journal* 207, 215.

[39] CA MacKinnon, 'Pornography, Civil Rights, and Speech' (1985) 20 *Harvard Civil Rights-Civil Liberties Law Review* 1, 21.

[40] [1985] 771 F.2d 323.

[41] *Ibid.,* 329.

which affirms the communicative element of such material,[42] but went on to say that 'Indianapolis seeks to prohibit certain speech because it believes this speech influences social relations and politics on a grand scale, that it controls attitudes at home and in the legislature.'[43] Mickelman rightly says that:

> 'Pornography is political expression in that it promulgates a certain view of women's natures and thus of women's appropriate relations and treatment in society; the Indianapolis ordinance is precisely designed to suppress that particular view by censoring pornography; therefore the Indianapolis ordinance is an instance of both the general social evil (governmental restrictions on political expression) and its particularly obnoxious manifestation (viewpoint-discriminatory suppression).'[44]

This political argument is narrow on these specific facts, but serves to highlight the difficulties encountered in excluding pornography from the legal ambit of speech. The reasons advanced for its regulation elevate its expression into the realm of political speech.

A robust defence that pornography should fall within constitutionally protected free speech clauses has thus been advanced based upon the application of free speech theories and in showing the ill-defined and incoherent nature of the two-tier system excluding obscenity. Schauer[45] meets these latter criticisms by saying that the initial inclusion of all speech would necessarily result in hierarchical categorisation which would weaken the protection of all speech essentially diluting constitutional protection, and moreover, that functional protection of speech for the lower categories would be the same as exclusion from protection altogether.'[46] Schauer addresses the obvious rebuttal of the creation of a chilling effect upon speech by drawing a distinction between constitutionally protected speech and that which falls outside its range, saying that 'unconstitutional chilling occurs only when the chilled material is itself material worth

---

[42] F Mickelman, 'Conceptions of Democracy in American Constitutional Argument: The Case of Pornography Regulation' (1988-1989) 56 *Tennessee Law Review* 300.
[43] n 39, 33.
[44] n 42, 302-303.
[45] F Schauer, 'Speech and "Speech"- Obscenity and "Obscenity": An Exercise in the Interpretation of Constitutional Language' (1978-1979) 67 *Georgetown Journal of Legal Ethics* 899.
[46] *Ibid.*, 907.

protecting.'[47] Burger CJ for the majority in *Miller*,[48] agreed with Brennan J dissenting in *Paris*[49] that '[t]he problem...is that one cannot say with certainty that material is obscene until at least five members of this Court, applying inevitably obscure standards, have pronounced it so.'[50] The uncertainty of the dividing boundary between speech and obscenity rebuts Schauer's defence, since the category of the chilled material cannot be determined until it risks prosecution, creating the chilling effect of potentially constitutionally protected material. Therefore, the case for *prima facie* single-tier inclusion is a strong one.

Restrictions on Pornography

The argument does not require the inclusion of all sexually explicit material within constitutional safeguards to ensure its adequate safeguard. Even if there are no good reasons for including such material within free speech clauses, it does not follow that censorship in this area should necessarily be applied; it simply means that protection of the material rests upon weaker justifications. Furthermore, initial inclusion within a protective provision does not necessarily prevent censorial incursions into such material, as most free speech clauses allow justifiable limitations. The underlying rationale is that free speech is not an absolute right, but is one which needs to be balanced against other interests and protected speech may still be justifiably limited according to the relevant test in the jurisdiction.

Article 10(2) of the ECHR emphasises the rights and duties associated with the exercise of free speech and allows limitations which are 'prescribed by law and...necessary in a democratic society' for the most exhaustive and expansive list of competing interests available under the Convention. The ECtHR application of this is exemplified by *Wingrove*[51] where no violation of Article 10 for the UK to refuse an application of certification for the film was found. In reaching this conclusion, the Court accepted that the restriction was prescribed by law based on the existence of blasphemy laws in the UK before moving on to the 'legitimate aim' limb. This test is one of strict liability, as it has

---

[47] *Ibid.*, 931.
[48] n 9, 28.
[49] n 15, 92.
[50] *Ibid.*, 92.
[51] [1997] 24 EHRR 1, paras [37]-[65].

to be 'in such a manner "as to be calculated (that is, bound, not intended) to outrage."'[52] and was unmoved despite even the accepted discriminatory nature of the prescribing law. [53] The final limb of 'necessity in a democratic society' was then considered. The ECtHR had 'consistently held that Contracting States enjoy a certain but not unlimited margin of appreciation' and that it is 'for the European Court to give a final ruling on the restriction's compatibility with the Convention...by assessing...whether the interference corresponded to a "pressing social need" and whether it was "proportionate to the legitimate aim pursued".'[54] The Court noted the hierarchical categories of speech which protected political and public interest speech the most (per *Lingens v Austria*)[55] whilst granting a wider margin of appreciation to speech which is 'liable to offend intimate personal convictions within the sphere of morals or, especially, religion.'[56]

Importantly, the Court stresses that this 'does not...exclude final European supervision,'[57] a concept which is elaborated upon in the earlier case of *Handyside*:

> '[T]he Court's supervision would generally prove illusory if it did no more than examine these decisions in isolation; it must view them in the light of the case as a whole, including the publication in question and the arguments and evidence adduced by the applicant in the domestic legal system and then at the international level.'[58]

A final safeguard on restrictions is found in Article 18 which states that limitations on Convention rights may only be used for the purpose for which they are provided.

A cynical view of this approach is that this is empty rhetoric masquerading as the effective judicial oversight of rights, and indeed recalls Schauer's claim that in practice, due to the hierarchical nature of speech protection in the single-tier system, the protection of speech is the same in effect as the level of protection afforded by two-tier

---

[52] *Ibid.,* para [48].
[53] *Ibid.,* para [50].
[54] *Ibid.,* para [53].
[55] [1986] 8 EHRR 103, para [42].
[56] n 4, para [58].
[57] *Ibid.,* para [58].
[58] n 2, para [50].

systems.[59] Single-tier protection may even be detrimental to speech protection due to its ability to legitimately proscribe speech in the process of balancing competing interests and in granting the wider margin of appreciation to Contracting Parties. The ECtHR is, however, an international court, and this supranational status limits its enforcement abilities. Granting a margin of appreciation to the High Contracting Parties is necessary, per *Handyside*: 'By reason of their direct and continuous contact with the vital forces of their countries, State authorities are...in a better position than the international judge.'[60] Moreover, the legitimacy of its rulings relies heavily upon the consent of its Member States, severely limiting its ability to intervene in areas such as expression where a strong European paradigm has not crystallised. Thus, although ECtHR case law is illustrative of the theoretical shortcomings of the single-tier system highlighted by Schauer, it cannot fairly be compared with the US Supreme Court position due to their different roles and statuses.

The Canadian jurisprudence is perhaps a better comparator to its neighbour than Europe. As mentioned above, all forms of expression are covered within Charter s2(b), and limitations must satisfy the reasonable limits clause in s1 as Charter rights are guaranteed. To demonstrate the application of s1, an analysis of the *Oakes*[61] test in *Butler*[62] will be conducted.

The two limbs of the *Oakes* test are that there must be a 'pressing and substantial objective,' and that the means must be 'proportional' - the latter limb dividing into three subcategories: the means must be 'rationally connected to the objective', there must be a 'minimal impairment of the rights,' and there must be 'proportionality between the infringement and objective.' Legally, it is a balance of probabilities test with the onus of proof resting upon the party seeking to apply the limitations and is therefore very similar to that applied by the ECtHR above.

Butler involved s163(8) of the Criminal Code which provides the definitive test for obscenity; the exploitation of sex is its dominant

---

[59] n 45.
[60] n 2, para [48].
[61] n 6.
[62] n 7.

characteristic and further, must be 'undue.'[63] Helper JA gave a dissenting judgment when the case was heard by Manitoba Court of Appeal[64], noting that the terminology of the provision 'left the criteria for the application of the standard to the judiciary. It is not the judicial function to define the material or actions which are to be proscribed by law' and the vagueness of this law would fail s1 scrutiny.[65] The Supreme Court went ahead to refine the obscenity test despite this challenge.

This 'undue' standard is unique in that it deals with material that Canadians would not tolerate others being exposed to, as opposed to simply what they would find intolerable.[66] Sopinka J for the majority, held that a determination of material that is 'undue' utilised the harm test, dividing pornography into three categories: 'explicit sex with violence; explicit sex without violence but which subjects people to treatment that is degrading or dehumanising; and explicit sex without violence that is neither degrading nor dehumanizing.'[67] A spectrum is thus created where the first category will almost always be 'undue', whereas the second category requires a substantial risk of harm, and the latter will only fall foul if children are involved in its production.

It was held that s163(8) violated the Charter s2(b), but since it imposed a reasonable limit and provided an intelligible standard, was saved by Charter s1.[68] Importantly, this overriding effect was not to be based upon moral objection but is rather upon the avoidance of harm and this crucial theoretical difference sets it apart from the jurisprudence of the ECtHR. The Canadian position is more coherent due to the high premium placed upon the protection of expression which should require the substantial societal detriment of harm to justify its limitation, but the supranational status of the ECtHR limits its ability to set such a high threshold due to other considerations and thus accepts a plethora of potential reasons for restriction. The Canadian position on the restriction of sexually explicit material is particularly commendable since it would draw obscenity restrictions in line with hate speech limitations, creating theoretical cohesion to the area.

---

[63] *Ibid.*, para [44].
[64] [1990] 60 CCC (3d) 219.
[65] *Ibid.*, 266.
[66] n 7, para [47].
[67] *Ibid.*, paras [49]-[54].
[68] *Ibid.*, paras [128]-[134].

Furthermore, its adoption would be feasible in two-tier systems since the test is essentially similar and would only require transference of the onus of proof to the party limiting to seek the restriction, creating a higher level of expression protection generally.

Gonthier J's concurring opinion in *Butler*, generally agreed with Sopinka J, but disagreed regarding morality as a limitation justification, since the 'avoidance of harm is but one instance of a fundamental conception of morality,' [69] making it subject to certain criteria. [70] Interestingly, he explicitly referred to the ECHR listing morality as a ground for restricting the freedom of expression for support. [71] He concluded that 'attitudinal changes certainly qualif[y] as a "fundamental conception of morality"...[which] is well grounded, since the harm takes the form of violations of the principles of human equality and dignity.' [72] This dilution of the strict harm criteria has a detrimental effect to expression protection as it allows for incidental effects of material to justify limitations. In other words, harm may be caused even if it is not regarded as harmful. This is reminiscent of MacKinnon's feminist argument for the proscription of pornography considered above; 'to the extent pornography succeeds in constructing social reality, it becomes invisible as harm. If we live in a world that pornography creates...the issue is not what the harm of pornography is, but how that harm is to become visible.' [73] This argument is extremely convenient in that the very act of refuting the necessary visibility of explicit harm negates the need for causation to be proven empirically, and indeed precludes the possibility of challenges against it.

The position of the majority in *Butler* is preferable to the minority view due to its firmer theoretical grounding and the coherence of its result with comparably justifiable limitations. The foundation upon avoidance of harm strikes fairer balance between the high premium placed upon speech with other serious societal concerns.

---

[69] *Ibid.*, para [165].
[70] *Ibid.*, paras [168]-[169].
[71] *Ibid.*, para [166].
[72] *Ibid.*, para [170].
[73] n 39, 20.

Justifications

The justifications provided for incursions into the realm of speech in the context of sexually explicit material must now be considered in terms of proportionality and breadth of coverage. One of the most problematic issues encountered with restricting pornography is that it amounts to a content-based restriction - especially intolerable due to its ability to suppress a particular perspective, and which the constitutional protection of speech was designed specifically to combat.[74] When this is coupled with the nebulous nature of obscenity, the incursion into expression is potentially extremely grave, resulting in a disproportionately large chilling effect which requires a high threshold of competing societal interests, such as actual and severe harm, to justify.

The problems of prior restraint also enter the area as shown by the *Little Sisters* case and where the import of explicit materials is otherwise restricted. Ryder notes that these are usually administrative decisions which are hidden and unaccountable with no judicial hearing involved, resulting in a drift towards censorship.[75] In *Freedman v Maryland*, 'the censor's business is to censor, there inheres the danger that he may well be less responsive than a court...to the constitutionally protected interests in free speech.'[76] This effect encourages high levels of self-censorship resulting in a disproportional chilling effect of material which is liable to fall foul to such restraints. The preferred position would be to allow judicial oversight of such restrictions, as the independence of courts insulate them from the undulating opinion of everyday politics. Moreover, since a definitive position on this issue need not be adopted permanently, but may gradually evolve to suit shifting societal norms, the oversight of the courts is favoured over administrative departments for the regulation of explicit material.

Despite this, judicial oversight has proved to be far from the panacea it promised to be. The most significant problems are that criminal sanctions can be imposed for offences related to the uncertain and potentially overbroad category of obscene material as Douglas J

---

[74] n 42.
[75] n 38, 220-222.
[76] [1965] 380 US 51, 57-58.

emphasised in his dissent in *Miller*.[77] According to general principles of criminal law, crimes must be both well-defined and foreseeable and that conviction can only follow if the presumption of innocence is overturned beyond reasonable doubt. Thus, the full implications of obscenity laws and their potential to be violative of fundamental criminal law principles has been understated both within the case law and by commentators in the area; these silencing laws arguably fail to satisfy the protective safeguards required before the force of the criminal law is applied. The legitimacy lent by the legal process further cloaks the severity of this stance. The adoption of a strong presumption in favour of speech protection where material is criminalised or otherwise restricted only on narrow and explicit grounds may aid the resolution of this legal inconsistency.

It is further submitted that any restrictions upon speech should be based upon empirically observable harm causally linked to the speech in question, analogous to the position adopted for restricting political speech in *Keegstra* and *Chaplinsky*, and that implied harm falls short of the standard since it cannot be evidentially refuted. Interestingly, MacKinnon cites recent (in 1985) experimental research linking pornography to measurable harm through attitudinal changes, and 'all pornography...acts...to diminish one's ability to distinguish sex from violence.'[78] It is conceivable that such implicit harm may therefore qualify as explicit harm and that scientific research has simply not managed to develop the relevant techniques to establish the empirical casual link. Despite this possibility, the requirement of explicit harm should be the benchmark for justifying restrictions to keep the threshold both at a high and consistent level to ensure that adequate protection of speech.

Oft ignored aspects of competing interests are ones in favour of expression protection, such as that of privacy. In *Stanley v Georgia*,[79] Marshall J, for a unanimous US Supreme Court, held that the First and Fourteenth Amendments prohibited the criminalisation of private possession of obscene material, '[f]or also fundamental is the right to be free, except in very limited circumstances, from unwanted

---

[77] n 9, 37.
[78] n 39, 52-55.
[79] [1969] 394 US 557.

governmental intrusions into one's privacy.'[80] The legal prohibition of the production and dissemination of such material would interfere disproportionately with this privacy right such that any restrictions should necessarily fall within the limited exclusions of this right as well as those of the First Amendment.

Conclusion

It is important to reemphasise that within the legal systems considered, sexually explicit material is generally covered within the constitutional conception of speech except where it satisfies the criteria which categorises it as obscene. The two disparate methods of restricting obscenity both have their problems and inconsistencies. That pornography is protected within speech provisions is of dubious value due to the unclear dividing line between protected pornography and excluded obscenity.

The two polar positions of total inclusion and total exclusion of protection for expression can be dismissed quickly - free speech has never been considered to be absolute, and the constitutional position adopted by the jurisdictions considered above created a strong presumptive protection of expression. Positioned on the spectrum between these extremes are the disparate solutions exemplified by the US on the one hand, and Canada and the ECHR on the other. The fundamental benchmark upon which to judge the success of these approaches is the desired strength of expression protection compared to the importance of other rights and interests.

The US two-tier approach can be seen to value the interests competing against free speech the most, which may explain the possibility of holding certain categories outside of the First Amendment altogether - the presumptive protection of speech is weak enough that competing interests may oust obscenity from the ambit of constitutional protection. This idea is supported by the vagueness of the *Miller* test which allows space for judicial manoeuverability and which results in a strong chilling effect. This is inconsistent with the high levels of speech protection afforded by the First Amendment in other areas such as the regulation of hate speech.

---

[80] *Ibid.*, 563.

The Canadian single-tier approach provides the highest level of expression protection through its initial inclusion of all forms of expressive material which puts the burden upon the party seeking the limitation to justify it. Thus, the presumption is that all speech is protected, and so the onus of proof rests upon the party seeking to set limits upon it to show otherwise; legitimate competing interests are required to satisfy the high threshold test of the speech in question producing demonstrable harm before entitling its curtailment. This combination thus requires very substantial justifications to be shown before the courts will allow a limitation of protected speech.

Occupying the middle ground is the European position. At first glance, Article 10 of the Convention appears to grant expression protection on a similar level to that of Canada as a result of its inclusion of all forms of expression. Subsection 2, however, allows for the longest list of legitimate competing interests of any of the Convention rights and substantially weakens the Article's protective abilities. Indeed, it appears feasible that a legitimate interest can be found for any limitation as these grounds are so expansive. It is questionable whether Article 10 provides greater substantial protection for pornographic materials than the First Amendment as a result. The application of the margin of appreciation doctrine complicates the position further as Member States are granted a wide margin in areas such as morality where there is no European consensus, so allows for greater latitude of measures restricting sexually explicit materials. This weak position is exacerbated by the supervisory nature of the ECtHR; it is not an appellate court and so can only ensure that the various issues are considered at the national level.

The constitutionally protected status of speech excludes it to a significant degree as an area where the people and politics can interfere. This creates a unique problem in the context of pornography, which is widely regarded as an issue of morality or decency which the state, influenced by the people, is allowed to dictate. This paper has subjected the legal solutions of various jurisdictions to the problems found in this intersection to scrutiny. There is unlikely to be a clear conclusion in favour of one or other perspective since law is informed by the culture of a society, and it is precisely this culture which determines the legitimacy of limiting factors upon the freedom of speech, regardless of the words in constitutional texts. It is likely that this cultural difference is what accounts for this spectrum of solutions, and if this is the case, there cannot be one preferable solution.

Is Positive Discrimination a 'Very Blunt Solution to a Complex Problem', and Does it Fight 'Unfairness with Unfairness'?

JACK SIMSON CAIRD[*]

Introduction

At the time of writing, two of the most populated democracies in the world, South Africa and India, are about to conduct general elections in which positive discrimination will play a remarkably large role. This above quotation questions the ability of positive discrimination to solve problems of inequality by describing it as 'blunt' and advances that it is unfair. My response locates arguments supporting each accusation, relates them to the example of positive discrimination in first chamber legislatures and tests them on the examples of India and South Africa. In this discussion, I advance that certain historical circumstances can justify the use of positive discrimination to secure representation for certain groups in the first chamber of a national legislature. This is not fighting unfairness with unfairness. On the contrary, the entrenched nature of the disadvantage caused by certain circumstances means that without positive discrimination those groups would be underrepresented. Therefore fairness dictates that this is acted upon. However, in the examples of India and South Africa, the 'blunt' description of positive discrimination has particular purchase, in fact such is the extent of the limitations and unintended consequences that their overall justification is thrown into doubt.

In part one, I consider the unfairness of positive discrimination policies in the first chamber of national legislatures. To do this I locate, expand and critique arguments suggesting that all positive discrimination policies are unfair. I focus on the argument most applicable to the example of positive discrimination I have selected: that such policies are unfair as they depart from criteria based on merit. I present arguments and reasoning in favour of such a departure in

[*] Jack studied for the LLM at UCL Laws in 2008-2009.

certain circumstances. Finally, I consider the example of India's policy of electoral reservations in the Lok Sabha and highlight arguments which support the fairness of its positive discrimination policies.

In part two, I examine the claim that positive discrimination policies in the first chamber of national legislatures are 'blunt'. I begin by describing the use of such policies in South Africa's National Assembly. Rather than examining the justificatory arguments surrounding the policy, the focus is on the criticism presented in the informed article by Vincent in order to respond to the 'blunt' description, which is directly addressed by her.[1] A number of her arguments are then applied and tested in the Indian context.

Despite the importance of context and the use of an interdisciplinary approach in this discussion, I must stress its limitations. I am neither qualified nor able to describe or compare the situations facing discriminated groups in the countries that I consider. However, the gravity and existence of such circumstances are a vital part of some of the arguments presented. Further, it must be noted that despite a desire to depart from the generality of the question's quotation, my choice of example raises a number of other issues, especially to do with democracy, that I am unable to give adequate focus. I refer to first chamber national legislatures as the example for comparative reasons, as India only has positive discrimination at a national level in the first chamber and not the second, whereas South Africa has it in both of its two chambers. I understand positive discrimination in the broader meaning of the term and I do not recognise distinctions in terms of gravity between it and affirmative action. In keeping with this, I offer Fredman's definition of affirmative action to illustrate my understanding of positive discrimination: affirmative action denotes the deliberate use of race or gender conscious criteria for the specific purpose of benefiting a group which has previously been disadvantaged on grounds of race or gender. Its aims range from providing a specific remedy for invidious discrimination to the more general purpose of increasing the participation of groups which are visibly under-represented in

---

[1] L Vincent, 'Quotas: Changing the way things look without changing the way things are' (2004) 71 *The Journal of Legislative Studies.*

important public spheres such as education, politics and employment. At its most controversial, it requires that individual members of the disadvantaged group be actively preferred over the allocation of jobs, university places and other similar benefits.[2]

This definition refers to the area of positive discrimination I have chosen to examine, politics, and points to the importance of historical circumstances, both of which gives me confidence in my approach to this discussion.

1. The Unfairness of Positive Discrimination Policies in the First Chambers of National Legislatures

A source of the 'unfairness' accusation is what Fredman describes as the 'symmetrical' approach to positive discrimination.[3] This view submits that the moral prohibition against using race or sex as a criteria applies with equal strength to measures designed to help disadvantaged groups.[4] Fredman locates three core beliefs behind this approach. Firstly, justice is viewed as an independent concept unaffected by context, which is unaltered by distributions of advantage and disadvantage in a society.[5] Secondly, support for individualism that encapsulates a strong belief in meritocracy, merit being objectively quantifiable and race or gender neutral.[6] Thirdly, a commitment to state neutrality, that a state should not favour some citizens over others.[7] Each of these three basic propositions needs to be challenged in order to argue that positive discrimination can be fair.

Another position identified by Fredman challenges positive discrimination and is known as the 'equal opportunities' approach.[8] In contrast to the symmetrical argument, it permits race or gender based policies on the condition that they are used to take individuals to equal starting points.[9] This position regards policies that correct imbalances in society through quotas, in other words equality of outcome or

---

[2] S Fredman, 'Reversing Discrimination' (1997) 113 *Law Quarterly Review* 575.
[3] *Ibid.*, 576.
[4] *Ibid.*
[5] *Ibid.*, 577.
[6] *Ibid.*
[7] *Ibid.*
[8] *Ibid.*, 579.
[9] *Ibid.*

proportionality policies, as unfair on the basis that they depart from considerations of individual qualities.[10] A proponent of this view, Morris Abram, offers insight into its cultural and political origins in his article: 'Affirmative Action: Fair Shakers and Social Engineers'.[11] Abram submits that the original civil rights movement, which arose in the United States of America between the mid-1940s and the mid-1960s was concerned with equality of opportunity.[12] I suggest his argument is bound to this specific context. Abram notes that he became involved in the movement in an attempt to remove the barriers to equality of opportunity and reveals that he associates attempts to enforce policies justified by historical circumstances with the very racist regime that he was attempting to defeat.[13] This could also explain the symmetrical approach's emphasis on state neutrality. Abram's argument shares with the symmetrical approach a strong support for meritocratic principles, a neutral state and a context free vision of justice.[14] For Abram, meritocracy acts as a trump over any claim for proportional representation, because in his view: 'uneven distribution, however, is not necessarily the result of discrimination'.[15] He outlines that the operation of meritocracy is a legitimate explanation for the discrepancy between the actual achievements and the opportunities available to previously discriminated groups, he illustrates this by the variable records of success of different ethnic groups in American society.[16] This approach is outdated, context bound and self-contradictory. Many of his arguments are intended to only apply to the American scenario, however it is important to emphasise their cultural and political origins to illustrate the difficulty of applying such arguments outside of their context. This difficulty weakens his and the symmetrical support for justice as a context neutral concept in so far as the difficulties in exporting their approach seems to contradict that belief. Further, it seems hypocritical for the equality of opportunity or symmetrical

---

[10] *Ibid.*
[11] M Abram, 'Affirmative Action: Fair Shakers and Social Engineers' (1985-6) 99 *Harvard Law Review* 1312.
[12] *Ibid.*
[13] *Ibid.*, 1314.
[14] *Ibid.*
[15] *Ibid.*, 1315-6.
[16] *Ibid.*

approaches to criticise positive discrimination measures of any type for taking account of circumstances when much of their own view seems informed by a particular context. It is difficult to understand why Abram would use evidence of different racial groups 'performance' to prove an argument which is based on a distrust of racial categorisation. Despite these reservations, the emphasis placed by both Abram and the symmetrical approach on positive discrimination's departure from meritocracy and the neutral state are clear challenges that need to be addressed.

Balkin and Siegel introduce the terminology of anticlassification and antisubordination to the debate on positive discrimination in their article: 'The American Civil Rights Tradition: Anticlassification or Antisubordination'. [17] The anticlassification principle is particularly useful for our analysis as it encompasses both the equality of opportunity and symmetry perspectives outlined above. Anticlassification opposes the use of group classification for the purpose of the distribution of goods and opportunities.[18] Balkin and Siegel's analysis breaks down the popular over simplistic narrative of the triumph of anticlassification over antisubordination in the American context.[19] They contest whether the anticlassification perspective can espouse an objective and determinate rule, which can be applied neutrally.[20] If the anticlassification principle is to be applied in reality, a number of decisions have to be made, as to how this will be achieved and in doing so which values, political or legal, will inform those decisions.[21] As they point out: 'the principle that social goods should not be distributed on the basis of group membership is not self-implementing'.[22] Further, they demonstrate that the principle has been applied in a number of different ways, using a number of different viewpoints including antisubordination itself, depending on the historical and factual context facing the American legal system.[23] This

---

[17] J Balkin and R Siegel, 'The American Civil Rights Tradition: Anticlassification or Antisubordination' (2003) 58 *University of Miami Law Review* 9.
[18] *Ibid.*, 15.
[19] *Ibid.*
[20] *Ibid.*
[21] *Ibid.*, 16.
[22] *Ibid.*, 15.
[23] *Ibid.*, 16.

observation has important consequences for two of the core arguments identified in support of the claim that positive discrimination is unfair. It shows that even when a state adopts an anticlassification perspective, it takes into account context specific factors, and in my view this prevents the state claiming it maintains either its own 'neutrality' or a context unaffected vision of justice. If this is the case then it makes it difficult to argue that positive discrimination policies are unfair as they depart from such principles. It appears that their own alternative fails to an extent in regard to those principles. However, arguments on such a practice's unfairness, on the basis of a departure from individual merit remain, at this stage, uncontested.

The charge that positive discrimination is unfair because it departs from meritocratic principles is the strongest and the most relevant argument for my example of the use of such policies in national legislatures. Bacchi notes that in a wide range of contexts the argument is made that affirmative action and electoral quotas in national parliaments bypass competitive processes and ignore the merit principle.[24] In response Bacchi submits that the nature of the task of political representation means that positive discrimination is more justifiable in this arena than for university professorships for example, as in political representation, gender or other group membership can be counted as a merit, given that representative political systems should reflect the views of a wide range of the population.[25] Bacchi also argues that the strength of the merit argument is related to an individual state's overall attitude to positive discrimination, as if positive discrimination polices are treated as exceptions to anti-discrimination law, then the meritocratic argument is likely to prevail and prevent the use of positive discrimination in the national legislature.[26] Phillips offers an alternative response to the meritocratic argument and presents a strong case in favour of the use of positive discrimination in national legislatures.[27] Phillips sees the distorted distribution of legislative seats as evidence of

---

[24] C Bacchi, 'Arguing for and Against Quotas: Theoretical Issues' in D Dahlerup (ed.), *Women, Quotas and Politics* (Routledge, London 2006) 33.

[25] *Ibid.*, 33-34.

[26] *Ibid.*, 34.

[27] A Phillips, 'Democracy and representation: or, why should it matter who our representative are?' in A Phillips (ed.), *Feminism and Politics* (Oxford University Press, Oxford 1998) 229.

intentional and structural discrimination, and submits that the gender parity in terms of population should be reflected in the political representation as a matter of justice and fairness.[28] Her emphasis on the unfairness caused by meritocratic criteria provides a strong case for intervention justified by fairness. Phillips emphasises that using such policies requires an historically specific analysis of representation together with the conditions of political inclusion in the political system in which they are going to apply.[29] On the issue of the historical conditions, Mansbridge outlines certain historical contexts that are likely to give rise to claims for descriptive representation and consequently presents a challenge to the group neutral meritocratic criteria for representation envisaged by the unfairness argument:

> 'In the contexts of group mistrust, uncrystallized interests, a history suggesting inability to rule, and low de facto legitimacy, constitutional designers and individual voters have reason to institute policies that promote descriptive representation, even when such implementation involves some losses in the implementation of other valued ideals.'[30]

All four contexts correspond to the following representative functions, in order: adequate communication, innovative thinking, creating a social meaning of 'ability to rule' and increasing the state's de facto legitimacy.[31] These functions illustrate the potential substantive benefits that can follow from descriptive representation. In turn, these functions demonstrate the positive consequences that can follow from the use of positive discrimination in national legislatures to secure descriptive representation for groups affected by the historical contexts referred to above. The nature of the role of a member of a national legislature makes it susceptible to arguments in favour of a departure from a strict criterion of merit, as group membership can be an influential attribute regardless of whether positive discrimination is used to ensure that it does. Despite this acknowledgment, it is still a radical step for a

---

[28] *Ibid.*

[29] A Phillips, *The Politics of Presence: The Political Representation of Gender, Ethnicity and Race* (Oxford University Press, Oxford 1995) 46.

[30] J Mansbridge, 'Should Blacks Represent Blacks and Women Represent Women? A Contingent "Yes"' (1999) 61 *The Journal of Politics* 628-9.

[31] *Ibid.*

democracy to restrict the candidates for a number of its most important legislative seats to members of a particular group.

Article 330 of the Indian Constitution secures seats in the Lok Sabha (House of the People) for Scheduled Caste (SCs) and Scheduled Tribes (STs) according to a percentage calculation of their population in each State or Union Territory.[32] As it sits today, 120 seats in the chamber, out of a total of 543 are reserved, 79 for SCs and 41 for STs.[33] On the 11th of March 2009, the Electoral Commission announced that the 15th Lok Sabha constituted on the 28th of May 2009, after the general election, will have 11 more reserved seats, raising the total to 131, which represents 24% of the total number of seats, 5 more for SCs and 6 more for STs respectively.[34] It is important to note that the reserved seats do not use separate electorates. As Galanter notes: 'the seats are "reserved" in the sense that candidates who stand for them must belong to the specified groups, but the entire electorate participates in choosing among candidates so qualified.'[35] The reservation of such a large number of the most important legislative seats in India is a bold step away from a group neutral meritocratic criteria and it is therefore unsurprising that the arguments supporting this and other positive discrimination policies are of an equally bold nature.

The Indian Constitution appears to confirm Bacchi's observation above, that a state is more likely to accept and acknowledge a departure from merit, through a policy such as that pursued in Article 330, and recognise the value of symbolic representation if its overall attitude to positive discrimination is not framed as an exception to anti-discrimination law. India is a pioneer, in respect of positive discrimination, as Dushkin notes: 'nowhere else is so large an underprivileged minority granted so much special treatment'.[36]

---

[32] The Constitution of India, Part XVI, Article 330, pages 200-201.
[33] Source: *The Hindu News* Update Service, available at http://www.hinduonnet.com/ (accessed on the March 12 2009).
[34] *Ibid.*
[35] M Galanter, 'Compensatory Discrimination in Political Representation' (1979) February *Economic and Political Weekly* 437-438.
[36] L Dushkin, 'The Backward Classes: Special Treatment Policy' (1961) 1661 *Economic Weekly* XIII 1667.

Mackinnon outlines India's position in relation to positive discrimination and antidiscrimination law:

> 'India's Article 15 (3) specifically suggests a substantive recognition of women's unequal social status by permitting special provisions to rectify their inequality. As a result, steps to end the hierarchy of men are not cast as violations of an equality rule that are nonetheless permitted. Rather, because such steps promote equality, they are not exceptions to an antidiscrimination rule; they are not discrimination at all.'[37]

This position is replicated in relation to caste. Within the equality articles 15 and 16, positive discrimination in favour of SCs and STs is expressly permitted. [38] On first reading, it may appear that the permissions are cast as exceptions, however, when read within the context of other constitutional provisions such as Article 46, which directs state policy to promote the interest of SCs and STs, it is clear that such measures are more than exceptions.[39]

Galanter offers three themes to explain the Indian justification for positive discrimination, which in turn offers important context specific arguments for Article 330. [40] The non-discrimination theme justifies positive discrimination by arguing that despite the use of legal provisions to remove invidious discrimination, subtle and yet powerful discrimination persists which prevents the realisation of the norm of equal treatment as guaranteed in the Constitution.[41] Therefore, group specific criteria is used to identify those individuals who need protection to ensure that their merit is given equal weight and this 'assures fairness to every applicant'.[42] Applying this argument to Article 330, I can relate this to Phillips's argument in favour of such measures on the basis of justice. Individuals from a traditionally under represented group deserve, as a matter of justice, to have a place

---

[37] C Mackinnon, 'Sex equality under the Constitution of India: Problems, prospects, and "personal laws"' (2006) 4 *International Journal of Constitutional Law* 189-190.
[38] The Indian Constitution, Part III, Fundamental Rights, Articles 15 and 16, pages 7-8.
[39] The Indian Constitution, Part IV, Directive Principles of State Policy, Article 46, page 23.
[40] M Galanter, 'The "Compensatory Discrimination" Theme In The Indian Commitment To Human Rights' (1986) 13 *India International Quarterly* 77-94.
[41] n 35, 83.
[42] *Ibid.*, 84.

reserved for them because otherwise they are likely to be discriminated against and excluded from the chamber. The general welfare theme conforms to the worst nightmares of Abram, it seeks to achieve social goals through positive discrimination and creates standards quite apart from personal desert for the roles to which it is applied.[43] This theme justifies positive discrimination in India by recognising that certain roles, such as in the Indian civil service, carry with them strong 'symbolic, representational and educational aspects'. [44] Such an understanding supports and reinforces Bacchi's recognition that for certain roles, including those guaranteed by Article 330, group membership could be considered as a merit. Alternatively, the general welfare theme could be said to demonstrate an appreciation of the transformative quality of membership of a national legislature, directly securing benefits for SCs and STs through the existence of Article 330. Vincent notes on this point:

> ... [I]n certain contexts, namely where there has been a history of discrimination and exclusion, it is important to shift perceptions both on the part of the members of the excluded group and on the part of the advantaged groups and having members of the disadvantaged group present in representative structures can help to do this.[45]

An understanding of the representative role and the arguments outlined by Galanter above provides a justification for the use of positive discrimination to guarantee representation of traditionally discriminated groups such as the SCs and STs in India.

The final theme and most important element of the justification of the policy contained in Article 330 is the reparations theme. Galanter views it as the most important, in the Indian context, as it underpins all other justifications of positive discrimination.[46] Galanter states:

> '... [T]his is a fairness argument, rather than a welfare argument. But it emphasises groups as the carriers of historic rights rather than as

---

[43] *Ibid.*

[44] *Ibid.*

[45] L Vincent, 'Quotas: Changing the way things look without changing the way things are' (2004) 71 *The Journal of Legislative Studies* 75.

[46] n 35, 77.

indicators of individual victimization. And it looks to a very different time frame. Welfare arguments are prospective; non-discrimination looks at the present situation and seeks to refine out lingering inequalities. The reparations theme sees the present as an occasion to reckon accounts for past injustice.'[47]

The reparations theme captures those historical contexts referred to by Mansbridge, the extent of their presence in the Indian context cannot be described here; Galanter's stress on this theme provides the necessary evidence for these purposes. India has embraced the attitude alluded to by Galanter in the above quotation. This proactive attitude is the driving force behind Article 330 and other provisions in the Constitution.[48]

Article 330 highlights that India appreciates that merit, in a group, race or gender neutral sense, will never be the sole criteria for the selection of representatives within the Lok Sabha. Hence to prevent the unfair effect of engrained disadvantage denying members of the SCs and STs the representation which their population would otherwise create, they have secured a fair level of representation for these groups. This course of action contradicts the question's quotation by fighting unfairness with a fair solution.

2. Positive Discrimination in First Chamber National Legislatures as 'Blunt'

In this part, I focus on criticisms of the use of positive discrimination policies in the first chamber of a national legislature which could give weight to the 'blunt' description. The example of South Africa provides evidence to indicate that using positive discrimination in this context can be ineffective to such an extent that the justificatory arguments in regard to such policies fairness are weakened.

The use of positive discrimination in South Africa's first chamber, the National Assembly, provides a strong contrast to India's Lok Sabha in both form and content, highlighting the diversity in this area. Rather than being within the Constitution, the relevant measures

---

[47] *Ibid.*, 85.
[48] For example see the abolition of untouchability contained in Article 17 of the Indian Constitution.

have been adopted within the internal structure of the overwhelmingly dominant political party: the African National Congress (ANC). [49] Before the first democratic elections in 1994, the ANC's National Executive Committee pushed through a quota requiring 30 per cent of elected positions to be reserved for women.[50] This has had the effect of steadily increasing the proportion of women in the National Assembly. In the last general election in 2004, the ANC secured 69 per cent of the vote for the National Assembly, giving the party 290 out of the total of 400 seats available.[51] The ANC's policy resulted in the house containing 132 female members, placing it seventeenth in the world ranking of percentage of women with 33 per cent. [52] In 2007, at the ANC conference in Polokwane, the party vowed to achieve 50 per cent gender parity across all structures where the ANC is represented.[53] With a general election due on the 22nd of April this year, there is a prospect of the ANC internal policy having even greater impact on the gender composition of the house. It should be noted that the nature of the South African election system for the National Assembly, proportional representation with closed lists, means that there is little doubt as to the outcome of the ANC's policy as voters cannot choose not to vote for women as they do not get a vote for individual candidates, only a party.

Louise Vincent presents a number of arguments against the use of quotas based on the South African experience, she notes: 'despite their much heralded success, and here South Africa is a case in point, quotas (electoral) are a blunt instrument'.[54] Vincent acknowledges the strength of the justice argument as advanced by Phillips, however, she does not believe that the answer to the problem is the type of positive discrimination used by the ANC, as she argues that positive discrimination in this form simply covers up the injustices that cause imbalances in representation rather than actually removing them. [55] Vincent does not suggest how the requisite change is to be achieved. A

---

[49] n 45, 75.
[50] *Ibid.*, 76.
[51] Source: Inter-Parliamentary Union website available at: http://www.ipu.org.
[52] *Ibid.*
[53] J Duarte, 'Burst-the-patriarchal-bubble' *Mail Guardian*, available at http://www.mg.co.za/ (accessed 25 March 2009).
[54] n 45, 71.
[55] *Ibid.*, 73.

similarly destructive criticism is made of the essentialist nature of such policies: 'not just with the fact that there are all kinds of women but with the fact that the kinds of women who tend to be present in political elites are frequently drawn from a narrow layer of women.' [56] Having argued that the nature of the role of membership of a first chamber of a national legislature meant that in certain contexts group membership could be counted as merit or could justify a departure from merit, it would be hard to maintain that position if it could be shown that the persons selected were not or could not be representative of the group they were selected from. Partly in contradiction to her support for the essentialist critique, Vincent actually supports the argument advanced by Mansbridge in favour of symbolic representation in the historical context of group mistrust, so as to improve the legitimacy of the group, however, in regard to the ANC's policy she finds a problem.[57] Vincent recognises that under apartheid there was a history of discrimination against women, only 15 women elected in 40 years, however, she emphasises that gender subordination is a secondary issue in relation to racial subordination.[58] The ANC, as the party of liberation, is able to dominate the candidate blind electoral system to such an extent that gender identity is afforded little opportunity to make its presence known to the voter.[59] In South Africa, the potential benefits of the positive discrimination policy are muted by a combination of the electoral system and one-party dominance which leaves the policy operating within a vacuum without popular support or the ability to effect change at a higher level.

Vincent acknowledges that many would argue that women have made great progress since independence, however, she disputes that quotas have been a causal factor behind any progress and the actual extent of the progress.[60] Vincent refers to a number of policy failures and although they cannot be analysed here, the arguments presented illustrate why the quotas have failed to achieve the desired effects and

---

[56] *Ibid.*
[57] *Ibid.*, 75.
[58] *Ibid.*
[59] *Ibid.*
[60] *Ibid.*, 85.

hence can be described as 'blunt'. [61] Firstly, Vincent questions the impact of the ANC's policy because it is not the result of a wider societal shift, but has its origins within a political party.[62] This raises two related features that can impact on the success of a policy of positive discrimination in the first chamber of the national legislature: the legal or political level it occurs and the extent of the consensus that leads to the policy being adopted. Secondly, Vincent bemoans the failure to enmesh the policy with other structural and institutional reforms and feels that this has dulled the impact of the quotas both for the female members of the National Assembly themselves and for the citizen. [63] Thirdly, Vincent notes that the presence of marginalized groups, under positive discrimination policies, can engender an attitude where legitimacy is not created through decision-making, but rather simply through presence.[64] Vincent notes that this can have the effect of marginalising the issues specific to the included group as it is felt that their problems are solved by their presence rather than policies. [65] Fourthly and most importantly, related to her essentialist critique, Vincent argues:

> 'The improved presence of women in South Africa's national legislature due to ANC's quota has done little more than advance the careers of a select group of already well educated, politically highly well connected women.'[66]

In Indian politics, this is known as the 'creamy layer' problem, and it represents a major element of the 'blunt' criticism, attacking the very fundamentals of a positive discrimination policy. If such a policy cannot provide representative individuals of the targeted group then it seems based on a flawed premise. The South African experience and Vincent's piercing critique has elaborated the 'blunt' argument in relation to positive discrimination polices in first chamber legislatures. Her arguments enable an attempt at comparison with the Indian experience

---

[61] n 45.
[62] *Ibid.*, 93.
[63] *Ibid.*, 94.
[64] *Ibid.*, 84.
[65] *Ibid.*
[66] *Ibid.*, 95.

and assessment of whether the problems and limitations challenge the justifications presented in part one.

The 'creamy layer' problem pervades all aspects of the extensive positive discrimination programme in India, the term refers to the tendency of reserved posts to go to a thin upper layer of the identified group in need of preferential treatment. Despite this, the situation in India and the Lok Sabha does not appear as straightforward as that described by Vincent in South Africa. McMillan notes that members who hold reserved seats in the Lok Sabha have distinctive backgrounds from those elected to general seats, being younger, less well-educated, having less parliamentary experience, more likely to be from an agricultural background and less likely to be from a professional background.[67] At the very least, this indicates that the reservations are guaranteeing the presence of individuals who are more similar to SCs and STs than the average MP. However, McMillan notes that these differences do not mean that the holders of reserved seats are actually representative of the SCs and STs population, in general, rather, they have been described by Guru as a 'bourgeoisiefied microscopic middle class'.[68] From this evidence, the symbolic representation argument is weakened by the practical problem of finding individuals capable of being truly representative of the identified discriminated group. However, the lack of success of SCs and STs candidates in non-reserved seats, Galanter notes in the first six Lok Sabhas there were only a handful of successes, puts this problem into perspective.[69] In the absence of regular electoral successes for SCs and STs candidates outside of reserved seats, positive discrimination in the Lok Sabha remains justified despite the creamy layer problem, as it is unlikely that group neutral criteria would provide more representative individuals.

Despite the issues surrounding their representativeness, the question that needs examination, is that which spawned so much of Vincent's critique; to what extent have members who have benefited from Article 330 been able to perform the role envisaged by advocates of such policies? Both Galanter and McMillan note that there is a

---

[67] A McMillan, *Standing at the Margins: Representation and Electoral Reservation in India* (Oxford University Press, Oxford 2005) 300.

[68] *Ibid.*, 301.

[69] n 35, 439-440.

pattern of members from reserved seats having limited roles in debates, committees and government membership.[70] However, the causation of such trends is unclear and cannot be placed solely on Article 330. Political parties do have a major impact on the operation of the policy.[71] Galanter makes the point:

> 'Representatives who occupy reserved seats can be expected to elevate the interests of Scheduled Castes, etc. over those of their constituents only to the extent that one assumes the Scheduled Castes representatives will be more responsive to the pull of ascriptive ties than to the experiences of gaining and holding office.'[72]

Those elected through Article 330 have a symbolic role in representing those groups, however, McMillan notes that the substantive representative role is dominated by the political parties.[73] The extent to which members in reserved seats have been able to act together has varied depending on political context, or in other words the beneficiaries of Article 330 seats have not defended SCs and STs interests consistently.[74] Macmillan notes that with the decline of the formal role of the Lok Sabha, personal networks have become a vital part of Indian politics and in that sense Article 330 has widened the channels of patronage and influence.[75] Overall, the picture is one where MP's selected through Article 330 are constrained by party politics to the extent to which they can substantively represent SCs and STs interests.[76] Galanter observes a similar problem to that which Vincent notes in South Africa, the presence of members who are deemed to represent SCs and STs relieves other members of the Lok Sabha of the requirement to deal with their interests and encourages 'compartmentalisation' of issues.[77] The problems of elitism and political parties raised in the South African context are relevant to the Indian,

---

[70] *Ibid.*, 443; n 67, 302.
[71] n 67, 303.
[72] n 35, 442.
[73] n 67, 304.
[74] *Ibid.*, 305.
[75] *Ibid.*, 307.
[76] *Ibid.*, 310.
[77] n 35, 444; *Ibid.*, 309.

although the location of the policy at the constitutional level, supported by other policies and by consensus seems to buffer it from Vincent's other criticisms.

Conclusion

The nature of the example selected in this discussion of the question's quotation directly challenges one of the major criticisms of positive discrimination policies: that they depart from meritocratic principles and consider irrelevant factors. Membership of the first chamber of a national legislature is not the sort of role where an individual's ability to perform is easily assessed, and even in ordinary circumstances symbolic representation forms an important part of a candidate's qualities. For traditionally under represented and discriminated groups, such as the SCs and STs in India or women in South Africa, symbolic representation is more important than in ordinary circumstances. For these groups simply being present in more proportionate numbers than in the past is a major achievement, it also provides evidence of their respective nation's commitment and determination to overcome the injustices of the past that weigh so heavily on their national consciences. The entrenched disadvantage and ensuing under-representation that is likely to exist without interference provides a fairness justification for the use of positive discrimination in the national legislature and India, in particular, illustrates this point. The failure of the unfairness arguments can be blamed on the specificity of their own context and a failure to appreciate that for certain roles and in certain historical circumstances a deference to merit will perpetuate unfairness rather than secure fairness.

Despite establishing that policies of positive discrimination in the first chamber of national legislatures can be fair, the problems in the operation of the policies point to the conclusion that they must be described as 'blunt'. The desire for immediate change described by Galanter above, can mask a failure to instigate the sort of reforms that could result in a more fairly proportionate chamber in the long term. Even worse, Vincent has explained, in the South African context, that they can be detrimental to the cause of the group identified as needing extra representation. South Africa's policy suffers in comparison to India's due to its location at the party political level and the ensuing isolation within the political context. Both policies are blunted by the reality of their respective political contexts in which the machinery of politics works against the possibility of positive descriptive representation occurring at a level to satisfy the theoretical arguments. The blunt allegation highlights issues which question the very basis of representation in modern democracies that I was unable to answer in adequate depth. Despite this limitation and the failures of the policies I have examined here, I ultimately recognise that no state desires the contexts that give rise to claims for positive discrimination. Therefore any state which attempts to combat and confront the problems created by those contexts and find a more inclusive and fairer solution than those offered by the established perspectives on representation and equality must be applauded for their intent.

War Crimes in the Conflict in Pakistan

NIAZ A SHAH[*]

Pakistan is an important battlefield in the war on terror.[1] The United States has included direct drone attacks in the tribal areas of Pakistan in the new strategy in the fight against Taliban in Afghanistan[2] and is sending more troops to Afghanistan as reinforcement.[3] The US forces are increasingly using the Iraqi counter insurgency tactics in Pakistan and Afghanistan: gathering actionable intelligence and taking out the target.[4] The Afghan government wants to go after militants inside Pakistan.[5] The Pakistani government said it would not accept from militants anything less than to lay down their arms and accept the writ of government.[6] The Pakistani government made it clear that it wants to expel foreign militants from its tribal areas but would not allow direct military engagement against militants by another country.[7] The

---

[*] University of Hull.

[1] GW Bush, Lecture at the National Defense University's Distinguished Lecture Program, Discusses Global War on Terror, 9 September 2008.
http://www.whitehouse.gov/news/releases/2008/09/20080909.html (accessed 11 September 2008).

[2] M Mullen, 'Attacks inside Pakistan is necessary' *BBC Urdu*, 10 September 2008 available at http://www.bbc.co.uk/urdu/pakistan/story/2008/09/080910_mike_mullen_as.shtml (accessed 12 September 2008) and A Iqbal 'US includes Fata in its area of concern' *Dawn*, 11 September 2008.

[3] MR Gordon and T Shanker, 'Plan Would Shift Forces from Iraq to Afghanistan' *The New York Times*, 4 September 2008 available at http://www.nytimes.com/2008/09/05/world/middleeast/05military.html?partner=rssnyt (accessed 15 September 2008).

[4] 'US using anti-insurgency tactics of Iraq in Fata' *Dawn*, 9 September 2008.

[5] H Karzai, 'Karzai issues warning to Pakistan' *CNN*, 15 June 2008 available at http://edition.cnn.com/2008/WORLD/asiapcf/06/15/afghanistan.pakistan.index.html (accessed 15 September 2008).

[6] YR Gilani, 'A Conversation with Yousaf Raza Gilani', 29 July 2008 available at http://www.thenews.com.pk/pm_interview_usa.htm (accessed 25 September 2008).

[7] A Kayani, 'Foreign Force cannot Attack' *BBC Urdu*, 10 September 2008. http://www.bbc.co.uk/urdu/pakistan/story/2008/09/080910_kiyani_us_forces_pak.shtml (accessed 12 September 2008) and A Kayani, 'Defending Territorial Integrity under new Leadership' *BBC Urdu*, 12 September 2008 available at

government of Pakistan thinks itself 'capable of taking an effective action within the boundaries.'[8] The Prime Minister of Pakistan[9] has warned the United States to stop violating the Pakistani border as it is not only against the Charter of the United Nations but is also counter productive in Pakistan's war against militants. The United States says it has a right to cross the Pakistani border to pursue militants,[10] but in April 2009 it came to light that both governments have a tacit understanding on the issue of drone attacks inside Pakistan.[11] In June 2009, the US resumed surveillance flights over Pakistan.[12] In May 2009, the government of Pakistan changed its conciliatory stance towards militants: armed groups shall be fought until they are defeated,[13] as they have become a threat to the survival of Pakistan.[14] The Pakistani security forces started Operation Rah-i-Rast to 'clear' Swat of militants.[15] Operation Rah-i-Nijat was launched to 'clear' regions of

---

http://www.bbc.co.uk/urdu/pakistan/story/2008/09/080912_corps_commander.shtml (accessed 12 September 2008).

[8] Y Gilani, 'Pakistan capable to tackle terrorism within its boundaries' *The News International*, 12 September 2008 available at
http://thenews.jang.com.pk/updates.asp?id=55067 (accessed 12 September 2008).
[9] 16th September 2008.
[10] R Gates, 'Gates acknowledges US strikes inside Pakistan' 23 September 2008 available at http://www.defensenews.com/story.php?i=3739002&c=AME&s=TOP (accessed 25 September 2008).
[11] *The Washington Post*, 15th February 2009.
[12] Schmitt and Mazzetti 'U.S. Resumes Surveillance Flights Over Pakistan' *The New York Times*, 30 June 2009 available at
http://www.nytimes.com/2009/06/30/world/asia/30drone.html (accessed 1 July 2009).
[13] A Zardari, 'No turning back on Swat offensive, says president' *Dawn*, 10 May 2009 at http://www.dawn.com/wps/wcm/connect/dawn-content-library/dawn/the-newspaper/front-page/no-turning-back-on-swat-offensive,-says-president-059 (accessed 30 June 2009) and A Zardari, 'Operation to continue till militants eliminated: Zardari' *Dawn*, 30 June 2009 at http://www.dawn.com/wps/wcm/connect/dawn-content-library/dawn/the-newspaper/front-page/zardari-praises-soldiers-operation-to-continue-till-militants-eliminated-069 (accessed 30 June 2009).
[14] Y Gilani, 'Swat operation a fight for Pakistan's survival' *Dawn*, 9 May 2009 available at http://www.dawn.com/wps/wcm/connect/dawn-content-library/dawn/the-newspaper/front-page/swat-operation-a-fight-for-survival-of-pakistan-pm-059 (accessed 30 June 2009) and Y Gilani, 'Time for dialogue with militants over: PM' *Dawn*, 29 June 2009 available at http://www.dawn.com/wps/wcm/connect/dawn-content-library/dawn/news/pakistan/13+time+for+talks+with+militants+over+pm-za-14 (accessed 29 June 2009).
[15] Inter Services Public Relations (2009) Post peace agreement situation. Available at http://www.ispr.gov.pk/front/main.asp?o=t-press_release&date=2009/5/8 (accessed 29 June 2009).

Waziristan of militants.[16] Most of the world media, human rights organisations and experts do not focus on the conduct of conflict by the security forces of Pakistan. The focus tends to be on the conduct of conflict by the Tehrik-i-Taliban Pakistan (hereinafter, TTP) and its affiliated armed groups. As a result of this tendency we see only partial exposure and analysis. We need full exposure and analysis of how this conflict is conducted by both parties.

The purpose of this article is to investigate two aspects of the conflict: (a) whether war crimes have been committed by the security forces of Pakistan and the TTP's fighters; and (b) if war crimes have been committed, have the war criminals been prosecuted or is there a real prospect of their prosecution?

1. Status of the Tribal Areas

We need to identify the parties to the conflict and the legal status of the tribal zone in order to determine the nature of the conflict and appropriate applicable laws. There is a great deal of confusion about the legal status of the tribal areas which is why it is important for our discussion to shed light on the point. The conflict zone in Pakistan is in the tribal areas bordering Afghanistan. These areas consist of regions governed by the central and provincial governments. The Federally Administered Tribal Areas – FATA - are part of Pakistani territory under Article 1 of the 1973 constitution of Pakistan. The people of FATA are represented in the National Assembly[17] and the Senate[18] but administratively it remains under the direct executive authority of the President.[19] Laws framed by the parliament do not apply to FATA unless so ordered by the President. Most of civil, criminal, custom and laws related to terrorism are extended to FATA.[20] The President is also empowered to issue regulations for the peace and good governance of the tribal areas.[21] The President has the power to cancel the current status of these areas after consultation with the tribal people through

---

[16] Khan, 17 June 2009.

[17] Article 51.

[18] Article 59.

[19] Article 247.

[20] F Hussain, (2005) 'Testing FCR on the Touchstone of the Constitution'. In: Human Rights Commission of Pakistan, *A Bad Law Nobody can Defend*.

[21] Article 247.

their council of elders (*Jirga*). Today, FATA is governed primarily through the Frontier Crimes Regulation 1901 (hereinafter FCR). The Governor of the North West Frontier Province (hereinafter, NWFP) administers FATA in his capacity as an agent to the President of Pakistan, under the overall supervision of the Ministry of States and Frontier Regions in Islamabad, the capital of Pakistan.

2. Parties to the Conflict

The two main parties to the conflict are the security forces of Pakistan and the TTP. The security forces include the armed forces, the Frontier Corps, the police and in some cases the levies (government forces also known as Khasadars) of different tribal regions. Most of the operations, apart from sporadic skirmishes, are conducted under the overall supervision of the army. The local tribal lashkars (a group of village fighters), supported by the security forces, also fight the TTP in the Dir and Buner areas (see 4.3). The TTP, which is discussed below, has affiliated armed groups which carry out suicide bombing and take part in fighting against the security forces. These groups include Lashkar-i-Jhangvi, Sipah-i-Sahaba Pakistan and Jaysh-e-Muhammad. They have a different origin and history than the TTP and are often described as the Punjabi Taliban.[22] These organisations operated under state patronage rather than challenging the writ of the state and were, until very recently, focused on the struggle in Kashmir. In 2002, former President Musharraf banned these organisations, however they remained active and some joined the Taliban in Afghanistan and Pakistan. Other sectarian Shia and Sunni groups and criminal gangs, such as the Mangal Bagh group of Dara Adam Khel, also commit violence but their activities are not discussed. The main armed group and party to the conflict is the TTP, which warrants detailed discussion.

2.1 Tehrik-i-Taliban Pakistan

During the US-led war against Taliban, prominent Taliban and Al-Qaeda figures found shelter in the tribal areas of Pakistan. Pakistan as an ally of the US provided extended support to the US-led coalition. Al-Qaeda branded former President Musharraf of Pakistan as a 'traitor'

---

[22] H Abbas, 'Defining the Punjabi Taliban Network' *CTC Sentinel*, April 2009.

and called on Pakistanis to rebel against him.[23] The Pakistani forces started military operations to flush militants out of the tribal areas but some tribal figures resisted the Pakistani effort. This initiated a direct conflict between those who now constitute the TTP's leadership and the Pakistani security forces. At the start of the Afghan conflict in 2001, allies and sympathisers of the Taliban in Pakistan were not identified as 'Taliban' themselves. The transition from being Taliban supporters and sympathisers to becoming a mainstream Taliban force in the tribal areas of NWFP initiated when many small militant groups operating independently in the area started networking with one another. Soon, many other local groups started joining the Taliban ranks in the tribal areas: some as followers while others as partners. During this process, the Pakistani Taliban never really merged into the organizational structure of the Afghan Taliban under the leadership of Mullah Omar. Instead, they developed a distinct identity. These independent militant groups now banded together and created a space for themselves in Pakistan by engaging in military attacks on the one hand, and cutting deals with the Pakistani government to establish their autonomy in the tribal areas on the other.[24]

Baitullah Mehsud is thirty four years old, slightly short with black beard; a warrior belonging to the South Waziristan Agency. He hails from the Mehsud tribe. He shuns media and does not want to be photographed, but in May 2008 he invited media to his stronghold in South Waziristan.[25] He came to prominence in 2005 when he signed a deal with the Pakistani government. As part of the deal, he had pledged not to provide any assistance to Al-Qaeda and other militants and not to launch operations against government forces.[26] The deal was short

[23] O Bin Laden, 'Bin Laden Declares War on Musharraf in New Audiotape' *Fox News*, 21 September 2007 available at http://www.foxnews.com/story/0,2933,297401,00.html (accessed 1 May 2008) and H Siddique, 'Bin Laden urges uprising against Musharraf' *Guardian*, 20 September 2007 available at http://www.guardian.co.uk/world/2007/sep/20/alqaida.pakistan (accessed 1 May 2008).
[24] H Abbas, 'A Profile of Tehrik-i-Taliban Pakistan' *CTC Sentinel*, January 2008.
[25] BBC 'Meeting Pakistan's most feared militant', 27 May 2008 available at http://news.bbc.co.uk/1/hi/world/south_asia/7420606.stm (accessed 9 July 2008).
[26] H Rashid, ('Jirga (Council of Elders) is waiting for government confirmation' *BBC Urdu*, 31 January 2005 available at http://www.bbc.co.uk/urdu/pakistan/story/2005/01/printable/050131_waziristan_agreement_am.shtml (accessed 9 July 2008).

lived. Since 2006, he has virtually established an independent zone in parts of South Waziristan Agency. Mehsud commands a force of around two thousands militants[27] and has moved aggressively against Pakistan's army in recent months, especially when he captured around three hundred army soldiers in August 2007.[28] The soldiers were returned only when the government released twenty five militants associated with Mehsud.[29] Of the fifty six suicide bombings in Pakistan in 2007, thirty-six were against military related targets, including two against the Inter Services Intelligence (ISI); two against the army headquarters in Rawalpindi; one aimed at the air force in Sargodha; and one directed at the facility of the Special Services Group (SSG) in Tarbela. For many of these attacks, the government blamed Baitullah Mehsud and his associates.[30] This reveals the fact that the TTP has additional resources and geographic reach. The then pro-Musharraf government has charged Mehsud with the assassination of Benazir Bhutto[31] but Mehsud denies any involvement.[32] The new government, which consists of the late Bhutto's party, has warned that it is premature to accuse Mehsud.[33] The government of Pakistan banned the TTP on 25 August 2008 under the Anti-Terrorism Act 1997 but the TTP spokesperson termed the move as ineffective.[34]

To sum up the position of the TTP, it is a newly founded organisation of Pakistani origin based in the tribal areas at the border between Pakistan and Afghanistan. They have effective control of most of the tribal areas.[35] They have established Islamic courts in Mohmand,

---

[27] BBC 'Profile: Baitullah Mehsud', 28 December 2007 available at
http://news.bbc.co.uk/1/hi/world/south_asia/7163626.stm (accessed 9 July 2008).
[28] *Ibid.*
[29] D Wazir, 'Waziristan: army men release expected' *BBC Urdu*, 4 November 2007.
[30] H Abbas, 'A Profile of Tehrik-i-Taliban Pakistan' *CTC Sentinel*, January 2008.
[31] S Malik, 'Warrant for Baitullah and five others issued' *BBC Urdu*, 10 March 2008 available at
http://www.bbc.co.uk/urdu/pakistan/story/2008/03/printable/080310_bb_accused_remand
_ra.shtml (accessed 9 July 2009).
[32] R Orakzai, 'We did not attack Benazir, says Taliban' *BBC Urdu*. 22 October 2007.
[33] 'Qazi courts set up in Mohmand' *Dawn*, 15 July 2008 available at
http://www.dawn.com/2008/07/15/top4.htm (accessed 23 July 2008).
[34] 'Tehrik-i-Taliban Banned' *Dawn*, 26 August 2008 available at
http://www.dawn.com/2008/08/26/top12.htm (accessed 18 September 2008).
[35] J Perlez & PZ Shah (2008) 'Pakistani Forces Appear to Push Back Militants' *The New York Times*, 30 June. http://www.nytimes.com/2008/06/30/world/asia/30pstan.html (accessed 10 July 2008).

Khyber, Orakzai, Bajaur and South and North Waziristan agencies.[36] Any security posts vacated by the Pakistani forces are occupied by the TTP fighters.[37] The TTP's influence is also emerging in other provinces such as Punjab[38] and Sindh.[39] The TTP has its own command structure and a clear mission: to fight and expel foreign forces from Afghanistan.[40] The TTP does not want to fight Pakistani forces but if fighters of the TTP are attacked or prevented from Jihad in Afghanistan, they will fight back in self-defence. The government of Pakistan recognises the TTP as a force and had signed several peace agreements with the TTP.[41] These agreements, however, do not affect the TTP's mission in Afghanistan.[42] On 30 June 2009, Mullah Nazir and Hafiz Gul Bahadur terminated their agreements with the government of Pakistan after the security forces launched operation Rah-e-Rast.[43]

3. Existence of the Conflict and Applicable Laws
3.1 Existence of Armed Conflict
The application of the law of armed conflict is triggered when there is an armed conflict of an international or a non-international character. Before examining the nature of the conflict, we need to establish whether an armed conflict exists inside Pakistan. The existence of armed conflict is a question of fact, but the statements of the Pakistani

---

[36] 'Blaming Baitullah for Benazir Murder premature: Qureshi' *Dawn*, 14 July 2008 available at http://www.dawn.com/2008/07/14/top2.htm (accessed 16 September 2008) and A Kakar, 'Sharia courts set up in tribal areas' *BBC Urdu*, 15 July 2008.
[37] R Orakzai, 'Taliban take over vacated border posts' *BBC Urdu*, 25 July 2008.
[38] A Sulman, 'Taliban threat in south Punjab' *BBC Urdu*, 30 July 2008.
S Tavernise and I Ashraf 'Attacked, Pakistani Villagers Take on Taliban' *The New York Times*, 10 June 2009 available at
http://www.nytimes.com/2009/06/10/world/asia/10pstan.html (accessed 30 June 2009).
[39] A Sabir, (2008) 'Taliban: government must take steps' *BBC Urdu*, 5 August.
[40] M Fazlullah, 'Suicide bombers ready' *Dawn*, 28 July 2008 available at
http://www.dawn.com/2008/07/28/top9.htm (accessed 26 September 2008).
[41] R Orakzai, (2006) 'Government and Taliban Agreements' *BBC Urdu*,
http://www.bbc.co.uk/urdu/pakistan/story/2006/09/060905_waziristan_agreement_ur.shtml (accessed 10 July 2008).
[42] A Kakar, 'Agreement won't apply to Afghanistan, says Taliban' *BBC Urdu*, 16 May 2008 and R Hamdani, 'Taliban attacks from Pakistan' *BBC Urdu*, 16 May 2008.
[43] 'TTP claims it bombed Lahore, Nowshera and Peshawar' *Dawn*, 12 June 2009.
http://www.dawn.com/wps/wcm/connect/dawn-content-library/dawn/news/pakistan/11-ttp-claims-it-bombed-lahore--nowshera--and-peshawar--il--06 (accessed 30 June 2009).

government are also examined together with the factual conditions on the ground.

The factual conditions on the ground indicate that it is a full-fledged armed conflict of a non-international character. The TTP and its affiliated armed groups are inflicting heavy losses on the security forces of Pakistan. The Pakistani forces are using tanks, jets and gunship helicopters to suppress the TTP's fighters in Swat, Buner, Dir, Kurram Agency and North and South Waziristan. Thousands of people have left their homes and taken refuge in the neighbouring areas of Afghanistan and some settled districts of the NWFP.[44] The ICRC[45] has declared Dir, one of the tribal agencies, as a war zone and consistently refers to the situation as an armed conflict. The Security Council[46] suggestively refers to the situation as an armed conflict as this urges respect for international law. The essential conditions of an armed conflict of a non-international character, as applied by the International Criminal Tribunal for former Yugoslavia in *Prosecutor v Ramush Hardinaj et al*,[47] are all present in the conflict in Pakistan.

The initial statements of the Pakistani officials do not provide a clear picture of the situation. The Ministry of Interior always regard the conflict in the tribal areas as a law and order issue. The official statements of the Pakistani army also refer to the conflict as a law and order situation.[48] The President of Pakistan, however, said that we are in a state of war.[49] The Prime Minister[50] also said it is not a normal but rather a guerrilla war. The position of the government became clearer in May and June 2009 when the security forces were called in to eliminate the militants. Since then, the language of war has been used. The factual conditions and the statements of the President and Prime Minister of Pakistan strongly suggest that an armed conflict of a non-international character exists in Pakistan.

---

[44] UNHCR, 6th October 2008; 26th June 2009.

[45] 1st October 2008; 26th June 2009.

[46] 2008.

[47] 2008, paras [49] and [99].

[48] A Kakar, 'Swat operation in one year' *BBC Urdu*, 15 October 2008.

[49] A Iqbal and M Haider 'We are in a state of war: Asif' *Dawn*. 25 September 2008 available at http://www.dawn.com/2008/09/25/top2.htm (accessed 25 September 2008).

[50] 12th July 2008.

3.2 Nature of the Conflict

Many armed conflicts these days have the characteristics of both international and non-international armed conflict.[51] But the conflict in Pakistan is clearly a conflict of a non-international character. The Pakistani security forces are fighting the TTP and its affiliated armed groups and some foreign fighters in the ranks of TTP. The TTP is a well-organised armed group and exercises full or partial control over certain regions of Pakistan. The intensity of fighting can be gauged by the use of war machinery by the security forces, the number of deaths and displaced persons, and the destruction of property.

3.3 Applicable Law: International Law

In general, the law of armed conflict, customary law, human rights law,[52] international criminal law[53] and the municipal laws[54] are applicable to an internal armed conflict. Pakistan is not party to Additional Protocol II, 1977 but is party to the four Geneva Conventions of 1949. Therefore, Common Article 3 applies. Pakistan is not a party to the Rome Statute of the International Criminal Court of 1998 but Article 8 (2(c-f)) might apply as it is reflective of custom. Pakistan has not ratified or acceded to many human rights conventions but has signed the International Covenant on Civil and Political Rights 1966 on 17 April 2008. Pakistan has also signed the 1984 United Nations Convention against Torture and Other Cruel, Inhuman or Degrading Treatment or Punishment on 17 April 2008. It is less important here whether Pakistan has ratified these human rights instruments, as most of the principles contained therein have acquired the status of customary international law or *jus cogens* binding all states. In no circumstances can these norms be violated.[55] In addition, as we shall see

---

[51] Prosecutor v Tadic IT-94-1 [1999] ICTY 2 (15th July 1999).

[52] W Abresch, 'A Human Rights Law of Internal Armed Conflict: The European Court of Human Rights in Chechnya' (2005) 16(4) European Journal of International Law 741 and EL Haye, *War Crimes in Internal Armed Conflicts* (Cambridge University Press, Cambridge 2008).

[53] A Cassese, *International Criminal Law* (Oxford University Press, Oxford 2008) and A Zahar and G Sluiter *International Criminal Law: A Critical Introduction* (Oxford University Press, Oxford 2006).

[54] APV Rogers, *Law on the Battlefield* (Manchester University Press, Manchester 2004) 216

[55] Office of the UN High commissioner for Human Rights (2008) Human Rights, Terrorism and Counter-terrorism. Fact Sheet No. 32 available at http://www.ohchr.org/EN/PublicationsResources/Pages/FactSheets.aspx (accessed 16

later, most of these human rights principles are recognised as fundamental rights in the constitution of Pakistan.

For our discussion, Common Article 3 of the four Geneva Conventions is the most important one. It is described as a 'convention in miniature'[56] or as a 'convention within the convention'[57] dealing specifically with armed conflict not of an international character. It outlines certain basic humanitarian provisions which each party to the conflict must adhere to. 'The obligation is absolute for each of the Parties and independent of the obligation on the other Party.'[58] An internal armed conflict, in the sense of Common Article 3, must occur within the territory of a State Party between the government forces and one or more armed group or between the armed groups. The conflict in Pakistan fits neatly within the Common Article 3 paradigm. The conflict also fits in well within the 1977 Additional Protocol II's definition of an internal armed conflict of non-international character.

Article 1 describes non-international armed conflict as a conflict 'which take[s] place in the territory of a High Contracting Party between its armed forces and dissident armed forces or other organized armed groups which, under responsible command, exercise such control over a part of its territory as to enable them to carry out sustained and concerted military operations and to implement this Protocol.'

As stated above, Pakistan is not a party to Additional Protocol II but those principles which are reflective of custom do apply. Common Article 3 obliges each party to the conflict to treat humanely 'in all circumstances' and without distinction those who are taking no active part in the hostilities, including members of armed forces who have laid down their arms and those placed *hors de combat* by sickness, wounds, detention, or any other cause. Common Article 3 not only protects civilians but also those who had laid down their arms for whatever reason. Discrimination on the basis of religion, colour, race or

---

September 2008) and S Borelli, (2002) 'Casting light on the legal black hole: international law and detention abroad in the "war on terror"' (2002) 85 *International Review of the Red Cross* 39.

[56] J Pictet, *Commentary on Geneva Convention (I) for the Amelioration of the Condition of the Wounded and Sick in Armed Forces in the Field. Geneva, 12 August 1949* (ICRC, Geneva 1952) 48.

[57] F Kalshoven and L Zegveld *Constraints on the Waging of War: An Introduction to International Humanitarian Law* (ICRC, Geneva 2001) 69.

[58] n 56, 51.

'other similar criteria' e.g. nationality etc is prohibited.[59] Common Article 3 prohibits 'at any time and in any place whatsoever' (a) violence to life and person, in particular murder of all kinds, mutilation, cruel treatment and torture; (b) taking of hostages; (c) outrages upon personal dignity, in particular humiliating and degrading treatment and (d) the passing of sentences and the carrying out of executions without previous judgement pronounced by a regularly constituted court affording all the judicial guarantees. It is obligatory to collect and care for the wounded and sick. Three broad categories of people may benefit from the provisions of Common Article 3: civilians, those who are *hors de combat* and the wounded and sick. Common Article 3, however, does not preclude the application of municipal law. Captured militants, whether national or not, may be tried for offences they have committed provided the requirements of Common Article 3 are observed.[60]

There are certain principles of customary international law which are applicable to an armed conflict of non-international character.[61] It is not always easy to determine the content of customary law applicable to internal conflict; however, the basic guide should be the principles of military necessity, humanity, distinction and proportionality.[62] The right of the parties to the conflict to choose the methods and means of warfare is not unlimited.[63] The current law of the armed conflict is consistent with the economic and efficient use of force. The argument that in some cases the law of armed conflict might be ignored to achieve the purpose of the war is obsolete as the modern law of warfare takes into account military necessity.[64] The principle of humanity forbids inflicting unnecessary sufferings.[65] All military operations shall be based on the principles of distinction, i.e. a clear distinction must be made between military targets and civilian population and objects.[66] The law of armed conflict, however, does not

---

[59] *Ibid.*, 55
[60] United Kingdom, Ministry of Defence *The Manual of the Law of Armed Conflict* (Oxford University Press, Oxford 2005).
[61] *Prosecutor v Tadic* 2nd October 1995, para [127].
[62] n 60.
[63] Hague Regulations 1907, Article 22.
[64] n 60.
[65] n 63, Preamble.
[66] Additional Protocol 1 (1977), Articles 48 and 49(3).

require that civilians and civilian objects shall never be damaged. For instance, civilian casualties are acceptable if they are proportionate to legitimate military goals. Any military attack must be proportional 'to the concrete and direct military advantage anticipated'.[67]

3.4 Applicable Law: Domestic Law

On a domestic level, the 1973 constitution, Frontier Crimes Regulations of 1901, Pakistan Penal Code 1860, Code of Criminal Procedure Code 1898, the Pakistan Army Act 1952 and the Anti-Terrorism Act 1997 shall apply. Most of the constitutional provisions are applicable to everyone at all times within Pakistan but chapter two – dealing with fundamental rights - is the most relevant for our discussion. Article 4 states that it is the inalienable right of every individual to enjoy the protection of law and to be treated in accordance with the law. No law shall be made which is inconsistent with or derogating from fundamental rights recognised by the constitution.[68] These two articles override any other laws or customs which might conflict with fundamental rights. All citizens are equal before the law and are entitled to equal protection of the law.[69] The constitution guarantees the security of person and life.[70] No one shall be arrested and detained without being informed of the grounds for such arrest. An arrested person shall have a right to consult a lawyer of his/her choice and must be produced before a magistrate within twenty four hours of such arrest. This, however, does not apply to those who are kept under preventive detention for acting against the security or integrity of Pakistan. Such a person may be detained for up to three months and his/her detention may be extended only by a review board.[71] The dignity of the individual is inviolable and the use of torture for extracting evidence is prohibited.[72] Those imprisoned shall not undergo compulsory service which is of a cruel nature or incompatible with human dignity.[73]

---

[67] *Ibid.*, Article 51(5)(b).
[68] Article 8.
[69] Article 25.
[70] Article 9.
[71] Article 10.
[72] Article 14.
[73] Article 11.

These constitutional provisions are applicable to everyone irrespective of domicile or nationality. These rules, therefore, equally apply to foreign fighters in the tribal areas of Pakistan. The President of Pakistan has the power to declare a state of emergency in case of war or internal disturbance.[74] During such emergency, fundamental rights, specified in the order, may be suspended by Presidential Order but such order must be approved by the joint session of the parliament.[75] At the moment, an emergency is not declared in the tribal areas of Pakistan and therefore, fundamental rights remain in force. As we shall see in 4.2, most of the constitutional protections are blatantly violated by the security forces of Pakistan.

The Pakistan Penal Code, 1860 (PPC) takes effect throughout Pakistan.[76] Every person acting contrary to the provisions of the PPC, within Pakistan, shall be liable to punishment.[77] The phrase 'every person' comprises all persons without limitation and irrespective of nationality, religion or creed.[78] Most of the provisions of the PPC overlap with constitutional and Common Article 3 guarantees. The most relevant provisions of the PPC are offences against the state,[79] offences affecting the human body such as murder,[80] offences related to kidnapping and abduction[81] and offences related to mischief by causing fire or explosives.[82] The amended Anti-Terrorism Act of 1997 is a special and perhaps the most relevant law[83] which extends to the whole country including tribal areas. The Pakistan Army Act 1952 is mostly concerned with the organisation and discipline of the armed forces but some of its provisions prohibits wilful damage and destruction of property,[84] plunder[85] and conduct of cruel, indecent or unnatural kind.[86]

---

[74] Article 232.
[75] Article 233.
[76] Section 1.
[77] Section 2.
[78] PLD 1958 Supreme Court (Ind.) 115.
[79] Sections 121-130.
[80] Sections 299-338.
[81] Sections 359-368.
[82] Sections 425-440.
[83] On terrorism law, see S Fayyaz, 'Responding to Terrorism: Pakistan's Anti-Terrorism Laws' Pakistan Institute for Peace Studies, 28 April 2008.
[84] Section 25.
[85] Section 29.
[86] Section 41.

4. War Crimes in the Conflict

In the conflict between the security forces of Pakistan and the TTP, the law of armed conflict and other applicable laws are violated on an almost daily basis. The following accounts show that both parties to the conflict have committed and continue to commit war crimes under Common Article 3 and customary law and crimes under domestic law.

4.1 War Crimes by the TTP

The TTP seems to believe that they act according to Islamic law of armed conflict. The Taliban in Afghanistan has a *Jihad Manual*[87] whereas the TTP has no such written rules but it can be safely assumed that the TTP closely follow the Afghan Taliban's *Jihad Manual*. This assumption is made on the basis of the similarity of conduct and avowed alliance between the two groups. Both groups also have a close ideological, territorial and cultural nexus. Here, however, the conduct of conflict by the TTP is examined under international law of armed conflict. It is very difficult to pinpoint who is behind a particular incident of violence but we will examine those incidents for which either the TTP has claimed responsibility or has issued warnings that it will attack particular targets such as foreign NGOs[88] and later those targets were hit. Since early summer 2008, the TTP stepped up their activities against the government forces. The modus operandi is that the TTP would give a warning to the government to stop operation in a particular area against the TTP, if the warning is not heeded, the TTP would attack the security forces, civilians and civilian objects.[89]

4.1.1 Targeting Civilians

Since 2002, the TTP has targeted civilian objects and killed hundreds of civilians. In some cases killing civilians is deliberate, while in others civilians are killed and property destroyed as a result of indiscriminate firing and suicide bombing. Targets have included government officials, pro-government tribal elders, health and foreign aid workers. It is

---

[87] 2006.
[88] D Wazir, 'NGO attacked in Wana [Waziristan]' *BBC Urdu*, 25 November 2007.
[89] M Omer, 'Wah attack is a reaction' *BBC Urdu*, 21 August 2008.

difficult to note all such cases but a few are stated here by way of example. Those killed are either kidnapped or shot dead on the spot.

On 9 November 2007, Federal Minister Amir Muqam's house was hit by a suicide bomber killing four people including three security guards. He was threatened a few days before the attack.[90] On the 2nd of April 2006, the dead body of Zahir Shah, a pro-government religious scholar, was found in South Waziristan. Several bullet wounds were found in his body.[91] On 28th April 2007, Federal Interior Minister Aftab Sherpao's election rally was attacked in Charsada where thirty-one people died and dozens were injured.[92] On 27th January 2007, a suicide blast in Peshawar killed thirty-one people and wounded thirty others. Deputy Inspector General of Police, Peshawar and two local council chairpersons were among those killed in the blast.[93] In February 2007, Doctor Abdul Ghani of the Health Ministry of the NWFP was killed during polio campaign in Bajaur Agency. In August 2008, the TTP commanders in Swat valley threatened several pro-government politicians and officials to put pressure on the government to spot operations against the TTP. The members of the Awami National Party – which has formed a government at the provincial level - were specific targets. The TTP attacked the house of the brother of a ruling party MP with rockets in Shah Derai area of Tehsil Kabbal, Swat killing ten people. The TTP spokesman for Swat chapter, Muslim Khan, said the attack was in revenge of innocent people killed in the Kabbal operation.[94] On 9 June 2009, militants attacked Pearl Continental hotel in Peshawar killing 11 people and wounding another 55.[95] After two days, the TTP took responsibility for the bombing and said it was in

---

[90] A Yusufzai, 'Suicide attack in minister's house: Amir Muqam escapes unhurt' *Dawn*, 9 November 2007 available at
http://www.dawn.com/2007/11/10/top2.htm (accessed 26 September 2008).
[91] A Kakar, 'Waziristan: pro-government scholar murdered' *BBC Urdu*, 2 April 2006.
[92] I Khan and G Khan 'Sherpao survives suicide attack' *Dawn*, 29 April 2007 available at http://www.dawn.com/2007/04/29/top1.htm (accessed 26 September 2008).
[93] 'Police chief, 12 others killed in Peshawar blast: Second suicide attack in two days' *Dawn*, 28 January 2007.
[94] 'MPA's brother among 10 killed in Swat rocket attack' *The News International*, 25 August 2008 available at
http://thenews.jang.com.pk/updates.asp?id=53088 (accessed 22 September 2008).
[95] I Khan and S Masood 'Militants Strike Hotel in Pakistan, Killing 11' *The New York Times*. 10 June 2009 available at
http://www.nytimes.com/2009/06/10/world/asia/10peshawar.html (accessed 30 June 2009).

retaliation to shelling on seminaries in Hangu and Orakzai a few days before.[96]

4.1.2 Targeting Civilian Objects

Tehrik-i-Taliban Pakistan has attacked several girls' schools and music shops in different tribal agencies of the NWFP. These attacks are systematic and seem to be part of the TTP's policy. The modus operandi of these attacks, however, is different from those of the Afghan Taliban in that these schools are attacked during the night when no civilians are present at the premises. On 2nd August 2008, two girls' schools were blown up. The Taliban's spokesperson, Muslim Khan, accepted responsibility.[97] On 30th July 2008, the Swat chapter of the TTP took responsibility for blowing up a girls' school, an army guest house and a tourist hotel. In a separate attack on a girls' school, a letter was left warning parents not to send their children to these schools because English/Western style education is given in these schools.[98] Letters of this kind are distributed during the night and are known both in Pakistan and Afghanistan as 'night letters'. Four schools were set ablaze in Dir district in June 2008.[99] 'At least 39 girls' schools were blown up or set ablaze by militants in Swat [in June 2008].'[100] Attacking music shops has become a routine in the NWFP in which several civilians are either killed or wounded.

4.1.3 Suicide Bombing

Suicide bombing in armed conflicts has a very long history. It has been committed by the followers of many religions and in different time and regions of the world.[101] 'Suicide attacks are increasingly becoming alien to nowhere and no people. Worldwide, the number of terrorist groups employing them has grown over the past twenty-five years. In some of

---

96 'TTP claims it bombed Lahore, Nowshera and Peshawar' *Dawn*, 12 June 2009 available at http://www.dawn.com/wps/wcm/connect/dawn-content-library/dawn/news/pakistan/11-ttp-claims-it-bombed-lahore--nowshera--and-peshawar--il--06 (accessed 30 June 2009).

97 A Kakar, 'Swat: two girls' schools set ablaze' *BBC Urdu*, 2 August 2008.
98 A Kakar, 'Another blast in girls' school' *BBC Urdu*, 13 June 2008.
99 *Ibid.*
100 H Khan, 'Girls' school, shop blown up in Swat' *Dawn*, 26 July 2008 available at http://www.dawn.com/2008/07/26/top3.htm (accessed 26 September 2008).
101 R Pape, *Dying to Win: The Strategic Logic of Suicide Terrorism* (Random House, New York 2005).

the world's conflict areas they have come to be widely accepted, and even supported, by populations who presumably might once have recoiled at the idea.'[102] More than twelve hundred people have been killed in attacks mainly suicide in Pakistan since the beginning of 2008.[103] The TTP recruit and train individuals, mostly youths, for suicide missions. They proudly claim to have a large number of suicide bombers waiting for orders to go and kill.[104] The TTP's suicide bombers are known as 'Fidayeen Squad'. The TTP started suicide bombing as a tactic against the Pakistani forces in 2002. There were terrorists' attacks and bomb blasts before 2002 but they were of sectarian nature: Shia and Sunni groups attacking each other.[105] For instance, the attack on a shrine on 27 May 2005 in Islamabad killing twenty people was of sectarian nature. But since 2002, suicide bombing seems to be the new face of militancy.[106] Targets are usually military objects to achieve military objectives. The attacks on military targets results in some civilian casualties. There, however, are many instances where civilians were targeted intentionally. Three major incidents of brutal suicide bombing follow. The common features of these incidents are: intentional killing and injuring dozens of civilians and the TTP taking responsibility describing it as a revenge for killing TTP's fighters. On 21st August 2008, Pakistan Wah Ordnance Factory, when civilian employees were leaving the main gates immediately after the closing hours, was hit by two suicide bombers. The blasts killed seventy people while injuring sixty nine others. The TTP claimed responsibility saying that it was sad over the deaths of civilians, but that the government forces were killing the women and children of the TTP.[107] The Ordnance factory was a military target, but the TTP chose the time and

---

[102] UN Assistance Mission in Afghanistan, 2007:3.

[103]   *The   News   International,*   20th   September   2008   available   at http://thenews.jang.com.pk/updates.asp?id=55840 (accessed 23 September).

[104] M Fazlullah, 'Suicide bombers ready' *Dawn,* 28 July 2008 available at http://www.dawn.com/2008/07/28/top9.htm (accessed 26 September 2008).

[105] R Sohail, 'Rising tendency of suicide attacks in Pakistan' *BBC Urdu,* 18 July 2006. R Hamdani 'History of suicide attacks in Pakistan' *BBC Urdu,* 9 November 2007. Reuters 'Chronology of major incidents of violence in Pakistan', 11 July 2007 available at http://www.alertnet.org/thenews/newsdesk/B80845.htm (accessed 31 July 2008).

[106] 'Suicide bombing, new name of terrorism' *BBC Urdu,* 19 December 2002.

[107] A Iqbal and M Asghar 'Taliban claim 'credit' for Wah carnage: At least 70 killed, 67 injured in   twin   suicide   blasts'   *Dawn,*   22   August   2008   available   at http://www.dawn.com/2008/08/22/top1.htm (accessed 22 September 2008).

place of attack such that the casualties were mostly civilians. In addition, civilians working at the Ordnance factory do not lose their civilian immunity. They might be at risk of being attacked, but they cannot be targeted.[108] On 20th August 2008, a hospital (a protected place under customary law) in Dera was attacked by a suicide bomber killing 32 people while injuring 26 others. The TTP claimed responsibility and threatened more attacks if the government failed to halt operations against the TTP.[109] The most recent and devastating suicide attack was on the Marriot Hotel, Islamabad which killed 57 people, including foreigners. It is not surprising that the TTP was initially suspected, but two days later a lesser known organisation, Fidayeen Islam, accepted responsibility for carrying out the attack while threatening further attacks.[110] Fidayeen Islam is believed to be an auxiliary group of the TTP who had claimed responsibility for suicide bombing in the past.[111]

Attacking civilians and civilian objects is prohibited under customary law and the 1949 Geneva Convention. The TTP's argument that the security forces of Pakistan are killing their fighters as well as their innocent family members is not tenable. As we shall see later, the TTP is correct about the killing of civilians by the security forces of Pakistan; but one legal violation cannot be remedied by another violation. The immunity of the civilian is absolute until their civilian status is lost. The TTP's suicide bombers are posing as civilians when they attack the security forces of Pakistan. Their behaviour is perfidious, and perfidy is a war crime.[112] The indiscriminate killing of people through suicide bombing violates the principle of distinction. Targeting protected civilians objects such as girls' schools by the TTP is

---

[108] n 60.

[109] M Nawaz, '32 killed in DIK hospital suicide blast' *The News International*, 20 August 2008. Available at http://www.thenews.com.pk/top_story_detail.asp?Id=16710 (accessed 22 September 2008) and I Mughal, 'Suicide bomber hits D.I. Khan Hospital: 32 killed, 55 injured; Tehrik-i-Taliban claims responsibility for the carnage' *Dawn,* http://www.dawn.com/2008/08/20/top1.htm (accessed 22 September 2008).

[110] I Mehr, 'Fidyeen Islam accepted responsibility' *BBC Urdu*, 23 September 2008 available at http://www.bbc.co.uk/urdu/pakistan/story/2008/09/080922_marriott_claim_rh.shtml (accessed 23 September 2008).

[111] H Rashid, 'New organisation of suicide bombing' *BBC Urdu*, 16 February 2007 available at http://www.bbc.co.uk/urdu/pakistan/story/2007/02/070216_fidayan_islam_ns.shtml (accessed 23 September 2008).

[112] Hague Regulations 1907, Article 23(b)

a war crime. The ICRC[113] reminded 'all those involved in the armed conflict of their obligation to comply with international humanitarian law. In particular, they must ensure that the civilian population is respected and protected in all circumstances and take all feasible precautions to spare civilians from the effects of hostilities.'

4.1.4 Hostage Taking and Kidnapping

Hostage taking and kidnapping by the TTP has been common practice since 2004.[114] Its members kidnap members of the security forces, government officials and those they regard as pro-government individuals. The majority of hostages are killed, but the lucky ones might get swapped for TTP's fighters in the government's captivity or in some cases by paying ransom.[115] The government usually denies paying ransom and tries to attribute the release to the bravery of the security forces which most Pakistanis doubt. In many cases torture and inhuman treatment is reported. The list of abduction incidents is long, but three cases of civilian abduction incidents are mentioned by way of example. On 2nd September 2008, the TTP claimed that four missing Chinese engineers were in their custody and that its Shura (Council) was preparing a list of demands for the government of Pakistan to meet.[116] They were released in 2009 but it is believed that the government paid a ransom. Tariq Azizudin, Pakistan's ambassador to Afghanistan was kidnapped on 11th February 2008 while on his way to Afghanistan. The TTP took responsibility by issuing a video tape asking the government of Pakistan, through the ambassador, to meet the TTP's demands.[117] He was released on 18 May 2008 under a deal with the local Taliban but the government of Pakistan denies any such deal.[118] A Polish engineer was kidnapped in Pakistan on 2nd October 2008. The TTP claimed that he was in their captivity. On 15th October

---

[113] 22nd August 2008.
[114] R Orakzai, 'Kurram Agency: 44 FC personnel released' *BBC Urdu*, 1 July 2008.
[115] D Wazir, 'Government and Taliban swap prisoners' *BBC Urdu*, 14 May 2008.
[116] H Khan, 'Taliban claim Chinese in their custody' *Dawn*, 3 September 2008.
[117] A Kakar, 'Taliban: kidnapping for ransom, a new strategy' *BBC Urdu*, 19 April 2008 available at
http://www.bbc.co.uk/urdu/pakistan/story/2008/04/080419_taliban_ambassador_ms.shtml (accessed 26 September 2008).
[118] I Khan, 'Azizuddin is home after 97 days' *Dawn*, 18 May 2008 available at http://www.dawn.com/2008/05/18/top1.htm (accessed 26 September 2009).

2008, in a video released by the captors, he said: 'I'm in the hands of the Pakistani Taliban ... I demand that all those watching and listening to me, including Poles, put pressure on the [Pakistani] government to free those [Taliban] who are jailed. In this way, I will also be freed.'[119] He was killed in early 2009. Hostage taking is specifically prohibited by Common Article 3 and is a war crime.

4.1.5 Killing Suspected Spies

Under the law of armed conflict, spies are not entitled to prisoner of war status, but they must be treated humanely. They are at the mercy of the capturing power subject to the right of a fair trial.[120] The TTP do have their own courts (a court of the Taliban is mainly a council of few men) in the areas under their control. They usually claim that the spies confessed before the TTP's council to their crimes of spying. The practices of the TTP are against the law of armed conflict for two reasons. First, it is highly likely that the 'confessions' obtained were done so under duress. Second, the type of justice the TTP is administering in the case of suspected spies is not even near the requirements of a fair trial under international law.

4.2 War Crimes by the Pakistani Forces

Since 2002, when small and large scale operations against militants in the tribal areas began, the public has been given the impression that the security forces of Pakistan are engaged in a war for the security of Pakistan. The implied message was that everything done need not be questioned. Militants are portrayed as the enemies of Pakistan who needed to surrender or be killed to save the country. This sense of Pakistan's security being on the line made it difficult for commentators to question the conduct of various military operations whether these are within the legal framework: the law of armed conflict and domestic law. Commentators also do not want to run the risk of being branded as being pro-militant and so get into trouble with the security forces and intelligence agencies. There was and is a genuine belief that

---

[119] 'Polish engineer urges govt to accept demands of Taliban' *The News International*, 15 October 2008 available at
http://www.thenews.com.pk/top_story_detail.asp?Id=17818 (accessed 15 October 2008).
[120] HR IV 1907, Articles 29-30.

militancy must be eliminated but we also need an objective examination of the way the security forces conduct operations against militants. What follows is a brief account of how the war against militants is conducted. The purpose here is not to discuss whether Pakistan should fight militants but it is to see how different military operations are conducted.

4.2.1 Indiscriminate Killing

It seems that on many occasions the intelligence regarding militants is not sound and the security forces act on doubtful evidence. It also seems that no proper evaluation has been made of the concrete military advantage to come out of hitting particular targets. If the Pakistani security forces kill an important militant but civilians are also killed during the attack, such incidental loss of civilians is permitted. However, the principle of proportionality needs to be strictly followed. The incidental loss of life and property must be taken into account and weighed against prospective concrete military advantages.

4.2.2 Operation Silence: Red Mosque Operation

One of the operations where the most serious violations of the law of armed conflict and human rights occurred is Operation Silence or the Red Mosque Operation. The security forces started operation against the alleged militants inside the Red Mosque early in the morning on 10 July 2007. During the operation, around eight security personnel were killed whereas over a hundred students including the Imam of the mosque were killed.[121] The security forces did not give exact figure of how many were militants and how many were civilians. Several dead bodies were buried in a single mass grave during night by the government personnel.[122] Not a single militant was identified among the dead bodies. On 3 June 2008, General (Rtd) Gulzar Kayani said that phosphorus bombs were used against the students which was cruel and un-necessary and called for an inquiry.[123] The Human Rights

---

[121] Rashid, H. '102 dies in operation' *BBC Urdu*. 13 July 2007.; see Dawn 'It's all over as Ghazi is killed'. 11 July 2007 available at http://www.dawn.com/2007/07/11/top1.htm (accessed 22 September 2008).

[122] I Mehr, 'Doubts over the deaths' *BBC Urdu*, 12 July 2007.

[123] J Kayani 'Inquiry for Lal Masjid and Kargil' *BBC Urdu*, 3 June 2008.

Commission of Pakistan[124] also joined the call for inquiry into the loss of innocent lives as the then Musharraf government tried to cover it up.

4.2.3 Missing Persons

After the attack on Afghanistan on 7th October 2001, the Bush Administration offered hundreds of thousands of dollars as head money for key Al-Qaeda and Taliban figures. The government of Pakistan, as an ally, started arresting suspected militants and made a lot of money. 'We have captured 672 and handed over 369 to the United States. We have earned bounties totalling millions of dollars.'[125] 'The phenomenon started with the great sweeps for al-Qaeda suspects after September 11, but has dramatically increased in recent years, and now those who disappear include home-grown "enemies of the state" - poets, doctors, housewives and nuclear scientists, accused of terrorism, treason and murder.'[126] Under the law of armed conflict and domestic laws of Pakistan, the security forces are allowed to detain militants but they should keep record of those arrested and let their relatives know the whereabouts of the detainees. There is no government record available to show the detention of these people, which is why these detainees are called 'missing persons'. Amina Masood Janjua's husband, Masood Janjua, was apprehended by Pakistani security forces in July 2005, along with another man, Faisal Faraz. The security forces have detained them since without filing any charges against them, and in some cases, even denying their detention. The two men (and even some children) are among hundreds of victims of enforced disappearance in Pakistan, held beyond the reach of the law or any outside monitoring. Their families continue to fear for the lives of their loved ones, aware that torture and other ill-treatment are routine in Pakistani places of detention. Those forced to fear for the fate of the 'disappeared' are also victims of Pakistan's plague of enforced disappearances.[127] There are

---

124 11 July 2007.

125 P Musharraf, *In the Line of Fire: A Memoir* (Free Press New York 2006).

126 D Walsh, 'Without a trace' *The Guardian*, 16 March 2007 available at http://www.guardian.co.uk/world/2007/mar/16/alqaida.pakistan/print (accessed 15 October 2008).

127 *Denying the Undeniable: Enforced Disappearances in Pakistan* (Amnesty International) July 2008, http://www.amnesty.org/en/library/asset/ASA33/018/2008/en/d3e8181d-631c-11dd-9756-f55e3ec0a600; and *Pakistan: Human Rights Ignored in the "war on terror"* (Amnesty International)

reports that some terror suspects in the custody of Pakistani intelligence agencies were tortured.[128]

The security forces of Pakistan have used jets and gunship helicopters in the fight against militants. On many occasions sound intelligence was not collected which led to hitting the wrong targets killing civilians. On numerous occasions, disproportionate force was used. The firing was indiscriminate resulting into the deaths of civilian and destruction of civilian property. Hundreds of persons are arrested and detained without charges. The relatives of those detained do not know their whereabouts. Most of these people were kidnapped or picked up by the Pakistani secret agencies. Torture is reported in several cases. Indiscriminate firing and use of excessive force is against customary international law. Torture and inhumane treatment is against Common Article 3. Detention without charge and trial is against the fundamental rights recognised by the constitution of Pakistan. The Security Council[129] has consistently condemned acts of terrorism in Pakistan. It has, however, at the same time consistently stressed to states that 'any measures taken to combat terrorism comply with all their obligations under international law, in particular international human rights, refugee and humanitarian law'.

4.2.4 Local Lashkars

A local Lashkar is a group of armed men who get together to defend themselves or take a revenge for wrong done to them by the TTP. A lashkar consists of young men carrying whatever arms they can lay their hands on and are guided by motives of self-help and revenge. A lashkar is usually led by tribal leaders. In the past, the government has tried to empower such lashkars[130] by providing arms, while no training on the

---

September 2006 available at http://www.amnesty.org/en/library/info/ASA33/035/2006 (accessed 22 September 2008).

[128] I Cobain and R Norton-Taylor 'Whitehall devised torture policy for terror detainees' *Guardian*, 19 February 2009 available at
http://www.guardian.co.uk/world/2009/feb/16/pakistan-torture-mi5-agent-binyam (accessed 30 June 2009).

[129] Presidential Statement, 22nd August 2008.

[130] I Ashraf, 'Tribesmen on their own' *Dawn*, 17 June 2009 available at
http://www.dawn.com/wps/wcm/connect/dawn-content-
library/dawn/news/pakistan/provinces/16-tribesmen-on-their-own-hs-05 (accessed 30 June 2009).

laws of war or use of weapons is given. In many cases, the TTP came back and killed many members of the lashkar. On 5th June 2009, the TTP's suicide bomber killed 33 worshipers in a mosque in Upper Dir. As a response, the local people formed a lashkar of 700 men to avenge the deaths of their loved ones.[131] The lashkar claims to have killed dozens of militants, burnt their houses and the houses of their sympathizers.[132] In August 2008, the TTP killed 6 policemen, took their weapons and disappeared into the mountains of Buner. The people of Buner formed a lashkar and attacked militants' hideouts and killed most of them. 'A video made on the cellphone showed six militants lying in the dirt, blood oozing from their wounds.'[133] On 29th December 2008, the TTP struck back: a suicide car bomber set off an explosion in a school where polling was taking place for the election of the National Assembly. More than 30 people were killed and more than two dozens wounded.[134]

The problem with the lashkars is that they are not part of the security forces of Pakistan. They do not have any formal or informal training in the law of armed conflict or use of weapons but the government encourage local tribesmen to raise arms against the militants. The TTP is working outside the law and so are lashkars by taking the law into their own hands. As their only motive is revenge, there is a greater risk that the law of armed conflict will be violated. This can be seen in instances where the lashkars killed even the sympathisers of the TTP. As a retaliation, militants attack villages and kill indiscriminately. The security forces do not come to the aid of

---

[131] Z Jan, 'Tribal lashkar kills two militants in Upper Dir' *Dawn*, 29 June. Available at http://www.dawn.com/wps/wcm/connect/dawn-content-library/dawn/news/pakistan/provinces/19-upper-dir-lashkar-kills-two-more-foreign-militants-01 (accessed 30 June 2009).

[132] n 132; Inter Services Public Relations 15 June 2009, available at http://www.ispr.gov.pk/front/main.asp?o=t-press_release&date=2009/6/15 (accessed 30 June 2009).

[133] J Perlez and PZ Shah 'As Taliban Overwhelm Police, Pakistanis Hit Back' *The New York Times*, available at http://www.nytimes.com/2008/11/02/world/asia/02pstan.html (accessed 30 June 2009).

[134] RA Oppel and PZ Shah 'Taliban Hit Pakistan Town that Fought Taliban' *The New York Times*, 29 December 2009. Available at http://www.nytimes.com/2008/12/29/world/asia/29pstan.html (accessed 30 June 2009).

lashkars.[135] The security forces have the duty to protect civilians rather than encouraging them to pick up guns and take revenge. It is promoting lawlessness and potential war crimes.

5. Prosecution of War Crimes

It is clear from the above discussion that war crimes and crimes against domestic laws are committed by the TTP as well as the security forces of Pakistan. The key question to examine is whether those guilty of war crimes are prosecuted. The security forces of Pakistan were able to arrest key members of the TTP but unfortunately none of them has been either charged or prosecuted for war crimes. They were kept in captivity for a few days or weeks and then either mysteriously released or swapped for members of the security forces imprisoned by the TTP. The top lieutenant of Baitullah Mehsud, Rafiuddin, was arrested but released after cutting a deal with the government. In September 2008, he was rearrested under FCR.[136] The intelligence agencies of Pakistan arrested hundreds of persons but they are neither charged nor prosecuted. They are simply missing. The violation of the law of armed conflict and other relevant laws by the security forces is not an issue of concern for the security forces and the current civilian government. There is no record showing that someone from the ranks of the TTP or the security forces of Pakistan is charged for war crimes.

There no reasonable prospect for the prosecution of war crimes. There are two reasons for this. First, the security forces believe that they are fighting for the security and future of Pakistan. Whatever damage they can inflict on the TTP is legal. Their view is supported by the civilian administration. This might be true but the question is not whether the TTP is a legitimate target. The question is to prosecute those who violated the law of armed conflict and domestic law in

---

[135] S Tavernise and I Ashraf 'Attacked, Pakistani Villagers Take on Taliban' *The New York Times*, 10 June 2009. Available at http://www.nytimes.com/2009/06/10/world/asia/10pstan.html (accessed 30 June 2009).

[136] A Saboor, 'Mehsud's deputy and two aids re-arrested' *Daily Times*, 13 September 2008. Available at http://www.dailytimes.com.pk/default.asp?page=2008/09/13/story_13-9-2008_pg7_21 (accessed 26 September 2008) and see PZ Shah and J Perlez 'Taliban Threaten to Kill Officials Held Hostage' *The New York Times*, 19 July. Available at http://www.nytimes.com/2008/07/19/world/asia/19pstan.html (accessed 26 September 2008).

carrying out operation against the TTP. The second reason is that the TTP is a lethal force. The fighters of the TTP routinely kidnap government officials and members of the security forces. The TTP usually ask the government to release the detained TTP's fighters in return for the release of government officials. The government is usually inclined to swap captives with the TTP. In some cases, ransom is paid to the TTP. This scene of quid pro quo prevents the successful prosecution of the TTP's members involved in war crimes. The government also understands and fears that prosecuting a top TTP's commander will cause strong retaliation from the TTP.

6. Conclusion

The conflict in the tribal areas of Pakistan is bitter and violent. The law of armed conflict and domestic laws are violated. The conflict seems to intensify further which could mean increase in war crimes. The media portrayal and governments of countries such as Pakistan, the United States and the United Kingdom tend to argue that it is only the militants who violate the law. This is a half-truth. Both parties to the conflict have committed war crimes. Militancy in the tribal areas is serious and genuine but should be fought only within the limits of municipal and international law. No matter how much we dislike or disagree with the TTP's agenda, we still need to play by the rules to defeat them.

The Year in Human Rights

In association with the UCL SHRP Bulletin

Compiled by Harriet Holmes

AUGUST 2008

29 August 2008
R (on the application of Binyam Mohammed) v Secretary of State for Foreign and Commonwealth Affairs **[2008] EWCH 2100**
(Admin)
Divisional Court: Thomas, LJ and Lloyd Jones, J

The claimant (BM) applied for judicial review of a decision of the defendant secretary of state to refuse to disclose certain information relevant to his defence of terrorist charges in the United States. BM also claimed the provision of information and documents under the principles set out in *Norwich Pharmacol* [1974] AC 133 or a duty said to exist under customary international law.

BM was an Ethiopian national with refugee status in the UK. He had been arrested in Pakistan in 2002 whilst attempting to leave for the UK using the passport of a British national. He had been interviewed there by the US agents and UK security services about possible links to terrorism. From the period of April 2002 until May 2004 his precise whereabouts were unknown to the UK security services. Any requests for information made by the UK services to the US authorities either received no response or stated that direct access could not be facilitated at that time. As a result, the UK services submitted questions to be put to BM.

In 2004, BM had been transferred into US custody and made several confessions. He was then charged in 2008, in the US, with terrorist offences carrying the death penalty.

The matter at issue in this case was whether the Secretary of State was entitled to a public interest immunity certificate in disclosing the documents and information about the detention, treatment and rendition of BM by the US authorities for the purposes of his defence to the criminal charges in the US. The documents and information had previously been ordered to be disclosed.

BM had sought disclosure of documents in the possession of the Secretary of State that supported his claim that he had confessed to terrorist offences as a result of torture. The Secretary of State claimed that disclosure would seriously harm the existing intelligence sharing arrangements between the United Kingdom and the US and thereby cause considerable damage to the national security of the UK.

BM argued that (1) the change of position of the US authorities about disclosure of the documents was insufficient as he was not assured of timely disclosure and would not have disclosure of the documents to be able to make submissions to the convening authority; (2) the public interest immunity certificate and sensitive schedule had failed to address the abhorrence and condemnation accorded to torture and cruel, inhuman or degrading treatment.

On the facts, the Court considered that the agreement of the US authorities to supply the documents to the authority and to BM if charges were referred meant BM had achieved all that the Court could have ordered; as well as being all that is essential for a fair trial. The only deficiency was that BM would not have disclosure to be able to make submissions to the convening authority. The effect of this would have to be considered by the Court when performing the balancing exercise in relation to public interest immunity and the exercise of its discretion to order disclosure.

The Court held that BM's allegations of torture had not been dealt with either expressly or impliedly in the public interest immunity certificate. The secretary of state had, therefore, failed to show that he had taken a material matter into account. Nonetheless in light of the pressure of time and speed at which matters had developed amongst other factors, it was just to allow the respondent to amend the certificate.

SEPTEMBER 2008

2 September 2008
R v O **[2008] EWCA Crim 2835**
Court of Appeal (Criminal Division): Laws LJ, Jack J and Sir Charles Gray

The appellant was arrested on attempting to leave the country using false documentation. The custody record indicated that although the appellant insisted she was older, she appeared to be a juvenile, and subsequently informed her solicitors she was 17 years of age. Further, she claimed that she had been a victim of sex-trafficking, which was documented in writing by an outreach worker in counsel's brief. At the Crown Court she pleaded guilty with neither the discrepancies about her age, or trafficking claims being explored further.

Upon appeal to the Court of Appeal, it was held that there was a complete absence of a fair trial. The failures by both the Crown, in investigating the apparent youth of the appellant, and defence counsel, in failing to raise the issue of the trafficking as a possible defence of duress, were shameful and the conviction was quashed.

Furthermore, the Court stated that when prosecuting immigration offences involving defendants who might be the victims of people trafficking, prosecutors had to be aware of the protocols contained in the Code for Crown Prosecutors requiring them to consider whether the public interest was best served in continuing the prosecution.

3 September 2008
Kadi v Council of the European Union **[2008] ECR I-6351**
European Court of Justice (Grand Chamber): Vassilios Skouris (President)

This case concerned a joint application made to the ECJ in respect of asset freezing orders made against certain individuals, who were suspected of terrorism.

Pursuant to Security Council Resolution 1267, it was felt by the EC Council that Community action to implement the Resolution was required, and subsequently Regulations were passed allowing, amongst other things, assets of individuals to be frozen.

The Court allowed the appeal in part. First, they held that fairness required that the authorities communicate to the individual concerned at least the grounds upon which orders made under the Regulation to freeze assets were made, so that there could be an effective judicial review. As the Council has not afforded the individuals the right to be informed of evidence against them, there had been a breach of their right to be heard, and a violation of the principle of effective judicial protection. Secondly, the Court held that the argument accepted by the Court of First Instance, that because the regulations were passed in accordance with Security Council authorisation there could be no review of their lawfulness, was wrong in law.

The Court held that even where Security Council authorisation is concerned it must undertake a full review of any action taken in light of fundamental rights.

12 September 2008
Murungaru (Kenya) v SSHD [2008] EWCA Civ 1015
Court of Appeal (Civil Division): Sedley, Jacob LJJ and Lewison J

The contractual right to receive private medical treatment is not property or possession for the purposes of Article 1 of Protocol 1. Indicia of possessions for the purposes of establishing a property right under Article 1 of Protocol 1 of the European Convention on Human Rights include: tangibility, whether the possession is assignable, transmissibility, and economic value, and the possession must be capable of being described as an 'asset'.

The claimant was a former government minister in Kenya. He had a multiple entry visa for the UK which was revoked without notice about three months after it had been granted. He wanted to travel to the UK to continue his private medical treatment, but was unable to do so. This case concerned his challenge of the revocation by means of judicial review. One of his arguments was that the revocation interfered with his rights under Article 1 of Protocol 1 of the Convention, the right to peaceful enjoyment of his possessions, that is, to his contract with his doctors.

18 September 2008
R (Thomas) v Havering LBC [2008] All ER (D) 18
Queen's Bench Division (Admin): His Honour Judge Pelling QC

This case concerned applications made challenging the decision of the local authority to close residential homes as being a breach of the positive obligation under Article 2 (the right to life). The principal reason according to the claimants being that moving individuals with dementia and other ailments had a statistically significant adverse effect on mortality rates.

The Court held that the decisions were neither unreasonable nor contrary to Article 2.

OCTOBER 2008

2 October 2008
R (on the application of C) v Ministry for Justice [2008] EWCA 2671
Court of Appeal (Civil Division): Pill LJ, Silber J

The appellant appealed against a decision refusing to quash the Secure Training Centre (Amendment) Rules 2007. The respondent Secretary of State had sought to amend the Rules so as to permit physical restraint of young persons at such centres where restraint was thought to be necessary for the purposes of ensuring good order and discipline.

The Court of Appeal held that the failure to conduct a racial discrimination enquiry into the use of physical restraint and into its effects on children was a significant procedural defect. The rule of law as well as the proper administration of race relations required the amendments to be quashed.

Moreover, a system of physical control in care was found to engage Article 3 (freedom from torture and inhuman or degrading treatment) by its very nature, and therefore there was a *prima facie* breach or at least a significant risk of breach of Article 3. Lastly, the Secretary of State could not establish that such a system was necessary in a democratic society and it was thus a violation of Article 8 (right to privacy).

3 October 2008
L v Human Fertilisation and Embryology Authority [2008] EWHC 2149 (Fam)
High Court, Family Division: Charles J

The case concerned claimant (L) who sought declarations that the sperm of her deceased husband (H) could lawfully continue to be stored and used in the United Kingdom or be stored for export and use abroad.

H and L had wished to have a second child. However, H died unexpectedly. Following H's death, a declaration was made that the hospital could lawfully retrieve sperm from H, which was carried out. Once they had learnt of the Court's declaration, the defendant authority indicated that it was for the Court to determine whether the relevant statutory provisions had been satisfied. The decision to export H's sperm was suspended pending a decision by the Divisional Court.

The claimant submitted that an absolute bar on the use and storage of H's sperm based on effective consent, under the Human Fertilisation and Embryology Act 1990, was unsustainable and incompatible with the Article 8 of the European Convention on Human Rights. She further argued that the effective consent requirement was an unjustified interference with rights under the EC Treaty.

The Court found in favour of the defendant. The judge assessed the provisions contained within the legislation. Firstly, Charles J held that the need for effective consent to storage in the UK was not incompatible with L's convention rights, following the decision of the ECtHR in *Evans v United Kingdom* (6339/05), where it was held that a fair balance had been struck between competing rights in the legislation concerned.

Secondly, he placed weight on the fact that the discretionary power vested in section 24(4) to permit export meant that the Act was not in absolute terms. The section enabled the authority to grant a special direction authorising storage or further storage pending a decision by it on export.

Thirdly, Charles J outlined the position of the Court in proceedings of this nature. Outside of the bounds of judicial review, the

Court had limited jurisdiction to fill any gap pending a decision by the authority. Without a special direction, storage without effective consent was not permitted and was a criminal offence. The Court could not authorise the commission of a criminal offence or give consent on behalf of H to modify conditions of the relevant licences.

Finally, the authority should consider whether the Court had the power to make a declaration on the legality of the retrieval. It was not possible to lawfully remove or authorise the removal of gametes from a dead person who had not given effect advance consent.

R (Bancoult) v Secretary of State for Foreign and Commonwealth Affairs [2008] UKHL 61
House of Lords: Lord Hoffmann, Lord Bingham, Lord Rodger, Lord Carswell and Lord Mance

In disagreement with the Court of Appeal, the House of Lords – by a 3 to 2 majority (Lord Bingham and Lord Mance dissenting) – upheld the Government's decision not to allow resettlement of the Chagos Islands by their previous inhabitants, enforced through two Orders in Council.

The islanders had been compulsorily removed in 1971 so that the islands would be used as a US military base. The majority found no constitutional right to one's abode and thereby no violation of any fundamental constitutional principle by the executive decision. Although Orders in Council are susceptible to judicial review on ordinary principles, the majority held that it was not for the Court to assess whether the Crown, as legislator for the particular non-self-governing colonial territories, exercised its powers for their stated purpose, namely for the "peace, order and good government" of the territories. Rather the majority considered the wording to confer unrestricted authority to the Crown rather than place limits on its legislative capabilities.

Lastly, the majority found that a prior decision not to challenge an earlier successful application for judicial review by the islanders did not give rise to a legitimate expectation because there had been no clear and unambiguous promise to allow resettlement. Hence, no constitutional right or legitimate expectation was found to be breached by the Government.

NOVEMBER 2008

4 November 2008
Demski v Poland (22695/03) (2008)
European Court of Human Rights: Nicolas Bratza (President)

The applicant was convicted of raping a 17-year-old girl, and sentenced to four years' imprisonment in Poland. Relying on Article 6 (right to fair trial) he complained that he was not able to examine the victim who is the main witness in the criminal proceedings against him. The witness had not appeared before the court in Poland as she was living in Germany and had failed to appear when summoned.

The Court considered that Mr Demski's conviction had been to a decisive extent based on the depositions of the victim whom he had had no opportunity to have examined either during the investigation or at the trial. It was ruled that the authorities had failed to make every reasonable effort to determine her actual address in order to obtain her attendance at the trial despite the fact that the victim resides abroad. The Court unanimously concluded that there had been a violation of Article 6.

This decision is in accordance with a previous House of Lords case: *R v A (Sexual Offence: Complainant's Sexual History)* [2001] UKHL 25.

4 November 2008
Balsyte-Lideikiene v Lithuania (72596/01) (2008)
European Court of Human Rights: Josep Casadevall (President)

The applicant was a Lithuanian national who formerly owned a publishing company. In 2001, she published and distributed the 'Lithuanian Calendar 2000' which had been ruled to be in breach of the Code on Administrative Law Offences by domestic courts for promoting ethnic hatred. An administrative warning was given to her and unsold copies of the calendar were confiscated.

The applicant made two claims in the European Court of Human Rights against the domestic courts' decision. These applications were upheld in part.

First, relying on Article 6 (right to fair trial), the applicant complained that her case had been examined by the first-instance court without the experts being summoned to the hearing. This claim was successful. Although experts were appointed to produce relevant reports to investigate whether the calendar contained promotion of ethnic hatred; the applicant had not been given the opportunity to question the experts in order to subject their credibility to scrutiny. Thus there had been a violation of Article 6.

Secondly, the confiscation of the calendar and the ban on its further distribution was in violation of Article 10 (freedom of expression) of the Convention. However, this claim was unsuccessful. The Court considered the fact that after the re-establishment of the independence of the Republic of Lithuania in 1990 the questions of territorial integrity and national minorities had been sensitive. Whilst the applicant argued that the interference had been disproportionate, the Court noted that the calendar had caused negative reactions from official representatives of some neighbouring States, who had complained about the map denoting some of the territories of those countries as 'ethnic Lithuanian lands under temporary occupation'. Thus, the Court felt that the calendar did give the Lithuanian authorities cause for serious concern, and that there was a pressing social need to take measures against the applicant. Hence, it concluded that the interference with the applicant's right to freedom of expression could reasonably have been considered necessary in a democratic society for the protection of the reputation or rights of others. As such, it was unanimously held that there had been no violation of Article 10.

12 November 2008
Demir and Baykara v Turkey (2008) 48 EHRR 54
European Court of Human Rights: Christos Rozakis (President)

The case concerned the failure by the Turkish Court of Cassation in 1995 to recognize the applicants' right to form trade unions as municipal civil servants, and the annulment of a collective agreement between their union and the employing authority.

In 1993 the trade union entered into a collective agreement with Gaziantep Municipal Council regulating all aspects of the working conditions of the Council's employees. The trade union brought proceedings against the Council under the agreement in the Turkish civil courts. It won its case in the Gaziantep District Court, which inferred a right for trade unions to enter into collective agreements by reference to international treaties such as the conventions of the International Labour Organisation (ILO). However, the Court of Cassation subsequently ruled that the freedom to join a trade union and to bargain collectively could not be exercised in the absence of specific legislation.

The Grand Chamber of the ECtHR held unanimously that there had been a violation of Article 11 (freedom of assembly and association) on account of an interference with the exercise by the applicants, municipal civil servants, of their right to form trade unions. Article 11 was further violated on account of the annulment, with retrospective effect, of a collective agreement between the trade union and the employing authority that had been the result of collective bargaining.

18 November 2008
M Tosun v Turkey (33104/04) (2008)
European Court of Human Rights: Francoise Tulkens (President)

The applicant (T) was arrested in November 1995 because he was suspected of attempting to undermine the constitutional order. T was transferred to a prison where he was detained pending criminal proceedings. The 2002 judgment that he was convicted and sentenced to life imprisonment was quashed on appeal in 2003 but he was not released on bail before May 2006. The retrial is still pending.

The Court held unanimously that there had been a violation of Article 5(3) (right to liberty and security) on account of the excessive length, nine years and almost eight months, of the applicant's detention on remand and a violation of Article 6(1) (right to a fair trial within a reasonable time) on account of the excessive length, 13 years and still pending, of the criminal proceedings against him. Mr Tosun was awarded EUR 13,500 in respect of non-pecuniary damage.

20 November 2008
Brunet-Lecomte et Sarl Lyon Mag' v France (13327/04) (2009)
European Court of Human Rights: Rait Maruste (President)

This case concerns the publication of an article in a magazine (Lyon Mag') criticizing the teaching methods used by L, a lecturer at Lyons III University, and the subsequent publication of a written reply by L accompanied by comments in which the term 'maniac' appeared twice. The applicants were prosecuted for public defamation of a civil servant and were ordered to pay a fine. Consequently, the applicants complained that their conviction for defamation entailed a breach of Article 10 (freedom of expression) of the Convention.

The Court took the view that the term 'mania' could not by itself be considered defamatory in the circumstances and that the comments in question had not exceeded the degree of provocation generally allowed to the press. Furthermore, that the comments had not been serious and had concerned a subject of topical public interest. Secondly, the protection of L's office as a civil servant could not take priority over the right of the public to receive information. Finally, the applicant's conviction amounted to disproportionate interference with Article 10 (right to freedom of expression). Thus there was a violation of Article 10.

26 November 2008
R (on the application of JL) v Secretary of State for the Home Department [2009] 1 AC 588
House of Lords: Lord Phillips, Lord Rodger, Lord Walker, Lord Brown, Lord Mance

The case concerned the near suicide of the prisoner, JL. Although the Secretary of State was aware that investigation into a suicide or near-suicide was required, due to resource implications he wanted clarification of the nature and extent of the investigation required to comply with an individual's rights under Article 2 (right to life).

The Lords decided that a near-suicide of a prisoner in custody which left him with the possibility of a serious long-term injury automatically triggers an obligation on the state under Article 2 to institute an enhanced investigation. That obligation cannot be discharged by an internal investigation of the facts. The profundity of the investigation would depend upon the circumstances. In some circumstances an initial investigation would satisfy the requirements under Article 2; in others further investigation would be required. The finding of fault was not instructive as to whether to launch a further investigation. As the object of the investigation went beyond ascertaining whether state agents had been at fault; its primary purpose was to learn lessons for the future.

If the investigation was to be impartial and seen to be impartial, it should be carried out by a person who was independent of the prison authorities. To satisfy the requirements of Article 2, besides being independent and involving the family of the victim, investigations must be initiated by the state, be promptly and expeditiously carried out, and provide for a sufficient element of public scrutiny.

DECEMBER 2008

4 December 2008
Dogru v France (2008) 49 EHRR 8
European Court of Human Rights: Peer Lorenzen (President)

The case concerned the applicants' exclusion from school as a result of their refusal to remove their headscarves during sports classes. On many occasions in January 1999 the applicants went to physical education and sports classes wearing their headscarves and refused to take them off. This was despite repeated requests to do so by their teacher, who explained that wearing a headscarf was incompatible with physical education classes.

The domestic court held that, by attending physical education and sports classes in dress that would not enable them to take part in the classes in question, the applicants had failed to comply with the duty to attend classes. Further, it was ruled that their attitude had created an atmosphere of tension within the school and that, on the basis of all the factors involved, their expulsion from the school had been justified and proportionate, regardless of the proposal they had made at the end of January to wear a hat instead of a headscarf. Relying on Article 9 (the right to freedom of thought, conscience and religion), the applicants complained to the ECtHR of an infringement of their right to practice their religion.

The ECtHR held that there had been no violation of Article 9. The Court referred to earlier judgments in which it had held that the national authorities were obliged to take great care to ensure that, in keeping with the principle of respect for pluralism and the freedom of others, the manifestation by pupils of their religious beliefs on school premises did not take on the nature of an ostentatious act that would constitute a source of pressure and exclusion. In the Court's view, that concern did indeed appear to have been answered by the French secular model.

Also, the domestic court's concern that the wearing of a veil was incompatible with sports classes for reasons of health or safety was not unreasonable. It accepted that the penalty imposed was only the result of the applicants' refusal to comply with the rules applicable on the school premises – of which they had been properly informed – and not of their religious convictions.

4 December 2008
S and Marper v United Kingdom (2009) 48 EHRR 50
European Court of Human Rights: Jean-Paul Costa (President)

The case concerned the retention by the UK authorities of fingerprints, cellular samples and DNA profile after individuals' release.

The first applicant, S, was arrested at the age of eleven in January 2001, charged with attempted robbery and subsequently acquitted in June 2001. The second applicant, Marper, was arrested in March 2001 and charged with harassment of his partner but the couple became reconciled and the case was discontinued in June. In both cases the police took the applicants' fingerprints and DNA samples and refused to destroy them on request of the applicants after the cases were closed. The Administrative Court rejected their application for judicial review and the Court of Appeal upheld that decision. In July 2004 the House of Lords dismissed an appeal by the applicants.

The applicants complained under Articles 8 and 14 of the Convention about the retention by the authorities of their fingerprints, cellular samples and DNA profiles after their acquittal or discharge.

The Court found that the retention of DNA and fingerprint data of persons that were suspected but not convicted for criminal investigation purposes constituted a violation of Article 8 (right to respect for private and family life) of the Convention.

The Court analysis of the Article 8 violation was as follows: In the case of DNA and cellular samples, given the highly personal nature of the information retained and the amount of personal information which it contained, the retention *per se* constituted an interference with Article 8(1). The retention was all the more sensitive as it provided a means of tracing genetic relationships and identifying ethnic origin, which were very susceptible of affecting the right to private and family life.

Retention of DNA samples constituted a greater interference with the right to private life than fingerprints. Nonetheless, in the case of fingerprints, the unique and personal information contained in them also made their non-consensual retention an interference with Article 8.

The Court examined whether the retention of DNA samples and fingerprint data of persons that were suspected but subsequently acquitted was justified under Article 8(2).

It held that whilst the retention of DNA and fingerprints by the police had a clear and sufficiently certain basis in UK law, it was essential to have clearer rules providing safeguards preventing any such use of personal data as could be inconsistent with the guarantees under Article 8. It accepted that the prevention of crime was a legitimate purpose for the interference.

The Court then examined whether the interference was legitimate in a democratic society. The retention of data had to be proportionate to the purpose and limited in time. The use of DNA techniques was necessary for the prevention of terrorism and crime. However, in all Contracting States, personal data retained by the police were removed or destroyed after acquittal of the suspect. The Court noted that England, Wales and Northern Ireland appeared to be the only jurisdictions within the Council of Europe to allow the indefinite retention of fingerprint and DNA material of any person of any age suspected of any recordable offence.

The Court was struck by the blanket and indiscriminate nature of these powers, which contained no limitations in time regardless of the gravity of the offence, criminal history of the subject or the degree of suspicion against him. The fact of storage in itself constituted interference regardless of whether the information was actually used. Moreover, the risk of stigmatisation, residing in the fact that the innocent suspects were treated like convicted persons, denied them the presumption of innocence to which every individual is entitled under the Convention. That risk could be especially harmful in the case of minors, such as S, given the importance of their development and integration in society.

Thus the retention of DNA samples and fingerprint data of persons that were suspected but subsequently acquitted was disproportionate for the purpose of Article 8(2). No separate issues arose under Article 14 of the Convention.

10 December 2008
TK (Burundi) v Secretary of State for the Homes Department [2009] EWCA Civ 40
Court of Appeal (Civil): Waller LJ, Thomas LJ and Moore-Bick LJ

The claimant was an asylum seeker who sought to appeal the decision of an immigration judge which ordered his removal from the UK.

Although the claimant posited that he had two children in the UK, the immigration judge held that he should be removed from the UK because on balance Article 8 of the Convention (right to respect for family and private life) was in favour of his removal given that no evidence was given by the mothers of the claimant's children and that the explanation for this absence was unsatisfactory.

Permission for appeal was granted but it came to light that at the time of the reconsideration hearing, the claimant's new partner was illegally in the UK as her asylum claim had been dismissed. Therefore, the claimant's claim to be entitled to family life on the basis of his family life with his second daughter and his intention to marry the mother was unsustainable.

The claimant appealed *inter alia* on the grounds that the immigration judge would not have come the decision he did if he had not speculated about the evidence brought before him, and instead had merely assessed the claimant's credibility in light of the evidence brought before him.

On appeal, the Court held that where evidence was readily available a judge may take into account failure to provide such evidence, and that if there was no credible explanation for the failure to produce the supporting evidence, it could be a strong pointer that the account given was not credible and a judge committed no error of law when he relied on that failure as the reason for rejecting the account of a claimant.

In the present case, the claimant had provided no credible explanation as to his failure to call his new partner or as to his misleading statement to the immigration judge as to her immigration status. The approach of the judge on the evidence before him was an approach he was entitled to take in assessing the claimant's credibility and in reaching his conclusion that the family life was not as strong as the claimant claimed. The Appeal was accordingly dismissed.

11 December 2008
TV Vest AS v Norway (2009) 48 EHRR 51
European Court of Human Rights: Christos Rozakis (President)

TV Vest, the first applicant television broadcasting company and Rogaland Pensjonistparti, the 2nd applicant political party, brought an application against Norway claiming a violation of Article 10 (freedom of expression).

TV Vest agreed to broadcast Rogaland Pensjonistparti's political advertisement. There was a statutory prohibition in Norway against broadcasting political advertisements. Despite an awareness of the statutory prohibition, TV Vest broadcasted the political advertisement, arguing it was entitled to do so due to the protection provided under Article 10 of the Convention. The Media Authority decided to impose a fine on TV Vest, for violation of the political advertising prohibition.

An appeal to the Oslo City Court was unsuccessful. TV Vest did not dispute that the content was political advertising and thus fell foul of the above-mentioned prohibition in the Broadcasting Act. However, the appellant submitted that this provision was incompatible with the right to freedom of expression in Article 100 of the Norwegian Constitution and Article 10 of the Convention.

A further appeal against the City Court's judgment to the Supreme Court, challenging its application of the law, was dismissed. The Supreme Court, by four votes to one, upheld the Media Authority's decision.

At ECtHR level, the applicants complained that the fine imposed by the Media Authority constituted a violation of Article 10 of the Convention. The parties shared the view that the impugned measure amounted to an interference with the applicants' right to freedom of expression as guaranteed by Article 10. They further agreed that the measure was prescribed by law, namely sections 3-1(3) and 10-3 of the Broadcasting Act in Norway, and pursued the legitimate aim of protecting 'the rights of others' in the sense of paragraph 2 of this Article. The Court saw no reason to hold otherwise. Although the parties were in disagreement as to whether the interference was 'necessary in a democratic society'.

The Court held unanimously that there had been a violation of Article 10 of the Convention. This decision was reached on the basis that the Court did not find a reasonable relationship of proportionality between the legitimate aim pursued by the prohibition on political advertising and the means deployed to achieve that aim. The restriction which the prohibition and imposition of the subsequent fine entailed could not therefore be regarded as having been necessary in a democratic society, within the meaning of paragraph 2 of Article 10 for the protection the rights of others. This was notwithstanding the margin of appreciation available to the national authorities.

21 December 2008

R (on the application of Wellington) v Secretary of State for the Home Department [2008] UKHL 72

House of Lords: Lord Hoffmann, Lord Scott, Baroness Hale, Lord Carswell and Lord Brown

The appellant Wellington was a drug dealer who killed two people in Kansas City (one of whom was a pregnant woman) by firing with guns on 13 February 1997. The appellant was charged with murder of the first degree in the State of Missouri (USA). On 29 January 2003 the appellant was arrested in London. The United States requested his extradition, undertaking not to impose the death penalty. On 13 June 2006 the Home Secretary notified the appellant that he ordered his extradition. Wellington applied for judicial review and his application was dismissed by the Administrative Court.

He further appealed to the House of Lords on the ground that the Home Secretary's order violated Article 3 of the European Convention on Human Rights (prohibition of torture and of inhuman and degrading treatment), on the basis that a sentence of life imprisonment without eligibility for parole is alleged to constitute 'inhuman or degrading treatment'.

The House of Lords dismissed the appeal. The majority (Lord Brown and Lord Scott dissenting) held that a 'relativistic approach' to Article 3 had to be taken in the context of extradition.

Lord Hoffmann, who gave the leading judgement, examined two main issues. The first was whether a sentence of imprisonment for life without eligibility for parole would constitute an inhuman or degrading punishment in the UK.

He rejected the philosophical approach according to which life sentence without parole constitutes 'inhuman or degrading treatment' in that it destructs a life without possibility of redemption and that it is justified only if the death penalty argument is justified, i.e. if the crime is so heinous that it can never be atoned for. He instead accepted the ECtHR's ruling in *Kafkaris v Cyprus* that a life sentence may breach Article 3 only if it is irreducible.

He held that on the facts of the case the punishment was reducible *de jure*. The fact that the Missouri Governor's powers to reduce it were rarely used *de facto* was not sufficient to make the sentence irreducible. It had to be accepted that the appellant's chances of release were poor: otherwise the more horrendous the crime, the stronger the claim not to be extradited. In his opinion, however, even an irreducible life punishment would not contravene Article 3 if it were proportionate to the crime committed.

Lord Hoffmann held that, in the circumstances of the case, a life sentence would not be disproportionate to the crime committed and that the English Criminal Law would also impose the same treatment on the appellant. In the circumstances, therefore, there was no inhuman or degrading treatment under Article 3.

The second issue was whether it makes a difference that the sentence will not be imposed by a United Kingdom authority but by the State of Missouri.

Lord Hoffmann took a relativist approach to Article 3, holding that, in cases of extradition Article 3 did not apply as if the extraditing State were responsible for any punishment inflicted in the receiving State. The creation of safe havens for fugitives would otherwise undermine the whole foundations of extradition. He also considered the absolutist approach to Article 3 in *Chahal v UK* as confined to torture cases and as not affecting the present case.

The minority, on the other hand, took the following view: Despite agreeing that there was no inhuman or degrading treatment, Lord Scott considered that an absolutist approach to Article 3 was required. He argued that if an exception could be made to absolute rights in the context of extradition, exceptions could also be made on other public policy grounds. Moreover two results would follow from Lord Hoffmann's approach: either a distinction would be made between torture and other 'inhuman or degrading' treatment – however, there was no basis for this distinction in the wording of the article – or a uniformly narrow approach to Article 3 would be taken but this was inconsistent with the Strasbourg jurisprudence: Article 3 had to be a floor, not a ceiling.

Lord Brown took adopted a different position to Lord Hoffmann. He held that a sentence would not be irreducible '*de jure* and *de facto*' if at some point in time its proportionality to the circumstances of the crime were reconsidered and that, according to *Kafkaris v Cyprus*, a life sentence 'may' but must not in principle violate Article 3 and that Article 3 is violated only when the prisoner's further imprisonment can no longer be justified. Furthermore, he disagreed with Lord Hoffmann's relativistic view. Lord Brown was of the view that the approach to 'inhuman or degrading treatment' should be analogous to the *Chahal* approach to torture: no one can be expelled if he would then face the risk of treatment or punishment which is properly to be characterised as inhuman or degrading. In his opinion extradition was not a sufficient factor to abandon the absolutist approach to Article 3.

JANUARY 2009

8 January 2009
Iribarren Pinillos v Spain (36777/03) (2009)
European Court of Human Rights: Josep Casadevall (President)

The applicant, IP, complained of injuries he had sustained during clashes with the security forces in 1991. The question for the Court was whether the nature of the police reaction constituted an interference with Article 3 (prohibition of torture and inhuman and degrading treatment); furthermore, whether the investigation that followed was in violation of Article 6 (right to a fair trail).

During the demonstration, protesters built barricades and lit fires and the police fired smoke-bombs and tear-gas grenades over a period of several hours. IP, who was one of the protesters, was seriously injured when he was struck by a smoke-bomb fired at very short range by the police. At the scene he had stopped breathing; part of his face was burned and was partly paralysed.

Over the course from 1996 – 2003, IP launched a series of complaints claiming damages in respect of the injuries he had sustained. In 1996, Supreme Administrative Court rejected his claim to the Minister of the Interior on the ground that the damage he had sustained could not be imputed to the administrative authorities. In 1998 Audiencia Nacional allowed part of IP's administrative complaint lodged in 1997. However, in 2003 the Supreme Court set aside that judgment and held at final instance that the reaction of the security forces had not been disproportionate and that the injuries sustained by the applicant had been due to chance.

The final course for IP was to approach the ECtHR, relying mainly on Articles 3 and 6. His main argument was that his physical and mental integrity has been interfered with through the disproportionate nature of the police reaction. He further argued that he was not given an effective investigation during the criminal proceedings, and that no additional investigation had been carried out by the administrative courts.

The ECtHR found in favour of IP in respect of both claims; both Articles 3 and 6 had been violated.

With regard to the Article 3 violation, the ECtHR noted that the Spanish criminal courts had not established whether the applicant shared any responsibility for the damage he had sustained. Moreover, the administrative courts had not carried out any further investigation during the administrative complaint proceedings with a view to determining the applicant's share of liability. The Court considered that he could not be required to bear alone the results of being hit by the smoke-bomb, that the Spanish courts had not determined whether the way the security forces had used the missile was strictly proportionate to the legitimate aim of ending the disturbances.

The Court further noted that the Supreme Court had not taken account of the administrative authorities' liability for the events as established by the criminal courts. Nor had it correctly examined the question whether the applicant had suffered actual, monetarily quantifiable damage or the causal link between the offence and the damage suffered.

Regarding Article 6, the Court held unanimously that there had been a violation of this article on account of the excessive length (11 years and ten months) of the proceedings complained of.

20 January 2009
Güveç v Turkey **(70337/01) (2009)**
European Court of Human Rights: Françoise Tulkens (President)

Relying on Article 3 (prohibition of inhuman or degrading treatment), the applicant, G, (a juvenile) complained about his detention in an adult prison and his trial before the State Security Court instead of a juvenile court. Although a juvenile, he had been placed in an adult prison, where he had remained for the next five years, and which had resulted in his repeated suicide attempts. Under Articles 5 (right to liberty and security) and 6 (right to a fair trial), he also complained that he had not been released pending trial and that he had not been tried fairly.

In 1995 the applicant was charged with undermining the territorial integrity of the State, an offence which was punishable by death at the time. That charge was later modified and, following a retrial, in 2001 the Court found the applicant guilty of membership of an illegal organisation (the PKK) and sentenced him to eight years and four months in prison. The applicant's conviction was upheld in 2002.

When questioned by the police, and subsequently by the prosecutor and the judge, the applicant was not represented by a lawyer. During the retrial, both the applicant and his lawyer were absent from most of the hearings.

In 2000 the prison doctor reported that the applicant had been suffering from serious psychiatric problems in prison and had attempted to commit suicide twice in 1999. The doctor concluded that the situation in the prison was not conducive to the applicant's treatment and that he needed to be placed in a specialized hospital. The applicant also alleged before the Court that, while detained in police custody, he had been given electric shocks, sprayed with pressurized water and beaten with a truncheon.

The Court first observed that the applicant's detention in an adult prison had been in contravention of the applicable regulations in force in Turkey at the time and of the country's obligations under international treaties. It further noted that, according to the medical report of April 2001, the applicant's psychological problems had begun during his detention in prison and had worsened there.

Consequently, given the applicant's age, the length of his detention in prison together with adults, the failure of the authorities to provide adequate medical care for his psychological problems, and, finally, the failure to take steps with a view to preventing his repeated suicide attempts, the Court entertained no doubts that the applicant had been subjected to inhuman and degrading treatment, in breach of Article 3.

The Court hence concluded that the length of the applicant's detention on remand had been excessive, in violation of Article 5. The Court considered that the applicant had not been able to effectively participate in the trial, given that he had not attended at least 14 of the

30 hearings both during the trials. Having considered the shortcomings of the criminal proceedings against the applicant, in particular the lack of legal assistance for most of the proceedings, the Court concluded that there had been a violation of Article 6.

20 January 2009
Sud Fondi Srl and Others v Italy (75909/01) (2009)
European Court of Human Rights: Francoise Tulkens (President)

The applicant companies have their head offices in Italy, where they own land and buildings. Relying on Article 7 (no punishment without law) and on Article 1 of Protocol No. 1 (protection of property), they complained that their property had been illegally confiscated.

One applicant, Sud Fondi Srl, was the owner of land on the coast of Italy which was planned to be urbanised which entailed building houses, offices and shops. It was claimed that at the moment of the approval of the housing development projects in question, no general town planning of the location was in force. In fact, it was alleged that the plan had expired by the time of the adoption of the projects, so that the documents did not coincide with the marked red zones on the plan.

The Court held unanimously that there had been a violation of Article 7 and of Article 1 of Protocol 1, as the confiscation had been illegal and unjustified. Each applicant company was awarded EUR 10,000 in respect of non-pecuniary damage and EUR 30,000 for costs and expenses.

21 January 2009
R (on the application of Black) v Secretary of State for the Home Department [2009] UKHL 1
House of Lords: Lord Phillips, Lord Rodger, Baroness Hale, Lord Carswell and Lord Brown

The case concerned an appeal by the Secretary of State seeking to have the decision of the Court of Appeal set aside. The question was whether the secretary of state's decision not to exercise a discretion held under Criminal Justice Act 1991 s.35(1) was in violation of Article 5 (right to liberty and security of person) of the Convention.

The respondent, B, had been sentenced to a total determinate sentence of 24 years' imprisonment. As a long-term prisoner, convicted of violent offences with no entitlement to automatic release, the appellant, after considering the recommendation of the Parole Board, retained a discretion under s.35(1) over whether B could be released on licence half-way through his sentence. The appellant had rejected the Board's recommendation for release leading B to seek judicial review of that decision.

The Court of Appeal found in B's favour. In their view, s.35(1) left a discretionary decision to release in the hands of the executive and was therefore capable of being applied arbitrarily. This amounting to a breach of Article 5(4), as that was the mischief at which the article was directed.

The Secretary of State appealed based on the argument that in all determinate sentences, the requirements of Article 5(4) are satisfied when the original sentence is imposed. Furthermore, he alleged that there could be no right to any further Article 5(4) determination unless new issues arose affecting the lawfulness of the detention.

The majority of the House allowed the appeal (Lord Phillips dissenting), taking the following view: The European Court had, throughout its case law, treated indeterminate and determinate sentences differently. With regards to the former, the Court in *Stafford v UK* (46295/99) had decided that both the tariff and post-tariff stages of sentencing had to be decided judicially rather than by the executive. The rationale behind this approach being that whilst the tariff stage – a part of sentencing - engaged Article 6, the decision on release in the post-tariff stage was to be taken by a court for the purposes of Article 5(4), as the elements of dangerousness associated with the original sentence could change over time. The European Court's approach to determinate sentences had been quite different, stating that the judicial supervision required by Article 5(4) was incorporated in the Court's decision to impose a sentence of imprisonment.

The early release from a determinate term was regarded as an administrative implementation of the sentence of the court, *Stafford* considered. The secretary of state's continued discretion in cases such as the instant had been described as an indefensible anomaly in R *(on the application of Clift)* [2006] UKHL 54. However the House stated that it did not follow that Article 5(4) had always been directly engaged whenever a determinate sentence prisoner had reached his parole eligibility date and that that had simply been overlooked. Article 5(4) could not be held to apply merely because it would be useful if it did; that would involve widening its reach beyond its proper limits.

Furthermore, the secretary of state's decision was judicially reviewable and could be struck down if found to be arbitrary or irrational. There was nothing intrinsically objectionable in Convention terms in allowing the executive, subject to judicial review, to take a parole decision, notwithstanding that it involved rejecting the Board's recommendation. There was no need for the Board to have been involved at all; nor did the fact that it had been involved necessarily engage Article 5(4). The Court of Appeal's declaration of incompatibility was therefore set aside and the original order dismissing B's application for judicial review was restored.

In his dissent, Lord Phillips stated that to require a parole board to make its decision first and then allow the Secretary of State to make a different decision was contrary to the requirements of Article 5(4). In normal circumstances, prisoners were released on licence before they had served the full term of their sentences. The imposition of a determinate sentence did not therefore render the detention of a defendant lawful for the full period of the sentence. Article 5(4) had to apply to enable a prisoner to seek a determination of whether the conditions for release were satisfied.

27 January 2009
Z v Secretary of State for the Home Department (2009) 106(6) LSG 1
Queen's Bench Division (Administrative Court): Collins J

The claimant an Algerian national had been the leader of a London based cell of the Groupe Isamique Armee (GIA), which was a terrorist organisation.

The Secretary of State served on the claimant a notice of intention to deport on the basis that his deportation would be conducive to the public good on the ground of national security. The claimant argued that he faced a real risk of serious ill-treatment in Algeria, such that his removal there would be a breach of the UK's obligations under Article 3 (right against torture and inhuman and degrading treatment) of the European Convention on Human Rights.

In response to the issue of safety on return, the Secretary of State relied upon assurances given by the Algerian authorities as to the treatment the claimant would receive if returned to Algeria. The plaintiff claimed that in obtaining assurances from the Algerian authorities, the UK authorities had acted in breach of confidence and in breach of the Data Protection Act 1998. The claimant sought damages.

The Secretary of State conceded that the claimant's Article 8 rights (right to respect for private and family life) had been engaged but argued that it was justified for the purposes of Article 8(2) of the Convention. The Secretary of State applied for summary judgment on the claim and for a strike out of the claim.

The issue before the Court was whether the disclosure of information was justified under Article 8(2) of the convention. The Court found in favour of the Secretary of State. It was held that the disclosure had been necessary for the purposes of Article 8(2) of the Convention. The Court noted that disclosure should only be made in exceptional circumstances. In the present case it was done to protect the individual's rights under Article 3 of the Convention, and as such was justified. A summary judgment was entered for the Secretary of State.

27 January 2009
Tatar & Tatar v Romania **(67021/01) (2009)**
European Court of Human Rights: Judge Zupancic (President)

The case concerned an environmental accident which occurred near to the home of the applicants (T). The Court was asked to examine whether the respondent country's dismissal of the applicant's claims had violated Article 2 (right to life), but after admissibility proceedings assessed the case under Article 8 (right to respect for private and family life).

T, a father and son, lived in Baia Mare (Romania). The company S.C. Aurul S.A., obtained in 1998 a licence to exploit the Baia Mare gold mine located in the vicinity of T's home. The company's extraction process involved the use of sodium cyanide. On 30 January 2000 an environmental accident occurred at the site. A United Nations study reported that a dam had breached, releasing about 100,000 m3 of cyanide-contaminated tailings water into the environment. The report stated that S.C. Aurul S.A. had not halted its operations.

After the accident Mr Tătar (the father) filed various administrative complaints concerning the risk incurred by him and his family as a result of the sodium cyanide used in the extraction process. He also questioned the validity of the company's operating licence. T also brought criminal proceedings against the company complaining that the mining process was a health hazard for the inhabitants of Baia Mare, that it posed a threat to the environment and that it was aggravating his son's asthma. All his claims were dismissed by the Romanian authorities.

On application to the ECtHR, T complained under Article 2 of the Convention that the activities carried out by the company put their lives in danger, and that the authorities had failed to take any action. In its admissibility decision the ECtHR ruled that the applicants' complaints should be examined under Article 8.

The Court observed that where pollution or noise interfered with a person's well-being, a claim could be brought under Article 8 and that the State had a duty to take the necessary steps to control industrial activities, especially those dangerous for the environment and human health, in order to ensure the protection of its citizens.

On the facts, the existence of a material risk to the health and well-being of the applicants engaged Article 8. Although the Court did not doubt the reality of the medical condition of Mr Tătar, it noted that the applicants had failed to prove the existence of a causal link between exposure to sodium cyanide and asthma. However, despite the lack of causal link the existence of a serious and material risk for the applicants' health and well-being entailed a duty on the State to assess the risks, both at the time it granted the operating permit and subsequent to the accident, and to take the appropriate measures. The state had not taken such action, allowing the company to continue its industrial operations even after a preliminary impact assessment conducted in 1993 had highlighted the risks entailed for humans and the environment.

The Court also stressed the authorities' duty to inform the public and guarantee the right of its members to participate in the decision-making process concerning environmental issues. The failure of the Romanian Government to inform the public, in particular by not making public the 1993 impact assessment on the basis of which the operating licence had been granted, had made it impossible for members of the public to challenge the results of that assessment. This lack of information had continued after the accident of January 2000, despite the probable anxiety of the local people.

The Court concluded that the Romanian authorities had failed in their duty to assess the risks entailed by the activity, and had failed to take the suitable measures to protect the applicants' rights under Article 8 and more generally their right to a healthy environment.

Fines were awarded to the applicants under Article 44 (2) of the Convention.

28 January 2009
Austin v Commissioner of Police of the Metropolis **[2009] UKHL 5**
House of Lords: Lord Hope, Lord Scott, Lord Walker, Lord Carswell and Lord Neuberger

On 1st May 2001 at 2 pm a crowd of demonstrators marched into Oxford Circus. The organisers had deliberately given no notice to the police of their intentions. They had the deliberate aim of creating destruction in the capital. Taken by surprise, the police tried to establish control by putting in place a cordon which was effectively in place at 2.20 pm. There was sufficient space within the cordon for people to walk but conditions were uncomfortable. It took about seven hours for the police to disperse the crowd, given the non co-operative attitude of the demonstrators. The appellant was among the crowd demonstrating, but she was not one of the organisers. She had planned to collect her baby that she had left in a crèche but was prevented from doing so, being caught into the police cordon. She brought a claim for false imprisonment and for breach of her right to liberty under Article 5(1) of the Convention. Her claim was dismissed by Tugendhat J and subsequently by the Court of Appeal. In the House of Lords the common law plea was abandoned.

The House of Lords unanimously dismissed the appeal and held that the plea did not fall within the scope of Article 5(1) of the Convention.

In the leading judgment, Lord Hope, stressed that a distinction is to be made between conditions which restrict one's movement (that fall under Article 2 of Protocol 4, not ratified by the UK) and conditions which amount to a deprivation of one's liberty (under Article 5). In this case the appellant's liberty of movement was restricted by the police cordon. However, the question is whether this was also a deprivation of liberty under Article 5. Article 5 is an absolute right and its restrictions are to be construed strictly.

Whether there was a deprivation of liberty, as opposed to a restriction of movement is a matter of degree and intensity which has to be considered within a range of factors. These factors are to include the specific situation of the individual and the context in which the restriction of liberty occurred. The ambit that is given to Article 5 as to measures of crowd control must take account of a fair balance between the rights of the individual and the interests of the community. Thus any steps that are taken must be resorted to in good faith and must be proportionate to the situation which has made the measures necessary. Anything that is done which affects a person's right to liberty must not be arbitrary. It would seem in principle that the more intensive the measure and the longer the period it is kept in force, the greater the need for it to be justified by reference to the purpose of the restriction if it is not to fall within the ambit of the article.

In conclusion, Lord Hope held that in this case, the length of time over which the cordon lasted was justified by the impossibility for the police, in circumstances that were beyond their control, to release everyone earlier. The measures of crowd control fell outside the scope of application of Article 5, so long as they were not arbitrary. Furthermore, the cordon was put in place in good faith, it was a proportionate measure and it lasted for no longer than was reasonably necessary. Therefore Article 5(1) was not applicable.

Lord Neuberger added *obiter* that the intention of the police is relevant, particularly in a non-paradigm case such as the present one. Moreover, if it were to transpire that the police had maintained the cordon beyond the time necessary for crowd control in order to punish the demonstrators then it could amount to a breach of Article 5.

FEBRUARY 2009

3 February 2009
Women on Waves and Other v Portugal (31276/05) (2009)
European Court of Human Rights: Francoise Tulkens (President)

The case concerns the Portuguese authorities' decision to prohibit the ship Borndiep (owned by an association called Women on Waves), which had been chartered with a view to staging activities promoting the decriminalization of abortion, from entering Portuguese territorial waters in 2004.

In this case, the Court held that there had been a violation of Article 10 (freedom of expression). However, it considered it not necessary to examine separately the complaints under Articles 5, 6 and 11 of the Convention and Article 2 of Protocol No. 4 to the Convention.

The Court observed that the applicant association had not trespassed on private land or publicly owned property. Also, it noted the lack of sufficient evidence of any intention on their part to deliberately breach Portuguese abortion legislation. It reiterated that as long as the person concerned did not commit any reprehensible acts, freedom to express opinions during a peaceful assembly could not be restricted.

The availability of alternatives was considered an important aspect of the case. In seeking to prevent disorder and protect health, the Portuguese authorities could have resorted to other means that were less restrictive of the applicant associations' rights. The Court suggested seizing the medicines on board as an example. It highlighted the deterrent effect for freedom of expression in general of such a radical act as dispatching a warship.

The Court decided that the situation complained of should be examined under Article 10 of the Convention alone. While the Court acknowledged the legitimate aims pursued by the Portuguese authorities, namely the prevention of disorder and the protection of health, it reiterated that pluralism, tolerance and broadmindedness towards ideas that offended, shocked or disturbed were prerequisites for a 'democratic society'. The Court considered that in this case, the restrictions imposed by the authorities had affected the substance of the ideas and information imparted. It was further highlighted that the right to freedom of expression included the choice of the form in which ideas were conveyed, without unreasonable interference by the authorities, particularly during symbolic protest activities. Since the interference by the authorities had been disproportionate to the aims pursued, the Court therefore concluded that Article 10 was violated.

3 February 2009
Ipek and Others v Turkey (17019/02 and 30070/02)
European Court of Human Rights: Francoise Tulkens (President)

The applicants are Turkish nationals who live in Diyarbakır, Turkey. The case concerned the alleged unlawfulness of their arrest and detention in police custody.

On the 1st December 2001 the applicants were arrested at the second applicant's house and taken into police custody in order to establish whether they had any link with an illegal armed organisation, the PKK (the Workers' Party of Kurdistan). The police were unable to find anything illegal or incriminating during searches of both the first and second applicant's houses.

Upon the request of the police, the Diyarbakır public prosecutor (DPP) extended the applicants' detention for two days on 3 December 2001. On the same day, the applicants were questioned by the police without the benefit of the assistance of a lawyer; the reason for this being that they were accused of offences falling within the jurisdiction of the State Security Courts (the SSC).

On the 4th of December 2001, the applicants were brought before the prosecutor and then taken to the SSC, where it was ordered they be remanded in custody. The following day, relying mainly on the basis of the applicants' statements obtained during the pre-trial investigation, the DPP filed a bill of indictment with the SCC accusing the second applicant of membership of an illegal organisation and the others of aiding and abetting that organisation. The charges were brought under Articles 168 and 169 of the Turkish Criminal Code respectively.

They were released pending trial on the 5th of February 2002.

Relying on Article 5 (right to liberty and security), the applicants complained in particular about the unlawfulness of their arrest and the excessive length of their detention in police custody.

The Court reached the decision that there had been a breach of the applicant's rights under Article 5 paragraphs 1, 3, 4 and 5 based on the following analysis:

With regards to Article 5(1), the applicants submitted that there had been no reasonable suspicion warranting their arrest.

The Court noted that reasonable suspicion meant: 'the existence of facts or information which would satisfy an objective observer that the person concerned may have committed the offence.'

Accordingly it held that there was no violation of Article 5(1) of the Convention in respect of the second applicant for there was reasonable suspicion warranting his arrest. He was arrested in the course of an investigation into an illegal armed organisation of which he was suspected of being a member, and of having gone to the city in order to conduct activities on its behalf.

The first and third applicants were not detained on reasonable suspicion, but rather in virtue of being at the second applicants' house. Thus in their case there had been a violation of art 5(1).

As for Article 5(3), the applicants complained that their detention in police custody had exceeded the reasonable time requirement.

The Court held that especially in view of the applicants' young age (16), that the government was not justified to keep them in detention for more than 3 days. It held that there had been a violation of art 5(3).

The applicants further alleged under Article 5(4) that there were no effective remedies in domestic law to challenge the lawfulness of their arrest and detention in police custody. The Court held that this right had also been violated.

Finally, the applicants complained under Article 5(5) that they had not had a right to compensation in respect of the unlawfulness of their arrest and detention in police custody. The Court held that there had been a violation of Art 5(5) of the Convention concerning the lack of an enforceable right to compensation for the breach of their rights under Article 5 paragraphs 1, 3 and 4.

5 February 2009
***Tabernacle v Secretary of State for Defence* [2009] EWCA (Civ) 23**
Court of Appeal (Civil): Laws LJ, Wall LJ, Stanley Burnton LJ

The appellant was a long-time member of the Aldermaston Women's Peace Camp (AWPC). The organisation had engaged in peaceful protests once a month for some 23 years by camping in an area owned by the respondent Secretary of State. These areas had been designated 'the Controlled Areas' by the Atomic Weapons Establishment (AWE) Aldermaston Byelaws 2007 (the 2007 Byelaws). The original challenge had been to the legality of paragraph 7(2)(f), (g) and (j) of the 2007 Byelaws which prohibits camping, attaching items to any surface, and acting in any way likely to cause annoyance to others on the Controlled Areas respectively.

The Divisional Court had upheld the appellant's application for judicial review in part. However, the lower court had dismissed the appellant's application seeking to challenge the legality of paragraph 7(2)(f). This paragraph of the 2007 Byelaws prohibits camping in the Controlled Areas from which, therefore, it bans the AWPC. The appellant journeyed to the Court of Appeal alleging that paragraph 7(2)(f) constitutes an unlawful interference with her right of freedom of expression guaranteed by Article 10 of the European Convention on Human Rights, as well as a violation of her Article 11 right to freedom of association. It was clearly established that paragraph 7(2)(f) constitutes in practice an interference with the rights of the AWPC pursuant to Article 10(1). The ultimate question in the appeal, therefore, was whether this byelaw was nevertheless justified by any of the considerations in Article 10(2).

The Court of Appeal unanimously allowed the appeal. Laws LJ, who gave the leading judgment, examined two main issues. The first was whether, in the legal setting, the byelaw is nevertheless justified by any of the considerations in Article 10(2).

He determined that the application of the supposed distinction between the 'essence' of a protest and the 'manner and form' of its exercise is dependent on the particular facts of a case. Strasbourg had established that where the case falls into the latter territory and not the former, the State may be granted a wider discretionary area of judgment. The manner and form might constitute the actual nature and quality of the protest, as it did in the instant case. The camp had been established for something like 23 years. It had borne consistent, long-standing and peaceful witness to the convictions of the women who had belonged to it. However, he considered that on these facts, the 'manner and form *is* the protest itself'.

Furthermore, the fact that the secretary of state was himself the source of the public's right to go on the Controlled Areas carried no weight. It was elementary that government property was held for the public good. There was no proper analogy with a private landowner's grant whereby he reserved certain rights to himself.

In light of all these considerations, Laws LJ considered that if the respondent was to show compliance with his obligations under the Human Rights Act, he must demonstrate a substantial objective justification for paragraph 7(2)(f) of the 2007 Byelaws, amounting to an undoubted pressing social need. The byelaw's interference with the appellant's rights is far from being weak or insubstantial, and the respondent did not enjoy a broad margin of discretion.

The second issue was whether the Secretary of State's justification of paragraph 7(2)(f) of the 2007 Byelaws demonstrated a substantial objective justification amounting to an undoubted pressing social need.

He rejected the Secretary of State's justifications as insubstantial, regarding the fact that no steps had previously been taken to put a stop to the camp over the 23 years of its existence as material. Furthermore, he considered the reasons for this inaction 'extremely feeble'. Laws LJ held that paragraph 7(2)(f) was not framed in the face of high profile public concerns of the nature contained in Article 10(2).

Finally, Laws LJ concluded that the effect of paragraph 7(2)(f) of the 2007 Byelaws was to violate the appellant's right guaranteed by Articles 10 and 11 of the European Convention on Human Rights and accordingly allowed the appeal.

Wall LJ sought to reinforce the judgment of Laws LJ by providing a short supplement. He held that the arguments propounded by the Secretary of State did not come anywhere near demonstrating a 'pressing social need'. Therefore, the interference had not been justified by the consideration contained within Article 10(2).

10 February 2009
Ireland v Parliament and Council (Case C-301/06)
European Court of Justice: Vassilios Skouris (President)

Ireland, supported by Slovakia, asked the ECJ to annul a directive adopted by the Council on the basis of Article 95 EC concerning the retention of data processed and stored in connection with the provision of publicly available electronic communications services or data in public communication networks for the purposes of the prevention, investigation, detection and prosecution of criminal offences.

Ireland argued that the directive had not been adopted on an appropriate legal basis – taking the view that the directive cannot be based on Article 95 EC since its 'centre of gravity' does not concern the harmonization of national laws to improve the functioning of the internal market but rather the fight against crime, and that measures of this kind ought therefore to have been adopted on the basis of the articles of the EU Treaty relating to police and judicial cooperation in criminal matters.

In April 2004, France, Ireland, Sweden and the UK submitted to the Council a proposal for a framework decision based on the articles of the EU Treaty relating to police and judicial cooperation in criminal matters. The Commission took the view that Article 95 EC, which permits the adoption of measures which have as their object the establishment and functioning of the internal market, was the appropriate legal basis for the obligations imposed on operators to retain data for a certain period. On a proposal from the Commission, the Council opted for the adoption of a directive based on the EC

Treaty. On 21 February 2006, the data retention directive was adopted by the Council by a qualified majority. Ireland and Slovakia voted against the adoption of that directive.

The ECJ held that the directive was correctly adopted on the basis of the EC Treaty. The Court noted that the action brought by Ireland related solely to the choice of legal basis and not to any possible infringement by the directive of fundamental rights resulting from interference with the exercise of the right to privacy. The ECJ observed that, following the terrorist attacks in New York, Spain and UK, several Member States had introduced measures aimed at imposing obligations on service providers in regard to data retention, but that those measures differed substantially, particularly in respect of the nature of the data retained and the respective retention periods. These obligations could have significant economic implications for providers by involving substantial investment and operating costs.

Therefore, the Court felt that the use of Article 95 EC was justified since disparities between national rules would create distortions of competition and effect the functioning of the internal market. Furthermore, it was found by the ECJ that the measures provided for by the directive did not, in themselves, involve intervention by the police or law-enforcement authorities of the Member States. The Court therefore concluded that the directive relates predominately to the functioning of the internal market, and so its adoption based on Article 95 EC was justified.

12 February 2009
Nolan v Russia (2512/04) (2009)
European Court of Human Rights: Christos Rozakis (President)

The complainant, N, a citizen of the US, complained that by detaining him at the airport and excluding him from Russia, the respondent state had breached his rights under Articles 5 (right to liberty and security), 8 (right to respect for private and family life), 9 (freedom of thought, conscience and religion) and Protocol 7 Article 1 (right to fair procedures for lawfully resident foreigners facing expulsion) of the European Convention on Human Rights.

N had moved to Russia in 1994 to work. Consequently, the Russian authorities granted him leave to stay in Russia on an annual basis. During this time N married and had a son (K), of whom he became sole custodian upon separating from his partner. From 2000, the regional government took the view that the church where N worked did not meet specified requirements and was to be dissolved. Nonetheless, the authorities granted N leave to stay in Russia on the basis of an invitation issued by the church. However in February 2002, the Russian authorities issued a report concerning the exclusion of N from Russia on the ground of national security. In May 2002 N took a brief trip to Cyprus, leaving K in the care of a nanny in Russia.

Upon his return, N was detained at the airport's passport control, overnight in a detention cell and then refused entry into Russia without explanation. An attempt at re-entry from Finland failed and N's complaints to the Russian administrative authorities were refused or ignored. This led to a 10 month separation from K until N was able to arrange K an exit visa.

N complained on four grounds. Firstly, his exclusion from Russia had been imposed because of his religious activities, which constituted an interference with his right under Article 9; secondly, the lack of advance notice as to the exclusion order and the consequent difficulties in arranging an exit visa for K from abroad constituted a breach of his right under Article 8; thirdly, that his detention at the airport was unlawful; and finally, the measures taken against him fell within the notion of "expulsion" and were therefore in breach of his rights under Article 1 of Protocol 7.

The complaints were upheld, with only Kovler J dissenting in part.

With regards to the Article 9 claim, the Court considered that there was no evidence that N was involved with any activities other than at the church. The general policy set out in the Concept of National Security was that foreign missionaries posed a threat to national security. Therefore, on the evidence N's exclusion was a restriction on his right under Article 9. Moreover, without evidence that he posed a security threat, there was no justification for that restriction. Hence Article 9 had been violated.

The Court also found a violation of N's rights under Article 8. the discovery of this breach hinged on the fact that there was a legitimate interest in K remaining with N, his only parent; that the state had a positive obligation to ensure the protection of children; and that the state had failed to enable N to prepare for his and K's departure as a family and failed to facilitate K's exit.

As regards Article 5, the conditions of N's detention were equivalent, in view of the restrictions he suffered, to a deprivation of liberty contrary to Article 5.

Finally, the Court stated that the concept of lawful residence under Article 1 of Protocol 7 did not mean that persons lawfully resident in a state ceased to be so each time they took a short trip abroad. N was lawfully resident in Russia at the material time and had a valid visa. There had been no deportation order against him. Therefore, he had been 'expelled' for the purposes of Article 1 of Protocol 7 and it followed that there had also been a breach of that provision.

12 February 2009
Denisenko and Bogdanchikov v Russia (3811/02) (2009)
European Court of Human Rights: Christos Rozakis (President)

This case concerned the alleged violations of Articles 3 (freedom from torture and inhuman and degrading treatment) and 5 (freedom of liberty and security)

On 1 March 2001 the applicants were arrested on suspicion of attempted murder and robbery by an organised gang.

Criminal proceedings were initiated against them in the period between 2 March and 4 July 2002. The second applicant was examined by a narcotics specialist, the district prosecutor of Moscow authorised pre-trial detention after which he was charged with attempted aggravated murder and several robberies committed in concert. He and his co-accused's detentions were further extended until 2 June.

The second applicant applied for judicial review of the lawfulness and reasonableness of his detention but his application was dismissed by the District Court of Moscow and on appeal by the Moscow City Court. The detention was subsequently extended by the prosecutor. This decision was not challenged. On 4 July 2002 the applicant was sentenced to twelve years' imprisonment.

The applicants also experienced alleged ill-treatment. Upon his arrest, the police officers had hit the applicant on the head with a pile of books and a plastic bottle, had hit him on the body with a wooden board, injuring his coccyx and, finally, had kicked him in the area of the kidneys and handcuffed him to a radiator, causing burns on his wrist. This treatment was carried out with a view to extracting a confession. Being unable to stand the ill treatment, the applicant had confessed.

His mother sent numerous telegrams asking for criminal proceedings against the police officers, but the investigator decided not to institute such proceedings. The applicant raised the ill-treatment issue at trial and requested the court to exclude his confession because obtained under duress, but the trial court refused to exclude the evidence.

The final area of complaint concerned the conditions of their detention. The applicants had been held in remand centre IZ-77/2 in Moscow; they were subjected to an overcrowded environment with unsatisfactory temperature and sanitary conditions. Moreover he alleged that, on the days of court hearing at the Khamovnicheskiy District Court, he would wake up at 5 am, he would not be given any food or drink, and would occasionally spend more than ten hours a day in the courthouse cell.

Having declared the second applicant's application inadmissible for being lodged out of time under Article 35 paragraphs 1 and 4 of the convention, the Court went on to consider the first applicant's pleas.

The Court first found a violation of Article 3 of the Convention on account of the first applicant's ill-treatment. The Court noted that the first applicant had used a domestic remedy which was apparently sufficient, thus he could not be expected to also have tried others that were probably no more likely to be successful. Thus the claim was admissible.

The Court found a violation of Article 3 under its procedural limb for failure by the Russian authorities to carry out adequate investigations into the applicant's allegations of ill-treatment. On the facts, the wrist injury amounted to an 'arguable claim' of ill-treatment. Although an inquiry was opened shortly after the applicant's complaint, the question before the Court was whether the investigation was effective. The inquiry did not take into account any submissions by the applicant, failed to consider some pieces of evidence, and it based the decision not to open a criminal case on the testimonies of the officers who had participated in the arrest, showing a lack of independence on the part of the investigator. It contained further inconsistencies and critical flaws which led the Court to the conclusion that the investigation was not sufficient to establish the relevant facts.

The Court also found a violation of Article 3 under its substantive limb for ill-treatment of the applicant. Some of the facts were undisputed by the parties and those facts concerning the treatment of the applicant between his arrest and his examination by a narcotics expert were sufficient to prove ill-treatment.

The Court stated that in the absence of any violent behaviour on the part of the applicant and having regard to the nature of the treatment, its duration and the resulting bodily injury, the Court considered that the suffering experienced by the applicant constituted inhuman and degrading treatment.

Further violations of Article 3 were found on account of the applicant's conditions of detention in remand centre IZ-77/2 in Moscow; particularly due to the level of suffering experienced in the cramp conditions over the duration of the detention (one year and four months). The Court further found a violation of Article 3 of the Convention on account of the applicant's conditions of confinement at the Courthouse.

The Court also assessed whether there was a violation of Article 5(1) on account of the fact that there had been no legal basis for the applicant's detention after March 2001.

The applicant's placement in custody was in compliance with the law. However, the 'lawfulness' of detention under domestic law is not always the decisive element. On the facts of the case, the Court agreed with the Government and concluded that the applicant's detention from 12 March to 27 April 2001 was 'lawful' for the purposes of Article 5(1) of the Convention.

The Court declared inadmissible the applicant's complaint under Article 5(3) concerning the period of his detention after 2 June

2001. Instead, the complaint concerning his detention before that date was declared admissible.

In this case, to justify the first applicant's detention the domestic authorities relied on the fact that the applicant had been apprehended 'in flagrante delicto' and that the victims had identified him as one of the perpetrators, on the gravity of the charges against the first applicant and on the risk that he might abscond and interfere with the establishment of the truth, and on the need to carry out further confrontations with the victims, obtain the results of several forensic examinations and secure his access to the case file. The Court found that these justifications were relevant and sufficient. The Court did not find any failure on the part of the authorities to act with due diligence and thus concluded that there was no violation of Article 5(3).

The Court ordered that the Russian Government pay the applicant EUR 5,000 in accordance with Article 44(2) of the Convention.

18 February 2009
RB (Algeria) v Secretary of State for the Home Department [2009] UKHL 10
House of Lords: Lord Phillips, Lord Hoffmann, Lord Hope, Lord Brown and Lord Mance

This case concerned joined appeals against decisions of the Court of Appeal on the lawfulness of deporting the appellants (B, U and O). In this case, the House of Lords were being asked to consider the Human Rights implications of potential torture of terror suspects.

The Secretary of State had ordered their deportation on grounds of national security. The appellants claimed that deportation would violate their rights under Article 3 of the Convention, because there was a real risk they would be tortured by the authorities on their return. O, who was likely to be retried in Jordan for terrorist offences, also claimed that he would be deprived of his liberty by unreasonably lengthy detention pending trial. He also argued that he would not receive a fair trial, because the court that would try him would not be independent of the government and would likely use the evidence of witnesses who had been tortured.

The Court of Appeal dismissed the appellants' appeals to the Special Immigration Appeals Commission (SIAC). The Court affirmed the Commission's decisions under Article 3, but upheld O's appeal on the ground that evidence obtained by torture was likely to be used against him at his trial.

The House of Lords unanimously held that the appeals by RB and U should be dismissed and the appeal of the Secretary of State in Othman be allowed, thereby reinstating the decision of SIAC in all three cases.

There was nothing in the Convention which prevented the UK from according only a limited right of appeal, even if the issue involved a Convention right. The Court of Appeal had no general power to review the SIAC's conclusions that the facts it had found did not amount to a real risk of a flagrant breach of the relevant Convention rights. The SIAC's conclusions could only be attacked on grounds of *Wednesbury* unreasonableness.

It was also held that the use of closed material in relation to the issue of safety on return would not necessarily render the process unfair or in breach of the principles of legality. The deportee would usually be aware of the information personal to him that bore on the question of whether he would be safe on his return. Therefore, B, U and O had not been denied a fair trial by reason of the use of closed material.

Furthermore, there was no principle that assurances must eliminate all risk of inhuman treatment before they could be relied upon. However, assurances should be treated with scepticism if they were given by a country where inhuman treatment by state agents was endemic. The issue of whether the assurances given in the instant case obviated the risk was a question of fact for the SIAC, whose conclusions could only be attacked on grounds of irrationality. It was held that the Commission's conclusions in relation to Article 3 could not be described as irrational.

Finally, it was decided that, before the deportation of an alien could violate Article 6, there must be substantial grounds for believing that there was a real risk of a fundamental breach of his right to a fair trial, and that that breach would lead to a miscarriage of justice that itself constituted a flagrant violation of his fundamental rights. The SIAC concluded that the deficiencies it had identified did not meet that exacting test. The HL agreed. There was no authority for a rule that, in the context of the application of Article 6 to a foreign trial, the risk of the use of evidence obtained by torture necessarily amounted to a flagrant denial of justice.

18 February 2009
Mitchell (AP) and another v Glasgow City Council (Scotland) [2009] UKHL 11
House of Lords: Lord Hope, Lord Scott, Lord Rodger, Baroness Hale and Lord Brown

The pursuers were the widow and daughter of Mr Mitchell (M) who had been killed by his next-door neighbour Drummond (D). M and D were neighbours and tenants of the local authority. One night M banged on D's wall to get his loud music turned down. D retaliated by smashing M's windows as a result of which he was arrested by the police. D then adopted an attitude of hostility to M making repeated threats to kill him, despite the pursuers' warning that if he persisted in this conduct they would take action to recover possession of his house. In 2001, the local authority invited D to attend a meeting to discuss a recent incident involving him. D attended the meeting and was told that a fresh notice of proceedings to recover possession would be served on him. D became abusive during the meeting; back home he fatally assaulted M.

The pursuers claimed a breach of duty of care in negligence and under Article 2 of the Convention, pleading that the local authority had a duty in negligence and under Article 2 to warn M of the risk that he could face after the meeting on July 31 and a duty to take the steps against D.

The lower court dismissed the action. On appeal the court allowed a proof before answer on the pursuers' case at common law and excluded from probation their averments that the local authority had acted incompatibly with Article 2 of the European Convention on Human Rights.

The pursuers cross-appealed against such exclusion. The local authority appealed to the House of Lords to dismiss the cross-appeal: the appeal was allowed and the cross-appeal dismissed.

The Court first tackled the common law claim: the pursuers had claimed that there had been an operational failure by the Council to warn M in circumstances where it was reasonably foreseeable that harm would flow to him if they did not warn him about their meeting with D. The Law Lords held that foreseeability of harm was not in itself sufficient to establish a claim in negligence. There needed to be a sufficient relationship between the Council and M such that in the circumstances it was fair, just and reasonable to impose a duty of care on the Council.

The issue before the Court was whether, given that the Council were M's and D's landlords, their relationship was such that it was fair, just and reasonable that they should be held liable in damages for an omission to warn. Another issue was whether the causative link between the meeting and the fatal assault was sufficient to cast upon the Council a duty of care to take steps to protect M.

The Court held that the Council's obligation to M was to act as a responsible landlord and to take steps to terminate D's tenancy in order to remove him from the locality where he was causing trouble and that that obligation did not justify treating the Council as having assumed responsibility for M's safety. There was consequently no sufficient causal link between the Council's omission and M's murder.

The Law Lords moreover emphasized the complex and far-reaching implications of imposing a duty to warn on the Council. It might deter social landlords from intervening to reduce the incidence of antisocial behaviour.

With regards to the Article 2 claim, the issue before the Court was whether the local authority ought to have known that, when D left the meeting, there was a 'real and immediate risk' to M's life (*Osman v United Kingdom* (23452/94) (2000) 29 EHRR 245).

The Law Lords held that, even accepting the pursuers' averments on this point without further proof, nothing showed that M's life was at real risk or at immediate risk. The real and immediate threat to M's life occurred about an hour after the meeting, when no Council officials were present or were under any duty to be present.

Moreover the Council, being only M's landlords, had not assumed responsibility for M by taking him into custody, imprisoning him or constraining his liberty by other means. As landlords, the

Council had fulfilled their duties by taking steps towards exercising their statutory power to recover possession of Drummond's house. The public authority with the positive duty to protect M from criminal assaults by D was the Police, not the Council.

19 February 2009
A and Others v the United Kingdom (3455/05) (2009)
European Court of Human Rights: Judgment was given by the Grand Chamber of 17 judges; Jean-Paul Costa (President)

The case began with 10 men who challenged a decision of the Special Immigration Appeals Commission (SIAC) to eject them from the country on the basis that there was evidence of them being a threat to national security. They complained that they were detained in high security conditions under a statutory scheme which permitted the indefinite detention of non-nationals certified by the Secretary of State as suspected of involvement in terrorism. All were detained under the Anti-terrorism, Crime and Security Act 2001. Part 4 of the Act allowed this procedure as well as deportation, both only for non-British nationals.

The applicants complained before the Court that their indefinite detention in high security conditions amounted to inhuman or degrading treatment. The SIAC, while acutely conscious of the difficulties faced by States in protecting their populations from terrorist violence, stressed that Article 3 enshrines one of the most fundamental values of democratic societies. Even in the most difficult of circumstances, such as the fight against terrorism, and irrespective of the conduct of the person concerned, the European Convention prohibits in absolute terms torture and inhuman or degrading treatment and punishment.

The uncertainty and fear of indefinite detention had to have caused the remaining ten applicants anxiety and distress. Furthermore, it was probable that the stress had been sufficiently serious and enduring to affect the mental health of certain of the applicants. However, it was noted that although the fear of indefinite detention had had this effect, the detainees were not without any prospect or hope of release. For example, they had been able to bring proceedings to challenge the legality of the detention scheme under the 2001 Act and had been successful in 2002. Further, each detained applicant had had at his disposal the remedies available to all prisoners under administrative and civil law to challenge conditions of detention, including any alleged inadequacy of medical treatment.

In those circumstances, the Court found that the applicants' detention had not reached the high threshold of inhuman and degrading treatment for which a violation of Article 3 could be found.

The Court then went further to consider whether the applicants had been lawfully detained in accordance with Article 5 (right to liberty). In the unusual circumstances of the case, whereby the House of Lords had examined the issues relating to the State's derogation and concluded that there had been a public emergency threatening the life of the nation but that the measures taken in response had not been strictly required by the exigencies of the situation, the Court considered that it would not accept the House of Lords' conclusion only if it found that it was manifestly unreasonable.

The Court, like the majority of the House of Lords, held that there had been a public emergency threatening the life of the nation. Before the domestic courts, the Secretary of State had provided evidence to show the existence of a threat of serious terrorist attacks planned against the United Kingdom. Additional closed evidence had been provided before SIAC. All the national judges had accepted that danger to have been credible. Although no al'Qaeda attack had taken place within the territory of the United Kingdom at the time when the derogation had been made, the Court did not consider that the national authorities could be criticised for having feared such an attack to be imminent. A State could not be expected to wait for disaster to strike before taking measures to deal with it. Moreover, the danger of a terrorist attack had, tragically, been shown by the bombings and attempted bombings in London in July 2005 to have been very real.

Although the United Kingdom had been the only Convention State to have lodged a derogation in response to the danger from al'Qaeda, the Court accepted that it had been for each Government, as the guardian of their own people's safety, to make its own assessment on the basis of the facts known to it. In this sense, margin of appreciation operates through the acceptance that Parliament, government and national courts are better placed to assess the evidence relating to the existence of an emergency.

However, the Court found that the derogating measures had been disproportionate in that they had discriminated unjustifiably between nationals and non-nationals. The Court considered that the House of Lords had been correct in holding that the extended powers of detention were not to be seen as immigration measures, where a distinction between nationals and non-nationals would be legitimate, but instead as concerned with national security. Part 4 of the 2001 Act had been designed to avert a real and imminent threat of terrorist attack which, on the evidence, had been posed by both nationals and non-nationals. The choice by the Government and Parliament of an immigration measure to address what had essentially been a security issue had resulted in a failure adequately to address the problem, while imposing a disproportionate and discriminatory burden of indefinite detention on one group of suspected terrorists. There was no significant difference in the potential adverse impact of detention without charge on a national or on a non-national who in practice could not leave the country because of fear of torture abroad.

The Government had argued before the Court that it had been legitimate to confine the detention scheme to non-nationals, to take into account the sensitivities of the British Muslim population in order to reduce the chances of recruitment among them by extremists. However, the Government had failed to provide the Court with any evidence to suggest that British Muslims had been significantly more likely to react negatively to the detention without charge of national rather than foreign Muslims reasonably suspected of links to al'Qaeda.

Concerning the argument that the State could better respond to the terrorist threat if it were able to detain its most serious source, namely non-nationals, the Court had not been provided with any evidence which could persuade it to overturn the conclusion of the House of Lords that the difference in treatment had been unjustified. The national courts, in fact, which saw both the open and the closed material, had not been convinced that the threat from non-nationals had been significantly more serious than that from nationals.

The Court therefore found a violation of Article 5(1) (right to liberty and security). The Court also found a violation of Article 5(4) (right to have lawfulness of detention decided by a court) with regards to some of the applicants and finally of Article 5(5) with regards to some of the applicants, on account of the lack of an enforceable right to compensation for the above violations.

The Court made awards under Article 41 (just satisfaction) which were substantially lower than those which it had made in past cases of unlawful detention, in view of the fact that the detention scheme was devised in the face of a public emergency and as an attempt to reconcile the need to protect the United Kingdom public against terrorism with the obligation not to send the applicants back to countries where they faced a real risk of ill-treatment. The Court therefore awarded, to the six Algerian applicants 3,400 Euros (EUR), EUR 3,900, EUR 3,800, EUR 3,400, EUR 2,500 and EUR 1,700, respectively; to the stateless and Tunisian applicants EUR 3,900, each; and to the Jordanian applicant, EUR 2,800. The applicants were jointly awarded EUR 60,000 for legal costs.

24 February 2009
MQ (Afghanistan) v Secretary of State for the Home Department [2009] EWCA Civ 61
Court of Appeal: Sir Andrew Morritt, Longmore LJ and Hooper LJ

The Claimant (MQ) was seeking asylum. MQ's family history put him at risk from the Afghan authorities. His father had been a member of a Mujahadeen group, the leader of which was S. S was a close friend of the current President of Afghanistan. The group had been involved in large scale massacres during the civil war. In 2002, MQ's father had been arrested, subsequently convicted of several murders and sentenced to death. MQ's brother had been killed at the family home and his associate in business severally attacked. An Amnesty International statement and the report of a 'Dr G' indicated that execution may have been an attempt by powerful political actors to eliminate a key witness to human rights abuses.

MQ sought refugee status and human rights and humanitarian protection on the basis that if he returned he would be at risk from the Afghan authorities and bereaved relatives of the individual's his father had murdered. His application was dismissed. Subsequently MQ's appeal was dismissed, as although the judge accepted the credibility of the claimant, he did not accept that MQ had a risk profile.

A second stage reconsideration was ordered to decide all the issues, except the credibility findings made in respect of the claimant which were to stand. At the second reconsideration the judge concluded that the claimant's evidence was purely speculative. He noted that there was no basis on which to find that the claimant would be of any interest to S or the Afghan authorities, and that there was no evidence to support the claimant's assertion that his brother had been killed by agents of the government. He dismissed the appeal.

The claimant appealed to the Court of Appeal, submitting that (i) the failure of the judge to consider the AI statement and 'Dr G's' report constituted an error of law; and (ii) the judge should have been bound by the order that the findings as to the claimant's credibility were to stand.

In this case, therefore, the appeal was allowed. It was held that (i) the judge had made an error of law and (ii) the judge was required to accept the claimant's account as credible.

26 February 2009
Kudeshkina v Russia (29492/05)
European Court of Human Rights: Christos Rozakis (President)

The applicant Olga Kudeshkina (K), a judge for more than 18 years, was in office at the Moscow City Court (MCC) at the relevant time. She claimed in 2004 that she was unlawfully dismissed from her position for having publicly accused higher judicial officials of putting pressure on her deciding a high-profile criminal case.

In 2003, while sitting as a judge on a criminal case of great public importance, K withdrew from the case in circumstances which are contested by the parties. K herself submitted that the President of the MCC removed her from the case on 4 July 2003 without giving reasons, while the Government claimed that the case was withdrawn from her and assigned to another judge on 23 July 2003 on the grounds that she had delayed its examination.

In early December 2003, K stated in several interviews and lodged a complaint to the High Judiciary Qualification Panel alleging that the President of the MCC had put pressure on her while she had been dealing with that case; suggesting manipulation on the part of the Russian courts. However, the panel decided not to bring disciplinary proceedings against the President of the MCC.

In the meantime, on an unidentified date, the President of Moscow Judicial Council sought to dismiss K from office, alleging that she had behaved in a manner inconsistent with the authority and standing of a judge, having made statements which had the potential to undermine the authority of the judiciary. In May 2004, the Judiciary Qualification Board of Moscow decided that K should no longer act as a judge, having committed a disciplinary offence.

K complained about her dismissal before the MCC, which heard her case at first instance. K subsequently asked the Supreme Court to transfer her case to a different court, as the city court lacked impartiality. On 19 January 2005 the Supreme Court, in a final judgment, dismissed K's request to have her case examined by any other court apart from the city court, and upheld the decision that K had to be removed from her judicial position.

The majority in the ECtHR stated that the decision to dismiss the applicant from her judicial office, given that it was prompted by her statement to the media, constituted an interference with her right to freedom of expression under Article 10 of the Convention.

The Court assumed that the measure was prescribed by law and had a legitimate aim in that it was directed to the protection of the reputation, authority and impartiality of the judiciary.

In deciding whether the interference was necessary in a democratic society, the Court examined the circumstances of the case as a whole in the light of the Court's established case-law. In particular, it reminded that on the one hand issues concerning the functioning of the judiciary constituted questions of public interest enjoying the protection of Article 10, but that on the other hand the judiciary's authority and reputation as an impartial institution was to be protected. Moreover, the Court emphasised that in the context of election debates the exercise of freedom of expression was only subject to a very low scrutiny.

As regards the matter of a justification, the Court saw nothing in the interviews that would justify the claims of disclosure which had been made by the Judiciary Qualification Board of Moscow. Noting that K's allegations of pressure had not been convincingly dispelled, that she had publicly criticised the conduct of various officials, and had alleged that pressure on judges was ordinary; the Court found that her statements raised a highly sensitive matter of public interest which had to be open to free debate in a democratic society. Therefore, in spite of the potential exaggeration and generalisation, the Court found that K's statements had to be regarded as a fair comment on a matter of great public importance.

On the other hand, the Court considered that K's fears as to the impartiality of MCC were justified, given the allegations she had made against the court's President. The Court concluded that the manner in which the disciplinary sanction had been imposed on K had not secured the required procedural guarantees.

Finally, the Court recalled the 'chilling effect' that the sanction imposed could have on the judges' exercise of their freedom of expression. The Court noted that the penalty imposed, Ms Kudeshkina's dismissal, had been capable of having this 'chilling effect' on judges wishing to participate in the public debate on the effectiveness of the judicial institutions. The Court therefore held that the penalty of dismissing the applicant from her functions had been disproportionately severe, and had violated Article 10.

3 judges delivered dissenting opinions. The first two; Judges Kovler and Steiner, emphasized the existing duty of loyalty for the judges. They pointed to the fact that K had disclosed specific factual information concerning the criminal proceedings having then had the opportunity to sit as a judge in a number of other cases. They thus submitted that having excluded herself from the community of judges, the imposition of the disciplinary sanction was justified. They added that the chilling effect of the sanction could not override the need to protect the judiciary's authority.

In addition, Judge Nicolaou pointed to the categorical nature of the applicant's statement and the potential it had to undermine the judiciary's authority. He submitted that such categorical judgements needed to be supported by substantial facts, and that the certainty of those facts was lacking. He further added that the procedural irregularity 'did not amount to anything' in this case.

MARCH 2009

2 March 2009
***R (on the application of LG) v Board of Governors of Tom Hood
School and others* [2009] EWHC 369 (Admin)**
Queen's Bench Division: Administrative Court: Silber J

The claimant sought on the basis of Article 6 (right to a fair trial) of the
European Convention on Human Rights to challenge the appeal
committee's decision regarding the exclusion of V (the claimant's son)
from school.

The claimant's son, V was involved in a fight at school. S, who
was the teacher who came upon the aftermath of the fight, alleged that
V had been verbally aggressive and that he had been in possession of a
knife. V admitted to the former accusations, but denied he was in
possession of a knife, claiming that he was wearing a silver bracelet
chain whose loose end hung into his hand and which he often grasped
when nervous by flicking his wrist to reach it. Initially V was
permanently excluded from school on the basis that he was seen by
staff and pupils to be carrying a knife.

The pupil disciplinary committee of the school's governing
body met to consider the exclusion and on three further occasions to
consider whether or not to order that V should be reinstated, deciding
that he should not. An appeal against that decision was heard by an
appeal panel, and was rejected.

The following issue, *inter alia*, arose: whether regulation 7A of
the Education (Pupil Exclusion and Appeals) (Maintained Schools)
(England) Regulation 2002, SI 2002/3178, (the 2002 Regulations)
infringed Article 6 of the European Convention on Human Rights on
the grounds that the standard of proof applied by an appeal panel in
respect of a claim against a pupil should be the criminal standard of
proof, that was, that they would have to be sure of the allegations
against the pupils before upholding them.

The application was dismissed on the following grounds. Article
6 only applied to a person in 'the determination of his civil rights and
obligations or of a criminal charge against him.' For the purpose of
establishing whether the decision concerned the determination of V's

civil rights and obligations, V was unable to establish that he had a right to continue the studies he had begun at the school. The contention that the hearing in front of the panel was 'a determination of a criminal charge' would also be rejected. In *obiter*, the judge found that even if Article 6 was engaged there was no reason why the standard of proof should not be the balance of probabilities. Even where the conduct alleged amounted to a criminal offence; it did not follow that proof beyond reasonable doubt would be required. The proceedings before the panel did not become criminal proceedings just because one of the disciplinary matters allegedly happened to have a criminal law dimension.

Furthermore, the panel had not failed to give effect to the statutory guidance. The panel had explained clearly that having considered the evidence it was satisfied that it was more probable than not that V had carried the knife and threatened a member of staff. There was no reason to believe that the panel did not consider that there was compelling evidence. In so far as the claimant was challenging the correctness of the panel's conclusion, judicial review was not the appropriate way for such a contention to be determined, although there was adequate evidence to justify the conclusion which the panel had reached.

3 March 2009
Aba v Turkey **(7638/02 and 24146/04)**
European Court of Human Rights: Francoise Tulkens (President)

Ms Sakine Aba, a Turkish national, brought an application against the Republic of Turkey under Article 34 of the Convention, relying on Article 5 (right to liberty and security of the person) and Article 6 (right to a fair trial). The applicant complained of the length of time she had spent in police custody, of a lack of legal assistance, and of the absence of the right to compensation.

The applicant lives in Istanbul. She was arrested and placed in police custody on suspicion of membership of an illegal organisation. During her custody period, she was interrogated by the police, the public prosecutor and the investigating judge respectively, in the absence of a lawyer. Relying on Article 5(3) of the Convention, the applicant argued that the length of her police custody exceeded the reasonable time requirement. Under Article 5(5), she further alleged that she did not have any remedy whereby to seek compensation for the time she had spent in custody; and, invoking Article 6(3)(c), she complained that she had not been allowed the assistance of a lawyer during this period.

The European Court of Human Rights, noting that the applicant had spent 5 days in police custody, relied on the case of *Brogan v UK* (1989) 11 EHRR 117, where it had been held that detention in police custody lasting 4 days and 6 hours without judicial control exceeded the time constraints of Art 5(3), even if its purpose was to protect the community as a whole against terrorism. Therefore, since the applicant had been detained for a longer period without being brought before a judge or another officer authorized by law to exercise judicial power, the Court unanimously found a violation of Article 5(3).

As for the complaint under Article 5(5) of a lack of an enforceable right to compensation for the breach of the applicant's right, the Court also found a violation, since they felt that there were no particular reasons why they should depart from established case law on this matter.

Similarly, it was unanimously held that there had been a violation of Article 6(3)(c) in conjunction with Article 6(1), referring to the case of *Salduz v Turkey* (2009) 49 EHRR 19. It was held in *Salduz* that the right to a fair trial under Article 6(1) required, as a rule, that access to a lawyer should be provided from the first interrogation of a suspect by the police, unless compelling reasons were shown to restrict this right. Even where compelling reasons may exceptionally justify denial of access to a lawyer, such restriction - whatever its justification - must not unduly prejudice the rights of the accused under Article 6. In this case, it was held that the lack of legal assistance to the applicant was an unjustified violation of her Article 6 right. Therefore, Ms Aba was awarded EUR 3,000 in respect of non-pecuniary damage on an equitable basis.

5 March 2009
Colak and Tsakiridis v Germany (77144/01 and 35493/05)
European Court of Human Rights: Judgment was given by the Grand Chamber of 8 judges; Peer Lorenzen (President)

Ms Colak complained about the fact that she had not been informed by her doctor that her partner was suffering from AIDS. The partner had asked the doctor not to disclose. It was revealed to Ms Colak after her partner's death that her partner had died of AIDS. She was soon diagnosed as HIV positive. However, she did not receive any damages on the national level, amongst other reasons, because an expert held that it was probable that the applicant had already been infected before her partner told their common doctor. The applicant relied on Articles 2 (right to life), Article 8 (right to respect for private life) and 6 (right to a fair trial) of the European Convention on Human Rights.

No violations of the Convention were found through the following analysis.

With regard to the applicability of Article 2 the Court reiterated that the first sentence of that Article requires the State not only to refrain from the 'intentional' taking of life, but also to take appropriate steps to safeguard people's lives. Moreover, the State's positive obligations under Article 2 require an effective independent judicial system so that the cause of death of patients in the care of the medical profession can be determined and those responsible made accountable.

An event, however, which does not result in death may, only in exceptional circumstances, disclose a violation of Article 2 of the Convention. These may be found in a lethal disease. Having regard to the particular circumstances of the present case, the Court started on the assumption that the present case raises an issue as to the applicant's right to life.

The Court then reiterated that the positive obligations under Article 2 may be satisfied if the legal system affords victims a remedy in the civil courts, either alone or in conjunction with a remedy in the criminal courts, enabling any liability of the physicians concerned to be established and any appropriate civil redress, such as an order for damages, to be obtained. The Court also accepted that a generic approach to conflicts of interest in Article 34 of the German Criminal

Code is sufficient in dealing with conflicts of interest as occur in the case of a doctor's duty of confidentiality to patients as against the duty to prevent the transmission of HIV.

In conclusion, the domestic authorities did not fail to comply with their positive obligations owed towards the applicant under Article 2 of the Convention. The German legal system provides for legal remedies which, in general, meet the requirements of Article 2 as they afford parties injured through medical negligence both criminal and civil compensation proceedings. For the same reasons, the Court considered that there has not been a violation of the applicant's rights under Article 8 of the Convention.

Concerning violation of Article 6, the Court reiterated that it is not its function to deal with errors of fact or law allegedly committed by a national court unless they may have infringed rights and freedoms protected by the Convention. Further, while Article 6 guarantees the right to a fair hearing, it does not lay down any rules on the admissibility of evidence or the way it should be assessed - they are primarily matters for regulation by national courts.

In so far as the applicant complained about the domestic courts' refusal to apply a less strict rule on the burden of proof, the Court is called upon to examine whether the concept of equality of arms, being an aspect of the right to a fair trial guaranteed by Article 6, was complied with. The principle of equality of arms implies that each party, in litigation involving opposing private interests, must be afforded a reasonable opportunity to present his case – including his evidence – under conditions that do not place him at a substantial disadvantage vis-à-vis his opponent. Nevertheless, it does not imply a general right to a reversal of the burden of proof.

The Court found that the provisions of German civil law relating to the applicant's compensation claims were interpreted and applied in the spirit of the Convention. The holding back or destruction of the medical files occurred only after termination of the compensation proceedings and the medical files had been available to the courts throughout. Even taking into account that patients may face difficulties in proving that medical treatment caused the damage suffered; the Court finds that the applicant was not placed at a substantial disadvantage vis-à-vis the defendant and that the principle of equality of arms was complied with.

In conclusion, the Court considers that, taken as a whole, the proceedings in issue were fair for the purposes of Article 6.

10 March 2009
HJ (Iran) v Secretary of State for the Home Department [2009] EWCA Civ 172
Court of Appeal (Civil): Pill LJ, Keene LJ and Sir Paul Kennedy

The case concerned appeals against the decision of the Asylum and Immigration Tribunal (AIT). The AIT had dismissed their appeals against the respondent Secretary of State's refusal to grant asylum on the grounds that they had not established a well-founded fear of persecution if returned to their home countries.

One of the appellants was an Iranian national who had practised homosexuality in Iran for several years before seeking asylum in the UK. The AIT decided that he could reasonably be expected to tolerate the position in Iran if he were returned there, since they felt that he would behave discreetly and could conduct his homosexual activities in Iran without serious detriment to his private life. The other appellant was a citizen of Cameroon, who had had two homosexual relationships there. He had been discreet except on one occasion where he was caught kissing in public and subsequently attacked. However, as with the other appellant, the AIT held that he would also be discreet on return to Cameroon, and that there was no real risk of persecution.

The first appellant argued that a person had a right to the normal incidents of sexual identity, which included a right to associate and live openly with the partner of his choice, not having to lie continuously about a core aspect of his identity, and, when single, openly seeking out the partner of his choice. He argued that refugee status could not be avoided by requiring the threatened person to appease his persecutors. He further submitted that the determination of what was 'reasonably tolerable' should not be country-sensitive. The second appellant submitted that the AIT had failed to consider whether he would in fact be discreet on return, and whether, if he was not, he would be at risk of persecution.

However, their appeals were dismissed. The test for determining how a person will behave on being returned to their home country required examining 'whether that will entail for him having to live a life which he cannot reasonably be expected to tolerate because to do so would entail suppression of many aspects of his sexual identity.' The Court of Appeal held that this test was an appropriate and workable test complying with the standard required by the Convention relating to the Status of Refugees 1951 (United Nations). The AIT in the case of the first appellant had understood the test and carefully considered the evidence in detail. Therefore, the CA did not find the tribunal's findings to be perverse.

Secondly, it was accepted that the need to protect fundamental human rights transcended national boundaries, but that in assessing whether there had been a breach of such rights, a degree of respect for social norms and religious beliefs in other states was appropriate. Therefore, analysis of in-country evidence was necessary in deciding what an applicant could expect on return and what was reasonably tolerable there. A degree of discretion could be required in all sexual relationships. Whether a requirement to respect social standards violated a fundamental human right was a matter of judgment for the tribunal. Finally, in respect of the case of the second appellant, the CA held that AIT had been entitled to find that, in the circumstances, a single attack following a one-off incident did not establish a real risk of persecution in the future.

10 March 2009
Times Newspapers (Nos. 1 and 2) v United Kingdom (3002/03 and 23676/03)
European Court of Human Rights: Lech Garlicki (President)

The case concerned an action by the company GL in defamation proceedings launched against Times Newspapers, stemming from the initial printed and subsequent internet archived article. The question for the ECtHR was whether the Internet Publication Rule was an unreasonable and unjustified interference with the applicant's rights under Article 10 (freedom of expression). The facts were as follows:

On 8 September 1999 and on 14 October 1999 The Times published two articles in the printed version of the newspaper alleging the involvement of GL in money-laundering through the Bank of New York. On 6 December 1999, GL brought proceedings against the applicant for libel in respect of the two articles printed in the newspaper. The applicant relied on the *Reynolds* [2001] 2 AC 127 defence of qualified privilege. A second action was also launched in response to the applicant's storage of the two articles in their online archive, alleging libel in relation to the continuing Internet publication of the articles. On 23 December 2000, the applicant added a preface specifying on each of the two archived publications that an action in defamation was being brought against them.

The defendant newspaper group were largely unsuccessful in the English courts. Initially, the High Court struck out the defence of qualified privilege in relation to the second action as the defendants had no reasonable grounds for contending that they had a duty to publish the articles on the Internet after lodging their defence in the first action. Furthermore, the Court rejected the argument that only the first publication on the internet should give rise to an action in defamation and stated 'the internet publication rule': in the context of the Internet, the common law rule according to which each publication of a defamatory statement gave rise to a separate cause of action meant that a new cause of action accrued every time the defamatory material was accessed.

The defendant's appeal to the Court of Appeal was also unsuccessful. The Court, dismissing the appeal, rejected their argument that the application of the common law rule to Internet publications could have a chilling effect on their readiness to provide Internet archives. They considered that the maintenance of archives was a relatively small aspect of the freedom of expression, and that it need not be inhibited by the law of defamation as the publication of a notice warning readers against treating potentially defamatory material as truth would normally remove any sting from the material. The House of Lords refused leave to appeal.

Thus the claim arrived in Strasbourg, in the form of a complaint that the 'internet publication' rule constituted an unjustifiable and disproportionate restriction of its right under Article 10.

Ultimately, the ECtHR did not agree, finding no violation of Article 10 on the following grounds:

Having reiterated the role of the press as a public watchdog, and reminded that the press do not enjoy an unrestricted freedom of expression, the Court went on to consider the margin of appreciation in this area. The ECtHR took the view that the margin of appreciation afforded to States in striking the balance between competing rights was likely to be greater for news archived, than for news reporting current affairs. In particular, the duty of the press to act in accordance with the principles of responsible journalism was likely to be more stringent in the absence of any urgency in publishing the material. It added that it was, in principle, for contracting States, exercising their margin of appreciation, to set an appropriate limitation period and to provide for any exception to the prescribed limitation period.

Moreover, the Court recalled how the Court of Appeal did not suggest that potentially defamatory articles should be removed from archives altogether, but instead that the attachment of a notice would 'normally remove any sting from the material'.

Finally, the ECtHR considered it unnecessary to examine the potential chilling effect of the Internet Publication Rule. Nonetheless, the Court emphasised that while individuals who are defamed must have a real opportunity to defend their reputations, libel proceedings brought against a newspaper after too long a period might well give rise to a disproportionate interference with the freedom of the press under Article 10 of the Convention.

Accordingly, there was held to be no violation of Article 10 of the Convention.

18 March 2009
Jansons v Latvia **[2009] EWHC 1845**
Divisional Court: Sir Antony May (President, QB) and Dobbs LJ

The appellant (J) appealed against the decision of a district judge ordering his extradition to the respondent requesting state pursuant to a European arrest warrant.

The day after the warrant had been issued; J had attempted to commit suicide whilst in prison. This attempt was almost successful;

therefore after the incident, J was kept in protective clothing in a gated cell. Psychiatric reports had diagnosed J with post traumatic stress disorder and depressive symptoms. The reports maintained that an extradition would make it very likely that he would attempt to take his life again. These contents were not disputed by the respondent state. Particularly as J had alleged that inmates in Latvian prison had made attempts to assault and kill him. However, the Latvian prison authorities had made arrangements to continue the kind of treatment and care that J had been receiving in the United Kingdom to restrain him from further self-harm.

The appellant's case was that he should be discharged under s21 or section 25 of the Extradition Act 2003. The respondent's view was that J would be unable to make a case that the extradition was in violation if his rights under Articles 3 or 8 of the European Convention on Human Rights. The basis of this response being that J would be unable to demonstrate the Latvian authority's inability to accommodate his mental health risk.

The judges found in the appellant's favour, ordering J's discharge.

On the facts of this case, the judges considered that there was a clear cut case indicating that if J was sent back to Latvia, his mental state would deteriorate and he would commit suicide. To order his return, therefore, would be 'oppressive' within the meaning of s25.

The Court was mindful in stating that reaching this conclusion was not a reflection on the ability of the Latvian authorities to protect and provide the necessary treatment for J, but rather the extent of the risk that he would succeed in ending his life whatever the steps taken.

This line of reasoning could also be applied to Article 8, in spite of the striking and unusual facts for the purpose of deciding whether there would be a disproportionate interference. Taking account of the seriousness of the offences, the need to honour international treaties and the finding that Latvian authorities would take all reasonable steps to protect him and weighing those against the extent of the risk of suicide, Article 8 would be infringed if J were extradited.

It was not necessary to consider the issue under Article 3, as the fact remained that if J were extradited he would commit suicide (following *Kwietniewski v Poland* [2008] EWHC 3121 (Admin)).

24 March 2009
Beker v Turkey (27866/03)
European Court of Human Rights: Francoise Tulkens (President)

The applicants are the mother, brothers and sister of Mustafa Beker, (MB) an expert corporal in the Turkish army, who was found shot in the head in his army barracks dormitory on 8 March 2001. The case concerned the applicants' allegation that, even though the official military investigation concluded that Mustafa had committed suicide, their relative had either been murdered or had died due to negligence.

MB was found, still alive, shot in the head. He was taken to the infirmary and died on his way to the hospital. The autopsy report issued on the same day concluded the cause of death was the destruction of the brain following a shot fired at point-blank range, just above the left eyebrow.

An inquiry was immediately launched and was closed on 8 November. The evidence uncovered included the discovery of a pistol that had fired two shots and seemed to have jammed on the third attempt. MB's fellow sergeants claimed to have not actually seen MB shoot himself. Thus the investigation concluded MB had shot himself due to being unhappy that his mother had opposed his marriage to his girlfriend.

Despite requests by the applicant and their lawyer, the authorities refused to divulge further information and failed to reply to a request to reopen the inquiry.

Relying on Articles 2 (right to life), 6(1) (right to a fair trial) and 13 (right to an effective remedy), the applicants alleged that their relative had either been murdered by agents of the Turkish State or had died due to their negligence.

The Court considered that given that MB was shot in his army barracks, that all eyewitnesses to the incident were members of the armed forces and that the inquiry was conducted by the military authorities (the family not being given permission to participate in the investigation), it was only the military authorities who had the means of establishing the cause of death and, if necessary, identifying and punishing those responsible. The death having occurred in an area under the exclusive control of agents of the State meant it was therefore up to the Turkish Government to provide a plausible explanation for the incident.

The Court had serious misgivings about the investigation into MB's death, misgivings for which no credible explanation had been given. These included questions surrounding how a third shot had been attempted, how he had shot himself in the left side of the head despite being right-handed, and how four trained officers present at the time of the shot had failed to see the incident.

The investigation carried out had therefore clearly been inadequate and left so many obvious questions unanswered that the Court was unable to accept the conclusion that MB had committed suicide. Indeed, in view of the apparent carelessness with which the investigation had been conducted, the fact that the conclusion reached defied all logic, the unwillingness to reopen the investigation, and the lack of satisfactory explanations provided by the Government, the applicants could be forgiven for thinking that a more sinister explanation, such as murder, was being covered up.

Accordingly, the Court unanimously concluded that the Turkish Government had failed to account for MB's death and therefore the State had to take responsibility for the incident, in violation of Article 2. Consequently, awards for just satisfaction made under Article 41. Therefore, the Court found no need to examine the case separately under Articles 6 and 13.

APRIL 2009

1 April 2009
Mr Tommy McGlynn v Welwyn Hatfield District Council [2009] EWCA Civ 285
Court of Appeal (Civil Division): Toulson LJ, Aikens LJ and Sullivan LJ

The case concerned a possession order issued against the appellant, M, who had a non-secure Tenancy Agreement with the Council; terminable by notice.

From about September 2003 the council received repeated complaints from a neighbour that M was, because of his drug dealing reputation, a magnet for noisy and ill-behaved visitors. On 30 April

2004 the council served a notice to quit on M. The voluntary organisation helping M recover from his drug addiction made a representation by letter to which the council replied on 2 June stating that their general policy was not to 'take action against a person's tenancy unless they are satisfied that there has been a significant breach that has caused a nuisance or annoyance to other residents in the locality' and stating further 'if we do not receive any further complaints of anti-social behaviour that can be linked to M or his property we will consider granting him a further non-secure tenancy'. From July 2004 to April 2005 however the complaints continued month by month. On 14 April 2005 the council issued a claim seeking an order for possession.

At first instance, the District Judge made a possession order. For the purposes of the hearing he accepted M's testimony, alleging that he had neither caused nor encouraged nuisance at his home. However, he held that since the appellant was not a secure tenant he had no defence according to the case of *Sheffield City Council v Smart* [2002] EWCA Civ 4.

M appealed contending that the Council could not have been satisfied that there had been a significant breach of the Tenancy Agreement. M was given a legitimate expectation that his situation would be fully investigated prior to any possession order, and the Council had behaved unreasonably in failing to investigate.

The issue before the Court of Appeal was whether it was seriously arguable that the council did not do enough to satisfy itself that there had been some significant further breach of the Tenancy Agreement.

The majority considered that the District Judge had taken an overly narrow view of the significance of the letter dated 2 June 2004 containing a statement of policy (see above). They noted that the Council was not required to conduct the equivalent of a judicial investigation.

They observed nonetheless that on the paucity of information available to the District Judge about the council's decision-making process and on such uncertainty as to whether M would be given the opportunity to answer the proceedings, it was wrong and insufficiently supported by evidence to conclude, as the District Judge did, that M's case was not seriously arguable.

2 April 2009
Muradova v Azerbaijan (22684/05)
European Court of Human Rights: Christos Rozakis (President)

The case concerned Ms Muradova's (M) complaint that she became blind in one eye after being hit by a police officer during a demonstration and that no effective investigation was carried out into the incident.

The injury was sustained at the demonstrations launched in opposition of the newly elected president in Azerbaijan. Anti-riot police and military personnel were deployed to disperse the demonstration. According to M, a police officer hit her right eye with a truncheon when she asked him for help in getting up from the ground. However, the authorities submitted that her injury was not caused by the police, but was the result of her having fallen down on a blunt object. Despite emergency treatment and surgery, M became permanently blind in her right eye.

In early 2004, M filed both a criminal complaint and brought civil proceedings. With regard to the former, no separate proceedings were launched; however, two forensic reports were issued in the proceedings bought by the prosecution into the public disorder. However, all eight eye witnesses denied having seen M and this action was discontinued due to a lack of evidence in support M's version of events. As for the latter, M called three witnesses who testified seeing a police officer strike her with a truncheon in the right eye, but M's claim was rejected due to lack of proof.

Relying on Article 3 (prohibition of inhuman or degrading treatment), M alleged that on 16 October 2003 she was hit in the eye with a truncheon by a police officer during a demonstration, and that the incident was not investigated adequately. The application was unanimously successful.

The Court considered that M had produced sufficiently strong evidence in support of her version of the incident, namely her medical records and witness statements. The Court was particularly astonished with the lack of reasoning in the domestic court's dismissal of M's civil claim for compensation; merely dismissing the witness statements as groundless. Further, the authorities had not justified the degree of force used against M, given that she had not been arrested or prosecuted for any violence during the demonstration and had tried to leave it to avoid danger. The Court therefore held that the force used by the police in respect of M had been excessive, in violation of Article 3.

Furthermore, the Court found that although a criminal investigation had been launched, it had been unclear whether it had actually examined the actions of the police during the demonstration. The investigating authorities had not attempted to seek or hear testimony from the witnesses presented by M during the civil proceedings. That omission in particular had contributed to the general ineffectiveness of the investigation. Accordingly, the Court held that the authorities had not conducted an effective investigation into M's complaint, in violation of Article 3.

Under Article 41 (just satisfaction) of the Convention, the Court awarded the applicant 25,000 Euros (EUR) in respect of non-pecuniary damage.

3 April 2009
R (on the application of Keith Lewis) v HM Coroner for the Mid and North Division of the Country of Shropshire **[2009] EWHC 661 (Admin)**
Queen's Bench Division (Administrative Court): Sir Thayne Forbes

The claimants sought judicial review of the rulings given by the defendant coroners in the course of the inquests following the claimant's relatives' deaths whilst in custody. The principal matter which fell to be determined in every case was whether the relevant inquest had complied with the procedural obligation imposed (implicitly) by Article 2 of the European Convention on Human Rights (right to life) for an 'effective official investigation' to be conducted into a death where 'agents of the state are, or may be, in some way implicated'.

In the first case the claimant's relative was found hanging dead in his cell. The coroner ruled that the jury could not consider questions relating to the actions of the prison service after the claimant's relative had been found on the ground and that the jury's role was limited to considering factual questions directly relating to the cause or contribution of death. The coroner held that because there was no evidence that the claimant's relative was alive when found, any acts or omissions by the prison service thereafter could not have contributed to his death.

In the second case the claimant's relative had set off his emergency cell alarm before hanging himself. The audible signal from the alarm panels had been disabled for some time and not repaired, and although the alarm light outside the prisoner's cell was lit, the alarm was not answered for around 15 minutes and officers then attending had not had the necessary tool to cut the ligature from his neck. The coroner held that it was not for the jury to decide whether there was neglect or not. The coroner stated that the jury could make factual conclusions, but they could not be judgmental in respect of any acts or omissions or use words like 'because' or 'contributed to'.

In the third case, at the inquest the coroner had similarly directed the jury not to be 'judgmental' in their conclusions and that that they may produce only an objective narrative verdict.

The claimants contended, *inter alia*, that a jury had jurisdiction to consider facts that were not directly causative of death as to be otherwise restricted would be bound to prevent valuable and important comment about practices, procedures and omissions in prison as required by a proper investigation within the meaning of Article 2.

The claimants further argued that a coroner was not permitted to prevent a jury from reaching and recording findings of a factual nature, and that directing a jury not to use words such as 'because' or 'contributed to' wrongly inhibited them from making judgmental conclusions of fact central to the issues raised. It was also submitted that the coroner in the second case had erred in failing to leave the verdict of neglect as there was sufficient evidence to do so.

The Court refused the first and third applications, but quashed the inquisition in the second case and ordered a new inquest. The reasoning as follows:

It was held that Article 2 was not prescriptive about either the precise scope or form of the investigation needed to fulfil the obligation, nor the level of scrutiny required in respect of 'non-causal' matters. There was no requirement under Article 2 that a jury reach factual conclusions on events that might cause or contribute to death in similar circumstances in the future. Compliance with the Convention did not require that the power of a coroner to alert the relevant person to take action where there was concern that future deaths might arise, pursuant to the Coroners Rules 1984, be exercisable by a jury.

The correct approach for the Court to take, when considering whether the conduct of an inquest and a coroner's directions satisfied the requirements of Article 2, was the narrow approach identified by the Secretary of State. The Secretary of State had disagreed with the Claimant's core submission that Article 2 imposes an obligation to leave questions to the jury concerning factors that cannot be shown on the balance of probabilities to have caused or contributed to the death in question, suggesting that the conclusions be limited to causally relevant matters. The judge considered it inconceivable that an investigation into the cause of death would be inadequate for the purposes of Article 2 because its conclusions were limited to causally relevant matters. Accordingly, whilst a coroner had the power and might well consider it appropriate to conduct a wider ranging investigation than was required for the verdict, Article 2 did not require an investigation of, or expression of the conclusions upon, events and matters that neither caused or contributed to the death in question in order to render the inquest Article 2 compliant.

In the second case, the coroner's directions had had the effect of preventing the jury from embodying judgmental conclusions of factual nature on a number of the disputed factual matters at the heart of the case. The inquest was not, therefore, an effective means for the proper discharge of the Article 2 obligation. The coroner had erred further in deciding not to leave the ancillary verdict of neglect to the jury as there was clear evidence of gross failures on the part of the prison and its staff which formed part of a clear and direct chain of causation leading or contributing to his death.

30 April 2009
R (on the application of JS (Sri Lanka)) v Secretary of State for the Home Department [2009] EWCA Civ 364
Court of Appeal (Civil Division): Waller LJ (Vice-president), Scott Baker LJ, Toulson LJ

J appealed against the dismissal of his application for permission to apply for judicial review of the Secretary of State's decision that he was ineligible for protection under the Convention relating to the Status of Refugees 1951 (United Nations). J was a Tamil and a citizen of Sri Lanka who had claimed asylum in the United Kingdom. He was a long-term voluntary member of the Liberation Tigers of Tamil Eelam (LTTE), having served in the intelligence wing.

J claimed that, if returned to Sri Lanka, he would face mistreatment because of his race and his membership of the LTTE. The Secretary of State found that the LTTE was responsible for war crimes and crimes against humanity. She found that J had been a highly-trusted member of that organisation and therefore had been complicit in its crimes. She thus considered him ineligible for humanitarian protection and protection under the Convention. The issue to be determined was whether her reasoning was sound.

J's appeal was allowed. The Court of Appeal considered that the starting point for the decision-maker was the Rome Statute of the International Criminal Court. The Secretary of State had to identify the type of crime, as defined in Articles 7 and 8, and then consider whether there were serious reasons for regarding the applicant as guilty of such a crime. In order for him to have committed the crime on the basis of joint enterprise liability, there had to be a common design amounting to or involving the commission of a crime provided for in the statute. The applicant must have participated in the furtherance of the joint criminal purpose making a significant contribution to the commission of the crime, and that participation had to have been with the intention of furthering one of the crimes provided for in the statute – *Prosecutor v Tadic* (ICTY) was considered.

Guidance given by the Immigration Appeal Tribunal in *Gurung* [2003] Imm AR 115, for determining whether there were serious reasons for considering a person guilty of such a crime was disapproved, since the Tribunal neither examined nor explored the principles of liability set out in the Rome Statute of the International Criminal Court Article 25, the Statute of the International Criminal Tribunal for the former Yugoslavia Article 7(1) and the decision in *Tadic*. Moreover, its approach to liability was potentially wider than that taken in those statutes and the cases under those statutes. It was clear that mere membership of an organisation committed to the use of violence to achieve its political goals was not enough to make a person guilty of an international crime. The Tribunal in *Gurung* had said that if an organisation was one whose aims, methods and activities were predominantly terrorist in nature, very little more would be necessary. The authorities showed that it could not be participation in activities that did not involve or promote the commission of international crimes.

While it was the purpose of some members of the LTTE to commit international crimes in pursuit of their organisation's political ends, the Secretary of State had wrongly presumed that J, as a member of the LTTE, was guilty of personal participation in those crimes. She should have instead considered whether there was evidence affording serious reason for considering that he was party to that design, that he had participated in a way that made a significant contribution to the commission of the crimes, and that he had done so with the intention of furthering the perpetration of them. Although his position in the organisation showed that he was trusted to perform his role, neither a significant contribution nor an intention to further the purpose of those members of the LTTE was shown.

MAY 2009

6 May 2009
R (on the application of Nasseri) v Secretary of State for the Home Department **[2009] UKHL 23**
House of Lords: Lord Hope, Lord Hoffmann, Lord Scott, Lord Brown, Lord Neuberger.

The appellant, N, was a failed Afghani asylum seeker who contested his removal to Greece on the grounds that his likely deportation from Greece to Afghanistan would violate his Article 3 rights. N had entered the UK illegally after having his asylum claim in Greece refused. Under Regulation 343/2003 the Secretary of State was empowered to remove failed asylum seekers to the country in which they first claimed asylum. The Secretary of State argued that Greece was on a list of 'safe countries' by virtue of paragraph 3 of Schedule 3 of the Asylum and Immigration (Treatment of Claimants) Act 2004.

At first instance, McCombe J held that paragraph 3(2) was incompatible with Article 3 as it precluded investigations into the risk of inhuman and degrading treatment and that this was a violation of Article 3. However, in the Court of Appeal this was reversed. The House of Lords affirmed this reversal on the basis that Article 3 does not impose procedural obligations. Following their decision in *R (Begum) v Denbigh High School Governors* [2006] UKHL 15, it was held that where a human rights claim is made the only concern for the Court is whether there has been a violation of a right. The Court is not concerned with the details of any decision-making process, which is the ordinary purview of judicial review. There is no 'process review' under the Human Rights Act 1998.

Further, it was held that there was no freestanding duty to investigate. The question is whether there has been a violation of a human right. The duty to investigate is parasitic on whether there had been a violation. A violation of Article 3 cannot be found simply because no investigation had occurred. On the question of whether Greece would be in violation of Article 3, it was held that there was no evidence to support that conclusion. Accordingly, the appeal was dismissed.

18 May 2009

R (on the application of Smith) v Oxfordshire Assistant Deputy Coroner [2009] EWCA Civ 441

Court of Appeal (Civil): Sir Anthony Clarke MR, Keene LJ and Dyson LJ

Private Smith died of hyperthermia in a UK Base whilst serving for the TA in Iraq. The accommodation space to which he was assigned was described as light and airy but lacking air conditioning. Temperatures reached an excess of 50 degrees Celsius.

Two issues were raised upon appeal. First, the 'Jurisdictional question': to what extent British soldiers serving in Iraq are protected by the European Convention on Human Rights. Second, the 'Article 2 question', namely as to whether the inquest in to the death of Private

Smith should comply with Article 2 of the Convention. If the inquest needed to comply with Article 2, two questions were raised. First whether Private Smith's death was caused by a defective system operated by the state to afford adequate protection to human life by ensuring, so far as reasonably practicable, that he was an appropriate person, with proper training and equipment, to expose to the extreme heat of Iraq. Second, whether there was a real and immediate risk of his dying of heatstroke and, if so, whether all reasonable steps were taken to prevent it.

With regard to the first 'jurisdictional' question, the Court decided in the affirmative. A British soldier serving the TA in Iraq, who dies on a UK base dies within the jurisdiction of the UK within the meaning of Article 1 of the Convention and thus can benefit from the rights guaranteed by the Human Rights Act 1998.

As for the Article 2 question, the Court distinguished between two types of inquest. First a traditional inquest and second an 'Article 2 inquest'. The essential difference between them is that the permissible verdict or verdicts in a traditional inquest is significantly narrower than in an Article 2 inquest. In addition, it is said that the scope of the investigation is or is likely to be narrower at a traditional inquest. The Court held that those who volunteer for the TA should be afforded protection under Article 2. The Court held that the precise limits of the inquest will be a matter for the coroner but expected that the coroner consider the questions: whether there were any systemic failures in the army which led to Private Smith's death and, indeed, whether there was a real and immediate risk of his dying from heatstroke and, if so whether all reasonable steps were taken to prevent it.

JUNE 2009

10 June 2009
Secretary of State for the Home Department v AF and others
[2009] UKHL 28
House of Lords: Lord Phillips, Lord Hoffmann, Lord Hope, Lord
Scott, Lord Rodger, Lord Walker, Baroness Hale, Lord Carswell, Lord
Brown

The appellants (AF, AN and AE) were appealing the decision of the
Court of Appeal ([2008] EWCA Civ 1148), arguing that the procedure
that resulted in the non-derogating control order being made against
them was contrary to their right to a fair hearing under Article 6 of the
European Convention on Human Rights because of its reliance on
evidence presented in closed courts and that the defendants had no
access to.

      The European Court of Human Rights had recently stated, in
the case of *A v United Kingdom*, that it was unacceptable 'for a court
assessing the lawfulness of detention to rely on [closed evidence] where
it bore decisively on the case the detained person had to meet and
where it had not been disclosed, even in gist or summary form,
sufficiently to enable the individual to know the case against him and to
respond.'

      While the Court recognised that it was for Parliament and the
Government to resolve any conflicts between the public safety and the
requirements of a fair trial, it felt bound to follow the jurisprudence of
the Strasbourg Court and to find that the use of closed evidence in this
case was contrary to the appellants' right to a fair trial under Article 6.

      A controlee needs to be provided with enough information on
the evidence held against them to be able to instruct their special
advocates on mounting a defence on their behalf. In this case even this
minimum standard was not met. Each case was to be remitted back to
the High Court for consideration in light of this decision.

16 June 2009
Author of a Blog v Times Newspapers **[2009] EWHC 1358**
Queen's Bench Division: Eady J

The applicant blogger applied for an interim injunction to stop the respondent newspaper from publishing any information that would or could lead to his identity being revealed to the public.

The applicant was a detective constable who wrote in his blog about his police work and what he thought about social and political issues surrounding the police and the administration of justice. The reason for his wish to remain anonymous was because of a significant risk of disciplinary action if his employer (the police authority) found out that he was disclosing information to the public about how police operations were being conducted. This behaviour was restricted by Police (Conduct) Regulations. However, the respondents had managed to discover the identity of the blogger by a process of deduction and investigation; mostly by using information available on the Internet. Therefore, the applicant argued that his anonymity should be maintained, since he had a reasonable expectation of privacy for his identity as the author of the blog, and because there was no countervailing public interest which justified its publication.

The application for an interim injunction based on Article 8 of the Convention was refused. The Court held that the applicant had not been able to demonstrate sufficiently that he had a legally enforceable right to stay anonymous. The Court considered previous cases where the claimant had been able to successfully restrain publication of private information, in the absence of a breach of confidence. The 'private' information in these cases had mostly been of a strictly personal nature; such as mental or physical health, sexual relationships, and the claimant's family or domestic arrangements.

However, in this case, the Court held that the applicant did not have a reasonable expectation of privacy over the information being published in his blog, since blogging is a public activity. Furthermore, the Court also felt that there was significant public interest in the applicant's identity being revealed. The respondents, who had successfully managed to discover his identity despite his own attempts to hide it, should be allowed to reveal it. Thus, on balancing the applicant's right to privacy and the respondent's freedom of expression, the Court held that the latter outweighed the former.

18 June 2009
R (on the application of Weaver) v London & Quadrant Housing Trust [2009] EWCA Civ 587
Court of Appeal (Civil): Rix LJ, Lord Collins and Ellis LJ

The appellant housing trust (L) sought to quash the decision of the lower court in subjecting them as a 'public authority' to human rights principles when terminating the tenancy of the respondent (W).

L was a registered social landlord regulated by the Housing Corporation under the Housing Act 1996. Their function was to provide social housing to those in need, funded by the income received from rents, private borrowing and grants allocated by the Corporation. Control over housing stock rested with L, but was subject to local authority allocation arrangements. Legal relationships between tenants and L were defined by the tenancy agreement. W was a tenant of L's and was served with an order for possession due to an accumulation of rent arrears.

She sought judicial review claiming that her eviction would interfere with her human rights. An issue arose as to whether L was a public body within the meaning of section 6(3)(b) of the Human Rights Act 1998.

This claim was successful. The Divisional Court found that L's act of management and allocation of housing stock was a public function. The act of terminating the tenancy was not a private act under the 1998 Act.

On appeal, the main issue was whether, when terminating the tenancy of someone in social housing, L was subject to human rights principles. W submitted that the act of termination was closely and inextricably linked to the function of allocation and that it would be artificial to separate it out and treat it as a private act merely because the tenancy itself was a contract. By majority (Rix LJ dissenting), the appeal was accordingly dismissed.

The lower court had focused on the wrong question, as it was conceded that L was a hybrid authority. The key question to determine whether W's human rights were engaged was whether the act of termination was a private act.

The means by which to determine an answer is to assess the context in which the act occurred; more specifically, the source and nature of the activities (following *YL v Birmingham CC* [2007] UKHL 27). The Court considered it material that L significantly relied on public finance and operated in close harmony with the local government. The provision of social housing was a governmental function, regulated to ensure government objectives concerning a vulnerable group were met. Hence through facilitating its provision, L was providing a public service with 'sufficient public flavour' to consider that action a public function.

As regards the act of termination, it was not purely incidental to L's principal public function of the provision of social housing. Termination was so inextricably linked with the provision of social housing. Once the latter was regarded as a public act, the acts involved in the regulation of the function were in themselves public acts.

The Court reinforced this position by assessing the alternative. If an act was necessarily a private act because it involved the exercise of rights conferred by private law that would significantly undermine the protection Parliament intended to afford to potential victims of hybrid authorities. It would severely limit the significance of identifying certain bodies as hybrid authorities if the fact that the act under consideration was a contractual act meant that it was a private act falling within section 6(5) of the 1998 Act. Accordingly, the act of terminating W's tenancy did not constitute an act of a private nature and was in principle subject to human rights considerations.

The Court went on to declare that the protection afforded by the 1998 Act would extend to all tenants of L who were in social housing. However, it did not necessarily follow that every housing trust providing social housing would be in the same position as L. The determination of the public status of a body was fact specific.

JULY 2009

16 July 2009
Féret v Belgium (15615/07) (2009)
European Court of Human Rights: Ireneu Cabral Barreto (President)

The Court held by majority (4 to 3) that there had been no violation of Article 10 (freedom of expression) of the European Convention on Human Rights in respect of the conviction of the applicant (F), chairman of the political party 'Front National', for publicly inciting discrimination or hatred, following complaints concerning leaflets distributed by that party during election campaigns.

F, chairman of the political party 'Front National-Nationaal Front' (the 'Front National'), is the Editor-in-Chief of the party's publications and owner of its website. He was a member of the Belgian House of Representatives at the relevant time.

Between July 1999 and October 2001 the distribution of leaflets and posters by his party, in connection with the election campaigns of the Front National, led to complaints by individuals and associations for incitation of hatred, discrimination and violence, filed under a law of 30 July 1981 which penalised certain acts inspired by racism or xenophobia. The leaflets distributed included urges to 'oppose the Islamification of Belgium' or to reserve the right to asylum to European citizens.

The applicant's parliamentary immunity was waived on the request of the Principal Public Prosecutor at the Brussels Court of Appeal and criminal proceedings were brought against him as author and Editor-in-Chief of the offending leaflets and owner of the website.

On 13 June 2004 the applicant was elected to the Bruxelles-Capitale Regional Council and to the Parliament of the French Community, both positions affording him new parliamentary immunity.

The public prosecutor reactivated the proceedings on 23 June 2004. On 20 February 2006 the Brussels Court of Appeal held a complete trial and on 18 April 2006 sentenced Mr Féret to 250 hours of community service related to the integration of immigrants, together with a 10-month suspended prison sentence. It declared him ineligible for ten years. Lastly, it ordered him to pay one euro to each of the civil parties.

The Court found that the offending conduct on the part of Mr Féret had not fallen within his parliamentary activity and that the leaflets contained passages that represented a clear and deliberate incitation of discrimination, segregation or hatred, and even violence, for reasons of race, colour or national or ethnic origin.

Relying on Article 10 (freedom of expression), Mr Féret alleged that his conviction for the content of his political party's leaflets represented an excessive restriction on his right to freedom of expression.

The Strasbourg Court found that the interference with Mr Féret's right to freedom of expression had been provided for by law (law of 30 July 1981 on racism and xenophobia) and had the legitimate aims of preventing disorder and of protecting the rights of others.

The Strasbourg Court observed that the leaflets presented the communities in question as criminally-minded and keen to exploit the benefits they derived from living in Belgium, and that they also sought to make fun of the immigrants concerned, with the inevitable risk of arousing, particularly among less knowledgeable members of the public, feelings of distrust, rejection or even hatred towards foreigners.

While freedom of expression was important for everybody, it was especially so for an elected representative of the people: he or she represented the electorate and defended their interests. However, the Court reiterated that it was crucial for politicians, when expressing themselves in public, to avoid comments that might foster intolerance.

The impact of racist and xenophobic discourse was magnified in an electoral context, in which arguments naturally became more forceful. To recommend solutions to immigration-related problems by advocating racial discrimination was likely to cause social tension and undermine trust in democratic institutions. In the present case there had been a compelling social need to protect the rights of the immigrant community, as the Belgian courts had done.

The Court noted that the authorities had preferred a 10-year period of ineligibility rather than a penal option, in accordance with the Court's principle of restraint in criminal proceedings.

The Court thus found that there had been no violation of Article 10.

24 July 2009
R (on the application of E) v Nottinghamshire Healthcare NHS Trust [2009] EWCA Civ 795
Court of Appeal (Civil): Moses LJ, Lord Clarke MR and Keene LJ

The case concerned the appeal by a number of appellants (P), who were or had been detained at Rampton high security psychiatric hospital. Their previous claims for judicial review of the ban on smoking at Rampton had been dismissed.

The Health Act 2006 required places of work, such as Rampton, to be smoke-free unless exempted by regulations. The Smoke-free (Exemptions and Vehicles) Regulations 2007 introduced a permanent exemption for smoking rooms in prisons, but only a temporary exemption in the case of mental health units.

In the Divisional Court, P bought claims for judicial review and under section 7 of the Human Rights Act 1998. They challenged the respondent NHS Trust's policy prohibiting smoking both inside and outside the buildings at Rampton. They claimed that the Regulations were discriminatory because of the difference in exemptions granted to prisons and mental health units, using Articles 8 and 14 of the European Convention on Human Rights upon which to hinge their claim.

Their appeal in this case consisted of a number of grounds: the lower court had erred in holding (1) that smoking was not an activity within the scope of the right enjoyed under Article 8, (2) the ban on smoking did not constitute an interference with Article 8 rights, (3) that the ban did not come within the ambit of Article 8 for the purpose of Article 14, (4) P's status as a detained mental patients did not constitute a personal characteristic for the purposes of Article 14, and (5) the Divisional Court was wrong to conclude that any interference was justified.

The Court of Appeal took a majority view (Keene LJ dissenting), that the Divisional Court had come the correct decision and the appeals should be dismissed.

The majority considered that the degree to which a person could expect the freedom to do as he pleased is contingent on the nature of the accommodation in which he lived. Article 8 sought to prevent state intrusion into the physical and private space which the concept of a home represented. Rampton was a public institution where the lives of patients were supervised and their activities were restricted. The majority considered the act of smoking, as well as the social interaction involved, to be not so integral to a person's identity to merit the protection of Article 8. In the Court's view, the prohibition on smoking at Rampton did not have a sufficiently adverse effect on the patient's moral and physical integrity.

The Court went further in concluding that if Article 8 was engaged, the trust's policy would be justified on the following basis: the ban was necessary and proportionate for the health of both the patients and others. They also considered that the difference in treatment between prisoners and detainees under the regulations was justified as reasonable and proportionate if Articles 8 and 14 were engaged. The basis for this conclusion was that the difference in treatment was the result of a considered judgment after extensive consultation by the legislature. Furthermore, since the right to smoke did not fall within the ambit of Article 8 standing alone, it could not come within the scope of Article 8 for the purposes of Article 14.

Keene LJ went on to outline his own position with regards to the interpretation of Article 8 in light of the Regulations. He considered that Article 8 was engaged, as the effect of the ban inside would be to completely ban those patients who are not allowed outside from smoking. In his view, this prohibition was disproportionate as it was more than was necessary to accomplish the public health objective of protecting people against second-hand smoke. Therefore, the regulations were in breach of Article 8 and 14. However, on the facts of this case, Keene LJ considered the position of the trust to be different, rendering their policy proportionate and not in breach of Article 8 and Article 14.

31 July 2009
R (on the application of Purdy) v DPP [2009] UKHL 45
House of Lords: Lord Phillips, Lord Hope, Baroness Hale, Lord Brown
and Lord Neuberger

The appellant Mrs Purdy appealed against a decision that found that the
absence of a crime-specific policy identifying the facts and
circumstances that the Director of Public Prosecutions would consider
when deciding whether to prosecute an individual for assisting another
person to commit suicide did not render section 2(1) of the Suicide Act
1961 unlawful and did not mean that it was not in accordance with law
for the purposes of Article 8 of the European Convention on Human
Rights.

Mrs Purdy, who suffered a debilitating illness, had declared her
wish to travel to a country where assisted suicide was lawful to end her
life when it became utterly unbearable. She sought information in order
to make an informed decision about whether to ask for her husband's
assistance in doing so. The DPP had declined to say what factors, other
than the general factors contained in the Code for Crown Prosecutors,
he would take into consideration in deciding whether, under section
2(4) of the Act, it was in the public interest to prosecute those who
assisted people to end their lives in countries where assisted suicide was
lawful. Mrs Purdy unsuccessfully sought judicial review and her appeal
was also rejected. She argued on two grounds; that firstly, the
prohibition in section 2(1) constituted an interference with her right to
respect for her private life under Article 8(1); and secondly that such
interference was not 'in accordance with the law' as required by Article
8(2), due to the absence of an offence-specific policy by the DPP which
set out the factors that would be taken into account by him and the
Crown Prosecutors in deciding under section 2(4) whether it was in the
public interest to bring a prosecution under that section.

The House of Lords allowed the appeal.

Applying the case of *Pretty v UK* [2002] 35 EHRR 1, they held
that the right to decide when or how to die was not excluded from
Article 8(1). The Code was found not to provide clear guidance as to
how the public interest test was to be applied where the offence was
aiding or abetting the suicide of a person who was terminally ill or

severely and incurably disabled, who wished to be helped to travel to a country where assisted suicide was lawful and who, having the capacity to take such a decision, did so freely and with full understanding of the consequences. The Code therefore did not satisfy the Article 8(2) requirements of accessibility and foreseeability in assessing how prosecutorial discretion was likely to be exercised in section 2(1) cases.

The DPP was required to promulgate an offence-specific policy identifying the facts and circumstances that would be taken into account in deciding whether to consent to a prosecution under section 2(1).

OCTOBER 2009

29 October 2009
R (on the application of L) v Commissioner of Police of the Metropolis **[2009] UKSC 3**
Supreme Court: Lord Hope, Lord Saville, Lord Scott, Lord Brown and Lord Neuberger

The appellant (L) had obtained a position as a playground assistant. In providing L with an Enhanced Criminal Records Certificate (ECRC), it was disclosed by the police that L had previously been accused of neglecting her child and non-cooperation with Social Services. Her employment was terminated. L claimed that the disclosure was a violation of her right to a respect for her private life under Article 8 of the European Convention on Human Rights, as incorporated by the Human Rights Act 1998.

The Court held that all ECRCs, by their very nature, would engage Article 8, and that this case was no different. Her ability to interact with others was impaired and it was damaging to her reputation, it was information held by public authorities that had been made public, and the information was related to private proceedings.

The Court stated that a two-stage analysis should be applied by the police when considering the inclusion of data in an ECRC: whether (i) the information is reliable and relevant; and (ii) it is proportionate to provide the information, in light of the public interest and the likely impact on the applicant.

The test for relevance could be found in the wording of the Police Act 1997; while proportionality would depend on a variety of factors such as the gravity of the information, the existence of an opportunity to make representations, the period that has elapsed since the relevant events, and the potential adverse effect of the disclosure (*per* Lord Neuberger).

In the present case, the Court determined that since the information released was both relevant, true and bore directly on L's suitability for the job, the interests of the children must take precedence over the prejudicial effects of disclosure. The appeal was dismissed.

BOOK REVIEW

Alison Young –
Parliamentary Sovereignty and the Human Rights Act[1]

JUSTIN LESLIE[*]

The classic account of the British constitution includes two important characteristics. First, the constitution is 'unwritten' in the sense that there is no singular codifying document which we can call 'the Constitution'. Secondly, Parliament, as the legislature, enjoys ultimate legal sovereignty which enables it to make or unmake *any* law it chooses. An important consequence of this classic account is that the constitution appears to be uncontrolled by *substantive* principles such as those associated with the protection of fundamental human rights and it is instead more concerned with *formal* rules. Such an arrangement means that the constitution focuses on identifying what is or is not law in a formal sense – i.e. whether it was enacted according to correct parliamentary procedure – and not whether law is normatively 'good'.

This classic account is closely associated with the work of Albert Venn Dicey who laid the foundations for our understanding of the modern British constitution.[2] An important part of Dicey's vision was to place the principle of parliamentary sovereignty at the heart of the constitution. This principle was subject only to the formal constraints of Dicey's second principle, the rule of law. However, as an approach to modern constitutional affairs, the classic account only tells part of the story. It appears to suggest that parliamentary sovereignty is an immovable, monolithic principle and in doing so forgets to emphasise the dynamic relationships which are a necessary part of any unwritten constitution. Several themes of recent years capture this

[1] Hart Publishing, Oxford 2009.
[*] Justin Leslie studied for an LLM degree in Public Law at UCL between 2008 – 2009. He now works for the Public Law Project.
[2] See AV Dicey, *Introduction to the study of the law of the constitution* (9th ed. Macmillan, London 1939).

dynamism such as the rapid development in judicial review principles,[3] the increased role of the judiciary in the political landscape,[4] the UK's accession to the European Union[5] and the incorporation of the European Convention on Human Rights into British law by virtue of the Human Rights Act 1998 (HRA). These changes are well documented[6] and each ask us to reassess our assumptions about how the constitution operates.

Alison Young's book is primarily concerned with aligning Dicey's understanding of parliamentary sovereignty with a post-HRA world. Young's argument is that the protection of human rights provided by the HRA is sufficient and can be defended by reference to a 'democratic dialogue' model of rights protection.[7] As such, Young seeks to provide ballast for the *status quo* but does so on the basis of careful exposition and analysis. Whilst Young calls this defence 'modest', a harsh critic might prefer the word 'unambitious'. However, it is important to note that if any work in this area wishes to be taken seriously it must recognise constitutional reality, particularly with reference to the enduring status of parliamentary sovereignty. Arguments for a wholesale usurpation of Parliament's central role in favour of shifting power towards the courts may be tremendously convincing – but ultimately, they will remain of academic interest only. As Jowell pointed out, good constitutional theory 'requires due regard to be had to a mix of principle and empiricism'.[8]

Young's book is divided into seven chapters. Chapter one introduces the reader to Dicey's notion of parliamentary sovereignty and indicates ways in which the HRA may undermine this principle. It quickly becomes apparent that there is a crucial distinction between 'continuing' and 'self-embracing' models of parliamentary sovereignty.

---

[3] For excellent overviews of these developments see M Supperstone, J Goudie and P Walker (eds.), *Judicial Review* (3rd ed. Butterworths, London 2005), chapters 1, 2 and 3 or more generally, P Craig, *Administrative Law* (6th ed. Sweet & Maxwell, London 2008).
[4] For instance, see R Rawlings, 'Review, Revenge, Retreat' (2005) 68(3) *Modern Law Review* 378.
[5] By virtue of the European Communities Act 1972.
[6] See generally J Jowell and D Oliver (eds.), *The Changing Constitution,* (6th ed. Oxford University Press, Oxford 2007).
[7] For a similar approach see T Hickman, 'Constitutional dialogue, constitutional theories and the Human Rights Act 1998' [2005] *Public Law* 306.
[8] J Jowell, 'Of vires and vacuums: the constitutional context of judicial review' [1999] *Public Law* 448, 460.

The 'continuing' model of sovereignty renders each Parliament as individually sovereign. Therefore, to ensure that each Parliament can exercise this sovereignty effectively, one Parliament cannot bind another. When Parliament #2 enacts legislation contrary to legislation passed at an earlier point in time by Parliament #1, the older provisions are impliedly repealed. The mechanism of implied repeal forms part of an inherent limitation on Parliament's sovereignty but also ensures that each Parliament is as omnicompetent as is logically possible. The 'self-embracing' model views all historical and future Parliaments as a whole. Parliament #1 can legitimately bind Parliament #2 since both are part of the same entity. This model allows implied repeal to be disabled in certain circumstances and suggests the possibility of a hierarchy of statutes.[9] However, the existence of implied repeal is a legal fact and therefore we must prefer the continuing model of parliamentary sovereignty. Young concludes chapter two by stating that stronger protection for human rights can apparently be achieved within the confines of the continuing model by modifying section 3(1) of HRA so that legislation 'took effect subject to Convention rights' and recasting section 3(1) as 'a dominant statutory provision'.

A reader of this section might be forgiven for thinking that this recommendation is such a subtle alternative to current arrangements that it is difficult to see what purpose it serves. Section 3 empowers the courts to give effect to legislation, 'whenever enacted', 'in a way which is compatible with the Convention rights' but only 'so far as it is possible to do so'. Section 3, therefore, is already a significant tool of statutory construction and as Lord Nicholls asserted in *Ghaidan*, in using section 3, 'a court can modify the meaning, and hence the effect, of primary and secondary legislation'.[10] Indeed, the principle of legality as enunciated almost a decade ago by Lord Hoffmann in *Simms*[11] – that in the absence of express words or necessary implication fundamental rights will not be overridden – appears to cover much of the same ground by way of a positive presumption in favour of rights as the 'entrenchment effect' which Young identifies.

---

[9] See further, Laws LJ in *Thoburn v Sunderland City Council* [2002] EWHC 195 (Admin) at [62] and J Laws 'Constitutional Guarantees' [2008] 29(1) *Statute Law Review* 5.

[10] *Ghaidan v Godin-Mendoza* [2004] UKHL 30 at para [32].

[11] *R. v Secretary of State for the Home Department Ex p. Simms* [2000] 2 AC 115, 131.

Whilst chapter two examines implied repeal, chapter three looks more closely at the relationship between the entrenchment of human rights and the models of continuing and self-embracing sovereignty. An important conclusion of Young's is that whilst entrenchment is a fairly straight-forward matter under the self-embracing model, entrenchment is not fundamentally precluded under the continuing model. However, 'entrenchment cannot occur through the actions of Parliament alone'. What is required is an alteration in the rule of recognition – Hart's rule which purports to define the criteria of legal validity – to require all law to comply with Convention rights.[12] Whilst Young assumes the position of soft positivism with little justification,[13] it is also recognised that such a shift may be difficult to achieve in practice – particularly because changing the rule of recognition in this way could be easily confused with a shift towards the self-embracing model.

In chapter four, Young analyses parliamentary sovereignty in terms of political, rather than legal, theory and concludes that the justification for the continuing model is rooted in the way in which it preserves democracy. The legitimacy of Parliament is premised on its representative nature since the membership of Parliament is – at least in part – democratically elected. Young lays the groundwork for what is a democratic justification of the HRA 'because it seeks to provide a protection of rights that is also sensitive to the need to preserve democracy'. This justification is by way of a 'democratic dialogue' model, which is argued for in chapter five.

The HRA is often credited with providing an important mechanism by which the courts can interact with the legislature. This is principally by virtue of section 4 which enables the court to issue a declaration of incompatibility. When the court is unable to interpret legislation to be rights-compliant under section 3, a declaration of incompatibility can be used to indicate to Parliament the need to amend or repeal the rights-breaching provision. Importantly, a declaration has no legal effect and does not compel Parliament to act. However, of the 26 declarations that have been made, in each case there has been some

---

[12] See HLA Hart, *The Concept of Law* (2nd ed. Oxford University Press, Oxford 1997).
[13] See MDA Freeman, *Lloyd's Introduction to Jurisprudence* (8th ed. Sweet & Maxwell, London 2008), ch 6.

positive government response.[14] A democratic dialogue model must carefully consider when section 3 or section 4 should be used. Young provides a thorough account arguing that the courts should use section 3 in 'easy cases'[15] whilst section 4 should be used in 'hard cases', where a rights-compliant interpretation requires a remedy which 'is beyond the institutional capabilities of the court' and where a rights-compliant interpretation would be impossible. Parliament is under a variable obligation to respond to section 4 declarations which depends on the circumstances in which it was made. In this way, Young emphasises the role of section 4 and argues that this model justifies the HRA.

In chapter six, Young seeks to see whether the current legal approach to sections 3 and 4 fit her model. The current approach is 'predominately linguistic' and was defined by the House of Lords in *Ghaidan* and, in Young's view, can be criticised if it promotes the excessive use of section 3. However, this chapter is more concerned with demonstrating how a balance can be struck in approaching the use of the sections 3 and 4 which promotes the interests of democracy. To this end, Young asserts that the HRA justifies the adoption of a 'weak' protection of rights. The problem with a 'strong' protection of rights is that this would inhibit democratic dialogue since such an approach would bring about a situation of one-way discourse in favour of the courts whereby 'the legislature feels obliged to approve all judicial decisions determining the scope of Convention rights'.

In the final chapter, Young brings together the strands of her arguments and concludes that both the continuing model of parliamentary sovereignty and the HRA can be justified because each 'facilitates inter-institutional comity'. Whilst Young is at pains to properly configure her model of the constitution in favour of Parliament due to its democratic legitimacy, her argument is not one of pure, unbridled power. This is because Parliament is necessarily limited by the doctrine of implied repeal and 'modification requires the acceptance of both Parliament and the courts'.

Young's book is a fascinating romp through the foundations of

---

14 See H Wildbore's article in this journal.
15 Young defines 'easy cases' as cases 'where the rights issue before the court is not contestable and it is not reasonable to disagree about the outcome'. A 'hard case' is 'where it is reasonable to disagree about the outcome'. See page 142.

parliamentary sovereignty and does much to illuminate this principle which is often stated without an appreciation of its many nuances. Whilst it is written with great clarity, this book has some demanding passages particularly at the more abstract points in the argument. As such, a prior understanding of constitutional theory and jurisprudence would enable the reader to fully appreciate Young's important insights. This emphasis on a conceptual understanding of the issues could have been balanced by occasionally focusing on the wider political circumstances which would help to ground certain aspects of the book. For instance, it is assumed that Parliament's representative nature entails that it has the strongest claim of democratic legitimacy in the constitution. However, whether Parliament is actually as representative as this would imply is open to question. First, half of the legislature – namely the House of Lords – is currently unelected. Second, voter turn-out can be low – at last general election it was around 60%, whilst in some constituencies it is as low as 40%.[16] Thirdly, the mode for elections to the House of Commons is unrepresentative with many votes wasted. Fourthly, the tribal system of politics, which is the hallmark of the Westminster village, often prioritises party patronage over the public interest.[17] Fifthly, a large number of executive decisions are made under the rubric of non-statutory powers (such as prerogative powers) which are not open to political participation.[18] Whether the laws which Parliament enact really have the level of legitimacy assumed by Young, is therefore, open to doubt. But it would be unfair to suggest that this weakness is fatal to the overall project of providing a democratic justification for the HRA.

As Lord Hope said in *Jackson*, 'our constitution is dominated by the sovereignty of Parliament. But parliamentary sovereignty is no longer, if it ever was, absolute.'[19] In unpacking the themes behind this statement, Young's book provides us with the tools to assess sovereignty a decade after the most constitutionally significant event of recent times – the enactment of the Human Rights Act. It is to be

---

[16] See http://www.ukpolitical.info/Turnout45.htm (Last Visited 31st October 2009).

[17] See D Oliver, *Constitutional Reform in the UK* (Oxford University Press, Oxford 2003).

[18] See M Cohn, 'Judicial review of non-statutory executive powers after Bancoult: a unified anxious model' [2009] *Public Law* 260.

[19] *R (Jackson) v Attorney General* [2005] UKHL 56 at para [104].

commended for its clarity of writing, the brevity of its prose and the poise of its argument. For anyone wishing to understand the British constitution in the twenty-first century, Young's book represents essential reading.

BOOK REVIEW

Dr Purna Sen (ed.) –
Universal Periodic Review of Human Rights: Towards Best Practice[1]

ANNABEL LEE[*]

The Universal Periodic Review Mechanism (UPR) is a recent innovation by the UN designed to tackle the problem of having a comprehensive overview of the state of the world's human rights. It began in April 2008 and forms one part of the radical changes introduced as part of the new UN Human Rights Council designed to overhaul the now defunct UN Commission on Human Rights. Under the process, States provide a report on the situation on human rights in their country once every 4 years, which is reviewed at a 3-hour meeting in Geneva by other member states.

This book, authored by Purna Sen, is divided into three sections: 'How the Universal Periodic Review Works'; 'What has been Learned?' and 'The First Year of the UPR: Analysis and Summary'. It aims to consolidate the lessons learned so far of the UPR and to provide an appraisal and evaluation of the effectiveness of the UPR.

The commentary in the book is a light read, stretching only to 57 pages. Most of the book is devoted to annexes detailing the constitution of the Universal Periodic Review Mechanism. Whilst citation of all the primary sources is informative, it is the commentary and the 'lessons to be learned' which will be of primary interest to those interested in this subject.

The shortcomings of the pre-existing Commission on Human Rights are well known. Kofi Annan has openly stated that 'States have sought membership of the Commission not to strengthen human rights

---

[1] Head of Human Rights, Commonwealth Secretariat, 2009.

[*] Annabel Lee studied for an LL.M degree in Public Law and Human Rights at UCL between 2008 – 2009.

but to protect themselves against criticism or to criticise others.'[2] The problem with the previous human rights regime was that the Commission was not seen as objective and impartial. So infamous was the reputation of the Commission that many sceptics were immediately suspicious of the new Human Rights Council.[3] The book certainly makes no attempt to mask the previous inadequacies of the UN Commission on Human Rights, for example by stating that 'The Commission was discredited by its perceived politicisation, which hindered constructive dialogue on human rights issues'.[4] This is to be applauded. Only from here can a genuine attempt at reforming the system be made. Whilst recognising these shortcomings, the book's emphasis is certainly forward-looking, towards the way in which the new UPR mechanism can help reform human rights monitoring.

There are three key features of Universal Periodic Review: as the title suggests, it is *universal*, it is *periodic*, and it is carried out by *peer review*. All of these features are to be welcomed.

There is much to be said in defense of the UPR mechanism. Some of this is said in the commentary. For example, the UPR seems to be a genuine attempt by States to address the problems inherent in universal standards monitoring. The fact that review is universal provides a grand vision for pulling together all the findings of numerous UN treaty bodies and for presenting an overall picture of the state of the world's human rights affairs. As Sen says:

'The word 'universal' in the Universal Periodic Review, is intended to indicate that *all states* are subject to the review process. Whilst this might seem obvious, one of the most powerful criticisms of the previous regime was that certain states could escape criticism by seeking membership of the Commission and effectively render themselves immune from review. Implicit in this new universality of review is the

---

2 In Larger Freedom: Towards Development, Security and Human Rights for All, Report of the Secretary-General, 21 March, A/59/2005.
3 E.g. N Schrigver, 'UN Human Rights Council: A New 'Society of the Committed' or Just Old Wine in New Bottles?' (2007) 20 *Leiden Journal of International Law* 809-823; B Rajagopal, 'Lipstick on a Caterpillar? Assessing the New UN Human Rights Council through Historical Reflection', (2007) 13 *Buffalo Human Rights Law Review* 7.
4 Page 5.

principle of equal treatment for all states – all have to go through the same mechanism and are treated in the same way procedurally'.[5]

The UPR mechanism ensures that all States are treated equally by subjecting them all to universal review.

Standards which are reviewed include the Charter of the United Nations, the Universal Declaration of Human Rights, the human rights instrument to which the State is a party and any voluntary pledges and commitments which have been made. There have been some concerns as to whether this new mechanism would step on the toes of individual treaty monitoring bodies. Whilst there is inevitably some overlap, the function of universal periodic review is not redundant. For a start, UPR ensures that there is an overall and comprehensive review of human rights which is not treaty specific. Human rights treaty bodies do not ensure the 'universality of coverage' as envisaged for by the UPR mechanism. The Charter of the United Nations and the Universal Declaration of Human Rights, the core of the human rights standards with which the UPR mechanism is entrusted with, have no specific treaty monitoring bodies. Instead, they are more concerned with broader principles and obligations.

Finally, and perhaps most importantly, the approach of the UPR mechanism in addressing human rights problems is one of dialogue rather than confrontation. As stated in the contribution by John Kissane from the UK Ministry of Justice, 'The spirit of the UPR is to encourage dialogue and not to be an examination. There are no right or wrong answers. Instead, the UPR promotes conversation between peers on prevailing human rights issues and how these can be taken forward'.[6]

Of course, the problem inherent in any peer review exercise is that States are both judges and being judged. It is stated on several occasions throughout the book that 'an ideal state report should be a genuine depiction of human rights at the national level'[7] and that 'states should undertake a genuine assessment of their human rights situation'.[8] That the emphasis throughout the book is on the need for

[5] Page 37.
[6] Page 15.
[7] Page 6.
[8] Page 55.

states to provide genuine reports is very telling of the underlying suspicion there is about States compiling their own reports. There is no guarantee that any information provided by a State under Review will in fact correspond to the true state of human rights affairs in that country. This concern underpins the need for the UPR mechanism to take the form of a dialogue, rather than of confrontation. Only then will States be prepared to discuss openly and honestly human rights concerns which are affecting their country.

So far, the response to UPR has been very positive, but it is early days. Success depends on the willingness of member states. This is both a credit to the UPR mechanism and a serious concern for some observers. Some critics argue that stronger compliance mechanisms are needed so that findings against States can be enforced. It is accepted that the State under Review is able to ignore recommendations if it wishes to.[9] However, as a general rule, such enforcement mechanisms do not exist in the context of public international law which is founded on the basis of consensus. In addition, the enforcement aspect would seem to detract from the idea that the UPR mechanism is a dialogue rather than a confrontation between states. This concern is not directly addressed in the book and represents a failing in the analysis. The UPR is certainly not a panacea for redressing all the world's human rights problems. However, set in the context of the limited capacity of the United Nations, relying on the good-will and cooperation of States, the UPR is truly ground-breaking. In the initial stages, it is important that cooperation between Member States is secured in order that a credible foundation is set for human rights review. Methods of ensuring compliance, whilst important, necessarily follow a sound basis of credibility.

The book is practical and informative. It serves as a useful introductory guide to the aims and procedure of the UPR. Although the mechanism is still in its early stages, there are many more positive comments to be made about the potential of the UPR mechanism which go unsaid. In an international climate where the legitimacy and efficacy of the UN is being doubted, it becomes all the more important that the positive aspects of the organisation are emphasised. The book falls somewhat short of this. It is hoped that future editions of this

---

[9] Page 40.

book will elaborate on the analysis and summary of achievements and lessons from the UPR.

SUBMISSION INSTRUCTIONS

The UCL Human Rights Review welcomes contributions for consideration by the editors with a view to publication. Contributions should be sent to hrreview@uclshrp.com, as should all correspondence, books for review and other communications.

The Board of Editors will only consider material which complies with the following guidelines:

1. The submission should be an original, unpublished work not currently under consideration for publication elsewhere.

2. The UCL Human Rights Review publishes articles which deal with human rights issues which are jurisdiction specific and international. The Review encourages the submission of innovative articles which are relevant to the area of human rights. Articles which do no more that rehearse well known and familiar material should not be submitted.

3. Articles should be no longer than 12,000 words in length. Book Reviews and case notes should not exceed over 3,000 words.

4. Authors should state their present academic or professional affiliation and indicate any professional or personal involvement in the subject matter of the article.

5. It is preferred that submissions are sent as email attachments in recognised software to hrreview@uclshrp.com. The submissions must conform to the Oxford Standard for Citation of Legal Authorities. Authors are asked to refer to previous editions for guidance. More detailed guidance will be sent on request.

SUBSCRIPTIONS
All subscription inquiries should be emailed to hrreview@uclshrp.com